CAPTURE THE
MOMENT

GREGG MATTE

CAPTURE THE
MOMENT

365-DAY DEVOTIONAL

B&H
PUBLISHING
NASHVILLE, TENNESSEE

Published by B&H Publishing Group
Nashville, Tennessee

Dewey Decimal Classification: 242.2
Subject Heading: DEVOTIONAL LITERATURE / CHRISTIAN
LIFE / SPIRITUAL LIFE

Cover design by B&H Publishing Group.
Cover photo by JUSTIN MULLET/stocksy.

1 2 3 4 5 6 7 • 25 24 23 22 21

To the congregation and staff of Houston's First, you are loved and cherished in the heart of your pastor. It is a joy to journey with you each day as we "Capture the Moment" together. You are a continual blessing to our family, Team Matte. Let's keep seeking the Lord, in the quiet times alone with Him and when we gather together as a church!

Foreword

A lot of days, I am in a rush, and don't feel like I have the time to warm-up for a workout. It seems like a waste of time. I'd rather just get on with it. But over the years, I've had unnecessary injuries and discomfort in my workouts all because I haven't taken the time to "warm-up" the muscles before doing the "real thing" with exercise.

Ever since college, I have used daily devotional books or Christian inspirational books as a "spiritual warm-up" for my daily time alone with God. They get the spiritual juices flowing so I can focus on God and what is important in life. *Capture the Moment* by Gregg Matte is a great spiritual warm-up for time alone with God through Bible study and prayer.

Here are a few reasons I think you will like it as a daily spiritual warm-up:

1. It is short. It won't take you long.

2. They include biblical verses and passages that allow God to speak to you from His Word.

3. Each one is relevant to everyday life. Whether it is dealing with anxiety about the future, discerning God's will, dreaming big, success, wisdom, marriage, prayer, ongoing temptation, love, having a healthy sex life, and many other crucial topics; every devotion speaks to life right where we live.

4. But most of all, so many of these devotionals focus on how to have healthy relationships with others and even more so, a healthy relationship with God. They help you understand what God is really like and who Jesus is. Since healthy relationships are a key factor to the fulfilled life, Gregg's insights are so helpful.

But there are a couple more huge reasons I am excited about *Capture the Moment*:

1. One is the man, Gregg Matte. He is the real deal when it comes to living the Christian life. He is authentic in what he writes. He is one of those special individuals whose spirit and character is so much like Jesus, whom he follows as his Lord. He doesn't just preach well and write well—he lives well—according to Jesus' way!

2. As just one example of that, he has designated all the royalties from this book to the compassion and relief ministry, Send Relief. It reflects his desire to build up Christ's kingdom

versus his own. It's another way for people to come to know Jesus personally.

In light of all of this, I urge those of you who are pastors to use *Capture the Moment* as a church-wide devotion for every member of your church. It can be a great unifier in keeping everyone on the same page as your church fulfills Christ's Great Commission.

So, enough about why I am excited about Gregg's book. It's time to get started. Whether it is January 1 or August 15, today is the day to begin using this "spiritual warm-up" to enrich your time alone with God through prayer and Bible study.

Bryant Wright, president of Send Relief

A New Year of Following

1 Corinthians 11:1

Happy New Year! It's a brand-new year and God has new moments for you! The calendar has turned, and now you have a brand-new 365 before you. Allow the beauty of the year to become obvious as you choose to follow Jesus each day. This year don't just tip your hat to God; tip your heart. God wants to use you as a person of impact, a leader of influence.

Everybody wants to make a difference, but to do so, we must first be a follower. Our living is based on our following. Paul told the Corinthians to follow him as he followed Christ. I don't think there is a greater example of a person who led people to be followers of Christ. Paul was someone who lived . . . by following. He followed the example of Christ and changed the world.

If you want to be a believer who lives well and has the characteristics and decision-making skills that Christ had, you have to be His follower. For this 365, read God's Word, understand Christ's teachings, "Capture the Moment" through our devotional journey, and know His heart so you can follow well to live well. The following of Jesus will impact your profession, your singlehood or marriage, your parenting, your church, and your joy. Live as a Christ-following believer here on the earth with a heart toward heaven.

What does God have planned for you this year? Ponder with anticipation. There will be highs and lows, but He will be with us every step. I'm honored to walk daily with you in these devotionals. God wants to bless us both and use us to make a difference in someone's life this year. So exciting!

Everyone has the ability to be a person of impact somewhere—in your house, your church, at work. If you're wondering this year how you can be the best mom, it is by following Christ. How can you be the best husband to your wife? By being a follower of Christ. How can you be the best employee? By being a follower of Christ. How can you be a single adult who honors God, it is by following Christ's example today. It is not about titles, money, personality, or things.

The word *leader* definitely sounds more powerful than *follower*. But true leadership is based on following. I encourage you to be a follower of Christ, just like Paul, so you can lead the way Christ desires for you. Let this new year bring a new you . . . a following-Jesus-closer-than-ever you. Lead others well by following Him even better.

Private and Powerful Praying

Matthew 6:5–8

One of the greatest aspects of being a follower of Christ is prayer. It's mind-blowing that we can talk with God! We want to deepen our lives of prayer, not just thanking God for the day or for our food. Instead, we should live as believers who call out to God in the good and the bad.

Usually, people feel they need to pray more. We all do. Jesus talked about being prayerful people. He tells us not to worry about the number of words we are using and there's no need to stand on street corners praying long, eloquent prayers for everyone to hear. Now, I know you're thinking, *Praying on street corners? That would get us ridiculed in today's society.* But that is what the Pharisees did 2,000 years ago. Jesus wants us to pray privately and individually at a time and in a place where we can connect and be intimate with the Father. In true prayer, private intimacy far outweighs public praise.

Followers of Christ choose the invisible power of God over the visible praise of man. It's not about how smart or spiritual we look when we pray in front of our friends or pastor. It is about pouring out our heart to God. Even when there's nothing to say, He knows what we're thinking. The prayers we pray today from the privacy of our own space can affect something that happens ten years from now. Do we realize God is answering prayers we might have prayed a while ago? Think seed planting, not drive-thru window. Before I was married, I was praying for my wife. Before I had kids, I was praying for my children. I love throwing prayers into the future. It builds my trust in Jesus today to know I'm going to walk in His answers for tomorrow. He meets us now and in the future. There's a power in the unseen prayer closet that is stronger than the Pharisees' prayers for personal praise.

Let's choose intimacy with God through prayer this year. Imagine looking back from December 31 saying, "I went to a deeper level of prayer this year and look at all God has done and seen me through." It's not about big words but about a big heart. Asking God to do something deep within us gives us clarity. Jesus spent a lot of time in solitude praying with the Father. He spent all night in the garden of Gethsemane praying to God.

Think about a marriage. A good marriage is not based on how good the couple is with a group of people but how they are when it's just the two of them. It's the same with God. It's not about your public life before others but your private prayer with Him.

This year . . . pray like never before. Start today by kneeling in private and call out to God from the depths of your heart for the year before you.

The Lord's Prayer
Matthew 6:9–13

In Israel, there's a church in the Mount of Olives called Pater Noster, which is Latin for Our Father. In the church, there are more than 100 plaques of the Lord's Prayer translated into various languages. Try to think of twenty languages. I bet you'll struggle to get there. I have been to Pater Noster, and I will say that it's amazing to see the Lord's Prayer translated into that many languages. It tells me the Lord's Prayer is a worldwide passion.

The Lord's Prayer meets all our needs. Isn't it incredible to think about that? Jesus was showing us through this prayer that this was the form to pray. He didn't need big words or prayers on the street. He was teaching us how to pray.

Now, for Jesus to teach the Jews how to pray was a huge deal. The Jews were people who prayed. They would spend all day praying on the Sabbath. They prayed three times a day, they prayed at their festivals, and even wore prayer shawls. And then, Jesus stepped forward and gave them the Lord's Prayer.

The Lord's Prayer is not just something you hang on your wall at home. It's a prayer from the heart of Jesus. It's telling God that He is holy and meets our every need, that we love Him, and we desire to be a prayerful person. We pray with the desire for God to do something great in and through us.

I encourage you to recite the Lord's Prayer today. We are so familiar with it, I encourage you to truly think about the words. Pray it slowly instead of saying it quickly. Let it seep into your heart as it comes out of your mouth, ponder as you pray.

Slowly pray from your heart, "Our Father who art in heaven . . ."

God Wants Intimacy
Matthew 6:14–15

Jesus spoke the Lord's Prayer to teach us how to pray. However, right after, He slipped in a verse that says to forgive others. He calls us to do the hardest thing we can do. It is so difficult—to forgive someone when they have wronged you. We're the ones who want to receive an apology, not give forgiveness.

Jesus is saying when you come from a place of intimacy with Him and the Father, you will realize how great He is. It means He is great enough to meet your every need and allow you to usher in forgiveness to others because you know the forgiveness He has given you.

You can turn to the Lord as your companion. Billy Graham put it like this: "Jesus prayed briefly in a crowd, a little longer with His disciples, and all night when He was alone."[1] Today, many reverse the process. We want to show off our prayers but don't make time to be alone with the Father.

Prayer with the Lord is for every moment of our lives. It's not just for times of suffering and joy, but prayers of place—the place where you meet God in genuine conversation. Remember, He knows your needs before you ask. You can really say anything you want as long as you pray with honesty and simplicity.

If you do an internet search for prayers written by children, you may learn a thing or two from them. "Dear God, I think the stapler is one of Your greatest inventions." "Dear God, in Bible times did they really talk that fancy?" "Dear God, I think about You sometimes, even when I'm not praying." Kids know they can be honest and say anything to God. That is intimacy, my friend.

God wants intimacy. He wants you to walk with Him, to know His heart deep enough to trust Him. That happens through prayer, not in a group, but individually, alone with God.

Physical Need or Spiritual Plea?

Matthew 6:16–18

As you start this year, let's take this a step further as followers of Christ. Are you inspired to take another step—one that requires application? It's going from level 101 to 201. This next step is fasting.

Fasting is moving from intimacy with God to being hungry for God. Here is the phrase I use: "No Food, Know Prayer." Fasting is not something weird or odd, or something done only in Bible times. It has nothing to do with diet and health. It's about our hearts.

There's something special about pulling back from our norm and our routines to fast, using the time we would normally spend eating to seek God. It's allowing the rumblings in our stomachs to be a hunger for Him. We turn to food for comfort and all sorts of stuff, but we've got to be able to show God we want deeper walks with Him.

Fasting is letting go of a physical need for a spiritual plea. It's hungering for something higher. Fasting is referenced more than seventy times in the Bible. When we fast, our aches for hunger become our aches for prayer.

Fasting is a sacrifice. It should be! Let me say something that seems incorrect in the Christianity of our day and age. Christianity involves sacrifice. It involves suffering at times. In this small place of sacrifice, we are telling the Lord that our hearts desire something bigger. We are saying that we want more than a hamburger; we want Him to move in our lives. You may think, *Of course we want God more than a burger,* but wait until you miss out on that burger. You'll feel the sacrifice.

Fasting is a statement that says, "We're more than physical beings; we are spiritual beings." It elevates heavenly needs over earthly needs. It's not only about removing food; it's about adding prayer. It's using your cravings and mealtime as prayer time. It's dining on true, heavenly bread. As you start the year, fast a meal or a day and call out to the Lord for His will to be done in your life this year—you won't regret it.

Everything for Life and Godliness

2 Peter 1:3–4

In 2 Peter 1:3–4, the apostle Peter tells us that God's divine power has given us everything required for life and godliness. He said by the precious promises of God, we can share in His nature and stay out of sin.

When we know Christ, we have all we need for life and godliness. It is not through us or what we do. Knowing Jesus is what will rescue us from living a life of sin.

At times we feel like: "I don't have the resources to do what God has called me to do in life." And yet Jesus is our resource. He has given us everything we need in life (Rom. 8:32).

When I need courage or wisdom, Jesus is my resource. When I need help in parenting or my marriage, He is my resource. For those who are single, He is your resource for singleness. He is your heart. He is your strength for life and godliness. I love that!

We often say, "Eh, I hope I can do this." Jesus is saying, "In My power, you've got this. You can do it. You can walk in a spiritually mature and godly way because I am your resource."

All of us struggle with sin. Some of us have such sweet or persuadable personalities that we can get mowed down by peer pressure. We say yes when we should be saying no. Stand strong. God has created you with a sweetness but He can also give you power stronger than what people think.

I want you to hear from the apostle Peter and from the Word of God so you have the strength to live for God. You don't have to sin. You don't have to follow that path. You have *everything* you need for life and godliness. When you need strength to follow Christ—not others—Jesus is your resource. When you need peace in the storm, Jesus is your resource. When you need wisdom in decisions, Jesus is your resource. It is through knowing Him that we are equipped to live a life for Him (Phil. 3:10).

Our Own Resources: Epic Fail

Colossians 1:25–29

Sometimes life can make us feel like a Swiss Army knife. We say, "Okay, I have these five or six little tools that will help me out. I have some education, some wisdom, some friends. I have a little bit of money and a job. I have this and that. With these tools, I can figure things out. I can do life, and I can do godliness." This would be a Swiss Army knife composed of our own strength.

But while we may have these five or six tools, the Swiss Army knife composed of the strength of Jesus is a tool and a resource for whatever we might need in a given situation. This Swiss Army knife wouldn't fit in your pocket or even your backpack! He has something for every circumstance, every problem, every joy, every concern, every moment when you are feeling down, and every moment when you are feeling up.

He says something like this: "You can have this tool that is Me in your heart through the Holy Spirit. It is part of the equal privilege you have as a citizen of the kingdom—just like Paul, just like Peter . . . just like the strongest Christian you know. I reside in your heart. If you will abide in Me and I abide in you, then you will accomplish much, and you will bear much fruit. But apart from Me, you will accomplish nothing" (see John 15:1–5).

Throw away your Swiss Army knife mentality with its five or six little tools and grab the greatness of the precious promises of God in your life.

It's scary to let go of our tools and take up the resources of Christ. But the Bible says "fear not" 365 times. There is a "fear not" for every day of the year, so you and I can stand—not on cultural myths and assurances but on the promises of God through knowing Christ (Isa. 35:4, 41:10–13; Matt. 14:27).

If you will, pray with me,

> *Lord, thank You that I can have equal access to You. Thank You that I can live a life pleasing to You. Thank You, Lord, that You're giving me just what I need for that meeting, just what I need for that presentation, just what I need for that school day, just what I need for that relational issue, just what I need for that emotional issue. You've given me everything I need, and I am going to stand on Your promises, God, trusting that You have provided for me all I need for life and godliness.*

God Is Faithful

2 Peter 1:3–4

Precious promises—don't you love those two words? Peter loved talking about the precious things of God. In his two letters, he talked about precious faith, precious promises, the precious blood, the precious stones, the precious rock, and the precious Savior. He is declaring that there is a preciousness of God.

We are to stand on the precious promises of God. We have equal faith among us all. We have the tool and the resource—Jesus Christ. We fall back and stand on the precious promises of God to live our lives.

God has never failed one single promise and He is not going to start with you. Do you ever feel like that's hard to believe? "Lord, I know You have been faithful to everybody in human history, but I am just wondering: Are You going to be faithful to me?"

God has not broken a promise and is not going to break a promise, because His perfect faithfulness would then be at risk. How much do promises mean in our culture today? Zilch. Zero. Nothing. Nada. Promises are broken all the time. But Jesus is saying, "I'll never break a promise. I have great and precious promises. Your life can fall, and I'll catch you on these promises: I am here with you. I live inside you. I am going to love you. I am going to guide you. I am going to take care of you. I am going to provide for you."

This is the truth of God. Live by the promises of God and stand strong on the promise of who He is. Our promises in today's world may mean nothing, but the promises of God mean everything. God is not like someone who has broken their promises to you. Your Father in heaven is not like a promise-breaking father on the earth. Your Father in heaven is not like an imperfect boss on the earth. Your Father in heaven keeps His promises.

Stand on the promises of God. His promises will take you through your darkest time, your best time, and the times in between. His promises are still strong in every situation. Jesus is strong enough to take you through anything! Thank Him for and trust in His promises today.

A Very Important Question

Philippians 4:13

How do we live the Christian life?

One word that pops up in the Bible is the word *through*.

Do you know how many of us are spelling Christianity? We are spelling it D-O—do. But it should be T-H-R-O-U-G-H—through. Through Jesus. How do we live our life? With Jesus living *through* us and us living *through* Him.

Our greatest desire is to live a life pleasing to God. Giving time and attention to Christ—listening, watching, seeking, and questing after Him—results in love and honor for Jesus. And when we love and honor Jesus, we live a life that is pleasing to God.

How do we live this type of life? Through Christ. He does it through us (Rom. 8:37). That happens when we surrender our time and attention to Him so we can love and honor Him.

You can't live through Him if you don't know Him. If you have never trusted Jesus Christ as your Savior and laid down your life at the cross, say this out loud: "Jesus, I want to trust in You. Not in my wisdom, not in my own way of doing life. I want You. I lay down my life at the cross and say, 'Jesus, I want You to be my Savior. I want You to wash me clean. I am trusting in You alone for salvation and forgiveness. Only You can take me to heaven when I die.'"

That's what it means to be saved. That's what it means to be born again. That's what it means to know Jesus personally. *Through* the cross and the resurrection of Christ, we received a relationship with God.

Maybe you already know Him as Savior but you're not walking in spiritual maturity. Walk in a pleasing way before the Lord because He loves you; let Him live His life T-H-R-O-U-G-H you as you live your life T-H-R-O-U-G-H Him.

Where Your Treasure Is

Colossians 3:3

A certain man received an inheritance from his aunt. While waiting for the reading of the will, he was thinking, *What am I going to get?*

Then, he read what his aunt said in her will: "To my beloved nephew, I bequeath my family Bible and all that it contains, along with the residue of my estate, after my funeral expenses and all the just and lawful debts are paid."

When everything was settled, the nephew got $200 and the family Bible. He was disappointed. In a short time, he spent the money, put the Bible in a trunk in the attic, and lived a good portion of the rest of his life in poverty.

Finally, he became an old man himself, and it was time for him to move in with another family member. So, he went up to the attic, opened the trunk, and saw that Bible. He pulled it out.

He opened the Bible for the first time and began to turn through it, only to find that his aunt had put cash throughout all the Scriptures in various passages of the Bible. There were thousands of dollars stashed inside that Bible.

Now, if you open your Bible, there likely won't be cash inside. But there will be treasures that will be greater than any amount of money you could ever imagine. Think about the symbolism this aunt was trying to show her nephew. He would be provided for as he walked through the Scriptures. The greatest treasure we will find when we open our Bible is Jesus. How do we walk in God's ways? Through Jesus and Him through us. That's how we realize the treasure of who He is.

Walk with Him. Love Him. Realize you have everything you need and that you are spiritually equal with the apostles of old and today. Stand on His promises. Give Him your time and attention today and you'll discover eternal treasure.

How Do You Respond to Anxiety?

Psalm 34:4

How is your stress level? How do you respond to anxiety? What's going on within you? Here is what I found out. Of all the people I asked, not one person said, "I don't know what you're talking about."

But when you talk about anxiety, nearly everyone says, "Yes, I know what that feels like. I feel it in the back of my neck, my lower back, and my shoulders. My stomach gets upset, I feel nervous. I worry, and I have fear."

I feel all these things too when anxiety comes around. I find it sneaking up on me. It's a buzz or catch in my heart. A feeling of the gas pedal being stuck in my life even when it is clearly time to relax. Surely there is one more thing *I need* to do or a problem around the corner. My mind continues to reach for things even when I should be at rest. We have all felt it in varying degrees, and today's culture amplifies it. We live in an anxious world with daily news reports of chaos, catastrophe, and crisis.

One way to see the depth of anxiety present in our society is the high level of irritability—anxiety frays our emotions and therefore makes us irritable. We're on the verge of upset all the time, it seems. In traffic, we honk and on TV, people bicker. We've made an entertainment industry out of irritability. How do we get through anxiety and irritability?

Throughout Scripture, we read things such as don't fear, don't be anxious, and cast your anxieties upon God. Fear, anxiety, worry—they are all in the same pile of feelings. What you and I are anxious about might be different, but the feelings are all the same. The psalmist said, "I sought the LORD, and he answered me and rescued me from all my fears" (Ps. 34:4). Over the next few days, we will explore fear as well as the anchors that are available to us when we are anxious. For today, give your anxious thoughts to the Lord. Let Him meet you where you are. Whatever you are concerned about, lay it at His feet.

What Is Anxiety?
Isaiah 41:10

Here is the clinical definition of anxiety: "Anxiety is a psychological, physiological, and behavioral state induced in animals and humans by a threat to well-being or survival, either actual or potential."[2]

That's a mouthful! It comes from the National Institutes of Health. It says anxiety is psychological—that means our minds. Our bodies start getting tight. We might seek out a chiropractor or massage therapist. In all honesty, we should add to the list a Christian counselor. Our mind is thinking that something is a threat. If it's a low-level threat, it's anxiety. If it's a medium-level threat, it's fear. A high-level threat, or something that is perceived to be so, is panic.

When I was in business school and studying for a final exam, I remember sitting down in class as my friend walked in and said, "What's the big deal?" I said, "What's the big deal!? Today is the final exam!" To which he replied, "Today is the test?!" I nodded. He immediately grabbed his desk and said, "This is not happening, this is not happening, this is not happening!" In a very Christian manner I said, "Oh yes, it is happening." The tests were passed out, and we both took the test. It was spring semester, and my friend was supposed to graduate and get married that summer. Now he was about to fail this test, which meant he would have to retake the class. Panic set in, the threat to his future sat on his desk in the form of a test.

Anxiety is not only psychological and physiological, it is also spiritual. Anxiety is rooted in unbelief and the unknown. It's a place where we believe God will *not* be able to take us through. So, we must be able to say, "Lord, I'm anxious about this, but I want to give it to You spiritually."

When we're able to think things through spiritually with a renewed mind in Christ, our bodies can follow. But we must be led by the Holy Spirit in order to be able to say, "Lord, I'm going to believe You. Even the flowers of the field don't worry about how they are clothed. So I'm not going to worry about how I'm clothed. Even the birds don't worry about how they're fed, so I shouldn't worry about what I will eat. Paul was in a jail cell by himself, but he said, 'The Lord stood with me' (2 Tim. 4:17). I don't have to worry socially because God is with me, no matter what comes my way."

Three Types of Anxiety

Isaiah 43:1–2

To find proper solutions, it is helpful to have proper definitions. There are three types of anxiety:

Chemical Anxiety: Chemical anxiety means there is a chemical imbalance in the neurotransmitters in a person's brain.

Reactive Anxiety: If a person has been in a state of constant stress for an extended period of time, the brain may not be able to shut off the anxious responses on its own. That's called reactive anxiety. In our society, anxiety has become the new normal. Maybe you have been in a constant state of stress, and your mind is unable to turn it off. Let me just be the chief of sinners here. This is the one I struggle with. I don't have time to rest and recover from one event to the next. When we've been in a constant state of anxiety and stress, and now when it's time to shut it off, we can't. The gas pedal is stuck.

Traumatic Anxiety: If the stimulus is sufficient to overwhelm an individual's coping mechanisms, then that person can experience psychological trauma. That's basically an extreme form of arousal. It's what happened in my hometown of Houston after Hurricane Harvey, whether someone's house was flooded or not. Trauma happened, to varying degrees in everyone who lived in Houston, and they were so overwhelmed. They saw the water rising, they saw all their belongings piled on the curb, and their coping mechanisms were overwhelmed.

We look at all the things happening in our city, our society, or our world and say, "What do we do now?" People end up looking for places to cope. And that leads perfectly to the message of the gospel because God wants your overwhelming feelings to draw you to Him. Jesus Christ was never overwhelmed, even by the grave. He rose from the dead! When you place your faith and trust in Jesus, you put your faith in the strongest One there ever was and ever will be. Jesus loves you even in the traumatic experiences.

Ambition or Anxiety
Proverbs 12:25

D id you know there can be a positive side to anxiety? I'm a hard worker, a go-getter. I like the adrenaline rush. But what was a blessing for me in my thirties is turning on me now in my fifties. Anxiety turns on you!

There is a difference between anxiety and ambition. If you are operating from an adrenaline rush and anxiety, you are going to crash. But if you are operating from ambition and pray, "God, I want You to do something great through the gifts You have given me," that's different. I have vacillated between the two and confused them more times than I can count. Am I doing this because I am nervous about approval? Or am I ambitious with godly motives and saying, "Lord, You do what You want to do."

We must pay attention because fleshly anxiety and godly ambition can be hard to distinguish. If it is anxiety, then we'll end up in reactive anxiety, creating a new norm. The slow day will come, and you'll say, "Wait a minute! Why can't I settle down? Why do I keep trying to find something to do? Why do I need a plan and continuous stimuli . . . on vacation!?"

We may feel more comfortable at work because we're in control. Outside of work, we are out of control. Addicted to producing, our vacations end up looking like a spreadsheet of tasks to accomplish instead of rest. Often, we break the commandment of honoring the Sabbath. That is one reason we are anxious; we don't "sabbath" well.

Sure, ambition can bring excellence and drive, but don't let it slip into anxiety pushing you forward. You want the power and will of God—not fear—to be the wind in your sails. So be careful of tilting from godly ambition to earthly anxiety. Turn to the Prince of Peace . . . today.

Lord, I have godly ambitions to fulfill all You have purposed for me, yet I can slip into stress and a task list with far too much. Lord, help me see the difference in godly ambition and earthly anxiety. I lay my heart before You . . . I ask for Your healing and helping work.

Seeking the Lord
Psalm 34:4

What will help dilute those anxious feelings? Do you drink or do drugs to take the edge off? With ambition, are you trying to gain a trophy for the shelf so you're safe in your worth? Where do we find help? We find help by seeking the Lord. He delivers us from *all* our fears.

We seek Him in a variety of ways. One is through assessing our own disposition. Are you tired? Are you sad? Maybe you're saying, "I'm exhausted. I've been going for so long." Or maybe, "I feel down." Is your disposition depression or fear? Is it hopelessness? Where are you coming from?

Second, what are you taking in? The world is after us in a lot of ways. It's molding our perspective. We might be afraid because we're taking in too much bad news over and over and over. Newsrooms fill us with news—not so much information but entertainment. Do you remember the days when TV went off the air at 11:00 p.m. or midnight? It would be awesome if that would happen again. It would be great if there wasn't 24-hour news cycle or unending updates—then we wouldn't always feel we were missing something. FOMO (Fear of Missing Out) is real.

For example, someone from a news station called a friend of mine and informed him that someone made some comment. The producer asked him, "Are you outraged about that comment?" My friend said, "Well, I don't like the comment, but I'm not outraged about it." The reporter then asked, "Can you be outraged by tomorrow morning?" My friend said, "I don't think I can." The reporter turned to someone else for the interview.

The news uses hyperbole and tries to get people excited with statements such as "It's an outrage" or "It's a bombshell statement." Then, we must ask ourselves if the phrase they used was an accurate description of what really happened. Most of the time, it is not.

When I was in college, one of my professors told the class, "If you find what people are afraid of, you can make a million dollars. You play to people's fears, and people will respond with the need for protection." That is exactly what happens all the time in our society. But God will deliver you from all your fears. The answer is not turning off the TV, although that may help. The answer, of course, is turning to Jesus.

The Good News
John 14:27

It's the gospel! Jesus meets my anxieties. Jesus meets my worries and my fears. I can come through any news report. I'm not going home until Jesus decides and I'll trust Him with every trial.

There is an upper story in heaven, not just the lower story of what's happening on the earth. As society disconnects from God, we get nothing but the lower story. The lower story is the earth aching with pains to declare that we need God in heaven through Christ to meet our needs.

If we only get a lower story, we will be hopeless and anxious. But if we get an upper story that God is at work in some way, we can rest. We can say, "I don't like what is going on, but I am praying the Lord's Prayer: 'On earth as it is in heaven.'" Let's bring some heaven down to the earth and let God do His work. He is the fixer. We're not the ones in control. God is the fixer of all things.

Corrie ten Boom wisely said, "Worry is a cycle of inefficient thoughts whirling around a center of fear."[3] I call that sideways energy—energy that is just leaking out. Get the right perspective; God is in control.

How do we seek God during anxiety? Bible reading, prayer, counseling, and never underestimating the power of hope. When you followed Jesus, you trusted that His death on the cross was for you and that His grace and forgiveness reached you. Now you can walk the rest of your life in hope knowing that God is who He said He is and will do what He said He will do. So let's walk in obedience to His plans and principles.

Our disobedience, on the other hand, will increase our fears. His power always accompanies His ideas. His power doesn't always accompany your ideas.

Realize there is a higher story taking place; something in the heavenlies is going on. Let's walk obediently and focused on the higher story in the midst of the lower story. His peace on our path.

Confess Your Guilt
Psalm 38:18

What are you worried about? Are you anxious about your marriage? Are you being obedient to Christ by honoring your wife or your husband? If you are obedient to the Lord and trust God with your marriage, you will have less anxiety. It will be a blessing instead of a burden.

Are you worried about finances? Are you faithful to God with your money? If you're not obedient on your finance path, you're going to be anxious about it. It's up to you. The best way to stop being anxious about money is to say, "God, it's all Yours, not just 10 percent but 100 percent. And I'm trusting You with it. I want to be faithful and able to give." It's not about giving to the church or a ministry or because God needs your money. It's about being at peace and trusting Him. If you're disobedient in your spending and always buy the biggest and the best, then of course you're going to be anxious because you're a servant to the next package on your doorstep instead of to Jesus.

How do we seek God during anxiety?

If our passion isn't Jesus, then we're asking for anxiety. We have to be passionate about the things of God. Seek first the kingdom of God. Do not worry about tomorrow. Seek first His kingdom and His righteousness. And then, as you're seeking them, you're letting God take care of tomorrow.

I seek the Lord, trust the Lord, and love the Lord, but I still wake up at 2:00 in the morning. I've got the right perspective, I'm walking the right path, I have passion for Jesus more than anything else, but at times, I'm still anxious. What do I do in those moments? I get out of my bed, kneel down, and call out to the Lord in prayer, "What am I worried about, Lord? What is going on here? What do I need to give to You?" And that prayer altar is where I lay things down. What do you need to lay down before Him today?

A Little Church History
Galatians 2:16

God is at work when we least expect it. On October 31, 1517, Martin Luther, who struggled with depression and anxiety, nailed his *95 Theses* to the door of a church in Wittenberg. He was trying to get an academic discussion going at the university where he was teaching. He wasn't intending to start a worldwide movement. He was speaking against indulgences. Leo X, the pope at the time, was a big spender. For example, he spent one-seventh of the Vatican's money on his coronation. He also wanted to raise a large sum of money to build St. Peter's Basilica in Rome.

Pope Leo X asked his people to sell indulgences to raise money. They were said to forgive sins or get someone out of purgatory. His friar Johann Tetzel went from town to town selling indulgences and proclaiming, "As soon as the coin in the coffer rings, the soul from Purgatory springs."[4]

When Leo X died, the church was bankrupt and had to borrow candles for his funeral from another funeral. Luther also spoke out against that, and in doing so, he brought about what came to be called the Protestant Reformation. Because of his protests, things changed. Ministers could marry (praise God!). Church services were in the native tongue, not Latin. The Bible was translated into different languages. Common people could own Bibles. Services were centered on preaching. People could read what priests were teaching from the Bible. There was also congregational singing. Lutheranism grew tremendously. The Protestant Reformation ended up with the Five Onlys (*Solas*). Each one is an anxiety killer.

Sola Scriptura: Scripture alone. The Bible alone is our highest authority.

Sola Fide: Faith alone. We are saved through faith alone.

Sola Gratia: Grace alone. We are saved by the grace of God alone. I don't have to work to get to heaven. So much of our anxiety comes from trying to be perfect. Grace. Grace.

Solus Christus: Christ alone. Don't look at humans; look to Jesus.

Soli Deo Gloria: To the glory of God alone. We live for the glory of God alone.

Five Anchors
2 Corinthians 10:5

It's surprising to hear that a powerful man of God like Martin Luther struggled with depression, but he did. We will all have dark days; some people have darker days than others. Here was Luther's advice when he was in the lows:

- Avoid being alone for long periods of time.
- Seek out people or situations that bring you joy.
- Sing and make music.
- Deliberately dismiss heavy thoughts.
- Make a list of all the things for which you can give praise.
- Exercise patience with yourself.
- Believe that depression can have a positive and fruitful side.

Luther's protest became Five *Solas* (Onlys). These five anchor points—the Bible, faith, grace, Christ, and His glory—are the anchors we can grab onto in times of need.

Are you giving your anxieties to Jesus, or are you just trying to stuff them down? Where is the place of unbelief in your life? You need to tell God that you have a place of unbelief. You need to believe that you are stronger than you think in that area of your life.

Where is the hope in your life? Are you just taking the negativity from the news intravenously? Or are you letting the IV of Jesus and His blood be your blood? Yes, the world is terrible. It is always going to be terrible. But Jesus Christ is Lord. He is always going to be Lord. He is always going to be above all the things that are happening. Praise the Lord! Jesus Christ has overcome the world! He is our Anchor in an anxious world.

The Welland River turns into the Niagara River, which turns into Niagara Falls. When the two rivers meet, there is a sign that says, "Do you have an anchor? Do you know how to use it?" God has given you an anchor. Do you know how to use it? If so, when the rapids come, use the anchor of Jesus . . . let it dig in deeply. Take your anxiety to the Lord and say, "God, I'm trusting You with this. Show me how to believe deeper. Increase my faith."

Give your anxieties to God right now, and trust in the gospel of Jesus Christ. He lives inside you, and He has overcome the world.

Great News! God Fights for Us!

Joshua 10:7–15

All of us go through seasons in life when we cannot see the light. Each day seems darker than the day before. Sometimes it is so dark that we may even wonder if the sun is there. Likewise, in the midst of trials and problems, we doubt if God is there for us. Today and all through the next seven devotionals, we will be inspired by an amazing story. The Creator of the sun and every other star you see in the sky (as well as those you cannot) is going to stop the sun and extend the day to fight for His people.

Yes, what you have just read is right! One day in history, God listened to a man named Joshua who trusted in Him so strongly that he bluntly prayed for God to stop the sun so he could finish a battle. Five kings of the Amorites were so afraid of Joshua that they came together to go against him and God's people.

In Joshua's time, the people of Israel were conquering the Promised Land. The Gibeonites, a people who lived in that land, sent word to Joshua asking him to help them because five Amorite kings were threatening to take one of the Gibeonite cities. Joshua had made a treaty with the Gibeonites, so the Israelites were forced to honor that promise. The Lord told Joshua, "Do not be afraid of them, for I have handed them over to you. Not one of them will be able to stand against you" (Josh. 10:8). Joshua marched all night with his entire army, took the five Amorite kings by surprise, and won the battle.

In our Christian journey, we, too, find ourselves in battles. We may feel surrounded by many enemies, just as Joshua did. But I have good news for you. No one will be able to stand against you! It does not matter how many enemies you are facing today. Do not be afraid because you are not alone. God is with you and not against you. God will journey with you through these battles so you can grow in your trust in Him. He knows that you are not perfect, but He does not turn His face away from you. God wants to show Himself to you in these moments. Do not be discouraged. The Lord will be with you, and He will give you the victory!

Whatever battle you are facing, know that the Lord's face is toward you.

Three Types of Struggles in Life
Joshua 10:7–15

Have you found yourself going through periods when it seems that everything and everybody is against you? Undoubtedly, you have. We all do. Can you remember a time when you desperately asked for help, and a friend or parent showed up and fought for you?

In our spiritual walk, we encounter different types of difficulties. They can be inconveniences, challenges, or battles. First, let's consider each of those words. An inconvenience is when our luxuries and comfort get pushed away. For example, "This line is so long. Why can't they open another register?" Or "Why can't the plumber come on Tuesday? I'll have to cancel my hair appointment." Do you see yourself here? These are not battles or challenges; they are mere inconveniences.

Challenges are different. They have to do with difficulties in marriage or parenting. Challenges are when we encounter incompetent people at work. It's when expensive bills arrive and you are facing difficult months ahead. These are challenges. You need time to find answers to the problem, and the solutions may be effort, discipline, and work. Still, you can find a solution and solve it yourself.

Battles are completely different. When you face grief, depression, anxiety, financial debt, illness, or a relationship crisis, you are in a battle. You cannot solve the problem on your own. You may not have the necessary skills to do that. You are either going to move forward or backward. You win or you lose. You need God's power. You need His intervention to go ahead. You cannot do it by yourself. It's important for us to properly define what we are facing. God is there to help in all three but particularly in the battles.

Joshua found himself in a battle. To win the battle, he needed God. He could not face five enemies and their armies with just one army of his own. He needed a miracle. God did three things for Joshua and the Israelites: He confused the enemy, He threw hailstones from the sky, and He made the sun stand still in the sky until the Israelites could defeat their enemies. Joshua 10:14 closes this way: "The Lord fought for Israel."

I wonder what your battle is. What is your impossible? It may look like you are surrounded and there is no way to address the matter. Expect a miracle!

January 22

Trust in His Promises
Joshua 10:8

I can honestly say that one of the hardest things to learn in life is to trust. I would dare to say that the more we know people, the more we tend to not trust. However, if we were to analyze the core of the problem, it does not have to do with the act of trusting. The real issue is the one in whom we place our confidence. When we trust, we rely on the character, ability, strength, or truth.

Trusting requires only one action: to stand still and do nothing but wait for the one in whom we have placed our confidence to act. It is so simple and yet so difficult! The only thing we have to do is wait and allow the person we trust to do what they have said they will do. But our instinct is to try to take the matter into our own hands. Nevertheless, when we face battles, we know we do not have the power to do what is needed. The only thing we can do is trust and wait for the One who has the necessary strength to step in and win the battle.

The amazing story of Joshua that we have been focusing on teaches us a crucial lesson. God told Joshua not to be afraid because no enemies would be able to withstand him. God made a promise, and Joshua believed and trusted in God's Word. The result: the Lord fought for Israel! Joshua did not have the ability or strength to win this battle. The first and only thing Joshua could do was trust God, who does not forsake those who seek Him.

The Bible has thousands of promises we can grasp. When the enemy surrounds your life and threatens to destroy you, when you cannot act, the first thing to do is set your mind on God's promises. Trust in God's power to deliver you from evil. It is your choice whether to focus on your ability or on God's. All of life is a chance to learn to trust Him more, to get to know Him, to really know Him.

All of life is a chance to trust Him more. Trust in His promises, in His ability, strength, power, and character. God does not forsake those who seek Him.

Prepare to Advance
Joshua 10:9

Imagine stepping into an NFL game without the proper equipment or training and having a linebacker run toward you. How is that going to work out for you? Some of us trust so much in our personalities, abilities, and experiences that we think we can go into battle unprepared. Fortunately, life teaches us that it takes preparation to succeed. It's a lesson we all learn.

The second truth we can learn from Joshua's story is to show up to battle prepared to advance. God promised Joshua that He would fight for the Israelites. After receiving this promise, after believing and trusting in God, Joshua and his army took the time to prepare for battle. They caught the enemy by surprise. They walked 25 miles and had to ascend 4,000 feet, from Gilgal to Gibeon. It took them the whole night to get ready for battle.

It makes you wonder how many times we show up for battle unprepared. How many times do we try to take matters into our own hands before spending time alone with God, before praying, or before studying the Word of God and meditating? It takes time to prepare for battle. It takes effort. You cannot face the enemy without preparation or you will fail and go backward. Remember that in combat, you either win or lose. There is just no other option.

The most significant spiritual battle that ever took place on the earth occurred at Gethsemane. It was the night before Jesus' crucifixion, and Jesus knew He was going to face the enemy at the cross. He did not show up to battle unprepared. His disciples, on the other hand, did not prepare; they did not bother to pray. And when they were tempted later in the battle, they sinned. Jesus prayed all night long. He did it so earnestly that His sweat was like drops of blood falling to the ground. This was the Son of God! If the Son of God Himself took time to pray before going to battle for you and for me, how much more do we need to pray before every battle. Allow this truth to sink in. Let us be humble enough to seek the Lord's face before facing our enemies.

Lord, help us to be humble and wise enough to realize that we need to prepare before stepping into battle. First we trust, and then we prepare to advance.

Trust His Time Frame
Joshua 10:12

How many of us get impatient easily? Do I hear a resounding "I do"? In our fast-paced generation, we want everything done five minutes ago. But in the spiritual realm, it is not always like that. Everything takes the perfect amount of time. Who determines this? An eternal God. Someone who is not restrained by time and space. In the book of Ecclesiastes, we read that there is a time for everything and a season for every activity under the heavens (Eccles. 3:1). We need spiritual wisdom to understand that God's timing is not our timing.

Another truth we can learn from Joshua's story is about spiritual wisdom when it comes to time. When we learn to trust God and believe in His promises, we can go through the valley of the shadow of death, knowing that He will fight for us. We also know that we need to prepare before stepping into battle. Joshua and his army marched all night long to prepare for battle and take the enemy by surprise. When the battle began, Joshua prayed and asked God to hold the sun still so they could finish the battle that day.

Clearly, when it comes to us, we would like to get the job on the first interview. We would love it if our kids took in a lesson from a twenty-minute conversation that took us twenty years to learn. If you were to battle cancer, you would likely pray for it to be beaten on the first round of chemotherapy. It is as simple as that. Not one of us desires to spend time in the valley of the shadow of death. We want to get out of there as soon as possible.

Nevertheless, in order for God to fight our battles, we have to trust His time frame. It is natural that we want victory in our battles as soon as possible. But we must give time for God to move. Allow Him to decide when to act. But remember, that doesn't give us a license for spiritual procrastination. There is a time to move. Joshua and his army did what they had to do, but they trusted God and allowed Him to do His part at just the right time.

For God to fight your battles, you have to trust His time frame.

Realize His Grace
Joshua 9:13–15

Our perspective of things causes us to make decisions based on what we can see and understand at any given moment. We are finite beings, so our understanding of situations is based on what we can analyze from what surrounds us, as well as our past experiences. Sadly, we often make decisions in a rush. We do not ask for counsel, and sometimes the people we love end up paying the price for our bad choices. Or they might help us solve a problem that wasn't theirs to solve. They do it because they love us. They decide to fight for us even though it is not their responsibility.

I want to share the background of the story we have been studying. We know that God fulfilled His promise and fought for His people, but why did they get into battle in the first place? It all started in Joshua 9:3. The Gibeonites were neighbors of the Israelites. When they heard about the victories the Israelites were having, they decided to trick God's people into a peace treaty, pretending to come from very distant lands. They did this because they were afraid of them. The battle that came later happened because Joshua made a treaty with these people before consulting God. Can you believe that? He was tricked into the treaty, so the Israelites had to keep their word and protect the Gibeonites.

This story is surrounded and covered in God's amazing grace. Joshua made a bad decision, and God, in His grace, fought the battle for Joshua anyway. Joshua didn't pray about that initial decision; he did not consult God or include God in his decision. But God, in His grace, decided to fight for His people. Every single battle the Lord fights for you and me will take place because of His grace. We surely do not deserve it, but that is what the cross is all about—love.

Someone who did not deserve to pay for our mistakes decided to take our place, to pay for our faults. That is how amazing God's love and grace are for us. May the realization of how much this cost Jesus teach us to make decisions and plans according to God's heart.

Realize His grace. Move by His plan, not your own perspective.

Surrender Your Battle
Exodus 14:13–14

Have you ever seen someone so deep in thought they are clueless to the world around them? They act as if nobody is watching them. In difficult times, we tend to focus so hard on our thoughts and limitations that the rest of the world seems to vanish. We cannot get our minds to think about anything else. We do not even care if we look like crazy people to those around us.

It is so hard to cast our cares on God and stop thinking about them! Yes, real surrender and trust are based on doing exactly that. It is not our problem anymore. It has become God's problem. That is what allowing God to fight for us means. All of life is a chance to trust Him more. Saint Augustine prayed like this: "You have made us for yourself, and our hearts are restless, until they find rest in you."[5] Find the rest you need in God. Let us pray together and surrender our cares to the Lord.

Here's our prayer for today:

> *I trust You, Jesus, with my battles. There is nothing in this world that can separate me from Your love. As I trust You, I know You will step in and save me. You will fight my battle for me. I need Your ability, strength, power, and character to intervene.*
>
> *I recognize that I do not have what it takes to win this battle, but Your grace is sufficient for me. Your power is made perfect in weakness. What I do know is that when I am weak, I am strong in You.*
>
> *Thank You, Jesus, because in spite of my bad decisions, You still fight my battles. You already won the victory over sin and death. Thank You for Your saving grace. I surrender my battles to You. Give me Your peace.*
>
> *In Jesus' name, amen.*

God keeps in perfect peace those whose minds are steadfast because they trust in Him.

God Is the Center of Attention

Psalm 84:10–12

Can you think of a better visual aid to get your attention than the sun? You cannot escape its grandiosity and power for about twelve hours of every day. It does not matter where you are or what you are doing. The sun is there, reigning over the sky.

Undoubtedly, when the psalmist was writing Psalm 84, he had a very clear and simple idea in mind. His purpose was to show us how important God is. He was affirming that the heavens declare God's glory and that God is like the sun. Mighty, overpowering, sublime, God is above everything else we can see or touch. God is the creator of the sun, and if God's creation is so powerful, just think about how strong and magnificent God is. Consider this, and let this image become the focus of your day and life.

God is so much more than the sun. He is the creator of everything and should therefore be the center of our focus and attention. Our most profound satisfaction should not be found in what we do or in the things we own. Our deepest satisfaction should be found in the companionship of God. If God is not the center of our lives, then sooner or later we will start looking for satisfaction in other places.

The problem is not that we may love our jobs, family, friends, or hobbies too much . . . but that we may love God too little. In John Calvin's words, "Man's nature, so to speak, is a perpetual factory of idols."[6] We tend to make idols out of good things and forget that we should love God first. He must be the center of our lives.

I wonder if this is true for us today. Is God the center of our lives? The focus of our attention? Usually, when this is not the case, we will feel empty, unsatisfied, and alone. If this is how you are feeling today, or if you know in your heart that God and His kingdom are not the number-one priority in your life, I urge you to meditate on the fact that the creator of the sun sent His Son, Jesus Christ, to the earth to die on the cross for you and for me. That is how important you are to Him.

Just as the earth revolves around the sun, so our lives are to revolve around the Son. Jesus is the only One who truly deserves to be the center of your attention.

The Path of Discovery
Psalm 25:4–5

Maybe you know where you are going. Perhaps your direction and objectives are clear. The only problem you may encounter is choosing which path to take to arrive at that destination without wasting time. As Christians, we know that God, the creator of the sun, sent His Son to earth to become our destination—the center of our attention.

In our Christian walk, we sometimes find ourselves asking difficult but honest questions. What happens when we do not feel satisfied in Christ? Why is it that we still have anxiety, pain, hurt, or fear? What does that mean? Does it mean that God is not satisfying? Does it mean I am walking in sin? We certainly would like to have the answers in as much detail as possible, but would that really help? We tend to remember and learn from what we experience, not from what someone clearly explains to us.

As a believer in Christ and you know that God is your number-one satisfaction, you are on the right path to discovering profound truth. We will never have the complete and ultimate picture or answer to everything until we reach heaven. The apostle Paul put it like this: "For now we see only a reflection as in a mirror, but then face to face. Now I know in part, but then I will know fully, as I am fully known" (1 Cor. 13:12). Paul was writing to Christians. He was saying that in our Christian path there will always be things we do not understand completely.

On the path of discovery, we may not have everything figured out, but that is why it is a path of discovery! Paul also gave this piece of advice:

> Not that I have already reached the goal or am already perfect, but I make every effort to take hold of it because I also have been taken hold of by Christ Jesus. Brothers and sisters, I do not consider myself to have taken hold of it. But one thing I do: Forgetting what is behind and reaching forward to what is ahead, I pursue as my goal the prize promised by God's heavenly call in Christ Jesus. (Phil. 3:12–14)

The most important word in these verses is *in*. Jesus is the center of attention, and *in* Him you have the answer to everything.

Stay on the path of discovery. Satisfaction is discovered in Christ.

The Path of Experimentation

Matthew 7:24

When considering what truly gives meaning to our lives, we may find ourselves either on the path of discovery or the path of experimentation with satisfaction. When you know that true satisfaction in life is found in Jesus Christ, then you are on the path of discovery. You may not have everything figured out, but you understand that Jesus is the reason for living and that ultimate satisfaction is found in Him. What happens when that is not where you are? Then you are walking down the path of experimentation.

When you take the path of experimentation, you are still looking for something. Possibly a foundation upon which to build your life? It can be spiritual or not. As teenagers, we usually look for approval or excitement. Single adults often crave accomplishment and companionship. If we already have that, we tend to look for stability and the blossoming of our loved ones. In adulthood, satisfaction and top priorities may come from comfort, consistency, and convenience.

Remember, these are all good things. However, they do not satisfy us completely. You may think that you would be truly satisfied if you could teach the Bible like your pastor, sing and worship like the worship leader, or have some other gift. When we think like that, we are walking down the path of experimentation. We believe that once we check off the points on our list, we will finally be satisfied. Unfortunately, we later realize that emptiness is still there and that satisfaction does not come from the outside. It is a matter of the inside, an internal and eternal foundation in Christ.

When you worship the wrong things, nothing else in life comes out quite right. But when you worship the only One who is truly capable of giving you real satisfaction, you will have a new sense of what really matters, and you will prioritize your life accordingly. I can promise you this: if you get off the path of experimentation, you will find yourself saying the same words written by the psalmist: "Better a day in your courts than a thousand anywhere else. I would rather stand at the threshold of the house of my God than live in the tents of wicked people" (Ps. 84:10).

When you stay on the path of discovery in Christ, true worship will flow out of your lips, and God's kingdom will be your number-one priority. Now, you are building on a firm foundation!

The Lord Is like the Sun, the Source of Unlimited Power

Psalm 147

Creation is a symbolic representation of a real and personal God. It's God's poem. God is the Creator, the artist. Creation is His work of art, a living poem.

Some people confuse the creation with the Creator and end up worshiping the things God created. When the psalmist wrote, "For the LORD God is a sun and shield" (Ps. 84:11), he was portraying God's grandeur. The Creator's supremacy and power are over everything.

Imagine if we were to buy all the energy the sun produces in twenty-four hours. We would have to cover the entire surface of the United States four miles deep with silver dollars. The amount of energy the sun produces could last thirty billion years. Can you imagine that? It is such a powerful image! God is portrayed as the source of unlimited power.

On the path of discovery in Christ, you may face anxiety, pain, hurt, or fear. Yes, that does happen to Christians. We may feel like we are living on the edge, but we have the power to overcome every situation. When Paul wrote his letter to the Philippians, he said this:

> I know how to make do with little, and I know how to make do with a lot. In any and all circumstances I have learned the secret of being content—whether well fed or hungry, whether in abundance or in need. I am able to do all things through him who strengthens me. (Phil. 4:12–13)

We all face different circumstances and trials. However, we can make it through things like depression through Christ who strengthens us. You can and will make it through hurts through Jesus who gives you strength.

We can overcome the world because we have believed that Jesus is the Son of God. He will give us the strength we need and the power to be content in any and every situation. I encourage you to keep this thought in your mind and heart today. Meditate on it and make it yours.

The Lord is greater than the sun. That source of unlimited power will give you all the strength you need in any given situation.

The Lord Is a Sun, Our Needed Light
Psalm 28:6–8

Many psalms were written for people on a pilgrimage. The people of Israel would travel from their homes to the temple in order to worship and be together in the presence of God. The journey was long and took many days. As soon as the sun went down, travelers had to stop and camp. It got cold, and they could not see the way, so they had to wait for the rising of the sun to follow the road. The sun was essential for them to know where to go and to keep them warm in the desert, where the temperature dropped significantly at night and a fire was needed to keep warm. You could not continue your journey until dawn.

As Christians, we, too, are on a journey. We are journeying through teenage years, singlehood, marriage, and adulthood. Sometimes we face moments, and the world becomes a very dark place for us. We desperately need light and guidance. In Psalm 23, King David speaks of those feelings like being in the darkest valley—the valley of the shadow of death, a place where there is no light. The road is not clear. So, what does the psalmist do in this situation?

First, the psalmist realizes that he is not alone—God is with him. Then he holds on to what he is certain of. For example, Psalm 119:105 says, "Your word is a lamp for my feet, and a light on my path." God's Word is the most certain, the safest, and the clearest ally when we face difficult times. Do you find yourself in a dark place today? Is your path unclear? God's Word is the right place to go. God's Word has the correct answer to every situation.

As pilgrims, we encounter dark places and valleys filled with shadows, but we are not alone. We also have this reassurance: 2,000 years ago, the Light of the world came to the earth and took our place on the cross. That day, at noon, darkness came over the whole land until 3:00 in the afternoon, for the sun stopped shining. Jesus paid the price so we could be reunited with the Father. The source of unlimited power shined His light to show us the way.

The Lord is a sun, our needed light. He is living and shining inside of you.

The Lord Is a Shield; He Is Protective Heat

Psalm 84:11–12

Our relationship with the sun is twofold: warmth and warning. On the one hand, I love the sensation of warmth covering every inch of my skin. On the other hand, once I start feeling that this warmth is going beyond a pleasant sensation, I take it as a warning and thank God for sunscreen. It is interesting that the psalmist used this powerful image—the Lord as a sun and a shield.

The psalmists use several images to describe God's protection around us. They describe it as a shield and even as wings that cover us with feathers (Ps. 91). When we are in God's presence, we feel protected. These are moments we all cherish and long for. His arms are around us, so nothing and nobody can harm us.

The Lord is a shield. He certainly protects us, and we feel safe and warm. However, this warmth is also a warning for us; it can become protective heat. In God's presence we encounter His holiness, and the Holy Spirit is in our hearts guiding us to all truth. Have you ever felt the Holy Spirit telling you, "Stop! Go away from this place!" The psalmist knew this when he wrote, "For the LORD God is a sun and shield. The LORD grants favor and honor; he does not withhold the good from those who live with integrity" (Ps. 84:11). When you walk with integrity, you understand that not only does God protect, but He also warns us regarding those things that are not good. That is why His Word is a lamp to light our way. We have freedom to do anything, but not everything is beneficial or constructive.

God does not withhold His blessings from those whose walk is blameless. It is our decision whether we want to live in God's presence or in the tents of the wicked. When we know that it is better to be one day in God's presence than a thousand elsewhere, we not only enjoy the warmth of His presence but also understand that we cannot play around with God. He is holy, and He will not withhold His blessings when we decide to live with integrity.

Worthy of Praise
Psalm 84:10–12

God's grandeur is portrayed throughout the Bible. Creation is God's poem. God the Creator made the sun, and the psalmist accurately used the image of the sun to remind us of God's magnificence and unlimited power. Allow this image to become the focus of your day and your life. The Father blessed and made the seventh day holy, because on it He rested from all His work of creation. Let us pray together and remind ourselves of our journey.

As I seek You, Lord, and make You the center of my life, I want to trust in Your unlimited power—even in the midst of difficulties and struggles. I can do all things through Christ who strengthens me.

In the valley of the shadow of death, tears, and sorrow, You will hold me and guide me with Your light. I need Your light. When my path becomes dark and uncertain, Your Word is a lamp unto my feet and a light unto my path. I need You to guide me as I walk because I am not perfect.

I need Your protective shield and heat, that warmth that comes and helps me understand that sin is never the path to satisfaction. I choose to pursue You above all else.

Thank You for sending Your Son Jesus to the earth to give His life for me. Thank You, Jesus, for taking my place and loving me. You truly are the light, the way, the truth, and the life. Thank You for not withholding Your blessings as I choose to follow You and live my life for You.

Lord, I trust You as I walk and continue on the path of discovery of who You are and who I am in You. I can say that it is better to spend one day in Your courts than a thousand elsewhere.

In Jesus' name, amen.

Don't Just Sit There . . . Worry

Psalm 34:4

There was a pillow in my wife's childhood that said, "Don't just sit there . . . worry." Intended to be a joke, it was all too true for most of us. That's why the Bible is filled with "Don't fear. Don't worry. Pray." We deal with worry every day.

Think about the different stages in life. Whether you are a student, single, married, a parent, an empty nester, or retired, each age brings some sort of stress. When we were in high school, we stressed about getting good grades so we can go to the university of our choice.

Once we get into college, we worry about graduating and getting a job. After landing a job, we have had enough of the single life, so we stress about finding "the one." We find Mr. or Miss Right, and then we feel like it is time to tie the knot. We get married, try to make it work, and realize that doing life with your soul mate isn't always easy. And all that produces anxiety. Then we think, *Let's have kids*. Now we are stressed about our kids and parenting. Finally, we get closer to retirement and worry we might outlive our money.

Remember the Word of God is full of verses that speak about worry and fears. Open it up and discover the treasures. The apostle Paul tells us in the book of Philippians to not be anxious about anything. All we must do is present our worries and fears to God; He is our counselor who gives us peace and consoles our hearts. He is our anchor of hope, a God who carries our burdens and gives us rest.

When we seek the Lord, He hears us and rescues us from our fears. God wants to grow our faith through anxiety and teach us to walk in His strength.

The Thrills and Threats
Psalm 56:3–4

Life is a combination of thrills and threats. How many times are we thrilled about something, and it slides into a secondary threat? You are invited to a fancy party . . . Yeah! But what is your next thought, that comes with a pinch of panic? Yep. *What am I going to wear?* Or maybe a new business deal is before you. What an opportunity! Ten seconds later . . . *What if it doesn't go through?*

Even a thrill can turn into some level of threat.

Remember, anxiety is a psychological and physiological state of arousal caused by the brain's interpretation of a stimulus as a threat. Arousal, stimulus . . . threat. It's an odd road. It's also physiological; it affects your body. A stiff neck, extreme fatigue, and even acid reflux can be due to anxiety. However, it's not only of the mind and body; it is spiritual as well.

Our worry is often rooted in unbelief. Life can be scary, and our plans often differ from God's. We think it is time for a rescue; He thinks it's time for teaching. We are ready for a voice from heaven, and He is content to just speak through verses of Scripture. It can be frustrating and faith building. We must keep walking, praying, and trusting. Only He knows when the clouds will part, or the road will smooth. Thankfully, in accordance to His timing will be in accordance to our best.

Through the thrills and threats, each can be a trigger of concern. Keep walking. Sometimes old fashioned perseverance is the only route. The saints of old showed grit we struggle with today. I'm always inspired reading a missionary biography, but do I have the fortitude to live it out? Some days yes, others no.

As crazy as it sounds, our struggles are also an opportunity for spiritual growth—a great opportunity. Your mind, body, and soul feel threatened, yet God is telling you to trust in Him. That is an opportunity. Trusting in God should happen not only in the good times but challenging times as well. Like weights on a barbell, the resistance becomes muscle.

A little self-examination: What area of your life can you believe God more? How would that shape your perspective, faith, feelings, and worry?

God Listens
Psalm 34:4–8

There's a psalm King David wrote about searching for God and God answering him. This is such an important factor when dealing with any form of challenge. David often wrote these psalms because he was concerned. We need to trust that God listens to us when we pray or cry out to Him.

My wife and I were having a discussion one day. You could call it a tiff. It's when one says, "What I meant . . ." and the other one says, "Well, what I thought . . ." enunciating each word so we get our points across. Finally, I said, "I feel like you never listen to me." It's embarrassing to admit that this is my code for "I'm losing the fight and need to pull an emotional string." Well, the one to whom I am a husband and her pastor responded, "Not listening to you? All I do is listen to you. For decades I've listened to you. I listen to you at home. I've traveled around the world listening to you. I listen to you multiple times every Sunday. People even quote you . . . to me. 'Pastor Gregg said . . .'" So yeah, I really lost the discussion because she was right, and she was listening. Truly, Kelly is a great listener.

Thankfully God is an even better listener. He listens to our prayers all day, every day. He also listens to our pain. When we are worried, fearful, or stressed, He is ready to listen, care, counsel, and respond.

Not only does He listen, but He already knows what we are going through. Have you ever heard someone say their thoughts and prayers are with you? The truth is that their thoughts don't get much done. Sure, it's a kind thing to say, but it's prayers that are seeking and speaking to God.

The silence of God is true in our feelings but not in fact. You will go through a time—numerous times—when you will feel God is silent. I have had those times and can guarantee I will have them again. It is part of the Christian experience. But you don't give up, because the fact is . . . He does listen.

Today, through your challenges, trust more deeply in your faith, realizing that God does listen. Are you stuffing your fears and anxiety, or are you truly giving them to the Lord?

Deep Questions
Psalm 62:5–8

Do you want to be a deep person? We have a very shallow society that is imploding. We are self-destructing before our eyes. We don't need any more rich or smart people. We don't need any more singers, preachers, or whatever talent you want to throw out there. This world needs more people of depth—people who walk deeply with God, ask deep questions, and give deep answers. Deep calls to deep.

We have the opportunity for growth. The author of the book of Hebrews says we have an anchor of the soul that is firm and secure. Anchors go deep into places we don't see. Do you have an anchor of depth in your life?

The answer is Jesus Christ. He came from heaven to die for our sins. It's not your willpower, money, talent, or knowledge. It is the good news of the gospel. Jesus lives inside you and can save your soul. You can place your sin on Him, and in return, He gives you righteousness and forgiveness. You can walk and live in greater depth through Him.

A lot of believers have Jesus as their anchor but do not know how to use it. Let's learn to see anxiety and fear as a place for deep, spiritual growth.

There are three things in this deep place:

Pour out your heart to Him. In Psalm 62:8 David says to pour out your heart and trust God at all times. Be honest with Him. His Word says He is our refuge. Morning will come.

Feel the feelings. The book of Psalms captures feelings. In times of fear, David would write down his feelings. It's okay to feel the emotions you're feeling.

Process forward. Don't worry about something over and over again. Take a step with it. Ask yourself what is stressing you and how you can move forward. Journaling your thoughts can help you process forward. It's a lot like David crying out to God in his psalms. Write down your prayers. Tell God you need Him. Use songs that have the exact lyrics you need to process forward. Our problems will require total surrender to God to move forward.

Using the Anchor
Hebrews 6:19

David wrote a psalm that says he searched for God, and God delivered him from all his fears. That's incredible! Jesus rescues minds and renews lives. That's the type of business Jesus is in. It seems that some people believe God is in the business of receiving perfect people, but that's completely false. God sent Jesus to rescue you in salvation and grow you in your faith. Anxiety is an opportunity for spiritual growth. We grow when we trust Jesus as our anchor.

Let's put our anchor of faith to work, holding us steadfast in the storm. There are a few things you can do with your anchor to help alleviate the stress you are carrying. First, develop new habits. Make lifestyle changes. Anxiety is physiological and psychological, but it also comes from a spiritual root. It affects your body. Ask yourself if your lifestyle is conducive for life. Is your schedule packed all the time? Do you constantly eat food that is unhealthy? Are you exercising? Do you sleep enough, or are you surviving on caffeine? Make lifestyle changes that will help you grow in your faith, not in your fears.

Then find good counseling and friendships. In Proverbs 12:25 it says, "Anxiety weighs down the heart, but a kind word cheers it up" (NIV). Ask your church for counseling. Get involved in a Bible study. Connect with people who will encourage you. There is nothing wrong with needing counseling. Anyone at a high level of leadership will have to talk to someone at some point. I sure have.

Finally, process the season from your heart. Heart work is soul work. Allow God to work in your heart. The truth is that if you do not allow Him to work in your heart, you will stuff it with anxiety. Eventually, all that stress will leak and affect the relationships around you.

Have you ever been so anxious that you got home and took it out on your kids? They were just being kids, but you were leaking anger and negativity. You've got to do the heart work. Once I made a list of verses about anxiety, and I've been reading them phrase by phrase. I'm not doing that because I'm in a horrible place. I'm actually in a better place because of this. Reading and meditating on the Word is great for the soul and the heart.

Let's take anxiety as an opportunity to grow our faith so we can rise up, minister to others, and walk in strength with Him. The strength is not your willpower, but God's power through you. He is the anchor for our souls in the daily waves.

God Loves Cities
Jeremiah 29:7

I'm a native Houstonian. I love our city. You don't get any more Houston than I am. I was born in the Houston Medical Center and raised in Houston. I've been here my whole life except for going away a little bit for college. A while back, somebody gave me a 1941 edition of a street guide to Houston. What's amazing about this guide is that the phone numbers in the advertisements are four digits. At that time, you only had to dial four numbers to get someone on the phone. There was also a map to help you find the businesses listed in the street guide. It looks like an old pirate's map.

I went to a couple of stores to see if I could find another one of these guides. I couldn't find one, but I did find an old travel map. The city had grown tremendously. Since the beginning, downtown has been the heartbeat of what was going on in the City of Houston. From 1841 to 1941 to 2007 to today, there was something happening in the city.

In 1900, 10 percent of the world's population lived in cities. In 2005, 50 percent lived in cities. Now, 80 percent of the world lives in cities. Cities are where people are going. On a planet filled with vast amounts of space, we congregate in cities. Cities are the heartbeat of the world. So, it is crucial for you to reach out to your city or town. And reach out to the suburbs as well. In the heart of your city, be willing to say, "I want to be part of what God is doing in the smack-dab middle of my city—the epicenter."

It is part of your heart and part of history to reach your city. Go to those difficult places and reach out in a great way. Peter encouraged the people of the city to go out and make an impact.

Here are the top five United States cities in population—pick two to pray for. (Pray for Houston too, since it's my hometown and we have become friends!)

- New York City
- Los Angeles
- Chicago
- Houston
- Phoenix

Pray, Give, and Go
1 Peter 4:7–10

Peter makes a declaration in the city of Rome. He starts off by saying, "The end of all things is near; therefore, be alert and sober-minded for prayer. Above all, maintain constant love for one another, since love covers a multitude of sins" (1 Pet. 4:7–8). What he wants us to understand is that because Jesus Christ is returning, we need to be focused. He desires for us to understand the importance of ministry and what God can do through us.

Praying, giving, and going bring focus. Peter is saying that if you understand that the end of things is near, you will be disciplined in prayer. This earth will have a completion moment. There will be a time when ministry will be done on the earth, and those who have trusted Christ will step into eternity with God.

Ministry is so important for us in this very moment. We can say, "Lord, I'm going for it because I know You're coming back." Did you know that for every prophecy in Scripture about Jesus' first coming, there are eight prophecies about His second coming? For every time one of them is mentioned—Christmas, Bethlehem, the birth of the Savior, the Messiah—there are eight prophecies about the return of Christ, the Messiah coming, and the end of time.

By looking at the world today—not just at your city or town, but everywhere—your heart should say, "I have to be even more diligent about praying, giving, and going because I am in the final days." Now, by no means am I trying to declare to you when the final day is. I do not know, but I know that it's closer today than it was yesterday. And Peter is saying that, with this in mind, we need to be focused.

What should we focus on? Peter gives us three things. He begins by talking about loving one another. Next, he says, "Be hospitable to one another without complaining. Just as each one has received a gift, use it to serve others, as good stewards of the varied grace of God" (1 Pet. 4:9–10). Peter is saying that we are to love well, be hospitable, and walk in our giftedness.

Love Well
John 13:34–35

Our life should be marked by loving well, being hospitable, and walking in your giftedness. Peter wants us to love "since love covers a multitude of sins" (1 Pet. 4:8). This doesn't mean that loving somebody gets their sins forgiven. That's not what he is saying. We're not Jesus. We can't forgive sins. It does mean that because of Jesus Christ in our life, because of the understanding that He's coming back, we are going to love well. John also continually speaks to the importance of love.

Let's put love into practice. The church should be known for loving well. Personally, I have a front row seat as a pastor; I love watching how the church loves. If you go through a difficult time, the church will come around and love you well. If you go through grief, they will love you. I hear people say it all the time that they don't know how they would get through difficult times without their church family. The church is a family that loves and you are a part of it. The touch of the church comes through the hands of the members trusting in the power of God.

Here's a great example. There was a man named Darren at our downtown campus. He had struggled with homelessness and addiction. He went to Open Door Mission, an organization our church has partnered with, and they told him about our Bible studies. Realizing he needed all the help he could get, Darren agreed to attend. Billy, one of our volunteers, is also an active member and a volunteer at Open Door Mission. She was waiting with open arms to connect to friends. She told him, "You need to get involved in a church." So, Darren showed up at our downtown campus, struggling with addiction and homelessness. The church is a place for the spiritually healthy and sick. Darren was eventually baptized and became a member of the family of God. The church has definitely loved him to the Lord. Now we celebrate with him!

That's a testimony of loving well, isn't it? God wants us to be out among the people of the city, being used by Him.

Hospitality and Gifts
Romans 12:9–13

The Lord wants us to be hospitable. What does hospitality mean? Hospitality is defined as the friendly, generous reception and entertainment of guests, visitors, or strangers. Hospitality shines with the love of Jesus Christ. Even if we're struggling, Jesus wants us to have a welcoming, hospitable heart. How can God use us to reach out to our friends and neighbors? How can He help us love others well and be hospitable?

Last summer, a couple at our downtown campus moved from the suburbs to the downtown area—the east downtown area called EaDo. They built a house from scratch, from the ground up. They built that house so they could be hospitable. Now, they're having married and young adult Bible studies there. They're hospitable by opening their home to men's and women's ministries and Bible studies. They're also planning to reach out to the poor and refugees. That's hospitality! Many of you have rooms in your homes that need to be redeemed, spaces where you need to say, "Lord, I want You to use this. I bought this house so I could have people over. Let's redeem it and give it to You." Be loving. Be hospitable. Be welcoming.

The Lord also wants us to walk in our giftedness. God has put a spiritual gift in you, and He wants you to put it to use. If you don't know what your spiritual gift is, you're missing out on the biggest joy of your life. Find out what it is. My gifts are leadership, teaching, and evangelism. So, if I wasn't teaching, leading, or sharing my faith, I'd be withering. If you can find your giftedness and put your service—even your vocation—around it, your life will be very different.

The Bible says that some of us have the gift of speaking. If that is your gift, you should speak as if you are speaking God's words. There are also gifts of encouragement, leadership, and teaching. Some have service gifts such as hospitality, mercy, and more. Go and serve in the ways you are gifted. But let God put it together for you. Allow the Spirit to guide you in your talents and gifts.

Loving Your City
Jeremiah 29:7

If you walk in love, in hospitality, and in your giftedness, you'd better look out for the great things God is going to do in your life!

If your desire is to reach your city, be about loving others, being hospitable, and walking in your giftedness. As I said, I am a native Houstonian and I love my city. I want to see God do amazing things there. The church is a key place for evangelizing the city. It says in the book of Genesis that the first city was founded by a man named Enoch. It says he was the builder of the city.

Right before the famous verse of Jeremiah 29:11, the Scripture says, "Pursue the well-being of the city I have deported you to. Pray to the LORD on its behalf, for when it thrives, you will thrive" (Jer. 29:7).

Do you know that Jesus Christ wept only two times? He wept when Lazarus died and when He prayed over the city of Jerusalem. The city is important to God.

If you love your city, you will want to see people come to Jesus Christ and will sacrifice and step forward to make that difference in somebody else's life. Peter says, "If anyone speaks, let it be as one who speaks God's words; if anyone serves, let it be from the strength God provides, so that God may be glorified through Jesus Christ in everything. To him be the glory and the power forever and ever. Amen" (1 Pet. 4:11). The key points are 1) God's glory and 2) His power.

Loving your city and others is about God's glory and power. It's not about loving your city because it has the best sports team or the best food. It's not about your ideas and service to the city. It's about God. It's about God wanting to use you so His love is known to the world. You have this moment before you. It is time you step out into the epicenter of your city and say, "I want to be about what Jesus wept over, and that's the city. Because the city is important to God; it is important to me."

Connect with Your City

Acts 1:8

Sociologist Rodney Stark said, "Early Christianity was primarily an urban movement."⁷ That is very interesting. The original meaning of the word *pagan* was rural person. Another way of saying that would be country hick. The term came to have religious meaning because, after Christianity had triumphed in the cities, most rural people remained unconverted.

Isn't that remarkable that pagan, meaning nonbeliever, was a word used for someone in a rural community because Christianity had so much to do with the city? Have you seen a shift in modern times where cities have gone away from Christ and smaller towns have stayed closer to Christ? Both are important, but we've lost the culture for Christ because we've lost the cities. From its earliest days, Christianity was mainly associated with the cities. Look at the book of Acts and the thrust of missions to the places teeming with people.

If your heart is desiring to get involved in your city, to volunteer and love others well, start by saying, "Lord, for Your glory, Your power, Your heart, I will reach my city." The fact is that Jesus is going to return. We've got to be people who love well, are hospitable, and are using our giftedness. Why? So, our lives can be about His glory and His power, about an impact that can outlast our lives. You are a difference-maker. You have a history-changing, Spirit-empowered, life-giving legacy to leave.

We can step out from simply attending church to being the church. So, step forward at this moment and go for it. This is about growing in our faith in Jesus Christ. This is about understanding that there is something bigger than our life and our plans. This is about being part of all the great things God is doing in your city. That is powerful. I invite you to pray, give, and go where God has placed you.

Imagine His Word through you where you live—small rural or urban. Imagine Los Angeles, New York, Chicago, Tokyo, London, and for me . . . Houston with a heartbeat for Christ.

Valentine's Day: First Step of the Journey
2 Peter 1:3–4

Happy Valentine's Day! Good news, God loves you! Knowing this gives us the incentive to grow in our trust. If you have been to any camp in the last twenty years, you've probably participated in a ropes course. And there is always a *trust fall*. In a trust fall, you stand on a platform, cross your arms over your chest, fall backward, and let your team catch you. If they don't catch you or you bend in half, instead of falling straight back, you hit the ground. You have to trust the ones who are catching you—trust them enough to hold your arms tightly and fall straight back into theirs.

In the apostle Peter's second letter, he wants us to trust the Lord enough so we are willing to fall backward and know that God is going to catch us. A spiritual fall. The letter is three chapters long, and Peter asks us a question in each chapter: *How do I live purely? How do I discern truth? How does this all end?* The letter is like an arrow shot from a bow. There is the tip that will hit the target, the center of the arrow that holds it steady, and finally, the three feathers at the end that guide it and allow it to fly straight.

The tip is hope and Peter is trying to use it to pierce our lives. The center part that holds it all together is diligent application. Peter also gives us three feathers, one in each chapter—warnings, reminders, and promises. Look again at the three main "trust falls" of 2 Peter:

How do I walk purely?

How do I discern truth?

Where is this whole thing going?

Trust fall into Christ with your purity, discernment, and future. He will help us. Peter tells us that He will. Is that enough for us to put our trust in the Lord?

The message in 2 Peter is a very important one, particularly for the younger generations, because this is a worldview message. There is a huge fight raging between two paths. Peter is asking us, "Which path will you take for your life?"—trust fall into the arms of Jesus or, our own plans? Today, trust Him, He will catch you.

Same Kind of Faith
2 Peter 1:1–2

The apostle Peter starts his second letter this way:

> Simeon Peter, a servant and an apostle of Jesus Christ: To those who have received a faith equal to ours. (v. 1)

It may say in your Bible, "A faith of a same kind."

So here we have this kickoff of equal faith and power. Peter says, "To those who have received a faith equal to ours."

Same kind of faith! Get that in your mind. Peter is saying that your Christianity and his are exactly the same. You have the same privileges that Peter had. Now, that blows my mind. Peter was the leader of the early church (Gal. 2:7–8). Peter walked on water (Matt. 14:29). Peter was with Jesus in the garden (Mark 14:32–33). Peter made mistakes but was right there at the transfiguration (Mark 9:2). And now Peter is saying that his faith and my faith are exactly the same.

I don't know about you, but every once in a while, I feel like, "Surely Billy Graham had a little more Holy Spirit than I have." "I know we are all equal, but surely some people are more equal than others." "Certainly, Peter had more faith than I have."

But here Peter is saying no, you are equal before the Lord. That is what we are all looking for in our organizations and societies. That is what we are all looking for in a world where people are always seeking equal rights and treatment. But that privilege only comes through God.

We are all trying to figure out how to get everybody to stop being prejudiced. And here is how: Let them realize that God has created them, and everyone else.

Created the Same
Colossians 3:8–11

When you're a believer in Christ, there is no room for prejudice because God has created every one of us the same. In His eyes, we are all equal—we all have equal access. It doesn't matter if you're rich. It doesn't matter if you are highly educated or graduated Magna Cum Laude or "Praise the Lordy." Every one of us steps forward with just as much Holy Spirit as Billy Graham, Peter, Paul, or anybody else.

There are no JV or varsity teams in Christianity. There is just the team of Christians, united in faith. But we often separate ourselves anyway—by what church we go to, what our giftedness is, whether we are good in public or not, the way we declare things, whether we're shy or bold, whether we are this ethnicity or whether we are that.

In God's kingdom, it's all one team (Col. 3:11). We are all equal. The Greek word for *equal* is used for immigrants who became citizens. They would have all the rights of natural-born citizens. Scripture tells us that God created all people equal in His eyes.

We have moved from darkness to light. We have moved from children of wrath to children of God. We have moved from outside the family of God to inside the family of God. We have moved from citizenship in the world to citizenship in heaven. We all now have the same rights and privileges and the same access to God (Eph. 4:7).

Every believer has the same value. What an amazing thought! That is a blow-your-mind-away thought. That answers so many questions related to what we are trying to do and how we are trying to act as a culture and as a society. If lived out, much tension in society is resolved.

Let's look at this thought that all people are loved by God. Every nation, tribe, people and tongue . . . all equal. We don't look down upon each other because of race or age or anything else (Gal. 3:27–29). We know God has created us all and loves every single one of us. So, we should also honor Him together (Rom. 8:16–17).

Civics and Creation?
Psalm 100:3

Are you familiar with the Declaration of Independence? The second paragraph starts like this:

> We hold these truths . . .[8]

Truths? Unfortunately, we live in a society based on opinions. The second paragraph goes on:

> . . . to be self-evident, that all men [humankind] are created equal . . .

Created? Oh, my! I wish this was taught in every school (Ps. 100:3).

Divinity and equality are connected—right there in the Declaration of Independence with the phrase "created equal."

> . . . that they are endowed . . .

That means graciously given by God. They didn't earn it. They were given it.

> . . . by their Creator . . .

Equality comes from realizing there is a Creator. Why do we have so many problems with prejudice and inequality? Because we have erased the Creator and made our own Declaration of Independence instead of recognizing that equality has been bestowed and endowed by God (Prov. 22:2).

> . . . endowed by their Creator with certain unalienable Rights, that among these are Life, Liberty and the pursuit of Happiness.

Imago Dei—we are all created in the image of God, and this value comes because of the truth of divinity. God has created us (Matt. 19:4), and He loves every single one of us.

Equal Spiritual Maturity

John 1:12–13

An amazing, godly, and generous friend of mine who passed away some years ago once told me that he was a member of a private club. In his typical generosity he said, "Gregg, I want you to go and have a great lunch and put it all under my name."

So, as he wished I took three friends to eat with and had a great time. For one meal I was equal to every member in that club, even though my bill was paid by another.

We all are endowed by our Creator, Jesus Christ, and because of His name, we are spiritually equal with Peter, Paul, and anybody else. It's on Jesus' account, through His death on the cross, that He provides that spiritual equality for us on the authority of His name. We all have the same spiritual privileges. But we do not have equal spiritual maturity. God loves every person on the earth. But that does not mean that everything done is pleasing to Him or we listen to Him with the same clarity or conviction.

We are all equal spiritually, and we can all go to God. But our spiritual intimacy and maturity isn't equal. I have the same access to God as Paul but I'm not quite ready to say I have the same intimacy as the apostle. Spiritual maturity develops as we live a life that is pleasing to Him (Matt. 16:24; Mark 8:34; Luke 9:23). We have the same spiritual privilege and access, and we are citizens of the same kingdom. But we are to keep growing in our spiritual maturity.

A change happens when we cease spiritually drifting because we have chosen spiritual growth. A heart that says, "My number-one quest is to live a life that is pleasing to the Lord" is on a growth path (Col. 1:9–11). A heart that is indifferent still has the same access to God but isn't growing at the same rate.

We all are equally loved. But we want to grow in our maturity (2 Pet. 3:18). That starts with desiring deeply our life to be pleasing to the Lord.

Jesus paid your bill at the most heavenly of clubs. Now we have access like every saint before us, so let's grab hold and never let go.

What Will Be Your Legacy?

Deuteronomy 34:5–12

I want to ask you a question. What will be the legacy of your life? Have you ever thought about that? What will you leave behind? Before you start thinking, *Oh, yeah. I'm going to leave my watch to so-and-so and my stocks to such-and-such,* that's not what I'm saying. I'm talking about looking back on your life. What will be the legacy that you leave? Will you leave a statement that says "I was here"? More important, "God was here through me." The life of Moses was one for the record books, but also the vision continued next in the life of Joshua. Moses impact continued on . . . strongly.

The most popular form of graffiti in the United States is "I was here." We want a statement that says, "I was here. I made a difference. There's my mark." But instead of doing it with a Sharpie on a bathroom wall, let's do it with our lives. Let's say, "God, You did something in me and through me."

In the 1700s, there was a man named Jonathan Edwards who was married to Sarah. Jonathan was an incredible preacher and part of the Great Awakening. You may have heard of his sermon "Sinners in the Hands of an Angry God." In the 1900s, a man named A. E. Winship researched 1,400 of Jonathan and Sarah's descendants. Here is what he found: They had eleven children. Among their descendants were one hundred lawyers, eighty holders of public office, sixty-six physicians, a dean of a medical school, sixty-five professors, thirty judges, thirteen college presidents, three mayors, three governors, three United States senators, one controller of the United States Treasury, and one vice president of the United States.

It's amazing! Their descendants affected even my own personal life. My pastor during college was a descendant of Jonathan Edwards. He baptized my wife. He is an amazing man of God who declared the Word of God over our lives. What will be your legacy?

Repetition Results in Remembrance

2 Peter 1:12

You want to leave a difference-making legacy. That's what Peter is telling us. He says, "I will always remind you about these things." I'm interested in leaving a legacy, and I know you are as well. To do that we need to be reminded. We need to hear truth repeated.

You remember things when you repeat them over and over. Legacy comes from repeated godliness—consistent living, godly discipline, the cumulative effect of time with God.

Have you ever gone to an unfamiliar website? Have you ever forgotten your password? You don't remember it because you don't visit the website or use the password often enough. However, if you pull out your phone and it's time to put in your password to unlock it, you don't even think about it. You don't even pause. You just put in the code because you have repeated that action so many times. Repetition brings remembrance.

Peter is saying that there's no harm in reminding you about what this whole thing with truth is about. Do you know that throughout Scripture, we see many references to remembrance?

Paul says, "I give thanks to my God for every remembrance of you" (Phil. 1:3).

"Jesus said again, 'Truly I tell you'" (John 10:7).

Matthew wrote, "Jesus said, . . . 'Again I tell you'" (Matt. 19:24).

Paul said, "As we have said before" (Gal. 1:9).

If you're at church and think, *I've heard this before*, that's awesome! It's great to have heard it before. The reason you know your phone number is because of repetition. That repetition can also have a negative effect, can't it? If somebody is continually saying negative things to you, it is easy to store that away in your memory. We need to rewire our mind to focus on what God is saying to us. "Rejoice . . . I will say it again: Rejoice!" (Phil. 4:4). I want you to declare those words out loud. Repeat and declare the words that God is saying to you in His Word.

Godly Purpose
Mark 8:36

What words are you repeating to others? Nobody has ever gone to marriage counseling and said, "You know what? My husband tells me he loves me all the time, and I'm sick of it." It doesn't happen like that. If anything, we don't say it enough, right?

Do you know what parenting is? It isn't found in some psychological journal, but parenting is basically being a parrot with a right heart. It's repeating the same things over and over but with the right heart. But what happens in parenting? We say the same things over and over and get ticked off about it, don't we? "I think I said pick up your shoes. Do I have to say this every day for the rest of your life?" Yes, you do.

Parenting is a continual repetition. But it's not just saying, "Pick up your shoes." It's also saying, "God has a purpose for you. God has a plan for you. God has a love for you. God can see you through this. The Bible is real. Yes, we're going to church when we're busy. Yes, we're going to be a worshiping family. Yes, we're going to declare the truths of the Lord. Yes, we're going to be generous. Yes, we're going to treat each other well even when it's not convenient."

As parents, we often have two goals: basic morality and earthly success. But these two are not enough. Of course, these goals are important, but God wants to do something deeper in our life. He wants us to have morals and earthly success, but He calls us first to set goals such as spiritual depth and seeking God's purpose.

"For what will it benefit someone if he gains the whole world yet loses his life?" (Matt. 16:26). It's about having spiritual success in this realm as well as the next. That doesn't mean your children have to be missionaries or pastors. What I'm saying is to be cautious that you are only satisfied with basic morality and earthly success in your life or others you love. Why? Because your goals will become what you repeat. What will be the result for your children? They will believe this: "I need to be successful. I need to make a lot of money to be valued."

What if your desire is to repeat spiritual depth into your friends and family's lives? I want godly purpose to be a goal in their lives. These profound goals keep your marriage together, keep your hearts together, and give you purpose in your singlehood. You could be absolutely miserable and tremendously moral. You don't have to be a believer in Christ to be successful. You want to go deeper than earthly success.

A Life of Camping
2 Peter 1:13–14

David Livingston, a missionary to Africa, said, "I will go anywhere, provided it be forward."[9] He means that he wants to continue to grow in spiritual depth and godly purpose. Why? Because that is where legacy comes from. Maybe you're thinking, *Well, I'm not spiritually deep. I don't even know what godly purpose is.* If you just keep on walking, the cumulative effect of walking with God, being in church, reading the Bible, and praying will give you spiritual depth and purpose.

Peter says, "I think it is right, as long as I am in this bodily tent, to wake you up with a reminder, since I know that I will soon lay aside my tent" (2 Pet. 1:13–14). Peter is saying that life is short, but our legacy is long. Even if you live for ninety years, that's a short life. All those years in light of eternity are short. Paul said, "For we know that if our earthly tent we live in is destroyed, we have a building from God, an eternal dwelling in the heavens, not made with hands" (2 Cor. 5:1).

What you have here is temporary. It's an earthly tent. That's how Paul and Peter speak about it, because 2,000 years ago, they lived in a mostly nomadic culture. They had buildings, but they had lots of tents. It was normal for them to put up a tent and take it back down. That's the image they are using to help us picture the short and temporary nature of our earthly lives. Then Peter describes his legacy as a remembrance for generations to come.

Your life, no matter your age, is a tent. It's a window that opens for a moment and through which you get to declare the truths of God. It's the door of Jesus that you get to go through. It's the opening in the heavens that you get to pray through. It is a short-term thing. Peter is saying that although your life is temporary, you can leave a legacy for years to come. What a powerful oxymoron—a tent that leaves a lasting legacy. When does that become true? When the things of truth are remembered in our lives and regurgitated through words and actions. When our goals are no longer just morality and earthly success but spiritual depth and godly purpose.

Your days as an earthly tent will eventually be over. The time goes quickly. God sets us up for a moment in time. We can have an impact for eternity. We have an opportunity to leave a legacy that will impact generations.

Difference-Makers

2 Peter 1:15

Our church has a difference-maker's declaration. We've said this out loud in worship hundreds of times. I want you to read it and declare it as well.

> *I was made for more than watching. I have a history-changing, difference-making, life-giving, Spirit-empowered legacy to leave. Jesus, I ask You to work deeply in me and clearly through me as I pray, give, and go in Your love. I am a difference-maker. In Jesus' name, amen.*

You are a difference-maker. God has put something in you . . . You were born an original. Don't die a copy. Walk with God and let Him use you where you are because you are a tent, a tent that meets with God. You're a tent that declares the praises of God. Live for what lasts as you live in what doesn't. This is confusing, isn't it? I have to do my taxes, and I have to go to the grocery store. I have to go to the dry cleaners, and I have to put gas in the car. All this stuff that's constantly around can overwhelm me.

I don't believe we purposely are so busy that we do not make time to impact others. Life happens. We have e-mails, text messages, this, and that. That's how life is, right? But instead, I encourage us to live for what lasts in the midst of everything that doesn't. Be in the world but not of the world. Live for a legacy.

What's your legacy? You may leave a legacy of treasure. That's what we think about sometimes, but most importantly, let's leave a legacy of truth. Peter says, "And I will also make every effort so that you are able to recall these things at any time after my departure" (2 Pet. 1:15). This Scripture tells us that Peter's mind was set on a legacy. It's not bad to leave a legacy of treasure. It's great to have a will and a testament but leave a legacy of truth as well.

John Maxwell said, "If you are successful, it becomes possible for you to leave an inheritance *for* others. But if you desire to do more, to create a legacy, then you need to leave that *in* others."[10]

Testament of Truth
Psalm 78:4

When we think of the things we are leaving to the next generation, we tend to think about money and heirlooms. Who's going to get the china? Who's going to get that pretty vase? Whatever it is, we all think about that. When we show up at our great-grandmother's house, we usually leave with stuff, right?

My wife and I have two children. Once everything has been taken care of with our kids and they're out of the house making their own money, we plan to leave an inheritance to a "third child" when we die. Our two children will each get one-third, and the "third child"—the kingdom of God—will get one-third. We've written that in our wills because we want to have an eternal significance. We'll take care of our children, but we want to give to the Lord as well. We communicated that to our kids, and they said, "That's awesome!"

Beyond our giving, I wanted to also state to my descendants clearly what was important to me. So, I rewrote the beginning of my will. Allow me to share it with you:

> I, Gregory John Matte, living in Houston, Texas, declare this to be my will and testament. I want all who read this to know that Jesus Christ is my Savior and there is no doubt in my mind that upon death I will enter into heaven. I will do so not on my own worthiness but through the merits of Jesus Christ our Savior and His death on the cross and resurrection from the dead. I ask that my children and grandchildren share God's Word with everyone and to always remember how much you're loved, knowing that God will provide for you. I encourage you to place your faith in Christ alone and never trust the world for your comfort. I look forward to seeing you again in the life hereafter where we will all live together with our Lord and Savior. May God grant you peace and love and strength as He guides you through this life. And then, at the end of time, we will be reunited in heaven as a happy family seeing Jesus face-to-face.

That's my testament I want to declare to generation after generation. Not just "here's my stuff, divide it up." This is the truth of my life. The stuff—who cares? The truth of God can change a legacy and a lineage.

Peter's Legacy
John 21:18–19

Where is your heart in your legacy? What's the last thing that's going to be spoken about you? Maybe you want to redo your will after yesterday's devotional, but my primary goal is to remind you of the legacy you have as a believer. It doesn't have a thing to do with earthly success or basic morality. The goal has everything to do with the heart of hearts.

Peter said he knew he was going to die. He was getting older, and Jesus had already told him that when he got old, someone was going to tie him up and take him someplace he didn't want to go. He was going to be martyred.

He knew his time was coming. He could see Nero's persecution and power on the rise. Peter knew he was going to be martyred and said, "I will also make every effort so that you are able to recall these things at any time after my departure" (2 Pet. 1:15). We're still recalling these things after his departure, more than 2,000 years later. It's absolutely amazing. Peter was killed right after Nero set Rome on fire and blamed Christians for it.

What is modeled is most remembered. It's not just about what you say. It's what you do. It's how you live. The legacy has to be more than show up early, stay late, build a great business, and be basically moral. It has to be about more. God has a purpose and a spiritual depth for us, and we want to honor Him.

This is what happened to Peter. Church history states that he was crucified upside down in St. Peter's Square in Vatican City. That's why they call it St. Peter's Square. His bones were buried under St. Peter's Basilica, a huge church right there in Vatican Square. In 1960, they excavated underneath the church and found the bones of a man they believe to be Peter.

Peter lived a life as a fisherman and a leader of the church. He was crucified upside down, and his tent was gone. His legacy, however, is his testament to being a witness to who Christ is, and that legacy is still alive today and part of the seeds that are going to change your life. That's a life worth living. That's what I'm calling you to do, to fall into the arms of Jesus and trust Him to do something through you. It doesn't matter if you ever become famous. The question is this: Will you be faithful?

ぁ.

Love First
Matthew 22:34–40

The Civil War was the most divisive time in our country. Have you heard of the Civil War wives Julia Grant and Varina Davis? Varina was married to Jefferson Davis, head of the Confederacy. Julia was married to Ulysses S. Grant, head of the Union. These two fought bitterly against each other in the Civil War. However, when both men died, these widows ended up moving closer to each other. Not only did they become friends, but so did their children. We are living in times when people are divided. We see racism again and again in our nation. Yet what our nation truly needs in times of hate and division is love.

When we choose to love instead of choosing negativity, hate, and division, powerful things can happen in our personal lives and in the lives of others.

Matthew teaches us that very thing. He takes us back to his journey with Jesus and lays a foundation for the church—a foundation of truth and love.

Receiving God's love for us is the first step toward loving God and others. First John 4:19 "We love because he first loved us." God is love. He sent His Son to die for us. The love God has for us does not compare to any other love you will experience. It's a love that impacts and transforms. When we choose to love God first, we can love others even when it may seem hard to do. God changes our hearts with love. He has the power to change hearts and draw others together, just as the Civil War wives did. God can do great things.

We reflect God's love when we choose to love our friends and, even more, our enemies. Often, we want to preach to them or change them. But what about if we just showed love to them? Showing love is a great start to sharing Christ with others. That is our greatest commandment—to love the Lord God with all our heart, soul, mind, and strength and love our neighbors.

Jesus Was God and Man

1 John 1:1–2

Jesus was a man—a real man who walked the dusty roads and ate food just like you and me. He was human! Believing that Jesus was a man is a crucial factor of our faith. The apostle John tells us so in 1 John. He lays that foundation to prepare us for what is next. He testified, "The infinite Life of God himself took shape before us" (1 John 1:2 MSG).

John wanted us to know that he saw, heard, and touched Jesus. Why did he find that so crucial for Christians to know? Because if Jesus did not exist in the flesh, He could not die the death He died. He could not bleed the blood that paid for our sins and rise from the grave to then take us to heaven when we die. We need Jesus to be a man to die for men.

But John does not stop there. He wants us to know that Jesus was also the Word of Life, God in the flesh, which means He can give us direction from heaven. He can breathe words of encouragement when we need them and in the direction we need. John said, "In the beginning was the Word, and the Word was with God, and the Word was God" (John 1:1).

Jesus is also eternal life. He wasn't *just* a man or a teacher. He is God. He is our Savior. As God, He came in the form of man. When we understand that Jesus was God and man, it means we are putting our trust and faith in God as our eternal life. He is our eternity. I'm going to break it down. Jesus was a man who was the Son of God, who is our Savior, who is the bridge by which we can connect with God. Jesus existed as a man to die for our sins. He is our Word of Life who takes us to God to be our eternal life.

Lift up a prayer of thanks for who Jesus is and what He does.

Connection
Psalm 55:14

People yearn for connection. Most of us—no matter our age, race, or socioeconomic class—desire to connect with people. We live in a society that is hungry for connections. Today, we share playlists. Or stay connected with old friends on social media or make new friends on Instagram.

Back in the day, hardly anyone took a taxi unless it was absolutely necessary. Now we have Uber. We Uber everywhere, even to grab a bite to eat. We stay connected with people because our natural being yearns for it. Nevertheless, the connections we make with people have to be more than a hobby or pass by. They have to be deeper than a Facebook comment or Snapchat. They have to be better than sharing our favorite sports team. They have to be from the heart.

Connecting from the heart requires vulnerability. It's sharing with a friend when you're hurting or healing. We may live parallel lives, but we are not connecting in the aspects of the heart. We want people to believe we have it all together and put up a wall that keeps us from having true connections with other people. Husbands and wives should not just be roommates but soul mates. They should not only share a house but their hearts. Families should be connecting. Put away your phones and connect with your children. Here are three points that can help us build a true connection from the heart:

1. *Time:* Give your time, whether it's to your children or a friend. Connection requires your time.

2. *Attention:* Be attentive when you're connecting with someone. We all know that you could be home and yet not present. Make sure your mind, eyes, and ears are present so you can have true connection from the heart.

3. *Resources:* We give our resources with true connection, sharing the resources of our hearts with vulnerability. We let others know our needs and thoughts. We also share our material resources when we connect. Whether it's giving someone a ride or blessing a friend who's in need with food or a gift card, we can have connections from the heart with our resources. Maybe a surprise gift or flowers to say thanks for being a friend.

Challenge your hearts to have a true connection with others.

Lord, connect us with You and others in a life-giving way.

Aquifer of Joy and Purpose
John 7:37–39

When you take a shower or pour a glass of water, most likely it is because of an aquifer. An aquifer is a far underground water source. Aquifers require deep digging to get to the water. Even in dry seasons, we still have water thanks to aquifers.

Jesus is our aquifer of joy and purpose. Here's what that means. The connection and fellowship you make with Jesus Christ when you accept Him as your Savior goes deep down. It does not matter if you're going through a difficult time in your life. He is the provider of joy and purpose. In the midst of trials, He can be your joy.

John testifies, "We proclaim to you what we have seen and heard, so that you also may have fellowship with us. And our fellowship is with the Father and with his Son, Jesus Christ. We write this to make our joy complete" (1 John 1:3–4 NIV). By sharing this, John says his joy was complete. It was not through receiving but through sharing. Obedience brings greater joy, not sin. Sharing with others, not taking from them, brings greater joy. Loving, not hating, brings greater joy.

Joy comes through Jesus Christ, the Son of God—who was 100 percent man and 100 percent God—coming into our hearts. And because of that, we can now have communion with Him and others. We can love and connect from the heart with others through the aquifer of joy and purpose. He digs deep down into our hearts, transforms us, and gives us joy, even in the midst of our circumstances and purpose here on the earth.

How can you live today at a deeper depth with Christ? How can you satisfy your deepest thirst in Christ alone?

Eternal Truths

Colossians 2:6–10

Are you acquainted with anyone who says, "I want to live my life according to a cleverly contrived myth"? Probably not. However, in his Second Epistle, the apostle Peter wrote, "We did not follow cleverly contrived myths when we made known to you the power and coming of our Lord Jesus Christ" (2 Pet. 1:16).

With just a sentence, Peter gives us a challenge, a significant question also posed in Colossians that we have to ask ourselves: Do we live by cleverly contrived myths or by eternal truths?

Why would anyone guide his own life according to a cleverly contrived myth? I don't think we choose to live by myths. Instead, we succumb to them because they are strong and convincing. Their influence is so pervasive that it is just a matter of time before we begin to live by them instead of by the eternal truths of God's Word.

Here's one way that can happen. In America, we watch a screen an average of seven hours per day, and very few of us read the Bible. Daily, we consume seven hours of cleverly contrived myths and very little eternal truths.

We are certainly not talking here about Greek mythology. We are discussing the cleverly defined myths that have been promoted by our culture for years. They have come to shape our perspective, our pleasure, and our purpose.

Have you felt it? After years of getting seven hours of myths and little or nothing of the Word, we can feel the shift in our minds and hearts. Now is the time to challenge ourselves: Are we following cleverly devised myths or eternal truths? The world's propaganda or God's truth?

To encourage, what you are doing right now is crucial. You are "Capturing the Moment" with God everyday through this devotional guide. This will be a huge blessing to your relationship with Christ.

Myths Debunked
John 8:44–45

We need to challenge every myth our culture sends our way. In the Scriptures, we find the eternal wisdom of God that defuses the enemy's lies. Here are some examples of the myths our culture beckons, each with its corresponding counter-truth rooted in God's Word.

Myth: Our worth is external. Women must look beautiful and dress in a way to gain attention. Men get their significance from success, money, or accomplishments.

Truth: You have an eternal identity in Christ. Your worth is eternal, not external. It doesn't matter what you look like. It doesn't matter how much you have earned or accomplished. What truly matters is that your identity is in Christ.

Myth: Happiness is our ultimate goal, and it justifies anything. If I am not happy in my marriage, I will get a divorce. If I am not happy with my job, I will quit. On the list goes . . . I am going to do whatever it takes to make me happy.

Truth: God wants your holiness more than your happiness (Rom. 6:11; 8:1; Heb. 12:10). We can have true joy in the midst of suffering. Some of the most significant challenges in our lives mold us to be the people God wants us to be. We grow in the hard times. Can we be happy? Sure. But is happiness or holiness our ultimate goal?

Myth: There is no longer right or wrong. Nothing is moral or immoral; it's just a personal decision. When there are no absolutes, everything is just a social construct; everything is up to you.

Truth: God puts limits, rules, and other people in our lives for our good and our joy. We will reap what we sow.

Have you spotted any cleverly contrived myth that has gotten in the way of how you think and live? Let's not follow cleverly contrived myths (2 Pet. 1:16). No matter how good the presentation is or how many people are doing it, let's follow eternal truths.

Eyewitness News
2 Peter 1:16–18

In his second epistle, Peter said the reason we come to know the truth is because of what we witness. He uses the transfiguration experience to say that we shouldn't follow clever myths. We should follow the eyewitness account. Peter heard God's voice. He saw Christ's brilliance. He saw Moses and Elijah. His testimony validated that Jesus is God's Son. This is why I believe—because of the eyewitness account.

Do you know your testimony? Can you share it? If you don't have one or know what it is, a testimony is sharing who you were before Jesus and who you are now that you have met Jesus personally. Sharing mine takes me only forty-five seconds, and I have done it thousands of times.

Eyewitness is crucial. In the Bible, it says more than 3,000 times, "We saw it." The ABC station in Houston calls themselves "Channel 13 Eyewitness News." Saying, "I saw it" gives credibility. It's as if Peter said as an on-the-scene reporter, "Eyewitness news! I saw it, and it changed me from a fisherman to a man used by God."

Eyewitness testimony can often be the most convincing thing in court. Consider how things are now in our culture. Every crime or incident is somehow on video. You will see more videos of accused acts in the next ten to twenty years than ever before. We have cameras in every building and cell phones in every pocket. People film things when they see them happening so they can say, "Here is the eyewitness testimony that this happened."

Peter is saying, "I saw it. I was there. It is true." Now, Peter is going to say even more than his testimony.

He says that the prophetic word in the Bible was strongly confirmed to us and that we will do well to pay attention to it. It's like a lamp shining in a dark corner until the day Jesus comes and He rises in our hearts. Then he adds, "Above all, you know this: No prophecy of Scripture comes from the prophet's own interpretation" (2 Pet. 1:20). They were not making it up. Prophecy never came simply because a prophet wanted it to. Instead, the Holy Spirit guided the prophets as they spoke.

Peter began by saying he saw it, and Jesus is real. But then he doubled down on it and said the Bible is true. Now let's go today as eyewitnesses as well to what Jesus has done in our lives.

The Bible Is Time-Worthy

2 Timothy 3:16–17

It has been said that Mark Twain once remarked, "The Bible is a book that everyone praises but few people read." If you say, "I haven't got enough time to read the Bible," then you are way too busy.

Lifeway Research took a look at Bible engagement within the church and found that 12 percent of churchgoers rarely or never read the Bible, 5 percent read it at least once a month, 12 percent read it at least once a week, and only 32 percent read the Bible every day.[11]

Which of these percentages represents you personally?

On average, Americans take in seven hours of talk radio, TV, media, and the internet every day. Despite all those hours, 68 percent of us don't read the Bible every day. It's not a surprise that we follow cleverly devised and contrived myths.

What does your Bible look like? If you have had your Bible for more than a couple of years and it doesn't have some wear and tear on it, you are not reading it enough. You will either have a worn-out Bible or a worn-out life.

Do you take your Bible with you on vacation, or does it stay at home? Let me get really in your business. Do you take your Bible to church? You know the pastor is going to preach out of it. Do you take notes at church? Do you want to learn, or are you just waiting for lunch?

If you don't have your Bible with you right now, do you even know where it is in your house? You have many versions of the Bible at your fingertips on apps or the internet. Think about this: we cannot follow eternal truths unless we read and study the Scriptures.

The Bible Is Trustworthy

Psalm 19:7–11

While I was preaching at our church, I heard a child call out from the crowd and then again. I couldn't make out what they were saying, so I kept rolling. Later, I found out they said with childlike investigation, "Pastor Gregg, how do we know the Bible is true?" Great question. Maybe you have wondered the same. Let me give you a couple of facts. First, more than 3,000 times in the Bible, the authors who were eyewitnesses to events said, "It is true, I saw it." Second, Christ fulfilled at least 300 biblical prophecies with His first coming alone.

Other people say, "Well, the New Testament has had all these changes and errors." That's actually not true. The New Testament is 99.9 percent pure to the original documents. The other 0.1 percent that may have shifted are little words that make no difference to the meaning.

If we talk about ancient literature, it stands out that there have been 24,000 partial or full copies of the New Testament discovered—24,000! In a distant second place is Homer's *Iliad* with 643 partial or full copies in existence. That's 24,000 versus 643. If a college student asks her English professor, "Do you think Homer wrote the *Iliad*?" the professor would certainly say yes. But if another student asks, "Do you think the New Testament is true?" the professor's answer might not be so positive. Yet remember: 24,000 versus 643.

Archaeological digs have proven the Bible's trustworthiness over and over. Dr. Nelson Glueck, one of the great modern authorities on Israeli archaeology, said this:

> No archeological discovery has ever controverted a biblical reference. Scores of archeological finds have been made which confirm in clear outline or exact detail historical statements in the Bible. And, by the same token, the proper evaluation of biblical descriptions has often led to amazing discoveries.[12]

A good archeologist in Israel would go with an Old Testament in one hand and a shovel in the other. That's because if the Bible says it's there, you'll find it if you just keep digging. The Bible has stood true and unchanged through the ages. We can be sure of one thing: the Bible is true. It is real. It makes a difference. Trust God's Word today.

A Fully Productive Life

2 Peter 1:5–8

Do you have a vision for your life? Are you purposeful? Are you productively working toward things of eternity?

Once we have trusted Jesus as our Savior, we are given everything we need for life and godliness, and the Holy Spirit lives inside of us (2 Pet. 1:3). That doesn't mean that instantaneously we are perfect in the sense that we never make mistakes. It does mean we are saved instantaneously. We are washed clean. We are forgiven. Now it is time to let that grow—in our sanctification and in our purity.

Peter tells us that in order to grow and build our new lives in Christ, we should make every effort to add six building attributes to our faith: goodness, knowledge, self-control, endurance, brotherly affection, and love (2 Pet. 1:5–8). We are going to focus in on this passage and these qualities for the next few days; to really sink our teeth into it.

Christian character is intentionally pursued, not passively received. We have to intentionally pursue Christian character (Rom. 6:19). You don't just show up at church, sit down, and all of a sudden become a stronger Christian. The process of growing is participating in worship. It is participating in the message. It is listening. It is trusting. It is knowing. It is letting God do His work in you and through you that makes the difference. You don't just become stronger by standing in a gym. Participation brings the fortitude.

When you trust in Christ for salvation, you start a new relationship with Him. Next you grow in this relationship. That is why Peter says that in order to grow, he wants us to add to our faith in these other six ways.

Don't think about building with these six attributes as a linear effort. You don't need to wait to achieve one and then, once you get past 101, move to 201, and then to 301, and on and on. This is more like putting them all together in the blender and hitting the button. This is godly and tasty—a stew, a wonderful recipe. Goodness, knowledge, self-control, endurance, brotherly affection, and love, each taking root in our lives in different ways and at different points in time. Ponder and pray for these attributes today.

Goodness and Knowledge

2 Peter 1:5

Growing in our character is like building a house. The first thing you need when you build a house is a foundation. Foundation is key. It says in Matthew that we shouldn't build on a sandy foundation of shifting sand. We are to build on a strong foundation of rock so our lives will make it through the storms (Matt. 7:24–27).

So, what is our foundation? Peter says the foundation of our lives is faith. Many people have not made faith the foundation but instead have made it just a part of their lives. Faith in Christ is a foundational aspect that will take you all the way through eternity.

The first pillar we are going to add to the foundation of our faith is goodness. Goodness is what we call moral excellence. When we hear moral excellence, many of us freak out and think, "Oh, no. Wait a minute. That means perfection." But that is not what Peter means. Moral excellence means we are going to walk in a way that shines with Jesus.

As we have the foundation of faith and the pillar of goodness, the second thing we need to add is knowledge. The knowledge spoken of here is not just about being book smart. It is not only about what's in our heads. There was a group of people written about in Scripture called Gnostics. They believed in knowledge, but they were not Christians and were not walking with God. It's a false teaching where all you have to do is retain information. In our American churches, we know a ton, don't we? But do we live it out?

We are not talking about just knowledge in our heads; this is also about knowledge in our feet. It is practical knowledge being lived out (Hos. 4:6). So, we want to know things, but we also have to apply things. James says that faith without works is dead (James 2:14–26).

Mark Twain put it like this: "It ain't the parts of the Bible that I can't understand that bother me, it's the parts that I do understand."[13] We know plenty in order to start moving and put our goodness and knowledge into action.

God, thank You for communicating so clearly with me. Please give me all the wisdom and willingness to diligently add goodness and knowledge to my faith.

Self-Control and Endurance

2 Peter 1:5–6

In the first chapter of his second letter, Peter gives us several characteristics that we are to add to our faith in Jesus Christ. The first two were goodness—our moral excellence—and knowledge—living out what we know (2 Pet. 1:5).

The next attribute Peter gives us to add to our faith is self-control, which can be defined as "not giving in" (v. 6).

Sometimes that applies to sin. We have a choice between sin and holiness, and we say, "I am not going to give in to sin." Sometimes self-control doesn't involve righteousness and sinfulness—just old-fashioned discipline. For example, we don't need to have chips and queso or a dessert at every meal. Maybe it's about accepting the fact that the alarm clock goes off and we have to get up, or that we have to go to bed on time.

You and I were made for much more than just feeding our natural cravings. So don't give in to "I am just going to eat like a crazy person; I am just going to sleep in." A lack of self-control is going to get you in the end.

The next thing Peter mentions is endurance (2 Pet. 1:6). Watch how these two tie together. Self-control is not giving in, and endurance is not giving up. Those who spend their lives giving in will ultimately be those who give up. The more you give in, the easier it is to give up (Heb. 12:1).

We are going to encounter many problems in our lives—sickness, mean people, a bad investment, a wrong decision . . . That's just how life goes. We never know how God is going to work us through it, but we can't give up (1 Cor. 10:13).

We want to be people who are walking with God in such a way that we are saying, "Lord, we want You to refine our desires. Instead of those worldly, fleshly things my mind or body say I need right now, what is my heart saying? What do I really need in my soul? What am I really looking for?" I've heard it said: "When a man knocks on the door of a brothel, he is knocking for God." It means that what he is really looking for is not sin but a soulful touch from God.

Don't give in and don't give up! You never know what God has for you around the corner.

Godliness

2 Peter 1:7

As we each go along our paths to build character, there is something God wants to develop in all of us: godliness. Godliness means to worship well. I'll never sing well. My friends and family will give testimony to that! But I can worship well. I'll never write a #1 song. But I can worship well.

Godliness is not found in being a pastor, a missionary, or a minister. You can be a plumber and worship well. You can be an accountant and worship well. You can be a student and worship well. You can worship God well through your hardest time, your easiest time, and every time in between. Allow godliness to blossom today by worshiping well in all you do (1 Tim. 4:8).

The next attribute that Peter gives us is brotherly kindness (some versions say brotherly love). The Greek word is *phileo*. It's why Philadelphia is called the City of Brotherly Love.

This kind of love means to show kindness to those around you in your workplace, in your home, on your street—to the person in the apartment next door or the house across the street. God wants you to live with brotherly kindness.

Finally, Peter ends with love. So why would he say brotherly love and then love? In the Greek, these are two different words. One is *phileo*, which means brotherly love (1 Thess. 2:8), and the other is *agape*, which means God's love (1 Cor. 13).

What Peter is doing here is spiking the ball and saying, "I want you to have these aspects in your life in a growing degree." We must have love for people and love for God.

You don't need to wait until you have one love to have the other. All these things can grow simultaneously. Yet we can also ask ourselves which one do we need to really concentrate on right now; goodness, knowledge, self-control, endurance, brotherly affection, or love? Pick one and personally ponder it today. It will bless you and others.

Unfinished
Philippians 1:3–6

Here is the truth and great news: God is not finished with you! I recently heard a song by Mandisa about trusting in God and empowering growth in our lives. The song is appropriately called "Unfinished."

> His work in me ain't through
> I'm just unfinished[14]

He is not finished with you yet. He who has begun a good work in you will be faithful to complete it. So we continue on the journey, not expecting to ever be perfect but saying, "Lord, on the foundation of my faith, I want to build these six pillars in my life: goodness, knowledge, self-control, endurance, godliness, brotherly love, and love" (see 2 Pet. 1:5–7).

And here is what is great. Jesus said in John 15:5 that if we abide in the Lord and He in us, we will bear much fruit. But it also says that apart from Him—we can do nothing.

Hebrews 11:6 says that without faith, it is impossible to please God, but He is a rich rewarder of those who place their trust in Him.

Faith is the foundation from which all these attributes spring. Do you know what these attributes really are? A lot of them are simply fruits of the Spirit. The branches of the vine aren't wishing, "Oh, make grapes. Make grapes. Make grapes." The branches just trust in the vine and its nourishment. Likewise, when you walk with God, just trust in His Spirit and yield to Him. The fruit will come, and you will grow up and mature. Everything will work as it is supposed to (Gal. 5:22–23).

We have all the things we need for life and godliness. Even though we are complete in Christ, in terms of spiritual growth . . . we are unfinished, with more fruit of our faith to come. From the foundation of our faith up, God will make more out of us than what He originally started with. If we let that happen, our lives are going to be something incredible.

Busy but Unproductive
2 Peter 1:8–9

As we have been studying, Peter tells us to add goodness, knowledge, self-control, endurance, godliness, brotherly love, and God's love to our faith. Peter also says these attributes will keep us from being useless or unfruitful in the knowledge of our Lord Jesus Christ.

Isn't that interesting? It's suggesting that if you don't increase in these qualities, if you don't make a concerted and intentional effort to add these things to your life, the moving sidewalk you're on is headed toward unproductiveness.

Peter is saying that if we add these things, we are going to reflect what we are supposed to reflect. We are going to be believers who look like believers, who accomplish what God desires.

Being purposeless doesn't mean you won't be busy. You will be very busy trying to keep the noise going so you never have to listen to the quietness of your heart as it calls out to God. But if we are to be truly purposeful and truly productive, it must come from a place of faith.

If I stand on the foundation of faith letting these intentional aspects come out in my life, I will be purposeful and productive. God will use my life for His purposes. It will be like the description in 1 Corinthians 3 . . . When the day of judgment and the fire come and everything is burned up, the only things that remain will be whatever is built on the foundation of Jesus Christ. We will be able to say, "Our Lord and God, you are worthy to receive glory and honor and power" (1 Cor. 3:11–15; Rev. 4:9–11).

Today, strive to be more than just busy but truly productive by shining with Christlike character.

Vision

Psalm 5:1–3

Look out the window, not just into the mirror. If you change your perspective in this way, you will walk with a grander vision for your life.

We often see this perspective in athletes. The quarterback throws a few touchdown passes. The reporter asks him, "How did you throw so many touchdown passes?" And he answers, "Our offensive line is incredible." He deflects the attention from himself and says, "The offensive line is the one who got it done."

Peter says that whoever lacks the building blocks of Christlike character "is blind and shortsighted and has forgotten the cleansing from his past sins" (2 Pet. 1:9).

It is really easy to say, "What is God doing in my life? What is going on with me?" However, when we get our line of vision up and look out and beyond ourselves, we can say, "Wow! Jesus has cleansed my sins. He is able to do miracles. He wants to use me to impact others." Instead of shortsighted, we see clearly to live for Christ. Christian character puts our focus on Him and others.

When somebody asked Phillip Brooks, an old pastor, "What would you do to revive a dead church?" he said, "I would preach a missionary sermon and take up a collection." Think about that. The revival here is not about money but about saying, "There is more, and you are part of it."

If I take off my glasses, I can't see clearly past a couple of feet. Since I'm nearsighted, things become fuzzy far away. When I remove my glasses, I become "shortsighted" focused only on what was near me. When you take off the lenses of who Christ is and what the purpose and productivity of your life really is, you are only going to see what is right in front of you. You are going to miss the grand and great vision of God long-term.

Peter is saying something like this: don't become blind. Don't become shortsighted. I want you to see far. That will show the world that you are God's children, that you are headed to heaven, and that you are already heaven-focused on this earth and sharing it with everybody else.

Put the lenses on of who Jesus is and the purpose of what He wants to do in you. Now you can see, clearly again, out the window—not just in the mirror.

An Upside-Down Tree
Ephesians 3:16–21

We build our lives by first putting the foundation of faith in place. Don't let faith just become a pillar. If faith is not the foundation, we will replace it with what we perceive as happiness. We can justify anything by saying, "This makes me happy." If the foundation is faith in Jesus Christ, happiness and joy will be all around you. But if you get the foundation wrong, you are not going to make it through the storm (Luke 6:46–49).

Peter gives us these building blocks—goodness, knowledge, self-control, endurance, godliness, brotherly love, and God's love—so we have purpose and true productivity in our lives. We can then see that this world isn't all there is, and we can also see who Christ is and who He wants us to be. So now our home, our church, and our lives are solid.

Warren Wiersbe, a former pastor of Moody Church in Chicago, said:

> Some of the most effective Christians I have known are people without dramatic talents and special abilities, or even exciting personalities, yet God has used them in marvelous ways. Why? Because they are becoming more and more like Jesus Christ. They have the kind of character and conduct that God can trust with blessing. They are fruitful because they are faithful; they are effective because they are growing in their Christian experience.[15]

Many of us are trying to grow down, and God is telling us to grow up. We are trying to start on the leaves and then push down to the roots. But is that the way a tree grows? Roots then fruit not the reverse. You may be asking: *What is the vision of my life? Where should I be? What should my job be? Whom should I marry? What should I do?*

If you will trust God to handle who you are, all of those other things will take care of themselves. Faith doesn't grow by your efforts; it grows by trusting in Jesus and saying, "You are the One. I want You to work in me and through me."

So just keep walking in faith. Keep focusing on all these things Peter speaks of; be intentional about them. Be patient with yourself and then all this other stuff will take care of itself. Feed the roots and you'll bear the fruit.

Be Angry but Do Not Sin

Ephesians 4:26–27, 30–32

As human beings, we can all relate to struggling with anger. It does not matter how patient, kind, or lovable we are. At any given moment, we can get angry. The Bible recognizes that this is a common reaction and warns us about its consequences.

A survey shows that 80 percent of high school officials and referees quit their jobs within the first three years. These referees agreed on their reason for quitting: pervasive abuse from parents and coaches. Here are the questions that arise from this survey: *Why* do we get angry at what is supposed to be a fun time for our kids? How is it possible that something that should be a pleasant and enjoyable time becomes a war zone?[16]

Our culture is filled with movies that show people getting mad and expressing their fury for various reasons and in various ways. Think about *Mad Max*, *Falling Down*, and *Anger Management*. The characters in these movies react with increasing violence as they face their frustrations. A well-known Latin saying states, *Errare humanum est, perseverare autem diabolicum*—to err is human, to persist is diabolical.

The Bible warns us, "In your anger do not sin: Do not let the sun go down while you are still angry, and do not give the devil a foothold" (Eph. 4:26–27 NIV).

It is crystal clear that the reaction of anger is normal, but the problem is that it can become sinful. The results of anger can hurt us and our relationships. In the next few devotionals, let's analyze the *why* behind our anger. Let's get to the root of it, expose it, and get rid of all the hindrances that stop us from walking in righteousness.

It's okay to get angry; it is not okay to sin in your anger. Ask yourself a couple of questions: "What am I angry about? More important, Why am I angry about it?"

Why Are You Angry?
Ephesians 4:26–32

When we think about anger, we could certainly conclude it is a secondary emotion. It is the result of another feeling. Anger is at the surface, but the emotion that triggers anger reveals the root. It is the difference between legitimate anger (not sinful) and illegitimate anger (sinful).

Here is the question we should ask ourselves: "*Why* am I angry? Is it because of the hinderance of my preferences, or God's purposes?" There is a vast difference between the two.

My Preferences Anger: When you get angry because your desires are not met, the reason behind your why is your preferences. There is something you want, but you are not getting it. It might be respect, love, the fastest lane on the highway, a parking space, the best table at a restaurant, and so on. Your selfishness is being confronted, and you want to fight back. You feel you deserve something you are not getting. You get frustrated because of unmet expectations.

God's Purposes Anger: You get angry because God's purposes are challenged. You see an injustice and that makes you angry. Some people call this righteous anger. For example, William Wilberforce headed the Parliamentary campaign against the British slave trade, until finally the Slave Trade Act of 1807 was passed. He and other evangelicals were horrified by the depraved and non-Christian trade and by the greed and avarice of the slave owners and slave traders. God created all people in His image and likeness. To see these truths challenged raised a righteous anger in these Christians who put God's purposes first.

Jesus is always the ultimate example of legitimate anger. The question we should all ask when anger arises is this: "*Why* am I angry?" The answer will allow you to realize its legitimacy or illegitimacy, righteous or sinful.

When we get angry, we need to ask ourselves: "*Why* am I angry? Is it because of my preferences or because God's purposes are being challenged?"

Results of Anger
Psalm 4:4

We have seen that getting angry is a common human reaction. We have considered that the Bible warns us regarding the root of the problem, the reason behind anger that triggers this emotion. Today, we are going to reflect on another question we should ask ourselves when considering if our anger is sin. *What* has resulted from our anger? Hurt or help?

When anger is the result of God's purposes being challenged, the result will be to help.

When William Wilberforce saw how slaves were treated, his anger resulted in efforts to abolish the slave trade in the United Kingdom. Jesus got angry when He saw that the Pharisees lacked compassion for someone in need. His anger resulted in a leper being healed. Another time, He flipped the tables in the temple because His house had become a market instead of a house of prayer. God's intent (purpose) was being challenged, and Jesus' anger resulted in the reestablishment of God's original purpose by helping those in need.

But when anger is the result of our preferences or the expression of hurt and pain, we end up making matters worse. Either our health or our relationships will be hurt. Long-term anger has been linked to high blood pressure, heart conditions, skin disorders, and digestive problems.

The hurt can stretch past the why and what of anger to the who—most likely you are not only hurting yourself but others—your spouse, kids, friends . . . Those we love the most can also be hurt the most by our anger.

The Bible clearly states that "human anger does not produce the righteousness that God desires" (James 1:20 NIV). We must pay attention to the fruit of our anger. If it does not result in helping others, then we must address it before the sun goes down. Our God is more than willing to forgive us and purify us from all unrighteousness (1 John 1:9).

When I get angry, I need to ask myself this: "*What* is the result of my anger? Hurting myself or others? Or helping right a wrong on the earth to the glory of God?"

The Devil's Opportunity
John 10:10

Have you ever had revenge conversations in your mind? Do you go back to discussions and rewrite the scene accordingly to include a stinger of a comment toward someone? We all have simmered with anger rehearsing a fight in our minds.

When we do not deal with anger before the sun goes down and when we carry it inside us, the Bible says we are giving the devil an opportunity to make things worse. Satan gets hold of us when we don't deal with anger as soon as possible. That's when revenge conversations begin to roll on repeat.

When we give the devil a foothold, he can expand small things and make them big. Remember, he is the father of lies, and he came to steal, kill, and destroy. When we choose to carry our anger, we allow Satan to hinder our relationship with God, others, and ourselves.

What is God's advice on the matter? First, make it right daily. Do not let the sun go down while you are still angry. Get over it as soon as possible. Small bricks build big walls. Walls separate us from our intimacy with God and others.

Second, choose to forgive. In Ephesians 4:31–32, we read, "Get rid of all bitterness, rage and anger, brawling and slander, along with every form of malice. Be kind and compassionate to one another, *forgiving each other, just as in Christ God forgave you*" (NIV, emphasis added). We can forgive because we have been forgiven.

Choose to forgive daily! Do not give the devil an opportunity to separate you from God and others.

Dive Deep into Your Heart

Psalm 139:23–24

One of the hardest things to do in life is to ask God to truly examine you. We read that the psalmist asked God to examine his heart: "Search me, God, and know my heart; test me and know my anxious thoughts. See if there is any offensive way in me, and lead me in the way everlasting" (Ps. 139:23–24 NIV).

Knowing that God's compassions are new every morning and that we can approach the throne of grace with confidence, we find that grace erases any doubt that God loves us. Having the assurance of God's love allows us to say "God, search me." We are so secure in His love, that we can be unafraid to lay before Him our flaws, weaknesses, and sins.

Let me encourage you to dive deep into your heart. "Why is it that I am anxious or angry? What has been the result of my anxiety or anger? Who has been hurt because of it? Have I been giving the devil a foothold in my life?" Ask God to search your heart and lead you in the everlasting way.

Heavenly Father, today I lay down my hurts and fears. Help me understand what is really in my heart. Help me see the result of my sin, if it has been helping or hurting others.

If I have hurt others, I ask for Your forgiveness. I confess my sin against You. Also, help me forgive those who have hurt me.

I do not want to give the devil an opportunity to hurt my relationship with You, Lord, or with others. Help me forgive. I choose forgiveness. And help me ask for forgiveness from others.

Jesus, teach me to understand Your purposes. Show me when Your original intents are being challenged, and give me the strength to address the problem righteously.

Holy Spirit, please remind me not to let the sun set on my anger or anxiety. Search me, and if there is any offensive way in me, lead me in the everlasting way.

In Jesus' name, amen.

The Sun Stopped Shining

Matthew 27:45–46

It was April 1984, and former President Ronald Reagan was flying to China to meet China's government officials when Air Force One lost communication with land. A series of sunspot explosions released so much gas into the atmosphere that it shut down communication between Air Force One and the earth. The airplane that never loses connection, lost communication. For hours, they were in the dark.

Every one of us at some point in our lives has gone through a dark moment. We have felt like communication was shut off. It doesn't matter if you are the most important and powerful person on the earth or the poorest and most helpless soul on the planet. You can be rich or poor, old or young. Sooner or later, you will face an unclear moment . . . alone, helpless, and overwhelmed by a burden that seems to crash your soul.

In those valley-of-the-shadow-of-death moments, you may find yourself saying, "God, I know You are there, but I can't feel Your presence. I believe You can help me, but please, can You do it faster?" It is precisely in those moments that most of us cry out, "Lord, where are You? Why have You forsaken me?"

Even Jesus endured a dark moment. Yes, Jesus the Son of God experienced a moment so dark that even the ambiance around Him changed. Darkness came over the whole world from noon until 3:00 in the afternoon. The earth became dark because the sun stopped shining. Can you imagine the most challenging moment of your life surrounded by darkness on the inside and the outside?

It was such an opaque and difficult time that Jesus cried out in a loud voice, "My God, my God, why have you forsaken me?" (Matt. 27:46 NIV). Are you in a valley of loneliness? Rejection? Failure? Addiction? Financial ruin? If you find yourself crying out as Jesus did, I want you to know that *you are not alone.* God is with you. Take this dark moment and turn it into an enlightening one. Embrace it as an opportunity to discover greater intimacy. Allow God to guide you through the storm and find rest under the shadow of the Almighty.

Remember that even in your darkest hour, God is with you!

March 21

The Cross
2 Corinthians 5:21

Nobody wants a trial in their life. Suffering is just not part of our nature. Very deep inside of us, something is telling us that this is not the way things are supposed to be. But Christianity is full of paradoxes. One of them is found in the book of Romans where it says that God will use everything that happens to us for good (Rom. 8:28). Consider trials, temptation, struggles, and difficulties as opportunities for God to show Himself to you.

The greatest paradox of all is found at the cross. In 2 Corinthians 5:21 we read, "God made him [Jesus] who had no sin to be sin for us, so that in him we might become the righteousness of God" (NIV). On one hand, we find our sin and the sin of the whole world. On the other hand, we find an innocent man who had never sinned. The righteous son of God took our place at the cross, and all the punishment we deserved fell on Him.

Can you imagine yourself carrying all the vile deeds, moral turpitudes, and lowness of the world? It was so dark and painful that even creation responded to the death of the Creator. There was an earthquake, and the whole land became dark for three hours.

The Bible tells us that the whole scene became a spectacle for everyone to see. Darkness covered the earth, and the Light of the world committed His spirit into the hands of the Father. Jesus canceled the charge of our legal indebtedness and nailed it to the cross. How amazing is that! The cross is, indeed, the centerpiece of Christianity. Jesus took His darkest moment and turned it into light!

Nobody wants a trial in their life, but God will bring what we *need* from what we do not want. Jesus asked the Father to let the cup (His suffering on the cross) pass from Him. He knew that the cross was not going to be easy. Nevertheless, He considered that the outcome of it all was worth it. In the New Testament, we are called to rejoice and exult in the midst of tribulations.

We do not know what we need, but God does. Therefore, He will allow trials and tribulations to come our way to produce in us the fruit of our faith. We will never realize that we need more perseverance, hope, proven character, or love for others. But God knows better than we do; He knows what we really *need*.

Do not waste the trials of your life. God will bring what you *need* from what you do not *want*! Make the cross the centerpiece of your trial, and let the Lord lead you through it.

The Veil
Luke 23:44–45

A series of miracles took place while Jesus was being crucified. One of those miracles was the temple veil was torn apart. In the Old Testament, before Solomon built the temple, people worshiped God in the tabernacle. It was a tent divided into three sections: the outer court, the holy place, and the most holy place—where the presence of God was.

Between the holy place and the most holy place, there was a veil. Nobody had access to the most holy place except the high priest who could enter only once a year after fulfilling a long list of ceremonial procedures. He represented the Israelites before God.

The veil was a symbol of the separation that existed between God (the Holy One) and humankind. We did not have access to God's presence because of our sin.

But the cross changed everything! Our relationship with God was opened. God wanted to make sure this event was recorded so we could rejoice and celebrate the fact that the separation between Him and us was, and is, over. It also demonstrated that only God could restore our relationship—the veil was torn in two, notice the direction . . . from top to bottom. God reached out to us. Jesus was the only One who could fulfill all the requirements of the law, which was a shadow of the things to come (Heb. 10:1).

Humankind could not reach God. It was God's initiative to restore our relationship with Him—top to bottom. At the cross, God pierced into our darkness, and the Light of the world established a new covenant. Greater intimacy with God was then and is now open wide. Moreover, Jesus now lives *in* us; our bodies are the temple of God.

So, when difficult times come your way, remember that nothing can separate you from the love of God that is *in* Christ Jesus our Lord. You will make it through. Trust in Jesus and allow Him to teach you what you need to learn from it. Do not waste the trial. Draw closer to the light of Jesus where everything is exposed. He will show you the way through the storm by the power of the Holy Spirit.

Greater intimacy is found and available in the midst of trials. Pull closer to Him! He understands what you are going through and is willing to help you.

Softening Our Hearts
Luke 23:47–48

When trials come our way, we have two *choices*: to soften or harden our hearts. We can choose to learn from the trial and draw closer to God, or we can try to get out of the storm as soon as possible, learning nothing from it and wasting the opportunity. We all know when we do not learn from our experiences, we tend to repeat our mistakes.

The events that took place during Jesus' crucifixion caused a series of various reactions among the people who belonged to very different social backgrounds. One of them was a centurion. These officers were respected and admired; they were the higher members of the Roman Empire Army. They were chosen by merit and remarkable for their deliberation, constancy, and strength of mind. The centurion who was by the cross said, after seeing what had happened before his eyes, "This man really was righteous!" (Luke 23:47).

At the same time, two criminals were being crucified beside Jesus. They had been thrown into prison for insurrection and murder. One of them, after seeing that Jesus was innocent and being unjustly punished, said to Jesus, "Remember me when you come into your kingdom" (Luke 23:42).

Two completely different people from two utterly distinctive backgrounds both softened their hearts and recognized that Jesus was the Son of God. It doesn't matter who you are, where you are from, or how important your status is in society. When it comes to the most critical decision you will ever face, you can choose when you stand before the cross to either soften your heart and recognize that Jesus is Lord of Lords or refuse to do so and harden your heart even more (as the other criminal chose to do). The cross gives all human beings equal footing.

When we go through difficult times, we are confronted with a choice. This choice is not to suffer but to choose God's will—whether it means suffering or not. Let us say as Jesus did, "Father, if you are willing, take this cup [suffering] away from me—nevertheless, not my will, but yours, be done" (Luke 22:42).

If you are facing a trial today, choose to soften your heart and pray that God's will be done in your life.

The Support Group
Luke 23:49–56

Difficult times give us an opportunity for growth. In Japanese, the word *crisis* actually means "opportunity." When you face a problem or when you are in the middle of a crisis, it becomes easier to realize who your real, loyal, and I-got-your-back friends are. The night before Jesus' crucifixion, Jesus was abandoned by all His disciples. Peter even denied knowing Jesus. Imagine how difficult that must have been for Jesus.

Nevertheless, at the darkest of hours, Jesus had a support group—a group of women who had followed Him from Galilee and stood at a distance watching what took place. As Christians, we are called to be a group of people who are willing to rejoice with those who rejoice and mourn with those who mourn. Sometimes it is difficult for us to find who those people are in our lives. You may even be asking God, "Lord, please show me who my support group is. I need help. Who are the people You have placed in my life to help me get through difficult times?"

We all need to be humble enough to say, "I need help, I need wisdom! Brother, sister, pastor, I need your guidance, your prayers." Faith, hope, and love are the greatest anchoring forces that you can experience when facing suffering and uncertainty. Jesus' support group was there for Him, and they were also there for each other. In the darkest moment they had to endure—the death of Jesus—they were *together*. A couple of days after, they went back to the tomb and found that it was empty, and Jesus had risen! They had mourned together, and now they rejoiced together!

The New Testament promises us that everything that happens is for our good. When facing trials, struggles, temptation, or difficulties, we have the assurance that God will make all things work out for our good. If God was able to turn the greatest evil ever committed (the crucifixion of His own Son) and use it for the greatest good (our salvation), imagine how capable He is to turn your crisis into an opportunity.

Trust *the cross*—Jesus' sacrifice was and is enough. Know that greater intimacy is open wide; *the veil* was torn. *Soften your heart.* Pray that God's will be done in your life, and *ask for help*! Gather with the community of believers who will mourn and rejoice with you!

Imagine
Revelation 21:15–21

It comes as no surprise that the concept of heaven permeates our culture. Phrases such as "I'm in seventh heaven" or "she moved heaven and earth to get something done" are part of our daily language. Music, films, and TV series also reflect our enthusiasm for such a place. Think about Frank Sinatra's "Pennies from Heaven" and Led Zeppelin's "Stairway to Heaven." And what about Netflix's *The Good Place*? The imaginary landscape of yesterday's and today's society presents a hunger for a place where everything is as it is supposed to be: perfect—just perfect.

Heaven is a place where there is no hunger, violence, war, poverty, suffering, tears, or illness. It sounds too good to be true, and yet it is true. This place we all long for and dream of does exist.

The Bible is very clear regarding the place Jesus is preparing for us. In the days before His death and resurrection, Jesus referred to it as "my Father's house" (John 14:2). It is also called paradise (Luke 23:43; 2 Cor. 12:4; Rev. 2:7), the better country (Heb. 11:14, 16 NIV), the kingdom of heaven (Matt. 25:1; James 2:5), the eternal kingdom (2 Pet. 1:11), the eternal inheritance (1 Pet. 1:4; Heb. 9:15), the Jerusalem above, the heavenly Jerusalem, and the new Jerusalem (Gal. 4:26; Heb. 12:22; Rev. 3:12).

Our faith tank will be entirely refueled by the wonderful promises God has left for us in His Word. Today, direct your attention to a city where there is no need for the sun or the moon to shine on it, for the glory of God illuminates it.

The understanding and profoundness of heaven are a treasure for our souls. It is like receiving a shot that contains all the vitamins we are in desperate need of. It will change the perspective of your life forever. Furthermore, this perspective will transform your attitude toward your plans, goals, and life itself.

You will be forever in the presence of your Creator—your loving God. Everything will be as He promised: perfect. A perfect me with a perfect you in a perfect place with our perfect God . . . WOW!

Jesus is preparing a place for us in heaven. May this eternal perspective of life be the driving force of our attitudes, plans, and goals.

Face-to-Face
Hebrews 10:19–23

In any relationship, we go through stages and develop different levels of intimacy. Thousands of books have been written about dealing with relationships and relationship problems. The most published and read book of all time, the Bible, tells the story of the Creator's relationship with us. From beginning to end, from Genesis to Revelation, this story presents the levels of intimacy we had, lost, and regained with our loving Father.

In the garden of Eden, God and human beings walked, talked, and spent time together face-to-face. In fact, the level of intimacy was so profound that, shockingly for us, Adam and Eve were naked and not ashamed (Gen. 2:25). Shame came after sin (Gen. 3:7). Besides being ashamed of their nakedness, they were afraid of God for the first time and hid from Him (Gen. 3:8, 10–11). God, in His mercy, provided garments for them but banished them from the garden of Eden (Gen. 3:21, 23). The purest and highest level of intimacy God intended to have with us was ruined because of sin.

In the Old Testament, we read that the closest people could get to God was through worship in special places that God intended for this purpose. This usually happened only on special occasions. In the desert, the people of God had the tabernacle, and later, Solomon built the temple. But no one could see God face-to-face (Exod. 33:18–20; Isa. 6:5), not even after fulfilling all the requirements the Law of God explained in such detail (Heb. 9; 10).

In the New Testament, the book of Hebrews masterfully explains to us how all the requirements of the Law were fulfilled—through Jesus' death and resurrection. Jesus' perfect sacrifice has allowed us to have a new level of intimacy with God. Now, we worship in spirit and truth, and God lives in us through the Holy Spirit (John 4:23–24; 1 John 3:24).

The Bible tells us that a day is coming when all things will be restored as God promised (Acts 3:21; John 5:28–29; Rev. 21:5). We will again be able to worship God face-to-face (1 Cor. 13:12). No more fogginess, no more shadows. We will have a glorified body, and we will be able to see Him, talk to Him, and walk with Him (Phil. 3:21). There will be no need for the temple or a special occasion to be with God. He will dwell with us (Rev. 21:3).

One day we will see Him face-to-face! Take a moment and let that truth sink in. Rejoice!

God's Glory in Heaven
Revelation 21:23

Do you know the sun radiates more energy in one second than all the energy humans have used since the beginning of civilization?[17] That is a powerful thought to ponder, isn't it? In light of this, let's consider the second truth about heaven.

Revelation 21:23 says, "The city [the new Jerusalem] does not need the sun or the moon to shine on it, because the glory of God illuminates it, and its lamp is the Lamb [Jesus]." In heaven there will be no need for light; God's glory will take care of that. You may be asking, "What does that mean? What is the glory of God?"

We certainly use the word *glory* a lot, but do we really grasp the whole sense of it? In the context of the verse we have just read, glory means God's essence. It is the sum of all of God's attributes (mercy, grace, truth, goodness, justice, knowledge, power, and eternity). All of them together are His glory; they represent the essence of who He is. God's glory radiates, enlightens, and spreads throughout all of heaven. It cannot be contained. It is like an explosion of beauty—all His attributes, His essence. Imagine a place where mercy, grace, goodness, justice, knowledge, power, and eternity are spread all over!

The second aspect of God's glory is that glory is intrinsic, not granted. What does that mean? Think about this: What makes water wet? Wetness is part of its essence. You see, a person's glory is not intrinsic to his or her nature; it is granted to him or her. Take any king or queen from the past to the present. Take away their crown, rope, scepter, and ring, and do not allow that person to bathe, shave, or practice personal hygiene for a month. Put that person next to any homeless person, and you will not be able to tell the difference. That is how weak our "glory" is. Our glory (beauty, fame, etc.) is granted, not intrinsic. It is not part of our essence. How humbling is that?

It doesn't matter what we drive, what school we attended, how much money we make, or how attractive we are. In the light of God's glory, our perspective of the things we value on the earth changes completely. There is no snobbery, prejudice, or racism in heaven. We all have the same value before God's eyes. The price Jesus paid at the cross was the same for all of humankind.

I want you to take a minute and reflect on this today. What "granted glory" are you giving importance or prioritizing in your life that does not reflect the perspective of God's intrinsic, eternal glory?

No More Night—
True Safety!
Revelation 21:9–14

Studies show that when people are going through difficult times, night is the hardest time. When everything gets quiet and there is no more activity, work, or errands to distract you, it is arduous. Your body relaxes, you are in bed, but your mind becomes an unstoppable force. It is like a fire alarm that just will not stop. You think, and think, and think. Your emotions awake, and rest is over.

For some people, sleep deprivation has to do with the sensation of not feeling safe. All of your fears arise like a sandstorm, and you think you cannot escape its voracity. We wish we could live in a closed-gated city with high walls and guards 24/7. Millions of dollars are spent on security every year, but we still do not feel safe physically, mentally, or emotionally.

The truth we will focus on today is true safety. "Its gates will never close by day because it will never be night there" (Rev. 21:25). The image of the holy city that comes down from heaven (Rev. 21:10) describes a city that never closes its gates. In ancient times, cities used to close their gates and have watchmen on the walls to guarantee security. In heaven, the gates will never be shut, for there will be no night there. True safety is guaranteed!

How is that possible? Revelation 21:27 says that "nothing impure will ever enter it, nor will anyone who does what is shameful or deceitful" (niv). God guarantees true security because nothing and nobody that does not belong there will ever enter heaven. Oh, how I long for my true home in heaven!

You may be saying, "Wow! That is very beautiful, but how do I deal with the difficulties I am facing right now?" In Romans 8:18, Paul says, "I consider that the sufferings of this present time are not worth comparing with the glory that is going to be revealed in us." That is the right perspective to have in the midst of suffering—an eternal perspective. The suffering we endure here on earth does not compare with the glory that awaits us in heaven because "we know that in all things God works for the good of those who love him" (Rom. 8:28 niv). Take comfort in God's promises and hold on to them.

I can lay down my burdens and trust that the suffering I may endure here on earth does not compare to the glory and true safety that awaits me in heaven.

The Book of Life
Revelation 21:24–27

The film was *Schindler's List*. Oskar Schindler was a German industrialist and a member of the Nazi Party. He is credited with saving the lives of 1,200 Jews during the Holocaust by employing them in his enamelware and ammunitions factories. The names of those 1,200 mortal Jewish souls were saved because they were on his list.

Can you imagine being spared from death for being on someone's list? There is another list, and it does not contain the names of those who belong to a country club, an exclusive university, or a certain church or denomination. It is more than a list; it is a book with the names of those who will enter heaven. It is the book of life. In Revelation 21:27, the apostle John writes, "Nothing impure will ever enter it [heaven], nor will anyone who does what is shameful or deceitful, but only those whose names are written in the Lamb's book of life" (NIV).

The book is not called "the good works book" or "the I-am-a-nice-person book." It is called the Lamb's book of life because the merit of being included in it only belongs to Jesus. When John the Baptist (a prophet) saw Jesus walking toward him, he said, "Look, the Lamb of God, who takes away the sin of the world!" (John 1:29 NIV). The only reason we will have total access to eternal life is because of Jesus' love for us (Rom. 5:8).

His sacrifice at the cross was made once and took away the sins of many (Heb. 9:28). You cannot write your own name in the Lamb's book of life, and, your name will not be written because of your good behavior, works, or intentions (Eph. 2:8–9). We have eternal life because Jesus' blood paid the full price of our redemption from eternal death. We have been saved from eternal doom because of God's grace and love. It is a gift. You cannot earn it; you can only receive it. Have you received it? Have you prayerfully asked Jesus to be your Savior and forgive your sins?

I pray that you will trust Him and have an eternal perspective of life so your goals, plans, and then your purpose will be aligned with God's eternal plans and promises.

If you have trusted Jesus as Savior, rejoice that your name is written in heaven!

Committing to Wisdom

Proverbs 1:20–23

We all need wisdom in our lives, and Proverbs is filled with it. Why is wisdom referred to as a woman in the book of Proverbs? The writer of Proverbs is using a literary technique.

He begins Proverbs with a woman of wisdom who we should listen to, declaring at the city gates. Later in the book there is the adulterous woman who continually sins because she does not listen to wisdom in Proverbs 2, 5, and 7. Then Proverbs culminates in chapter 31 with the ideal woman who shows what a life looks like walking in wisdom with God.

Take note, faith and wisdom go together. You can also see that in James where it says that if you lack wisdom, you should ask God who gives generously to all without finding fault. However, when you ask, you must believe and not doubt. Let's say that faith is the sail and wisdom is the rudder of the boat, both leading us in the right direction. Faith and wisdom work together, not in contradiction, because you need both to get to your destination.

What happens when I am being wise and bad things still happen? Let me respond with three words: *hang on longer.* All of us look at the short-term perspective, but we have to look at the long-term perspective. There is never going to be a time when you look back and wish you had been unwise and lacking faith. Wisdom and faith will always be the best choice. You might not see results on day one or even day 100, but you can be sure that God is going to do something.

The apostle Paul exhorts us to not become weary in doing good, for at the proper time, we will reap a harvest if we do not give up. Sometimes we just have to wait on God to show us what He is doing, even through bad times.

For the next several days, we will discuss the importance of wisdom. Are you ready to gain wisdom for every aspect of your life? Begin by asking God for wisdom today.

How Do I Get Wisdom?

Proverbs 2:6; 4:5

Do you want to be a wise person? Would you like to make wise decisions in your vocation, with your family and friends? All of us want wisdom, but what do we mean by wisdom? *Wisdom* is the capacity to understand in order to live skillfully. It's not a haphazard thing; it's God skillfully guiding you.

I want to parent skillfully. I want to be a husband skillfully. I want to minister in the church skillfully. I want to be a friend skillfully. Students should be skillful in the way they interact in school. Let me repeat, wisdom is the capacity to understand in order to live skillfully.

So how do we get it? Let's look in the book of Proverbs where King Solomon invites us to get wisdom and understanding and not forget God's words or turn away from them. He is inviting us to get wisdom.

Over the next days we will see there are three ways we can gain wisdom. First, we get wisdom from the Lord. We receive wisdom from Him through the Scriptures realizing there is truth higher and more significant than common sense. It's something that is not earthly but comes from the heavens. So we pray for wisdom, we read about wisdom, we ask about wisdom, we think about wisdom. And in doing so, we will grow in Christ. As we grow in Christ, we are getting to know Him more.

It is essential to spend time in the Word of God—reading it, studying it, memorizing it. The Lord gives wisdom, and from His mouth come knowledge and understanding. When Jesus was a young boy, He grew up to be filled with wisdom. Now He has become wisdom for us from God.

The first place we should go for wisdom is the Lord. James advises us to ask for wisdom because God gives generously to all. That is something we should pray every single day. I try to ask the Lord for wisdom every day. I want Him to lead me, and I want to be a good leader in my family and in my church. So put wisdom on your prayer list today.

Getting Wisdom
Proverbs 11:14

Yesterday we discussed the first place to gain wisdom: from the Lord. The second place we get wisdom is from other people. Wise counsel is greater than today's thought. There could be five subjects and fifty views, but wise counsel is greater than any of them. You can see ideas come and go, but society will never apologize and say, "Hey, we had a bad idea about twenty years ago." Instead, it just shoves in the next idea.

Wisdom comes from, of course . . . wise counsel. Do you have men and women in your life, people surrounding you, from whom you are able to get wise counsel? Parents, let's incorporate people into our kids' lives who are able to speak wisdom to them, people besides us to whom our kids can go in order to receive wise counsel.

When you come to a place where you do not know what to do, you should have wise people in your life. Wise counsel is so crucial. When I started pastoring years ago, I set up a wisdom team. I selected five godly men who loved the Lord and loved me. I called a different one every week to talk about what we were doing, decisions I had to make, situations we were facing, and so forth. I needed their wise counsel. Not the April fool's jokes of the world but the solid foundation of godly wisdom from a trusted friend.

The third place you get wisdom is from life. You learn from your mistakes, and you learn from the mistakes of others. The bad news is that we often make good decisions by first making bad decisions. Life will teach you lessons because no one is perfect. God is using those challenges to teach you. The Word of God says that gray hair is the crown of wisdom. You get gray hair through difficult decisions. A wise man learns by the experience of others, an ordinary man learns by his own experiences, and a fool learns from no one's experience.

We want to learn from the Lord, other people, and even through difficult times. Pay attention when somebody sins—how did it go? Learn from that. Watch when somebody makes a bad decision—learn from that. Learn from other people's faults and failures and other people's skills and success. Gain wisdom as God uses life to teach you.

Are there people in your life you can count on for wisdom? Are you wisely paying attention to the lessons of life?

A Decision Tree
Psalm 25:11–15

Let me give you a decision tree with three branches:

1. *What is best for me?* That is the lowest level of decision-making. Unfortunately, that is where our world lives—what is best for me. People usually care only about themselves.

2. *What is right or wrong?* What is moral, and what is immoral? Some of us as Christians think God is a great umpire in the sky and all He cares about is what is right. Well, He is righteous, but He also cares about your heart. He loves you. He does not want you to do what is right like a robot. He wants you to do what is right because you love Him and want to obey Him. So it is not just about what is right or what is best for me.

3. *What is wise and glorifies God?* For example, something may be legal or a crowd favorite but unwise and cease to glorify God.

So where are you on this continuum? Are you just asking, "What's best for me?" Are you asking, "What's right or wrong?" Just looking for a rule. Or are you asking, "What's wise?"

The ultimate tool for decision-making—the highest place, the best question—is:

What is wise and glorifies God?

That is the secret question to ask first, parents, if you want to teach your kids how to make decisions. Then all the other things will fall into the right place. What glorifies God answers all the other questions. What glorifies God is what is right because He is the King of righteousness. And what glorifies God is best for you. It might not always be what you want, but it will be best because He has come to give you life and give it abundantly.

Let's reverse the typical order by first asking, "What is wise and glorifies God?" Then we will be seeking His kingdom and righteousness first. And all the other things—what is wise, what is right, what is best—will be added unto you.

Glorify the Lord
Proverbs 4:6

In Proverbs, Solomon encourages us to not abandon wisdom because she will watch over us. We must love her, and she will guard us. He also tells us to love wisdom and obey wisdom. When you say you love wisdom, that shows desire. But when you say you obey wisdom, that means discipline.

In 2 Chronicles 1, the Lord comes to Solomon with a blank check asking him what he wants, anything in the world! What would fill in the payment line of a blank check from God? Many of us might say, "I don't want to pay taxes." Young people might say, "I want to be popular." A single person might say, "I want to get married." A businessperson might say, "I want to make a bunch of money." None of those would satisfy. Solomon decided rightly by saying, "I want to be wise." He chose wisdom. I hope we would choose the same.

The love of wisdom must result in the obedience to wisdom to really change our path. Proverbs says being wise requires discipline, not just desire. Sometimes God's wisdom and our emotions may be at odds. You may emotionally feel something, yet that might not be a wise decision. The secret is that we don't just live by our feelings, and that takes discipline. We live by the Word of God, and we walk in wisdom. So, when your feelings, desires, or emotions get the best of you, step back and ask yourself if it is really wise. Or ask a trusted friend. Many of us get in trouble because we walk in the fog of what we feel instead of clarity of what is wise. Feelings change, wisdom remains.

How would you assess your desires and discipline when it comes to wisdom in your life?

April 4

Elements to Gain Wisdom
Proverbs 9:9–10

There are qualities that bring wisdom into our lives. Reverence is one of them. So I acknowledge God and revere God. I fear the Lord. I say, "You are higher, You are better."

Humility is another quality that garners wisdom; it is a requirement for wisdom. You cannot be proud and wise. Humility brings wisdom. Think about teachableness. We need to be teachable and willing to learn. Consider a third one, diligence; it is the precursor of wisdom because you need to be careful and persistent and work hard in order to be wise. And then there is righteousness; you need to be morally right in order to act wisely. And finally, there is faith; it is always needed to receive wisdom from the Lord.

Now, let's look at the opposite of all of these to see if they will bring wisdom. What is the opposite of reverence? If you don't respect God, you will not find wisdom. The opposite of humility is arrogance. That is not going to get you wisdom. If you are not teachable, you are a know-it-all. That is not going to work. To be lazy instead of diligent is not a way to become wise. When you say, "I am going to choose sin, I don't want to be righteous," that is unwise. To be faithless instead of faithful will not gain you wisdom.

Wisdom is like an all-day pass that allows you to enjoy or endure all the rides at the amusement park. Can you imagine? You can ride as much as you want and enjoy everything for free. It is a pass for parenting. It is a pass for singlehood. It is a pass for marriage. It is a pass for joy and a pass for grief. It is a pass for a business decision. It is a pass for choosing what college to go to. It is a pass you will be able to pull out and say, "I want this pass to be my entrance into every ride of my life. I am going to love wisdom. I'm going to obey wisdom. I'm going to be disciplined by it."

Get the "wisdom pass" for your life through reverence, humility being teachable, diligent, righteous, and faithful! Ask the Lord today for wisdom in the_____ area of your life.

The Cost of Wisdom
Proverbs 4:7–9

For God, wisdom is supreme. Although it will cost all you have, get wisdom—get understanding. Cherish it, and it will exalt you. Embrace it, and it will honor you.

We can ask the Lord for wisdom as Solomon did. Wisdom for every day, for the things we cannot handle or should not handle in our strength. However, we need to know that though wisdom may cost us something, it will bless us far more than any sacrifice.

When Proverbs says to get wisdom, the author is using a word that means a business transaction, like when you pay for something you want. Wisdom has a price. But the price paid for wisdom will always be a trade up. The cost for sin is always a trade down; we will always lose when we choose to sin.

A wise decision may cost you friends, it may sacrifice entertainment, or exact its fee in time. When you get married or become a parent, it will cost you to walk in wisdom. Your time, hobbies, and money no longer are solely at your disposal. You will not be able to do all the things you used to do when you did not have children because your time is shared and wonderfully so! Wisdom has a cost, and when you pay that price, you will find it is a trade up, not a trade down. Wise ones gladly pay the price realizing the sacrifice is small compared to the value that is gained. Where do you need to walk in wisdom regardless of the cost?

If you want to live your life honoring the Lord, seek wisdom. Remember, the Bible says that if anyone is without wisdom, they should make their request to God, who gives freely to all, and it will be given to them.

Hard Times in God's Will

Job 1:20–22

God's people don't get passed over when it comes to hardship. But hard times are the part of His plan we'd almost always choose to omit if the choice were ours to make.

The hard times might be easier to understand if we could always trace our pain back to our own or others' sinful choices. But often we have no part in the struggles that can and do befall us. Sometimes the uproar of life is a natural result of choosing sin or selfishness, but just as often it is not. So how do we handle pain or heartbreak in a way that keeps us moving forward? Even if no 1-2-3 foolproof exit plan exists, can we at least hope in a higher way?

There is a spectrum of trials we can face—ones at work, home, financial, emotional . . . Yet God can see us through them all and even bring blessings from the pain. One of the hardest things my wife and I faced was a miscarriage. We already had a son and were trying for a second child. Excitement turned to tears in the doctor's office when we were told of the miscarriage.

But years later, Valerie came along. If we had not suffered a miscarriage, Valerie may not have been here. Obviously, conception is God's business. He is the giver of life. But in my and my wife's little microcosm of planning, the child now in heaven would have completed our family. We might not have tried again. Now a beautiful blonde-haired girl fills our life—and we can't imagine life without her.

Her presence speaks to a truth we all need to grip for dear life and savor well. The truth is God is working things out during those very parts of His will we do not want. He is crafting, shaping, and planning at a deeper level than we can see. He is looking through a lens or at a time line that stretches from eternity past to eternity future. We are looking through a straw at a tiny black dot on the line of life. God sees eternal joy while we only see today's pain.

God can be trusted to work all things out for our good and His glory. Hang in there! You never know what "Valeries" the Lord has around the corner tomorrow. Trust Him today and walk in faithfulness, even in the hard times.

Stay Put—He Is in Control

Exodus 13:17–18

When Moses and the children of Israel stood at the edge of the Red Sea with the Egyptian army closing in, they made an unbelievable tactical choice: they stayed put. They just stood in place. Why? Because God was crafting a story that a bridge across the water could not tell. The Israelites would have to walk *through the sea* to tell God's great story of deliverance. Surely there were other routes, other plans of escape. Certainly, battles awaited them on shorter roads too. But when they first left Egypt, God wanted to take them the long way. This meant the story would require unprecedented miracles—His leadership in a pillar of cloud and one of the parting of the Red Sea.

"Our whole perspective changes," wrote Robert J. Morgan in his book *Red Sea Rules*, "when, finding ourselves in a hard place, we realize the Lord has either placed us there or allowed us to be there, perhaps for reasons presently only known to Himself."[18] His goal for the hemmed-in Israelites was not the dot of the moment Moses must have seen through his straw-like perspective. But it would be a timeless story of God's greatness that would be told and retold throughout history.

When you and I begin to look at the whole of God's plan instead of the tiny part—the small dot—immediately in front of us, trust opens up. We can trust our great God to see us through. He has been faithful to those who have come before us, and He will be faithful to us. The psalmist wrote, "Your faithfulness continues through all generations; you established the earth, and it endures" (Ps. 119:90 NIV).

Martyrs, widows, orphans, the impoverished, the forgotten, the persecuted, and the wounded have all found Christ faithful. With such a rich history, God is not going to ruin His reputation by hanging us out to dry. He doesn't just act faithfully; He *is* faithful. That is who He is, and it is all He can be.

"He who calls you is faithful," Paul wrote to the Thessalonian church, and "he will do it" (1 Thess. 5:24). And to the church at Corinth he wrote, "God is faithful; you were called by him into fellowship with his Son, Jesus Christ our Lord" (1 Cor. 1:9).

When God has you on the longer path, keep walking!

Trust Deeply
John 6:66–69

In the most difficult times, we can trust deeply that the parts of His will we don't want are the very things He will use to accomplish His eternal plan. He is faithful not to wound us at random; He is faithful to save us forever. Throughout our lives, we will surely experience pain and heartache, but they are not meant to thwart the mission of the Lord. They are meant to further it!

Keep standing and keep trusting. Echo Peter's words as your declaration of truth in troubled times: "Lord, to whom will we go? You have the words of eternal life. We have come to believe and know that you are the Holy One of God" (John 6:68–69).

As Jesus drew closer to the cross and to His death, His disciples became more and more frightened and disoriented. They were hoping for something more secure. It's not surprising that some of His followers began to fall away. But Peter had it right. He understood that the best thing for them at the time was to press in even closer to Jesus than before. There was no better place for them to be.

Those times when we want to move just to keep from feeling trapped are the very times we need to be still and embrace His will. Don't leave— cleave! The more closely you walk with Christ in the uncomfortable of the unknown, the greater clarity of life you will experience. Are you confused? Hurt? Disoriented? Cling to Christ and His Word like never before.

Getting mad won't help, either. Anger is a secondary emotion. It doesn't achieve the will of God. In tough times, anger and resentment might be simmering. We imagine that by drifting away or giving God the cold shoulder we can teach Him a thing or two. We look for an ally whom we think will love us better than God. Some see alcohol or drugs as a ready friend offering quick comfort. Others believe a church switch where "people really understand me" will relieve their pain.

Coping mechanisms and strategies for handling hurts and disappointments abound. In those times join Peter in asking Jesus, "Lord, to whom will we go? You have the words of eternal life" (John 6:68). Keep turning to Jesus as you go through your day.

Closer to Christ
John 13:21–25

The trials of life are meant to push us closer to Christ. The night Jesus was betrayed, the apostle John laid his head on his Master's chest. When Jesus announced that one of His disciples would betray Him, wouldn't John's reflexive response have been to quickly lift his head and draw back in shock? In my imagination, I see Jesus placing His hand gently on John's head to draw him near again.

Near Jesus is exactly where I need to be when troubling words or wounding circumstances come. That kind of intimacy can feel a little uncomfortable for some, but the physical image points to a deeper spiritual reality. When one of my kids wanted to crawl onto my lap and press in close after a skinned knee or a scary dream, I can't help but be reminded of the tender love God has for His children. I am glad to be the one they run to.

Think about it. There is a short list of folks who have an open invitation to place their head on your shoulder or chest. My list includes only my wife and kids. No one else gets those kind of hugs because there is a depth of relationship that precedes such intimate contact.

When I am hurting, when I'm experiencing that part of God's will I do not want, He is the One I run to. The truth is, God has "rigged" this life to require Jesus Christ at its center. Faced with the painful parts of God's will, He is the One I draw close to, trusting that He is crafting a plan—even when I don't understand it.

Through that difficult morning of loss and heartbreak through miscarriage I shared about on April 6, Kelly and I learned immeasurable lessons in trust. We chose to pray and believe that God was in control. We returned home from the hospital and cranked up some of our favorite praise songs—we worshiped and we cried. We focused our attention on God and pressed into Him, hurting but knowing it was Him we needed most. We didn't like His will and did not want it, but He didn't ask us about that. He does not have to. He is the sovereign One. Our job is to lay our heads on His chest listening for His heartbeat and waiting for His plan to unfold.

More Than We Can Handle

John 16:33

Have you ever heard someone say, "God will never give you more than you can handle"? I'm guessing they're paraphrasing 1 Corinthians 10:13, which says God will not let you be tempted beyond what you can bear. But trials and temptation are two different things.

Sin is always a choice, not the inevitable result of crushing temptation. But somehow, that verse has been twisted to mean that we won't experience more trouble than we can bear. In fact, nothing could be further from the truth. God will often allow more than we can handle, but He'll never allow more than He can handle. Our whole lives are more than we can handle—that is why we need Christ!

I needed God to stay the course while I was in school. I needed Him when I was single and longed for a spouse. I needed Him when I sought a job. Now, with two kids, a marriage, friends, and a great church, I definitely have more than I can handle. Only in His strength and wisdom can I know what is best for my family and whether or not my desires are selfish or pure. In marriage, it is possible to win the fight but lose ground, a lesson most of us have learned the hard way. We need God in the important things and the mundane because life is too much; it's more than we can or were created to handle.

The bottom line is this: life is hard. I need God every minute of every day because I am often faced with more than I can handle. Paul understood that when he wrote these words to the Corinthians:

> We do not want you to be unaware, brothers and sisters, of our affliction that took place in Asia. We were completely overwhelmed—beyond *our strength*—so that we even despaired of life itself. Indeed, we felt that we had received the sentence of death, *so that* we would not trust in ourselves but in God who raises the dead. He has delivered us from such a terrible death, and he will deliver us. We have put our hope in him that he will deliver us again. (2 Cor. 1:8–10, emphasis added)

Shine

1 Peter 3:13–17

God will undoubtedly allow more than we can handle. Thankfully great pressure results in great reliance. Settle it and rely on Him. The I-can't-do-this sweat of life is where we learn to trust Him most deeply. "Trials and troubles are dumbbells and treadmills for the soul," wrote Robert Morgan. "They develop strength and stamina."[19]

God has used the pressures of life to draw us closer to Him. At the time, trials looked as uncrossable as the Red Sea must have looked to Moses. But such challenges cause us to rely on God more deeply than we might otherwise. Sadly, if we could handle these things without Him, many of us would try.

When was the last time you prayed for the strength to take a single step? Today, someone in a hospital or a physical therapy clinic is asking God for that much strength. That single step to them looks impossible. It is more than they can bear. They need their God so they can shuffle just a few feet forward. And when they do, the resulting celebration will be even louder than when someone else finishes a marathon!

Those parts of His will that we do not want cause the volume of our faith to get turned up. C. S. Lewis wrote, "God whispers to us in our pleasures . . . but shouts in our pain: it is His megaphone to rouse a deaf world."[20] Not only do we hear God more clearly, but our attentiveness to Him can also cause the ears of others to incline toward words of hope.

When my wife endured our miscarriage and in less than a year also lost her mom, she sought God like never before. You should see her Bible—ink-stained, pages curled, writing in every margin, torn cover. But the wear of her Bible also shows where the protection of her heart came from. Imagine a woman losing a child, caring for her cancer-ridden mother, and then speaking at her mother's funeral within twelve months. It was more than she could bear. But she trusted God to bear it for her, and He did. She leaned into Him and once again, He proved Himself faithful.

When God's will is not what we want, we have our chance to shine. So stay put and trust as you lean into Jesus. He will surely see you through.

Lights Out
Exodus 7:1–6

*B*am! *Zap! Pow!* and all of the other comic book words you can imagine. They described the moment when the power went out on July 13, 1977. New York City came to a screeching halt. Subways stopped, Times Square no longer glowed with neon, the evening Mets game against the Giants was cancelled, and Wall Street closed its doors.

The largest city in the United States was in the dark, literally. Powerless. That one word says it all. Even with all the state-of-the art technology and buildings reaching into the clouds, the lack of power resulted in thousands of people walking home from a shortened and purposeless workday.

New York City residents still had all of the appliances they had before the blackout, but they were now useless. No power, no progress; just sit and wait. Then it happened again. Ironically, on July 13, 2019, on the 42nd anniversary of the 1977 blackout, New York City again went dark—it was powerless once more.

New York needed a power source, and so do we. If our power source is Christ, then every Christ-follower and every leader can rest assured that God's will has God's power behind it. God's power may be manifested in quiet, steady ways or in dramatic, unbelievable miracles. Moses experienced both, but as he carried out his burning-bush assignment, he came to understand that God's will be done in God's way has God's power. Always.

Moses made it his business to know God's will. He followed God from the back side of nowhere to the courts of Pharaoh the same way you and I are called to follow Him: one step at a time. God demonstrated His power in spectacular ways when Moses came before Pharaoh. Why were those demonstrations needed? Because when Moses and Aaron asked Pharaoh for the release of the Israelites, Pharaoh resisted, just as God predicted he would.

It was that persistent hardness of heart that prompted God's mighty demonstrations of His power through a series of miraculous signs and terrible plagues. Some might argue that they were merely coincidental or caused by nature, but at least four factors mark the difference between a miraculous sign and a natural phenomenon: timing, location, purpose, and prediction. Those factors can determine what is a miracle and what is not. And those factors can also help us personally determine God's will. For the next two days we will look further into these four factors.

Timing and Purpose
Exodus 9:16–18

Let's look at four factors that mark the difference between a miraculous sign and a natural phenomenon: timing, location, purpose, and prediction. These factors also help us personally determine God's will. Today, we'll look at two of them: timing and purpose.

Timing: When Moses declared the plague of flies, he told Pharaoh, "This sign will take place tomorrow" (Exod. 8:23), and it did. When he said Egypt would be devastated by hail "tomorrow at this time" (Exod. 9:18), hail came down at that very hour. This precise and accurate timing indicated not a natural occurrence but a divinely planned one. God's timing is perfect. His miraculous timing rained down manna and quail from heaven to feed Moses and his sojourners. God in His perfect timing, through His magnificent power, accomplishes His eternal will in His time.

Purpose: The acts of God's power have a higher purpose that is missing from mere natural phenomena. When Jesus walked on water, He did not do so to prove He could float. He walked on water to demonstrate the power of God—that God could do anything He purposed, regardless of the laws of physics. When He rose from the dead, it wasn't a carnival trick but a permanent defeat of death and sin. God's miracles have a purpose. The *why* of the plagues and all miracles is to declare the greatness of God.

We must personally understand this. The miracle of God's guidance in our lives is not simply to bless us. We can easily slip into thinking that God's guidance is solely for our own pleasure. But when God is at work opening and closing doors, our lives shine with His greatness for others to see. We aren't the recipients of the miracle as much as we are the vehicles for it. Like a boomerang, it comes from Him through us and then back to Him.

Miracles are a combination of a Father lovingly blessing His children and showing His power to others. We are thankful for the blessing but realize the purpose is higher than our perspectives. In fact, He said so Himself in the message the Lord gave Moses to deliver to Pharaoh. He said the purpose was so "you will know there is no one like me on the whole earth" (Exod. 9:14).

Prediction and Location

Exodus 10:1–4

Moses predicted all the plagues. He clearly said the timing, location, and purpose of each miracle—before they happened. God uses the prophetic declaration of the future to establish credibility. More than 300 prophecies pointed to Jesus before He ever came. His birth, life, death, and second coming are all documented in the Old Testament hundreds or thousands of years before the manger.

Imagine if the news announced it would soon rain and that out of a dozen people on a certain sidewalk, rain would fall on only three of them. And then the news anchor would tell us which three they would be. If these things did happen as predicted, you would be less likely to attribute them to chance. Instead, you would likely think the news anchor possessed some supernatural power, and you would probably pay close attention to what was said next. The timing, location, purpose, and prediction of the ten plagues show it was God's power at work through Moses.

The plagues were specifically predicted in location, not randomly experienced. They affected the Egyptians, not the Jews. The plague of darkness covered all Egypt for three days, but all the Israelites had light where they lived. With the exactness of a GPS coordinate, the missiles of each plague struck on a dime.

These things can give us assurance on our burning-bush journey. God is in the know, even when we don't have a clue. Right now, God is orchestrating opportunities for you to discover Him more deeply. Tomorrow and the day after that may present you with a choice to be selfless or selfish. A decision is headed your way that your last fortune cookie cannot adequately prepare you for. That decision is not a surprise to God. His timing, location, purpose, and knowledge are acting in unison to lead you forward another step. His will always comes with His power.

Moses trusted God's ability to know the future. But will we take what we've seen and trust Him for our future? Corrie ten Boom wisely said, "Never be afraid to trust an unknown future to a known God."[21] The God we seek daily knows daily what is ahead. Understanding what makes a miracle miraculous helps us identify God's work in our lives. Personalizing these truths is the key to changing our day's headline from "Powerless" to "Powerful."

Where It All Starts
1 John 1:1–2

If you are like me, I also need more light and love to navigate the journey. John has an answer for us. First John was written by the apostle John around AD 90. There are two big thoughts throughout the book: 1) God is light, and 2) God is love. Along those lines, the book takes a firm stance against Gnosticism, which was a common false teaching at the time. And yet John is very loving in the way he speaks to these believers.

John writes about light and darkness, love of God or love for the world, the Spirit of Christ or the spirit of the Antichrist, righteousness or sin, and truth or falsehood. John wants us to make a change in our hearts. In today's society, we need to learn how to combine light and love so we can stand strong against things that are not true and, at the same time, be loving.

John starts with these words: "What was from the beginning" (1 John 1:1). Have you heard that phrase before? The beginning? We find it in the first verse of the Bible, Genesis 1:1, as well as in the first verse of the Gospel of John, John 1:1.

The second thing I want you to notice today is how John uses the words *heard*, *seen*, and *touch*. He wants us to live a life that is real. Now, think about that . . . he speaks of what he had seen. What did he see? He saw Jesus Christ on the cross. He walked with Him all those days in His time of ministry on earth. He saw Jesus.

He also heard Jesus preach the Sermon on the Mount. He heard Him declare the blind man healed. He broke bread with Him. He heard from Jesus. He touched Jesus. Who was the disciple that laid his head on Jesus' breast? It was John. He could say: "I heard His heartbeat. I've touched Him. I've seen Him for who He is. This is real. Jesus Christ is real."

The real life of Jesus is what gives us real life. We're not just playing games. There is a real eternity. A real life. A real Savior. A real God who wants to affect your heart as a real person. Talk to Him. Ask Him to touch your heart, speak to your soul, and show you His work in your life today . . . so you can say with John, "I've seen Him, I've heard Him, I've been touched by Him, Jesus Christ is real." Jesus is the light and love we are longing for.

Jesus Is Real!
Colossians 2:8–10

When John wrote his first letter, one of his main goals was to counter the effects of a false teaching known as Gnosticism. It said you had to have a special knowledge in order to connect with spiritual things. *Gnostic* means knowledge, a special knowledge. Gnosticism had this main tenet: physical things are bad; spiritual things are good. Therefore, if everything physical is bad and everything spiritual is good, then Jesus Christ must not have been a real man walking the face of the earth.

But Jesus had flesh. He was real. You could touch Him. The Gnostics said no; He can't be the Christ if He was a physical man. For them, Jesus had to be a spirit only. But we have to be clear about this. The physical death of Jesus, the physical life of Jesus, the physical resurrection of Jesus—they are all pivotal to our faith. The central aspect of Christianity is not just the teaching of the principles of Jesus. It is that Jesus Christ was a real man who walked on the earth, who lived a life we couldn't live, who died for our sins, and came back to life again.

It says in Hebrews that He was tempted in all things, but yet He was without sin so He could pay for our sins. He really went to the cross. Real nails went into His wrists and feet. The crown of thorns really hurt and drew blood. The spear went through His side. He really died. He really resurrected from the grave. That's why He said to Thomas, "Put your finger here and look at my hands. Reach out your hand and put it into my side" (John 20:27).

Why is this physical life of Jesus central to Christianity? Because you are a real person too. We are going to walk this life and will die one day. You and I need a physical Savior who lived a life we couldn't live and died a death we should have died so we could know we will rise again and spend eternity in heaven with God. So John, from the very beginning of his letter, said he saw, he heard, he touched. He said don't tell me He was a ghost. I was there. I laid my head on His chest and heard His heartbeat.

We all need a real encounter with Jesus. He is real. He is not a ghost. He is God's Son and is alive today. Trust Him with your life.

A Real Encounter with Jesus

John 20:28–29

One of the first things John wanted his readers to connect with was the truth that Jesus is real. He wanted us to know that Jesus really lived, died, and rose so we can have a real encounter with Him.

John's journey with Jesus was physical, but our journey is through faith. It would seem perhaps that John's journey was easier, but Jesus said to John and the other disciples that those who have not seen and yet still believe are blessed and full of joy. Jesus told them it was to their advantage that He would go away so He could send the Holy Spirit to dwell in their hearts. If you have trusted Christ as your Savior, the Holy Spirit lives inside of you.

Going to church is great, but have you had a real encounter with Jesus? Do you really pray? Do you talk to Him about the grand and ordinary things of life? Perhaps you are praying things like these: "Jesus, I'm nervous. God, I love You. God, I'm hurting. God, my marriage seems difficult. Lord, I'm so tempted by peer pressure. Jesus, I need You so badly right now."

Are you living a real life with Jesus? Do you really look at God's Word? When we read it, sometimes we don't understand everything. It's a difficult book at times. But it is of ultimate importance for you to be in it if you want to have a real encounter with Jesus. That's because Jesus Himself is the Word of God. It is sharper than any double-edged sword. It's able to pierce your soul and your spirit. It is alive and active. It doesn't return void. And it always accomplishes what it desires.

Are you having real fellowship with Jesus? Are you really trusting Him? When you get to heaven, nobody's going to ask you what denomination you were, who your pastor was, or what church you went to. The real question is going to be, "Did you have a real encounter with Jesus?"

Maybe you did many years ago and it has become stale. Or maybe you have just been to church so much or you are so busy that you're not having real fellowship with Jesus anymore. Maybe you need to have an encounter with Him once again. Or maybe your relationship with Him has never been better! Wherever you are on the journey, call out to Him with the deepest sincerity today.

I Was There

Luke 24:9–12

Have you ever seen or used virtual reality goggles? With the right gear, you can ride a roller coaster or go to Hawaii through virtual reality. When you look up, it looks up. When you look down, it looks down.

What God really wants is for you to have a real relationship with Jesus so you can say, "I've seen Him by faith. I've heard His voice through His Word and through His people. I've been touched by Him in the depths of who I am. And I have a heart that can say, 'I was there.'"

If you just do a few nice religious things, go to a certain church, and behave as you are supposed to, it's virtual reality. It's not spiritual reality. When you're walking around with virtual reality goggles, you don't see anybody else. When you move through spiritual reality, you begin to see everybody else in a totally different way, and you can share the good news you are a witness to.

Only when you can say, like John, "I was there" can you be a reliable witness to others. Nobody can tell you that it didn't happen—because you saw it, you heard it, and you were touched and transformed by it. And that's what we all want to say about our relationship with Jesus Christ. Salvation through Christ alone is reality. And then walking in the steps of Jesus Christ as He lives His life through you, touching and loving others—that's even more reality.

Pray. Care. Share.
Acts 2:42–47

We all long to share, to talk with people, be known, and know others. We don't want an isolated life without impact and connection. We want to have a life that makes a difference, a life that provides for needs and helps with hurts.

If you have a real experience with Jesus, the most natural reaction is to want to talk to others about the One you love. Seems that older generations shared Christ more freely. Unfortunately, we have become more silent today because our culture has become more aggressive.

It is still biblical to share your faith and tell somebody about Jesus, to say "I saw it and heard it. Jesus walked on this earth, died, and rose. He is the way, the truth, and the life." The world is hurting like never before. People are so stressed out, burdened, and afraid. And we have Jesus Christ, the Prince of Peace.

A real experience can't be kept in. You know Jesus is real, so share Him today with a friend or coworker in a way that's loving and kind without being obnoxious. How can we make a difference in somebody's life? Three words: Prayer, Care, and Share.

> *Acts 2:42 Prayer:* This is the first thing you can do for somebody. It can be for a person you work with, someone you live by in your neighborhood, a friend, or a family member. Begin to pray for that person. Say something like this: "God, I'm praying for my friend and I'm asking that You use me in their life. Would You do something wonderful in my friend's life? Would You speak to my friend, who needs a real relationship with You?"
>
> *Acts 2:45 Care:* What can you do to care for someone? How can you encourage them? Bring them cookies. Write them a note. Bring them some balloons. Be with them in the hospital or during a hard time. Show Christ's love and earn the right to be heard.
>
> *Acts 2:47 Share:* Now tell the one you've prayed and cared for the wonderful news about Jesus Christ.

Whose name comes to mind? God has placed you in that neighborhood, in that job, on that team, in that club for a purpose—to be able to reach out and love people. They need someone like you; who has had a real encounter with Jesus and who will love them well and share with them the Prince of Peace.

Fellowship with One Another

Acts 2:1

A real relationship with Jesus results in a real relationship with others. We will want to make a difference everywhere we go, not only with people we know. Togetherness opens the miraculous chapter of Acts 2.

There are people who need a word of encouragement or just a prayer. You will find them in simple interactions when you go shopping, sit in a restaurant, watch your kids practice sports, spend time in a waiting room, or even wait in line. You will see what the people around you are going through and seize the opportunity to chat with them or even ask for their permission to pray for them.

God wants to use you. Keep it practical, simple, and natural. Don't be obnoxious about it. Kindness and tact go a long way.

Maybe they are not going to pray and receive Christ at that moment. Or they may not make a big deal out of it at all. But you surely can pray, care, and share with strangers, new acquaintances, and people all around you. You will make a difference in that little moment right there.

When we share our testimony, people can have fellowship with us. What's fellowship? *Fellowship* is a Greek word that means "to share something or to connect." That's why you have a fellowship hall in church where you can share and connect with one another. We long for connection, we desire fellowship with one another and fellowship with God.

A quick word for parents . . . don't let school and activities raise your children. If we aren't intentional, busyness will devour family fellowship. Don't convey the idea that life is what happens outside your home. Get your family around your table and fellowship. Don't miss these years. Make sure you make time for each other.

Time is moving fast, let's not miss the blessing of true fellowship with family and friends.

Fellowship with the Father
1 John 1:3–4

Today may be a lazy day, or it may be a busy day. No matter which direction your day may take you, the most important part of your waking hours is to have fellowship with the Father through Jesus Christ. That means to take time to share and connect with Him, trusting Him each moment of your day.

Walking with Christ will enable you to have a real family life, a real single life, a real married life . . . one filled with depth, endurance, and joy.

That real fellowship comes from real fellowship with God the Father through Jesus Christ. Fellowship means to connect and share something in common. What do we have in common with God? Absolutely nothing. And that's why He sent Jesus Christ—a real person who walked on earth, lived temptations, but never sinned—so He could die on a cross and rise from the grave so you and I as men, women, teenagers, and kids could have real relationships with God with whom we have nothing in common. But Jesus Christ, our mediator, brings it all together.

What will be the result of this? Our joy will be complete.

The whole thing is about our joy. If you don't live a real life for Jesus and never share Jesus, fellowship with others, or fellowship with God, you are never going to experience real, complete joy. It is that kind of joy that luxuries, possessions, real estate, or fulfilling dreams can't bring—at least not permanently. The Holy Spirit is telling you and me that we have purpose and a relationship with God the Father through Jesus.

God Is Light
1 John 1:5

One of the themes found throughout Scripture is that God is light. Jesus said in the New Testament, "I am the light of the world" (John 8:12). In Matthew, at the transfiguration, Jesus' face shone bright like the noonday sun. And again, when Christ talked to John in Revelation, His face shone like the sun.

In the Bible, we see a contrast between light and darkness. Darkness is evil, and light is good. We can see that contrast in the way we talk about some things. If we see a movie and it is a dark one, it means there's likely some evil in it. But if it is a light movie, that means it has some goodness in it. God is light, and His primary attribute is holiness. God's holiness is linked to His light. He's bright. He's pure. He's without any blemish, without any darkness, without any smudge. His character is impeccable and perfect. He has never had an evil thought.

That's different from us. Our glory is granted. It is not intrinsic. Not so with God. God's glory and majesty are intrinsic to who He is and can never be removed. The more we know about who God is, the more we will understand about who we are and how to journey on this path. He is light. The book of Revelation ends with a new heaven and earth but no sun is needed. The glory of God is our light (Rev. 21:23)!

Before we get to heaven though, we are not going to have a perfect life. We will have to go through trials, judgment, discipline, and the consequences of sin. But whenever you think that God is doing something mean or evil, just dismiss it, because you know that everything God does is from a heart of light.

Let's Walk in the Light

1 John 1:7

God is light, and there is no darkness in Him. Walking apart from God is walking in darkness—walking in sin. Walking in darkness also brings self-deception and lies.

In many ways, our society walks in self-deception and lies. But before we blame society, we have to begin with our hearts. Why is society like it is? Because it reflects the human heart. Of course, society influences the human heart. But what is the problem with the world? The problem with the world is us. We are the ones who make up our society. This is not to say we are the worst of the worst. That wouldn't be completely true, either. Hopefully, we are trying to influence for good, but society and our hearts mirror one another in many ways. Darkness is strong in and around us and self-deception creeps in.

We end up deceiving ourselves because we have trouble admitting we are wrong. Why? Because pride is in us. We are prideful people. The root of sin is pride. Pride produces sin and darkness.

While humility produces light and truth, it doesn't produce wickedness. Pride does. When we say, "I'm going to have it my way, in my fashion, in the way I want it, and nobody's going to tell me I'm wrong," we end up prideful. That's how Satan fell from heaven, because of his pride—wanting to be above God (Isa. 14:12–15).

It is impossible to simultaneously choose sin and humility—light and darkness. When we are humble and walking in the light of God, it is the antithesis of choosing sin.

We have to desire to walk in His light. Today, let your desire to walk in the light become reality in your steps.

The Dark Side

1 John 1:8–10

In the first chapter of the apostle John's first letter, we see a fight between light and darkness. John says we are sinful and that we don't want to admit we are wrong. Sadly, the pride behind this condition is the path to deceiving ourselves. We end up creating a new reality so we can put together a world in which our sin is not wrong but normal.

Birds of a feather flock together—that's how we say it. Thieves hang out with thieves, drunkards hang out with drunkards, complainers with complainers, the materialistic with materialists, and the list goes on. We encircle ourselves with those who are like us. What started as "I know this is wrong, I know this is bad" ends up as "Everybody does it."

This delusion ends up being a sinful and prideful place where we have created a new reality where sin is no longer sin. It's where we call darkness light and light darkness. It's where we plant a garden of our lives, pick weeds, and call them vegetables. We say no, this isn't wrong. Why is it not wrong? Because, we say, everybody does it. And we get around folks who do what we want to do, and we end up with a new alternate reality. We have self-deception, deceiving ourselves. It's called justification. Many of us are Olympic gold medalists at justifying our sin. There is always a reason for our actions that makes sense . . . to us at least.

"I'm not materialistic. I just like nice stuff. Everybody likes nice stuff."

"I'm not selfish, I just like my way. I just like how I do things. I think that's the best way to do it."

Everybody likes their way. What happens when we create a self-deceptive place where we justify our sin? We slowly but surely begin to walk in the shadows, then in the dark until finally we circle ourselves with a group who will normalize our sin and make it no longer sin. Why? Because everybody does it. Then sin becomes normal, and we can't figure out how normal could be wrong.

The Bible tells us that when we walk in darkness, we walk in self-deception—and lies.

But our only hope is to walk in the light. Then we see life clearly.

Don't Give Up!

1 John 1:5–7

I think some of us have given up. We say, "Well, boys will be boys, and girls will be girls. That's just what they do."

Hear me loud and clear. You don't have to look at pornography. You don't have to have sex before marriage or get drunk or experiment with drugs. You don't have to cheat or lie. You don't have to cuss. You can be a godly man or woman and truly walk with God!

Some of us justify all these things with an everybody-does-it attitude. No. Not everybody. That is a normalization of something destructive. In fact, if everybody is doing it, that might be the very reason you shouldn't do it. Sin hinders our fellowship with God, and it hinders our fellowship with others. It messes with our relationship with our sons, our daughters, or our parents. No one in the history of the world has said, "My family is awesome because my dad had an affair. My family is incredible because my mom is selfish. The disobedience of our kids has brought us closer." No. Sin always separates. It is the real joy-killer.

Yet we create this dysfunctional world and try to justify our actions. Some folks living in self-deception have separated personal holiness from changing the world and making it better. Those two things must connect.

The younger generation is more into opposing human trafficking than any generation before. And yet this generation is also more into pornography than any other generation. We think these two don't connect, but they do—pornography is funding human trafficking. Rejecting personal holiness while working for a better world is like rallying against a corrupt politician and then donating to his or her campaign.

We change the world when we realize that personal holiness and societal impact are connected. Most of the abolitionists who helped end slavery were believers in Jesus and realized that God had placed equal, intrinsic value in every person. Hospitals were started by believers who wanted to help and minister to people in their greatest needs. Believers started orphanages because they realized kids are precious to God.

Do not be self-deceived. God is calling every one of us to walk in the light and change the world . . . realizing the two are connected.

April 26

Walking in the Light
Matthew 5:14–16

Through Jesus Christ, God forgives our sins and washes us clean. He is the only way we get to God. God sent Jesus to earth so He could be the substitute for you and for me.

When we walk in the light, our families and our friendships come together, our marriage or our dating is better. But you and I are pulled into the shadows over and over. What's the answer? To stand and say, "I'm going to walk in the light and trust Jesus who has cleansed me of sin."

Like the cross, there is a vertical relationship with God that makes our horizontal relationships better. When we walk in the light, we are better spouses, better friends, better employees, better neighbors. And that's because we aren't walking in the shadows, trying to justify and self-deceive ourselves.

When Hurricane Harvey hit Houston in 2017, a lady filled out a request for help on the church's website. One of our staff members called her and found out she was a single mom in need of diapers and pajamas. Then the lady added, "Our car was flooded too. If y'all have a car, that would be awesome." The people in our church started working on how they could help her. One staff member hung up the phone and said to another, "We need to help this single mom get some diapers and clothes. And you're not going to believe this, she even said, 'If you have a car, that would be awesome.'" The other person replied in celebration, "Five minutes ago, somebody called to donate a car to a single mom!"

When we called back the single mom and broke the news to her, she began to cry. An hour later, the single mom called back in shock, "Did I hear you right? Did you say a car?" We also had the opportunity to lead this single mom to Jesus Christ!

When you walk in the light, you love others differently. When you walk in the light, you hear God differently. When you walk in the light, you will be part of those kinds of stories. Is there any hero or hope in the darkness stories? No. The light stories are where God is doing great things.

Eyes, Friends, and Love
Matthew 6:22

We all want to walk in the light. The question is, how do we do it? You can begin by asking yourself three things.

1. *What goes into your eyes?* Jesus said that the eye is the lamp of the body and that if your eye is good, your whole body will be full of light. But He also said that if your eye is bad, your whole body will be full of darkness. What are you looking at? What's going into your eyes? If it's good, your whole body will be filled with light.

2. *Who do you run around with?* Who are you hanging out with? Paul asks us not to deceive ourselves; bad company corrupts good morals. I know we think this verse is for somebody else or maybe just for teenagers. We say, "They do XYZ or think XYZ but I don't." Just wait—all of us, at any age, can be influenced.

Bad company corrupts good morals because we create a circle of an alternate reality where our sin is normalized. This is not to say that we shouldn't hang out with unbelievers. As believers, we ought to hang out with people who need direction except without being influenced or partaking. Do you see the difference? I tell the students at our church, "Choose your Friday night friends carefully and there is no shame in hanging out with your family."

3. *What do you love the most?* Don't love the world or the things that belong to the world. Because if anyone loves the world, the love of the Father is not in him or her. What does our soul love? We love Jesus. We love His Word. We love God. If we love the light, we are going to walk in the light, and it is going to be attractive for us to walk in the light. Walking in the darkness brings self-deception and lies. Walking in the light brings fellowship with others and with God. It is easy to decide which one we want. Choose light today for your eyes, friendships, and deepest love.

Jesus, Our Rescuer
1 John 1:7–2:2

God is faithful. He is not fickle. He is truth and doesn't lie. But if we justify ourselves, we are calling God a liar. We might say, "Everybody else is saying it's okay. God, You say it is not. They're not the liars. You're the liar, God." But when we realize we have done that and walked in darkness, we need to repent and say, "Lord, I confess to You my sin. I've done wrong, and I am sorry."

C. S. Lewis wrote:

> Fallen man is not simply an imperfect creature who needs improvement: he is a rebel who must lay down his arms. Laying down your arms, surrendering, saying you are sorry, realizing that you have been on the wrong track and getting ready to start life over again from the ground floor—that is the only way out of our "hole." This process of surrender—this movement full speed astern—is what Christians call repentance.[22]

People think they just need to be enlightened. That is different from realizing there is wickedness in their heart. Jesus died on the cross to pay for our wickedness. I'm going to place my faith and my trust in His death on my behalf, and that's what's going to kill this pride in me—because now the Holy Spirit lives inside of me. He is faithful, He is righteous. When we confess our sins, He forgives us and washes us clean so now we can walk in the light.

We all need Jesus' forgiveness. If we say we haven't sinned, we have made Him a liar. Repentance brings self-understanding, fellowship with God, and fellowship with others. There is not a person who is without sin. If you think, *Well, that's me; I haven't sinned*, you're sinning right then in your pride. I'm not perfect. You're not perfect. We all dabble in the dark at times. But when we confess it, Jesus Christ is able to give us light.

It is only Jesus, and He is the One you have to call on. He's the only One. So don't live self-deceived. Don't live in lies. Don't walk in darkness. Walk in the light of Christ.

What Is Confession?

James 5:16

What comes to your mind when you think about confession? Is it someone famous who was caught red-handed and then said "I'm sorry" at a press conference? Is it a small booth and a chat with a priest? What is confession?

Confession means "to admit or acknowledge sin or wrongdoing"; it also means "to agree with someone or something." When we admit wrongdoing or sin, we pour out our hearts to God and to those we have wronged. When we say, "amen," to the pastor's message, we show agreement with a certain point or theology. Confession and theology go well together because when we confess our sins, we agree with God that He is right and that we have been wrong.

Doesn't it feel good when you confess? It takes courage. But self-respect is better than another person's respect. Sometimes, we ponder, *What are people going to think?* But it is better to just say, "Who cares what they think! I care about what God thinks, so let me confess this. I'm sorry I wronged you."

The importance of confession hit me square in the eyes when I was eight years old. My aunt and uncle loved to play tennis. When I visited them, we played a lot. I had a cheap racquet, but both of theirs were top shelf. One day I borrowed my aunt's racquet. I started hitting balls against the wall. After a while, I began hitting rocks. Then I picked up a piece of glass and hit it. When I looked down at the racquet, I saw that the glass had cut the string. I panicked, put it back in the case, quietly placed it next to where my aunt was sitting, and then walked away.

The next day, she said she had broken a string on her racquet while she was playing. She was pretty proud of herself that she had hit hard enough to break a string. The technician at the pro shop said, "The string was cut. You did not break it playing." My face went red, but I didn't say a word . . . for three years. Ugh!

Finally, I told her the whole story. She said, "That's okay, Gregg. You could've just told me right then. I love you."

Secrets make you sick. When we confess our sins, He is faithful and righteous to forgive us. Usually, others forgive us too.

A Statement of Change

Acts 19:18–20

Confession is not just about releasing guilt. It is also a statement of change. Think of all the Scriptures that say something like this: "I want You, Lord, to make me different."

In Acts, the Bible says there was a group of people involved in sorcery who came and confessed their practices because they intended to change. They even burned their old magic books. When Paul says to confess with your mouth that Jesus is Lord, it is a statement of change. We are saying, "I am going to follow Christ, not my own ways."

When confession happens, it is intended to break the cycle of sin. When we confess our sins to the Lord and to somebody else, and when we apologize, we feel relief from guilt because we have gotten things right. But it is also a statement of change because now we have been placed under accountability for our actions.

Often, we would prefer to confess only to God and not tell anybody else. That option gives us a little bit of an out. Nobody knows except God that we were wrong. But when we confess our wrongs to the person we have wronged, we place ourselves in accountability for change. Andy Stanley says in his book *Enemies of the Heart*, "Remember the purpose of confession is not to relieve your conscience. It's to effect change and reconciliation."[23]

Who do we confess to? Those we have hurt. We have hurt God because we have sinned against Him, so we confess to the Lord. Then we also confess to the person we have hurt. "I am sorry I did that. That hurt you. I apologize." Now we have been placed into accountability. So, we say, "Lord, give me the strength to not do that again. I know it is wrong, so I am going to strive not to do it again."

Confession is not just for us to feel better. It is to restore a relationship. Keep your lists short. You don't want to be on your deathbed apologizing to every kid, cousin, grandchild, and person coming to visit you. If you say something that could be taken as an offense, instead of staying up all night worrying about it, just apologize. Make sure things are right between you, God, and others.

Three Confessions
Romans 10:9–10

Let's talk about one more notch of confession. First, there is a confession to God that is unto salvation, a confession to continue the relationship with Him, and a confession to other people.

How does a person become a Christian? You confess with your mouth that you aren't in charge of your life anymore, and now Jesus Christ is in charge. Have you declared that to the Lord in a prayer like this?

> *Lord, I know I have sinned. I know I have done things wrong. Jesus, I know You are the Savior. It is not going to church, doing the right thing, or my willpower that is going to do it. I need a Savior. I need Your blood to wash me clean. I want to confess to You that I'm a sinner. I've wronged You, God. I place my life in Your hands. I trust You to be my Savior. Wash me clean of my sins. God, save me. I want my heart to be changed.*

Your only hope for forgiveness is the cross. If you believe in your heart that God raised Jesus from the dead and confess with your mouth that Jesus is Lord, you will be saved.

Second and third, we confess to God and to our fellow humans to restore and keep existing relationships moving in the right direction.

Let me give you an example. You wake up one morning a little grumpy. You get to the office and decide to let everybody else have it. To make it right, go back in your office and pray, "Lord, I've taken my grumpiness out on others instead of laying it before You. Change my heart." Then, walk out of your office and say to everyone, "I'm sorry, I apologize. Please forgive me."

What happened here is that you began throwing rocks horizontally because you didn't first get it straight with the Rock vertically. There will be times in all our lives when we say, "Lord, right now I'm feeling angry (or greedy, lustful, jealous), and I want to confess it to You before I take it out on anybody else."

There is one confession unto salvation when you become a Christian, one to cultivate deeper relationship with God, and one to make things right with others. Confession makes all the difference.

Confessions
James 5:16

When we don't confess our sins to the Lord and to one another, physical things can happen in our lives. We can even get sick. People have heart attacks, high blood pressure, and ulcers because of unconfessed sins, undisclosed faults, or chronic guilt. But when we get it out to the Lord and get it out to others, things change.

How does God respond to our confession? With anger or wrath? No. God's response to our confession is faithful and righteous forgiveness. He will cleanse us of our sins!

How does our trash make it to the street? In our house, we pull out the trash bag from underneath the sink. Then we tie it, put it outside the garage, and wait for one of the kids to take it to the garbage can. Hopefully, a squirrel won't rip it open, find something to eat, and leave the rest all over the place. When it finally makes it into the can, the garbage company comes and picks it up. So it went from under the sink to the garage, from the garage to the garbage can, and finally from the garbage can to the truck.

How does your horizontal confession work? Does it go something like this? "You know, I'm sorry if you felt like that." You just moved it to the kitchen floor. "Maybe I hurt your feelings, but I didn't mean too." You just moved it to the garage. "God, everybody does it." You have moved it outside, but you haven't taken care of your sin yet. You just moved it a little bit further. To get it emptied in the truck and carted off, you have to own it, "Lord, I'm sorry. I repent. I want to be different. Forgive me and renew my strength."

On the vertical side, let me tell you what Jesus does. He will take the trash straight to the dump at the bottom of the cross—instantaneously. Jesus is faithful and righteous to cleanse us from all our sin. Our forgiveness is based on His faithfulness and righteousness. Often our response to each other is retribution, but God's response to us is forgiveness and cleansing of all sin.

Cleansed and Made Clean

Matthew 3:4–6

The Bible says that when we confess our sins, God forgives us and washes us clean. King David said while expressing anguish in prayer: "Completely wash away my guilt and cleanse me from my sin" (Ps. 51:2). John the Baptist in the Jordan River, while the people confessed their sins, said, "I baptize you with water for repentance" (Matt. 3:11). With a towel draped around his waist, Jesus said to Peter, "If I don't wash you, you have no part with me" (John 13:8).

When we confess our sins to God, who is holy and blameless, we agree with Him. We admit we are wrong, and He washes us clean. Even our consciences are washed clean. We are forgiven, made spotless and beyond reproach. We are holy in His sight. We are His children, and Jesus cleanses us of all unrighteousness.

So when you come to confess, you come to a safe place. When you come to confess, you're restoring relationships with others. But when you keep it in, it burns you up inside. Secrets make you sick. But if you get it out, you can say, "Lord, take care of all my filthiness and sin. Cleanse me of all unrighteousness."

For example, juicing is a popular nutritional method nowadays. You take a bunch of fruits and vegetables and blend them together. After a lot of noise, a glass of 100 percent pure juice results. In one cup of juice, you're able to drink a huge amount of produce you wouldn't have been able to eat otherwise. But there are also juice cleanses that clean your whole system.

Which do you think is harder to clean? Your insides, your stomach, your intestines, or your soul? Jesus is faithful to cleanse you of all unrighteousness; He will cleanse the soul. Does it mean we will be perfect? By no means. But He cleanses our souls in such a way that we can then say, "Lord, I'm just grumpy (or angry, jealous, lustful, greedy, selfish, anxious, nervous) today, and I want to get this right with You. I want to confess it to You. I want to keep a short list, God, between me and You and me and others." He cleanses us completely.

When you and I confess what we already know is wrong, He's faithful and righteous to cleanse our souls. Can you think of a better deal? What needs to be confessed to the Lord today?

Who's Right—God or People?

1 John 1:10

One of the big questions of life, is Who is right—God or us? I believe that God is right. Therefore, instead of saying, "No, I haven't sinned. That wasn't that bad," I know in my heart when I am wrong. I go to Him and pray, "Lord, I am sorry. I don't want anything to hinder our relationship."

Parents, have you ever apologized to your kids? You should. There is no way you have ever been a perfect parent. What happens when you apologize? It teaches them that even their parents don't always get it right. Do you apologize to your wife, your husband, your boyfriend, your girlfriend, or somebody you work with? Are there faults you want to hide or sins you have tried to make time wash away but know in your heart they are still there?

Some years ago, I went through a weird season. For six months, numerous people confessed to me that they had been talking badly about me behind my back. It troubled me, and I wondered what was causing it. Part of it just comes with being a leader. To some people, you become a character instead of a person, so it's easy to throw rocks. "Keyboard courage" abounds on the internet as people type things they would never say in person.

To every one of them I said, "I forgive you. It is okay." They received the forgiveness, and I received the confession. Sometimes we will be on the receiving end of confession. We won't always be the person confessing but perhaps the person someone confesses to. Our response, then, must be as gracious as God's response to us: "It is okay. I love you." Then we will be able to make the connection that makes the difference in the future of our relationships.

If we confess our sins to God, He is faithful and righteous to cleanse us from all unrighteousness. But we must confess our sins to one another as well when we have hurt other people. What happens is this confession restores the relationship, and then we receive the cleansing that comes from Jesus.

Do you hide your sins and act like they don't exist? Is it eating you up? You have the opportunity to confess them to the Lord and others. Let's get it out and make it right!

Achieve
Ephesians 2:8–10

Great Work: How to Make a Difference People Love by David Sturt is a 2013 *New York Times* bestseller. It describes studies conducted by the O. C. Tanner Institute with Forbes Insights. The research found a fundamental mind shift in people who get groundbreaking results and achieve greatness. They have a specific mindset. Instead of seeing themselves as workers with an assignment to crank out, they see themselves as people who can make a difference and have an impact.

Are you one of those people? Do you have the potential to achieve greatness? In your vocation, do you see yourself as a worker with something to crank out? At home, do you see yourself as someone who is just checking items off a list? The lists are endless—dishes, laundry, cleaning, cooking, errands. How do you see yourself? Are you someone who completes a task, or are you someone on a mission? There's a huge difference!

In my book *Difference Makers: How to Live a Life of Impact and Purpose*, I dig deeply into what it takes to be a difference-maker. I want to be a person who makes an impact for Jesus. In our homes, in our schools, in our churches, in our neighborhoods, in our nation, and in our world, we need to be difference-makers. We are going to dig into this concept of impact for the next couple of weeks.

We do not need to just elect or vote for people who can make a difference. We cannot just hire difference-makers or ask someone else to do it. We need to *be* difference-makers. God has a call and a plan for every believer. At every age and stage, if you are breathing, God has a difference for you to make. If you are older, you cannot dismiss His call by saying, "Been there, done that." If you are young and do not know what to do, God still wants you to serve Him. Everyone in Christ is called to do the good works He prepared for them to do, to bring glory to Him by making a difference in this world.

Here is what our church calls the Difference-Maker's Declaration:

> *I was made for more than watching things happen. I have a history-changing, difference-making, life-giving, Spirit-empowered legacy to leave. Jesus, I ask You to work deeply in me and clearly through me as I pray, give, and go in Your love. I am a difference-maker. In Jesus' name, amen!*

Begin with the Heart
Matthew 9:1–8

After Jesus traveled to Capernaum, some men brought one of their friends to Him. Their friend was paralyzed and lying on a stretcher. What is the first thing Jesus said to him? "Have courage," He said. Some versions of the Bible say, "take heart" or "be of good cheer." What the original Greek is getting at is that Jesus wanted the man to be courageous, to be cheerful, to be bold, to stand up, and go for it. Difference-makers live with courage. The courage to live forgiven.

Christians often read this story and characterize it as a healing moment. But there is more to the story. Notice that Jesus starts with the heart. Before Jesus tells the paralyzed man to stand and pick up his mat, He says, "Have courage, son, your sins are forgiven." This has nothing to do with walking; it has nothing to do with being paralyzed. It's about his heart not his legs.

Jesus declares the man's sins are forgiven. He uses the present tense. He is not suggesting the man's sins were forgiven in the past or that his sins will be forgiven in some distant future when he gets to heaven. No, the man's sins are forgiven right then and there when Jesus speaks. By forgiving the man's sins, Jesus declared that He was God in the flesh. This was a statement of deity. And so the man received Christ's forgiveness. Sin is always the problem, and a right relationship with God is always the answer.

We tend to think wrongly about this. We tell ourselves something like this: "I've got to go to church more. I've got to do more to be holy, and I need to sin less. If I get all my little ducks in a row, I'll be a good Christian." But being a Christian is not about "getting your ducks in a row" (whatever that means anyway). Being a Christian is about your relationship with God.

Jesus started with the heart. To be a difference-maker, start with your heart. Have the courage to allow God to work in you to begin your spiritual transformation.

Make this your prayer today:

God, make a difference in me. Give me the courage to allow You to work deeply in my heart. Forgive my sins through Jesus. Renew me through Your Holy Spirit.

Courage to Change
Mark 2:1–5

The Gospel of Mark also tells the story of the paralyzed man. It says his friends had to lower him through the roof to get him close to Jesus. Sometimes we can help others get close to Jesus, as those men did. The paralyzed man's friends lowered him, and Jesus said to the man, "Have courage" (Matt. 9:2).

Believers are to live with courage. We live in a society where there is a lot to fear. A week or so ago, I took my kids to see a movie. As we went out the door, my wife said, "Have fun at the movie. Be safe." Being aware of your surroundings is smart. We live in a dangerous place and time. But I had never thought about safety at the movie theater before. Such a different time we live in today.

Crime and strife are in the news all the time. But what if there were no sin? There would be no crime. Trouble and disease would disappear. Sin rips us apart, but God brings us together. Jesus forgave the paralyzed man's sins and told him to have courage. Difference-makers are forgiven sinners who have the courage to change as God works in their hearts and minds.

A triangle is a symbol used to represent the Trinity: God the Father, Jesus the Son, and the Holy Spirit. In mathematics, a triangle also stands for change. To help us change, God uses the Bible. He speaks to us through His Word. He speaks to us through His Spirit, and He speaks to us through His people—generally in that order.

Often, we ask His people for advice before we consult the Bible. We ask our friends, "What do you think?" When we hear the answer we like, we go to the Bible to look for a verse to justify what our friends said. That is not the way to rightly relate to God. Start with the Word. Ask the Lord to confirm His Word with the Holy Spirit. And then ask Him to confirm His Word and Spirit with the wise counsel of His people. Do we have the courage to allow the Father, Son, and Spirit to change us?

Make this your prayer today:

> *God, grant me the courage to walk according to Your Word, with Your Spirit, and with Your people. I ask for the courage to allow You to change me.*

Take Action
Matthew 9:1–7

Imagine the paralyzed man on his mat. He was accustomed to it. His friends were used to seeing him on it and helping him get around. Maybe the paralyzed man was even comfortable, resigned to his lot in life. But Jesus said to him, "Get up, take your stretcher, and go home" (Matt. 9:6).

Now think about the fear the man felt as he stood up for the first time. Would his legs give out? Would he fall flat on his face? Was this a joke? The man had to have the courage to stand and take up his mat.

All of us become comfortable with things that we know are not best for us. It happens to everyone, Christians and non-Christians alike. God says, "Get up!" Maybe I respond, "Hey, I like my mat. It's comfortable." We like the mat, even though we know it is not God's best.

Change is hard, but to make a difference in the world, we have to change. We know we must have courage and take action. It is not easy. I try to eat right and exercise, but sometimes I rebel. Queso and tortilla chips will bring anyone to their knees. There I am, shoving it into my arteries. There are times when I don't want to do what is right. I like my mat, that's where I want to stay.

It isn't really about food. God speaks to us for our own good. You know what your mat is—it's that comfortable sin. Jesus tells us, like He told the paralyzed man, "Get up, take your stretcher, and go home." The man had the courage to obey. Do we? Are we living in faith, or are we living in fear? Are we getting up and walking with God, or are we comfortable on the mat? Do not stay in the comfortableness of sin. Take action. Get up.

Make this your prayer today:

> *Lord, give me the courage to change so You can make a difference through me. Help me put my sins and rebellion into Your forgiving hands so I can have the courage to stand up and walk with You.*

Point to Christ
Matthew 9:1–8

In Matthew 9, Jesus forgave and healed a paralyzed man. The crowd saw that man stand up, take his mat, and go home, and they were awestruck. The Bible tells us that they glorified God, amazed at the authority He had given to Jesus, the Son of God.

By forgiving the man's sins, Jesus declared Himself to be God. By healing the man, Jesus confirmed that He was the Messiah. When the crowd saw what Jesus had done, they celebrated the Savior. They gave glory to God and were awed by Jesus.

The crowd was not applauding the paralyzed man's steps. Scripture does not say that the people cheered as he danced or that he ran a marathon. They didn't select him to be on their soccer team because he would be the best runner and kicker. The paralyzed man walked, and the people glorified God. Heaven not earth captured the attention.

For the man's part, he exhibited great courage. Difference-makers aren't concerned with their success; they are concerned with doing what Jesus asks them to do, as the formerly paralyzed man did. If we are difference-makers who are courageous in faith, we need to let God have all the credit, and we need to glorify Him.

Difference-makers want to shine with their Savior. Jesus is not a route to fame or riches or our success. Jesus wants to shine through you. You cannot work for your salvation, but you do have to step forward in faith by God's grace to follow His leading.

We are all streaked and stained with our own desires and need for recognition, and we all want pats on the back. Sometimes we want some credit, but we need to let God have all the credit and be glorified. If we lack courage, if we refuse to get up, if we want the credit that properly belongs to God, we're not going to make a difference for eternity. Difference-makers have the courage to live for God, not for themselves.

Make this your prayer today:

> *God, help me know my own heart. Reveal the sins that hold me back and help me to live for You. Help me shine for my Savior. The focus is on You, Jesus, not me.*

Shine
Matthew 5:14–16

In Kenya, there is a place called the Maasai Mara. It's a national reserve, a grassland area where there are no billboards, fences, or power lines, and there's very few people. Instead, there are lions, elephants, zebras, giraffes, cheetahs, and many other creatures. It is a very beautiful place that borders the Serengeti National Park.

An older gentleman from our church went on safari there to shine the light of Jesus. He discovered that his guide, Thomas, was not a Christian, so he led him to Jesus. Thomas realized he had a call for his life. He began preaching under a tree and led half his tribe to Christ. Now, every Sunday, 200 people show up to the church that an American congregation helped him build.

Later, a mission trip was organized to support this work of God. Pastor Thomas received speakers, an amplifier and sound system, a screen, a projector, and even a motorcycle. Now he goes out to all the surrounding villages with a pile of equipment on his motorcycle and shows films that teach others about Jesus. Pastor Thomas is making a difference.

A school was built. Now, more than 300 children are being taught to read and write. Then a ministry team came to dig a well to give the people clean water. Each day, a thousand people go to that well. Excess water goes to a pool where cows can come and drink. None of it is wasted. People bring their buckets and fill them to get clean water—and they hear about Jesus, the living water. I'll never forget standing at this well with Thomas and praying with our mission team for God to use the water to quench thirst physically and spiritually.

All of this began with one man on a safari who decided to shared the gospel with his guide. God can use us to make a difference far beyond what we could expect or imagine. As we allow Jesus to give us courage, letting Him change our hearts and minds so we live for the glory of God, we can make a difference.

Make this your prayer today:

> *God, give me courage. Help me shine Your light so others might see and give glory to You. I have a history-changing, difference-making, life-giving, Spirit-empowered legacy to leave. Jesus, help me be a difference-maker in Your name.*

Reach Out
Matthew 9:9

No one likes tax collectors. No one says, "The IRS is my best friend" or invites tax collectors over for dinner and asks them to peruse their 1040s. In our day and age, we know tax collectors have a job to do and respect that, but we aren't waiting for them to ring the doorbell.

In Jesus' time, the Roman Empire would conquer a group of people and from that group choose individuals to collect taxes. Imagine, now your neighbor works for the conquering empire to take your money. It was such a heinous job that it was literally considered punishment. Tax collectors would not only collect money from their own people, but they would also take a little on the side for themselves.

Nevertheless, Jesus called a tax collector—Matthew—to follow Him. Matthew had been very far away from God, but Jesus was willing to go to his house, eat dinner with him, and be associated with him.

While Jesus was reclining at Matthew's table, many tax collectors and sinners came as guests to eat with Jesus and His disciples. Sitting at the table communicates, "You're part of the group." Even in our culture today, those folks who eat with us are different from those we say hello to when walking down the street. The people we invite into our homes receive a higher level of hospitality than those we meet at a coffee shop.

Jesus and His disciples are in Matthew's home, dining in great diversity. The Messiah and a tax collector, the Holy One and a crook, are in a sinner's home, speaking about the Savior's heaven. Connecting with people who need the Lord's love is clearly spoken. No one is outside the pursuit of Jesus; no one is outside God's desire to be present with them, to dine with them, to love them.

Jesus Christ is pursuing you and me in absolute love. He wants to sit with us, dine with us, and converse with us.

Make this your prayer today:

Jesus, please work in me as I seek to learn how to be a difference-maker in Your name. Show me people to reach out to today instead of judge.

Loving Clarity
Matthew 9:9–13

Difference-makers dine in diversity while speaking with loving clarity. There are two parts to this statement. It is amazing to dine in diversity. But it is also important to speak with loving clarity so we can step out and make a difference in a great way.

Jesus and His disciples were dining at Matthew's house. Notice the diversity of Jesus' dining partners. The disciples may have been nervous as they dined with Matthew and the other tax collectors and sinners. Then Jesus did something extraordinary. He did not condemn or condone those around Him. He spoke clearly.

Jesus came not to condemn or condone but to save. You and I sometimes dine in diversity without condemning, but we do condone. We act like everyone's chosen lifestyles are all great and wonderful: "Hey, come on to the table! It's okay. It is great you are a tax collector. Ripping people off is just part of your job." Our fear of confrontation or desire to please people can result in a lack of clarity about what is right. As we smile, we tend to condemn and judge them in our hearts or dismiss and condone their sin.

But Jesus didn't do that. He kept a wonderful balance. The Pharisees, however, thought by sitting at the table, Jesus and His disciples were turning a blind eye to sin. And they questioned Him.

How did Jesus respond to the Pharisees, these keepers of the law? He declared truth to them. He spoke clearly. He said He did not come to seek the righteous—as if the Pharisees were righteous—but sinners. We must speak with clarity by declaring the truth in love.

We all need to realize God loves us, no matter where we are or what we have done. Jesus Christ loves you. Jesus loved the disciples; He loved sinners, the Pharisees, and even Matthew the tax collector.

Matthew went on to have a tremendous, earth-shaking ministry. He was a tax collector who was changed because Jesus spoke with clarity about the powerful topics of love and righteousness.

Jesus, help me not to condemn people or condone their sin but, instead speak the truth in clarity, with love and grace.

Friends

1 Corinthians 15:33

As we continue our journey with Matthew, imagine you are in Matthew's house. The dinner table is set. Where will you sit? Which group are you in? Are you sitting with the disciples, in Jesus' group? Are you in the group of sinners and tax collectors? Are you outside, as one of the judgmental Pharisees? Are you walking with God, ministering with Him and His followers, or are you the ministry focus?

Which group is Jesus' inner circle? It isn't the sinners, tax collectors, or the religious Pharisees? Nope, it is the disciples. Jesus walked in full obedience to His Father. His inner circle shared His desire to walk in God's will. Particularly, if you are young in life or in belief, pay attention: your inner circle should be people who share your same heart for Jesus. Choose your friends very carefully. Who you hang out with on Friday nights will affect how you live out the rest of your life. As I said before, befriend everyone but choose your "Friday night friends" carefully.

Difference-makers dine with diversity but speak with clarity. But don't get mixed up. Some people tell themselves that Jesus ate with the tax collectors and sinners, so we can do the same. But it is important to have an inner circle of friends who can challenge and encourage you to pursue God's heart in those situations. It's true at any age, "Bad company corrupts good morals" (1 Cor. 15:33).

A cloudy heart brings a cloudy mind; a clear heart brings a clear mind. Do your close friends enable you to minister? Many who dine with diversity can fail to speak with clarity to their detriment.

Others are like the Pharisees. They can speak with clarity but never dine in diversity because they are judgmental. They don't want to be around "those people." The longer you walk with God, the harder it can be to dine with diversity because you have made a lot of Christian friends.

Christianity is when you put the two together—when you dine in diversity and also speak with clarity. So, eat lunch with everyone, hang out with all people, but stay close to Jesus. If you are dining with diversity, are you still able to speak with clarity? If you're speaking with clarity, are you still dining with diversity?

Jesus, help me dine with diversity, speak with clarity, and be someone who shares Your heart.

Please God
Mark 2:13–17

Difference-makers care what God thinks. They care more about what God thinks than what people think. As we look at Levi's dinner table from Mark's perspective, let's dig deeper into this thought. First off, Levi and Matthew are the same person. Matthew was his Greek name, and Levi was his Hebrew name.

The Pharisees who were watching Jesus thought He was doing wrong. They pulled the disciples aside to question them, but Jesus heard them. He told the Pharisees that those who are well do not need a doctor. Only the sick need a doctor. Jesus did not care what the Pharisees thought about Him, or that they did not like Him dining with tax collectors and sinners. Jesus cared more about doing God's will than about looking holy and righteous in front of the Pharisees.

It can be hard to tell others that we don't care what they think. That is appropriate to a certain level. But in fact, we do care what people think. If we don't care, then guess what? News flash: nobody likes you. They see you as impolite. There is a balance. We care about what others think so we are polite, but we care more about what God thinks.

The commandments are in the right order: "Love the Lord your God with all your heart, with all your soul, and with all your mind," and then "Love your neighbor as yourself" (Matt. 22:37, 39). Don't get them reversed. Keep the mindset of a difference-maker—not caring what the Pharisees think, caring more about what God thinks, and then caring enough to love and care for others.

Does caring for sinners mean that we blow our witness? Does it mean that we start dealing drugs to try to reach drug dealers? No. Difference-makers care about what God thinks. They share His heart for sinners. They dine in diversity while speaking with clarity about truth.

Remember what Jesus did. He reached out to a tax collector in such a way that Matthew became a disciple. Jesus was clear. He wasn't condemning or condoning. Jesus was secure in His identity and purpose. He knew. And declared, that He had come to seek and save the lost. He was a doctor on an eternal mission to help the spiritually sick.

God, help me prioritize Your desires over my need to be liked by others. Help me keep the mindset of a difference-maker.

Fast

Matthew 9:14–17

John's disciples came to Jesus, asking why He and His disciples did not fast. Jesus used the imagery of a wedding to answer them. The groom was Jesus, and the bride was the church. While the groom and His disciples and followers were together, they would feast together. The disciples rejoiced while Jesus was with them. Then, the ascension came, and Jesus was taken from them (Acts 2). Then they fasted. Jesus is not with us physically; He is in our hearts. So now, the church fasts. For the period Jesus is gone, however long it may be, we long for Him.

For the Pharisees, fasting was a badge. It said, "Look at me. Look how spiritual I am. See how I pray and fast. Look at my downcast face." But Jesus taught that when you fast, you should wash your face, look like you have taken a bath, and look happy. It is a prayer: "Let the ache in my belly be my ache for You, Jesus. I want to ache for You."

Don't be like the fasting Pharisees with long faces so people would ask what was wrong. A fasting Pharisee is like Eeyore in *Winnie the Pooh*, who moped around waiting for someone to ask what was wrong.

We Christians sometimes act like Eeyore or the Pharisees. We need to be honest about our emotions but not seek attention for doing what God says. Christians are Jesus' greatest testimony; and Christians can be His greatest hindrance. When we walk around with our spirituality or our suffering as some kind of badge, it is because we do not have spiritual depth in our lives. We are wearing our spirituality on our sleeves because we do not have it deep in our hearts.

I encourage you to fast a meal or a day this week. Seek God by using the time you would eat to spend in prayer. Let your hunger for food transfer to your hunger for God. Let go of physical need for a spiritual plea. Food typically has a hold on us. Switch the ache for God to have a hold on the situation you are fasting for. I can assure you God is better than the sandwich you will forego.

Go deeper with God. To have a wide ministry of dining in diversity while speaking with great clarity, we need to go deep with God.

Lord, I hunger for You. Deepen my walk with You.

Live Deeply
Ephesians 3:14–21

In his book *When a Nation Forgets God*, Pastor Erwin W. Lutzer wrote:

> I believe that the spiritual climate of America will never be changed unless we have . . . ordinary people living authentically for Christ in their vocations, among their neighbors, and positions of influence. We cannot look to a man [leader] or even a movement as much as to the common person who is committed to Christ and living for Him.[24]

I love the thought that ordinary people, not just leaders like a Billy Graham or Christian music artists, are the difference-makers. You do not have to have a big public ministry to change the world. We need a private depth. In my own life, my prayerfulness on my knees has a greater effect than any message I preach or devotional I write. To be difference-makers, we can have a wide reach but also need a private depth. We must be in a deep relationship with the Lord in order to be effective for Him. Difference-makers impact widely because they live deeply. Few of us will lead the masses but all of us can love the Lord.

In his book *Orthodoxy*, G. K. Chesterton wrote, "It is always simple to fall; there are an infinity of angles at which one falls, only one at which one stands."[25] You can fall backward, forward, or sideways, but there's only one position where you can remain standing. The disciples stood only with Jesus. Our strength, our gas in the engine, is not the width of our ministry but the depth of our life with God.

Do you see what difference-makers do? They dine with diversity but stand in love and great clarity. You don't have to condone. You don't have to condemn. But you do have to be clear about Jesus, especially in an ambiguous, crazy society.

God did not put you in your workplace so you could just make some money. He put you there so you could make a difference. You will likely spend more time at the office than anywhere else, so don't waste your time there. Wherever God has placed you, make a difference. And remember, difference-makers impact widely because they love deeply. Go deep in your relationship with God. Allow Him to use you right where you are.

Jesus, even though I am an ordinary person, help me live authentically for You.

Smiles
John 15:4–5

Reporting for *On the Road*, a segment on CBS Evening News, Steve Hartman shared the story of a difference-maker here in the United States. Jaden Hayes lost his father when he was four; his mother died in her sleep two years later. Jaden was heartbroken, but he decided he wanted to make sad people smile. He asked his guardian to buy toys so he could give them away to others, to cheer them up.

What would you do if a child gave you a rubber ducky or a dinosaur? You would probably do what the people in downtown Savannah, Georgia, did. They smiled. And some may have given Jaden a hug.

Though orphaned, Jaden decided he wanted to make a difference in someone's life. Instead of focusing on his misery, he chose to make it his ministry. That little six-year-old boy decided he was going to make a difference, and he stepped out and did it.

As Christians, we aim for smiles of the soul, not just smiles on the face. That is what is so great about being a believer in Christ. And, most important, we put a smile on God's face.

A church member who is in the oil business shared with me about missionaries in the Middle East. She wrote:

> They leave their home countries and their families behind because they are dedicated to sharing the love of Jesus in closed countries and in some of the world's most remote areas. The difference-makers I've met are insightful, hard-working, humble and incredibly courageous people with a passion for the lost. I've watched them preserve under tremendous pressures as they live like Christ in the toughest of circumstances.

Difference-makers reach out. They are about their personal Savior, not about their personal successes. They want others to know the difference Jesus can make in a person's life. Let God use your pain and hurts to be a catalyst for loving others.

Make this your prayer today:

> *I was made for more than watching. I have a history-changing, difference-making, life-giving, Spirit-empowered legacy to leave. Jesus, I ask You to work deeply in me and clearly through me as I pray, give, and go in Your love. I am a difference-maker. In Jesus' name, amen!*

Sunrise or Billboards?
Hebrews 12:1–2

In Houston, we are famous for energy, NASA, and the Astros. These are awesome things to have going for us. What we are not famous for are sunrises. You do not really see those in the City of Houston. Once in a while, people who live out in the suburbs might catch a glimpse of one, but not if you live closer in.

The best Houston sunrise you will see is when you are driving over an overpass you may get a quick look at a sunrise—so gorgeous! You have to go out in the country to get rid of distractions so you can really see a sunrise. There are too many buildings, billboards, and other things in your way.

The same is true for our relationship with God. We have so many distractions, we do not know how to be still. How do I slow down and know that He is God in my life? How do I really rest in Him and see the beauty of the sunrise in my darkness? Most days all I can see are the buildings and the billboards.

Our phones and our fears also keep us from seeing the beauty of God. Our hurry and worry keep us from seeing the sunrise of God in our lives. Now let's consider what "be still" means. We will remove the distractions so we can see the sunrise of God in all the circumstances of our lives.

Deep people are still people. They understand that God is in control of their pain in cancer as well as their pleasure when it is the greatest day in the world. In all our hustle and bustle, all our buildings and billboards, we can see the sunrise and know that He is God and that He is right there with us.

Do you need to see God more clearly? Do you need to rest more deeply? Are your fears and your phone keeping you frazzled and keeping you from being still? Are you running so busy that your hurry and worry are wilting your soul? God has a word for you today: "Be still, and know that I am God" (Ps. 46:10 NIV).

Stillness is a doorway to knowing your loving Father and Creator. Let's spend the next few days learning about stillness in order to know God more.

Being Still
Habakkuk 2:20

Stillness deepens our hearts and our lives. Deep people are still people. But when Monday morning comes, we all hit the pavement running because we have a lot of work to do. There is a rhythm to our lives—an ebb and flow. There is a put-the-pedal-down and tap-the-brakes mentality. Our lives have a neutral, a park, a reverse, and a drive.

Many of us are caught with the pedal down in drive, and we never truly rest or slow down. I am not talking about one email—it's about 100 emails. It's not one project at work—it's dozens of projects at work. It is not one phone call or text message—it's a life of phone calls and text messages.

Stillness is what we need because we need to deepen our hearts to deepen our lives. When we really get still, we finally begin to understand who we are and what we are really feeling.

One of the reasons we do not want to be still is because deep down we do not want to face what we are feeling inside. Maybe our anger, our hurt, our wounds, or our fears are too deep. If we slow down or get very still, we'll have to look at that sunrise in the face, and we're not only going to see the beauty of it, but we'll also see its brightness. The brightness of stillness reveals in our hearts what we are thinking, feeling, and going through. And that can be difficult.

We often get extremely busy and keep the noise and adrenaline flowing because we do not want to deal with what is going on. If we keep going and going, we're convinced we won't have to deal with it. We will not have to see the brightness of the sun. We can glance up and see the beauty every once in a while, but not the revealing brightness.

What do you really think about the things of God? What are your thoughts about your purpose in life? The hurry and the worry will keep you from recognizing God's thoughts toward you. But stillness brings an appreciation for His love and care for us.

Deep people allow stillness so they can truly see what they are feeling and thinking and understand who they are. Let's learn to be still.

> The LORD is in his holy temple; let all the earth be silent before him. (Hab. 2:20 NIV)

Deepening Our Hearts
Mark 1:35–37

Stillness deepens our hearts and lives; it deepens who we are. Stillness deepens our relationship with God; it deepens our relationship and understanding of the weariness, joy, hurt, or anger that we have when we really, really reflect.

My wife's grandmother's 100th birthday celebration was absolutely amazing. After the party, my family and I were sitting in the living room with Oma, as we called her, when I saw a pillow on her couch that had Psalm 46:10 on it: "Be still, and know that I am God" (NIV).

I said, "Oma, would you tell me the story about this pillow?"

She said, "Oh, yeah. I remember when Opa [her husband] was diagnosed with cancer. He went to sleep that night and acted like he wasn't worried about a thing. I walked the floor all night long, worried about him having cancer. What would happen? What would take place? And then, in that midnight hour, as I was just walking the floor praying, I heard this verse in my mind: 'Be still, and know that I am God. Be still, and know that I am God.' There's no way it could be anything else but the Lord speaking that to me." She continued, "I didn't even know the reference of it or where it was. I just knew I'd read it somewhere before. Be still, and know that I am God. I heard that verse, and then I got into bed, and I slept like a baby."

God deepens our heart. The deepness and peace of the Lord comes not just at 2:00 in the afternoon; it comes at 2:00 in the morning, at 4:00 in the morning, at midnight. They don't just come at birthday celebrations but also when there's a cancer diagnosis.

Stillness before Him is healing and helpful. It's more than a break from the busyness but a refreshment to the soul and reorientation of our purpose. It's ironic but we will accomplish more by being still. And we will do it in a healthy way by knowing God.

Get to Know God
Psalm 46:10

Let's keep digging into the treasures of Psalm 46:10. God wants to deepen our relationship with Him, and stillness deepens it. Psalm 46:10 does not just say "be still." It is not transcendental meditation. It is not a Caribbean vacation. It says, "Be still, and know that I am God" (NIV). It is a spiritual discovery. It is Christianity. It is saying, "Lord, I want to know You, and I want to get to know You better."

Be still. Cease striving. Be still. Stop fighting.

I love this verse in The Message version of the Bible. It says, "Step out of the traffic! Take a long, loving look at me, your High God, above politics, above everything." Step out of traffic, and take a look up. See the sunrise. See the beauty of the Lord in the heavens—what God is able to do. Our stillness lifts Him higher because now we are still enough to see how high He is. Depth brings height.

In my life, I want to walk in depth. So I put my phone and computer aside. I quit running errands and sit with Him, allowing Him to speak to my heart so I can fully understand what I am feeling. What am I actually going through? What am I truly joyful about? Why am I hurting? How can Jesus meet me there?

We need to be still and know that He is God. And then it says, "I will be exalted among the nations, I will be exalted in the earth" (NIV). He will be exalted everywhere. Missions and evangelism both begin with stillness. Our world will be different, not just by doing something about it but by first sitting still in true prayer.

I wonder if God sometimes thinks:

> *If you would just get out of the way, I could do so much more. You are asking Me to bless your ideas. Why don't you come discover My ideas? My ideas already have My blessing and My purpose. My ideas have your parenting and your marriage in its hand. My ideas have your singleness in its hand. As long as you keep trying to give Me your ideas to bless, you're going to miss it. Just let Me rise the sun in your life. Let Me begin another chapter in your life. And if you walk the floor at 2:00 a.m. in worry, hear Me say, "Be still and know that I am God. And then I will be exalted."*

Take a moment and be still before Him—think of His greatness.

Our Goal
Luke 5:15–16

God is the goal. Stillness before Him exalts Him in the nations and in the world so He can do His work. Our stillness lifts Him higher. How do we get still? It happens daily, weekly, monthly, and quarterly. Daily, we spend time with the Lord. Weekly, we have what is called a Sabbath. It begins with desire. Do we want to walk with God at a deep level? Do we want to know what is going on in our hearts and in our lives? Do we want to know that He is God? Then we have to get still.

There are three words that have become very special to me. I learned them from the book *Love Is Stronger than Death* by Peter Kreeft. Here they are: Stranger. Enemy. Friend. Here is what they look like: Stranger is the distant look; Enemy is the wall of deterrent that requires discipline and perseverance; and Friend is the blessing that comes when you accomplish the goal.

For example, let's take being still:

> *Stranger:* "Oh, I'd love to have some time where I could really think and ponder."
>
> *Enemy:* "I'm bored. Let's go to the mall. Let me check my phone. What else is going on?"
>
> *Friend:* "Wow, unplugging from the busyness has really refreshed my heart."

Resting:

> *Stranger:* "I wish I could have time to just rest."
>
> *Enemy:* "Oh, I don't like this quietness. I'm getting restless."
>
> *Friend:* "I really needed this downtime with the Lord."

If you break through the Stranger and the Enemy, you get to the Friend: breakthrough happens with stillness.

As an extrovert of all extroverts, I have loved and finally learned to become a friend of solitude. And I am an extrovert, full tilt. It was a stranger for years in my life. It was an enemy because I had FOMO—Fear of Missing Out. I would say, "What's everybody else doing?" After growing tired of my excuses in the Stranger stage and pushing through the Enemy stage, Solitude is now my Friend, and God is lifted higher in my life.

Stillness Is a Discipline
Exodus 31:12–18

Stillness is something we all need to learn. And the way to start is to have a great desire for it.

Then move on to application—with discipline. Begin with one day. Start small: fifteen minutes with God one day this week.

Stillness with the Lord might not be very familiar to you. Let that be part of cultivating your heart, to rest for fifteen minutes one day this week. Then take that fifteen-minute time with God and move it to fifteen minutes every day for a week. Then you might say from your heart, "You know what, Lord? I really desire to have an entire Sabbath day with you."

For me, my Sabbath is not Sunday. That is the biggest workday of my week. When I Sabbath on another day and rest, my soul is restored. It doesn't mean you can't do things or be part of things that day. Do things that refill you. Then you might say, "Oh, if I could just Sabbath for a month." Let me tell you something. You wouldn't know what to do with a month if you don't know what to do with an hour, a week, or a day alone with God.

Let a sabbatical heart happen on your Sabbath day. Honor the Sabbath and keep it holy. It is the only one of the Ten Commandments that uses the word *holy*. And throughout our nation, the Sabbath is probably the biggest Ten Commandment that's broken. And we are wilting and dying. We have not seen a sunrise or sunset or the beauty of the heavens of God in a long, long time.

What if you gave God your heart the same way you give forty to sixty hours to work every week? Put rest on the calendar, because guess what? If you do not put it on the calendar, it will not happen. I have it on the calendar every month that I spend a day with the Lord. One day a quarter might work for you. And do you know how many things battle for that day? When I put "Time with the Father" on the calendar, everything battles for that day. Persevere. Break through the enemy and find time alone with God as a precious friend.

The Right Kind of Crazy

Philippians 3:7–9

So what do you do on a Sabbath day? Take your Bible, a book you are enjoying, a journal, and headphones . . . get away and remove the distractions, all billboards and buildings that clamor for your attention. Sit with God and say, "Lord, I want to know You and sense Your presence."

To know God, and to know who I am in Him. Let me tell you, in today's society, that is crazy.

But . . . I want that kind of crazy. My kids and my wife need me to have that kind of crazy. My fears and my things melt with the wonderful crazy of connecting with God. We all need to put "Time with God" on our calendars. If you don't do this, your exterior pace will rob your interior peace.

When you can get a break, to see the sunrise, to step out of the traffic and let God do some work, then you will have peaceful rest in Christ.

Lord, I rest in Your finished work on the cross. I rest in Your blood that You shed for me. I rest in what You have done in my life. I want You to use me, God. I want You to empower me. Amen.

I challenge you to put "Time with God" on your schedule. You will be blessed. Allow God to still your life and your heart. Then Psalm 23 will become a reality for you:

The LORD is my shepherd;
I shall not want.
He makes me to lie down in green pastures;
He leads me beside the still waters.
He restores my soul. (Ps. 23:1–3 NKJV)

Try it. Put on your calendar "Time with God." It can be an hour, a morning, or a day. Start somewhere and see where God takes it. You have a good start with reading *Capture the Moment* each day—now add to it.

Sing to the Lord
Psalm 47:6–9

As you travel around the globe, you will see different things in every culture and every place, but there will always be singing. As humans we need to sing no matter the culture—music is the key ingredient. Singing is not just for good singers; it is for all of us. Our hearts need to sing.

As Christians, it's even better because there is Someone we sing to.

In today's verses, we hear the psalmist say the word *sing* five times. Sing praise to God! Throughout the Bible, we see praise after praise given to God. It is important that we do not just listen to praise music, but we sing praise to the Lord. When we sing praise to Him, it makes a difference in our lives.

A battlefield in the church has been worship wars over people's preferences. In the 1800s, Charles Spurgeon called the music department in his church the *war department* because everybody had a preference—a lot of different thinking about how they should praise. Also Spurgeon knew through our songs we were victorious in spiritual warfare.

Worship of God in song goes back to Genesis 4, where we learn that Jubal was the father of those who played the lyre and pipe. In Exodus 15, Moses and the people of God sang about the Red Sea washing over the Egyptians. In Nehemiah, choirs walked the wall and sang the praises of God to rebuild the city of Jerusalem. Two pillars of the Old Testament, Moses and David were songwriters—which conveys the intimate relationship they both had with God. Throughout the Scripture and history, there is a lot of singing—declaring the praises of the Lord—which brings us back to today's verses: "Sing praise to God" (Ps. 47:6).

God already knows what's in your heart, but He still loves to hear your praise. Sing to Him today!

Make Melody in Your Heart

Psalm 144:9

To correctly understand the present, we have to understand the past. Let's take an interesting biblical and historic stroll today. Both the Old Testament and the New Testament declare worship songs to the Lord. In the heavenlies, singing is taking place right now; the angels are singing out to God. In the New Testament, the apostle Paul, in his letter to the Ephesians, writes about "singing and making music with your heart to the Lord" (Eph. 5:19).

Right after the Lord's Supper, the Gospel of Matthew tells us that they sang a hymn and went to the Mount of Olives. Then Jesus Christ died and rose from the grave. And the church was persecuted for about 300 years. The early church encountered Roman emperor after Roman emperor with persecution upon persecution. Many of the first Christians died for their faith.

In AD 313, Constantine, the emperor of Rome, signed the Edict of Milan, which allowed Christians to worship freely. Everything that had been stolen from the church was given back to the church. All the house churches could come out of hiding and over the next 1,200 years, Christians built beautiful cathedrals. The acoustics of these magnificent structures let the songs of the people ring out loudly. Unfortunately, many of those worshipful buildings are tourist attractions today instead of houses of worship.

From the 300s to about the 1500s, the church was singing psalms in a Gregorian chant fashion. In 1517, the year of the Protestant Reformation, Martin Luther began to reclaim the teaching of the Scriptures. The church began to understand the Scriptures and sing about the Lord. They scandalously took melodies from the bars of Germany and put Christian lyrics to them. They were no longer just singing psalms; they were writing their own songs of praise. That was mind-blowing for the time period.

Singing is intricate to our Christian history and faith. We are to sing to the Lord from our heart today as well. Maybe there is a song or poem in you waiting for a pen and paper. Make a melody in your heart for the Lord. Sing to Him today!

Music Grows Our Vision of God

Psalm 72:18–19

M ost of our hymns were written in the 1700s and 1800s. But in the 1960s, everything changed. It was a watershed moment for the culture of the country. The Jesus Movement began in the late '60s and early '70s, and worship songs were like campfire songs played with one guitar.

Then, in the '70s and '80s, there was a worship war because part of the church was saying, "We want the 1870s hymns," and the other part was saying, "No, we want 1970s praise songs."

Thankfully, the battle is not going on as much now. Everyone still has preferences, although it's not quite like it was in the '70s and '80s. And that is a basic history of church music in America in a few paragraphs.

But the truth is that music is for the Lord. Music is to unify us. Isn't it interesting that Satan has so strategically assaulted music in the church? That's because music brings us together—and that is why he put it in his destructive crosshairs. Also, his goal is to thwart the worship of God by His people.

Singing grows our vision of God. He increases, and we decrease. We all need a decrease in conversation about ourselves, attention to ourselves, and our pride so He can increase.

When we sing praise to the Lord, it increases our vision of Him and decreases the vision of ourselves. Think about this prayer:

Lord, You are amazing. You are eternal. I'm just me. I'm singing to You. I want to be humble before You as I sing, as heaven is singing right now. Amen.

A Fair and Lovely Gift
Psalm 42:5–8

Singing to God softens our hearts and firms our resolve. There have been times when I was about to preach, and as I sang, I said, "Lord, this is going to be a difficult or controversial message. I'm not sure how it's going to go. I want to firm my resolve that I'm going to teach Your Word even though it's a difficult passage. I also ask you to soften my heart so that I speak the truth in love."

Martin Luther, the leader of the Protestant Reformation, said this when he was asked to recant what he had written: "Here I stand; I can do no other. God help me."[26] His faith had a firm resolve.

Luther also showed a soft heart as he commented on music:

> Music is a fair and lovely gift of God which has often wakened and moved me to the joy of preaching. . . . Next after theology I give to music the highest place and the greatest honor. . . . My heart bubbles up and overflows in response to music, which has so often refreshed me and delivered me from the dire plagues.[27]

God softens our hearts and firms our resolve through song. Remember in the book of Acts, Paul and Silas are singing in the jail cell at midnight. Maybe you have gone through incredibly excruciating, difficult times in your life, and I bet God has given you a song you can sing in your midnight hour of pain. God takes us through our hard times with a song in our hearts before Him in order to firm our resolve and soften our hearts. Here's a prayer for you today:

> *Even though I do not understand what You are doing, God, I am still going to walk with You. I know You are with me. I want a soft heart and firm resolve before You. Give me a song to sing to You. Amen.*

The Right Thing to Do
Psalm 47

As we've stated, singing praise grows our vision of God, softens our heart, and firms our resolve. Also, singing is the right thing to do. In America these days, often we do what we want to do instead of what's right. However, praising God through song is the *right* thing to do.

The book of Revelation says the Lord is worthy! If you are going to be a good husband, a good wife, a good friend, or a good employee or employer, you are going to have to do things because they are the right thing to do—whether you feel like it or not.

Show me employees who only work when they want to and not when it is the right thing to do, and I will show you some sorry employees. Show me a parent who doesn't do things just because it is the right thing to do but only when he or she wants to, and I will show you a lacking mom or dad. The Lord is worthy of your praise. Period. We need to be adults about it. We are going to do what is right, even if it is not easy. Worship through song is definitely a delight but also a discipline. If we don't cry out, the rocks will.

We also sing because it unifies us as a church. After the disciples took the Lord's Supper, they sang a hymn and went to the Mount of Olives where Jesus was arrested. They were unified in their singing as they lived through the most troublesome time of history: the cross.

In regard to the unifying power of music, think about a baseball game at the seventh inning stretch. Everybody stands up and sings "Take Me Out to the Ball Game." At an Astros game, we also sing "Deep in the Heart of Texas." The Red Sox fans also sing "Sweet Caroline." It is a unifying event in each game. Or you may go to a college football game, and when they sing the fight song, you suddenly feel part of a greater group. Everyone is there to support their team, together.

How much more should worship of the Great High King, the Lord of Lords unify our hearts?

Singing together with your church will open your eyes to see that you are part of the great kingdom of God with your brothers and sisters in Christ.

True Identity, True Songs

Ephesians 5:19–21

As the people of God, we can come together, sing praise to God, and be unified. We can conquer any worship war.

In the Old Testament, Abraham, Isaac, and Jacob—grandfather, father, and grandson—had the same job, wore the same clothes, lived on the same piece of land, and sang the same songs. That's not how it is today. The chances of liking our grandkids' music are slim.

We are called to sing *to* God, not just *about* God. We do not go to church to have Christian karaoke; we go to church to sing to God—sing to Him with all we have. It requires us to go beyond our personalities to our identities in Christ. If you are a believer in Jesus Christ, He has given you a song in your heart and praise to give back to Him. It is the right thing to do and a blessing to do it. Both a duty and a delight to sing to our King.

God has wired all of us differently. Some of us grew up singing every moment. Some always have a song in their hearts and whistle it while they work in the garden or doing dishes or always have the radio on. Others could take music or leave it. It is not really our thing.

You have to move past your personality to your identity in Jesus Christ—to your heart—your spirit. It does not matter if you are a good singer. I am talking about praising. I am not talking about vocal cords. I am talking about the cords of your heart. If you are a bad singer, who cares? But if you are a bad worshiper, that is a problem. If you are a bad keeper of a melody and a harmony, who cares? But if you are a bad giver of praise to God, it will affect your relationships, your marriage, and your way of life. It is about your heart as you are before the Lord, singing *to God*, not just *about God* or to other people.

Sing to Him. Get past your personality and preferences to your true Christian identity. We are not all great singers, but we can all be great worshipers, and that is what God is calling us to be.

Sing with Wisdom
Colossians 3:14–17

At the top of all his compositions, Bach wrote "J.J.," *Jesus Juva*, which meant "Jesus help me." At the end, he wrote, "S.D.G.," *Soli Deo Gloria*, which meant "To God alone be the glory." He was composing instrumental music and saying, "I want to praise God."

> All music should have no other end and aim than the glory of God and the soul's refreshment; where this is not remembered there is no real music but only a devilish hubbub.[28]—Johann Sebastian Bach

Worship is about what your heart is saying. Be a great worshiper before Him and sing a song of wisdom. Connect your head and your heart. Understand what you are singing, and feel what you understand.

There is a lot of music out there. You might be singing songs of praise that have a great melody but are incorrect theologically. Be careful, because what you sing is what you end up believing. For example, if you think the Holy Spirit comes and goes depending on feeling, you are going to miss that He indwells you and lives inside of you. In your deepest, darkest pain and in your greatest joy, He is with you.

Jesus said it like this: "Worship in spirit and in truth" (John 4:24). We need to sing with wisdom as we walk with God. As we get to know Him better, we sing to Him wisely with an understanding of who He is and what He is doing.

Psalm 47 says that the leaders of earth *belong to God*. Songs of praise remind us of *whose* we are, not *who* we are. If our world's leaders were to realize that they belong to God and worship Him as such, imagine the great things that could happen! Truly great leaders entrust themselves to the greatest Leader. And great leaders, great mommas, great daddies, great husbands, great single adults, and great employees and employers praise God—not themselves. They wisely sing *to the Lord*. Here's a prayer for today:

> *Lord, it is You I am entrusting myself to. I'm going to sing praise to You. I want to be wise enough to walk with You and trust You always, for Yours is the kingdom and the power and the glory. Amen.*

Dreams
Psalm 126

We have been studying the Psalms. The first series was based on Psalm 46 where we discussed our need to rest in the Lord. In the second part, we looked at the power of worship, of singing to the Lord as described in Psalm 47. We saw that you could be terrible at singing, but awesome at worship, making a joyful noise from your heart to the Lord.

This third part is based on a psalm that is not really famous. But I will tell you this: it has become one of my favorites. Psalm 126 is about dreaming big, and I am not referring to the dreams at night when you go to sleep. I am talking about dreams that make you think out loud, "What if this were to happen? What if that took place? What if God did this? What if the Lord moved in this way?" This psalm deals with the spectrum of emotions that we have in life—from joy and laughter to weeping and pain. It talks about how we can be part of the dreams of God.

As Americans, dreams are extremely important to us. One of the most famous speeches in American history is "I Have a Dream" by Martin Luther King Jr. It changed the course of our nation.

Almost every graduation, the speaker will declare, "Follow your dreams!" And your parents remind in response, "Make sure you can pay for your dreams."

Thankfully, we are a dreaming culture. But the key is that we need to be about God's dreams—not trying to get God behind our dreams. We need to get on board with His dreams and let His dreams take priority. Then we will see what it means to dream big and see it come to life.

Does God have a dream for you? For your kids? Does God have a dream where you play a part in His kingdom? Yes, He does, and He cannot wait for you to get on board.

The Dreams of God
Psalm 126:1–3

What does it mean to truly dream something and see it become a reality? How does it happen?

Keep dreaming of what God can do. God can do amazing, incredible things in your life and in your family's life. He can also use you to do incredible things, so keep dreaming of what God can do. Psalm 126 says that when the people were dreaming, their mouths were filled with laughter and joy. The greatest joy and laughter come when you get to be part of God's dreams.

God's dreams have to become our dreams—we have to want to do what He wants us to do.

Historically, today's verses are talking about the time when the people of Israel were released from Babylonian captivity after being enslaved for seventy years. In their new freedom they could return and rebuild Jerusalem. Psalm 126:1–3 says they were like those who dream. Declaring "What could God do now? I can't believe we're free. This is like a dream!" There were smiles and laughter.

God has not freed us from Babylonian captivity; He has done something even more extravagant. And it is almost like a dream. God has forgiven us of our sins through Jesus Christ, who died on the cross for you and for me and rose from the dead for us. When we place our faith and trust in Him, He washes us clean and gives us the right to be children of God. Wow! That is a dream come true.

We are free! Rightly relating before the Lord, connecting with God and talking to Him.

We do not get it all right all the time, but He always gets it right, so we keep following Him. It is like a dream. The psalm says that they began to laugh and had joy. What can God do? If He can free us from captivity and save our souls, what can God do in our lives, in our city, in our schools, in our friendships, and in our families?

They were "like those who dream" (Ps. 126:1). Today dream about what God can do through you.

God's Dream for You
Psalm 71:19–24

As we get older, life gets more serious, more stressful. When you are a kid, you laugh all the time. But when you get to be forty-two, fifty-two, and so on, life is not as funny as it once was. We laugh less and say things like, "Let's do something fun tonight." Fun has to be planned.

When you are a teenager, fun just happens. Fun is where you are. When we become adults, we get serious and begin to lack joy. Is that not peculiar? We have money to do things, we know who we are, we know what we do, and we understand all these things. There is a lot of security in our lives, but we are lacking joy in part because we have lost the ability to dream. We become more cynical than we thought we would.

Actually, we should dream bigger now. We know what our gifts are, where we have been placed, and what we are to do. We should be living light because we are trusting deep—fulfilling God's plan. There is a deep joy when we can say, "God, I will stop trying to talk You into being part of my plan. I want to be part of Your plan." The gospel sets us free from the captivity of our pride—of what we want—and we are able to be people who dream God's dreams.

I was at a board meeting when the person leading it began by saying, "If God answered every one of the prayers you're praying, what would happen?" That question really convicted my heart of this: I am not praying specifically enough in my life. I am praying ambiguously. It also showed me I was not dreaming anymore. What am I really dreaming and asking God to do?

So, if God answered every prayer you prayed, what would happen? Whose lives would be changed? God wants to use you in a great way. He has a dream for you. It might be to start an organization, club, or event. Or maybe it's just to introduce you to one person you are going to minister to and love on. It could be a new way of living that you have never experienced before. Today, laugh a little, do something fun, and dream about what God can do.

Dream Big
Zechariah 4:8–10

D o you have an idea? Do you have a thought? Let's jump out there and be like those who dream. What could God do if you took a step?

Let me share a couple of examples from my own life. When my son was in middle school, some dads and I decided to have a Bible study once a month with our sons before school. We called it "Dudes and Dads." One dad would bring a devotional, and another dad would bring donuts. We had two rules for the boys. They had to sit by their dads, and they had to hug their dads when they left.

For three years, it was one of the biggest blessings of my life. It was also a blessing to the other dads and the kids as well. When their high school years began, some dads got together and said, "Hey, what if we get together as dads and pray?" Once a month, we met at a little restaurant and had eggs, waffles, and all the syrup our wives wouldn't give us at home. Then, we would have a time of devotional and pray that God would do something great at the school. Often, we ended the time writing thank-you notes to teachers, coaches, and principals starving for encouragement. Usually, their in-box is filled with parental complaints. Instead, they would receive notes from dads saying: "I'm praying for you, and I appreciate you."

Then a handful of families had a wonderful idea. What if we kicked off the school year on a Sunday night in the school auditorium for a time of praise and prayer? With T-shirts made, yards signs placed in front of homes, and invitations extended, parents, teachers, and students gathered to ignite the school year with prayer and praise. It was a God dream come true.

Then parents and students from other schools decided to do the same. Now years later numerous schools host "IGNITE." The dream expanded further than we could have thought.

Let's make a difference, and let's be dreamers of what God can do.

Do not despise the days of small beginnings. Dream big. What could God start through you?

Great Things
Psalm 126:2–3

Psalm 126 says that the Israelites' mouths were filled with laughter and their tongues with joy. Then the nations around them saw the blessing and said, "The LORD has done great things for them" (v. 2). The people of God responded, "The LORD had done great things for us; we were joyful" (v. 3). The blessings and the source will become apparent to others and to us.

Are you aware of how many great things God has done in your life? How faithful has the Lord been to you? If God never did another thing for you, He has already done too much.

That is a whole different worldview, is it not? If God never did another thing for me besides releasing me, not from Babylonian captivity but from the weight of my sin, He has already done too much. I have been set free by Him! Yet from His abundant love, I still receive one gracious blessing after another.

He has given us the ability to dream, to think, and to be part of what His plan is. We can say, "Lord, You will do great things through me."

As an example, a ministry partner of our church operates in Asia rescuing young girls from the brothels where their moms work as prostitutes. If these little girls do not get out, they will end up doing the same. The ministry organization rescues and adopts these girls as their own, helping with school and everything else they need.

One of the rescued girls gave her testimony to our mission team. Her eyes filled with tears as she said thank you to our team. One of the members had been instrumental in this teenager attending college in the United States. A dream come true for both! When I think about her, I see a joyful dreamer. As she cried with gratitude, we cried with her and celebrated the dream and her future.

We couldn't help but say, "The LORD has done great things." Ponder and repeat that phrase throughout the day.

Seeds of Joy
Psalm 126:4–6

Psalm 126 reminds us that after the Israelites were filled with joy, they cried out to the Lord to restore their fortunes like the rain restores the water to streams in the desert. They knew even though they had sown in tears, they would reap with joy. Keep planting in hard times. We started this psalm with laughter and joy; we are ending with weeping and sorrow. That is the spectrum of life we will face at one point or another.

The Negev is a dry desert in Israel where there is nothing but crevices. But in the rainy season, at an unexpected time, a storm rolls in, and the crevices fill with water. The desert miraculously turns into rivers.

That happens in our lives as well. The healing and the finances come . . . The business deal happens . . . She was infertile and became pregnant . . . We did not know when it was coming, but the rain fell, and the living water filled up the dry cracks in our desert. God does immeasurably more than we could ask or imagine.

Salvation is very much like that. We did not earn it. We trusted in the living water of Jesus Christ to fill our dry and cracked hearts. Then streams of His living water flowed from us as believers to help others.

This psalm also speaks of hard walking. "Those who sow in tears will reap with shouts of joy" (Ps. 126:5). The psalmist describes someone with a bag of seeds who is throwing them out, weeping in their pain as they walk. Do not waste your pain; invest your pain. God will take your misery and make it your ministry. God will use you to give sheaves of joy to others as He gives them to you.

A family from church had a dear family member die. Their daughter was an organ donor. Later, the family opened a letter from the person who received one of the donated organs. They met and talked, and this family received great joy. Out of great tragedy, they walked and planted seeds, even in the midst of their grief. God can do amazing seed planting when it is watered by our tears. He can bring a harvest as you have never seen before.

Stand up and say, "Lord, step by step in my tears, I'm going to continue to throw out the seeds." And the joy will come.

Joyful Dreamers
Psalm 67

We are joyful dreamers who thank God and work faithfully. The Lord has done great things. Even in the midst of pain and joy, we work faithfully. We let God do something through us. God has a dream for you, your marriage, and your family. He has a dream for the schools you represent and for your business. God has a dream for you to be His dreamer on the earth, thanking God and working faithfully.

I am not calling you to start a big ministry or a new event. I am calling you to be a difference-maker, to dream and say, "God, You've placed me here. What's Your dream for this place?"

Parents, perhaps the dream is that you may be a prayer warrior on your kid's campus and realize that God has placed you there for a reason during this season of your life. Then you will march out as a joyful dreamer who thanks God and works faithfully.

Jesus is the living water from heaven filling your heart and soul. If your heart and soul are filled with Jesus, are you letting the river rage wherever He wants it to, or are you just building little dams to keep the course going the way you want it to?

The Lord has done great things for me. As the water courses fill the Negev (Psalm 126), as we sow in tears and reap in joy, we walk faithfully with the Lord. Pray this prayer:

> *Jesus, I love You and thank You because You are God, and You are the giver of dreams. I don't want to spend my life climbing a ladder and end up with it leaning against the wrong wall. I don't want to be successful and not joyful. I don't want to get You on my schedule. I want my life to be about Your dreams. Fill me with Your joy and laughter. Use me where You have placed me. I love You, Jesus. Amen.*

God Is Love
1 John 4:7–12

Regardless of what version of the Bible you choose to read, the word *love* is found countless times.

Have you ever asked yourself what true love actually is? Have you ever felt it? Have you ever really loved? We are going to focus on the love of God the next few days. We will discover some aspects of the love of God toward us, toward others, and toward Him.

First, let's define what love is according to the Bible. A perfect definition of what true love really is and means is found in 1 Corinthians 13. Love is not just a feeling or an emotion or a reaction to someone else's actions. True love does not change according to what the object of affection does or does not do. It is consistent through the valleys.

God is love. Everything He does and everything He did, is because of love. He is the purest form of love. He is the true measurement of love. Love was made by Him, for Him, and through Him. It is not until we get to know God that we can truly understand what love is.

God shows His love for us in many ways. He gave His Son as a sacrifice for the forgiveness of our sins because He loves us so much. He makes everything work together for our good because He loves us. He created everything for us to enjoy because He loves us. It does not matter what we do or do not do, God is love. And because He is love, He cannot go against Himself. It is who He is; it is based on His character, not on our actions. No matter what we do, He still loves us. Because love is from Him, He is love.

My prayer today for you is that you will get to know God in a deeper way, that through knowing Him more, you will experience a love like you have never felt before. I pray that you can understand what true love really is and that your life and the lives of those around you will be changed forever. What the love of God touches cannot remain the same.

June 9

The Love of God
Is Steadfast
Romans 8:38–39

We live in a world where everything changes; one day something is cool and the next day it is old-fashioned. Everything changes and keeps changing.

There is one thing, though, that will never change . . . the love of God. His love is steadfast. It is firm. It is unwavering. It is forever. It is always faithful. It will not change because God stays the same forever. He is love. He promises us His steadfast love many times in the Bible.

It might be hard for us to fathom the reality of the steadfast love of God—a love that endures forever—because nothing around us lasts forever. We are not used to thinking about things lasting forever in our lives, in our families, or in society. Sometimes, we do not want things that last forever; we want to move fast so we don't get bored. We buy cell phones knowing that in two or three years, we will be upgrading them for the new model. We buy clothes not because of their amazing lasting quality but because they are in fashion; but our souls need a forever, not a passing fashion.

If we really think about it, how amazing is it to know that the love of God is something that will never change, no matter what? It will not change even if we change. It will not modify if we do something or do not do something. His love for you does not alter with time. God's love remains firm forever.

> *Thank You, God, for Your unchanging love! Thank You for loving me with a love that will last forever, no matter what I do. Thank You for the security that is found in Your love. Thank You for a love I will always be able to depend on. Thank You for a love that always is and always will be!*

God's Love Is Irrevocable

Exodus 34:6–7

Have you ever wondered what could make the world a better place? To make it more peaceful? Have you asked yourself why the world is such a chaotic place?

The chaos of the world is because we have shunned the love of God. We have told God that we want our will and not His love. We want to do things our own way with our own wisdom and for our own glory. Thankfully His love is a love that is irrevocable, no matter what we or anyone else does. It does not depend on anything or anyone, only God Himself.

Human-to-human love is revocable; we are constantly taking back things we give, say, or do. But heaven-to-human love is irrevocable. I'm so glad the love of God is irrevocable. His love for us is not conditional on our works.

Irrevocable is a legal term. It is something you cannot take back. Think for a moment about these synonyms for irrevocable in terms of God's love to YOU: beyond recall, binding, changeless, definite, factual, final, indestructible, permanent, stable, certain, conclusive, and ironclad. That is what the love of God is for YOU. It is based on His character, not your actions.

We often think when we do something wrong or make bad decisions, God no longer loves us. Our guilt clouds our knowledge of the truth. We still believe His love never changes but guilt causes us to feel like it has shifted. But the love of God does not work that way. His love is always white-hot for us. It's not only because God is our Father; it's because it goes against who He is and all the promises He made us. In the times we've failed, His love is to be a catalyst to continue our walk with Him in obedience.

His love will never change, and He will never take His love back. That is a truth we must learn to accept and understand. There is nothing we can do to change it—it is wonderfully irrevocable.

God's Love Is Forgiving
Luke 15:11–32

There is a painting by Rembrandt that has always caught my eye. It is called *The Return of the Prodigal Son* and is believed to be one of Rembrandt's final pieces. The painting perfectly depicts the forgiveness of a father toward his son, and it is based on the parable of the prodigal son in the Bible. If you look at the painting closely, you can almost feel the love of the father by the way his hands are placed on his son's back and by the expression on his face. A quick internet search will let you see the painting for yourself.

The parable discusses a son who asks his father for his inheritance and then leaves and spends it all. It tells of the forgiveness of the father when the son returns. The son has no other expectation except to become one of his father's servants. But this father's love offers unexpected forgiveness and grace. It's the same for the love of God for us. Even when we least expect to be loved and forgiven, He still loves us and forgives us, repeatedly. That is who He is.

The forgiveness God gives us through His love is more complete than human-to-human forgiveness. He forgives us and never struggles with holding a grudge. His forgiveness is comprehensive; it forgets all wrongdoing. It is a forgiveness that goes deeper than what we can expect or imagine. And that is not because we did something to deserve such a forgiveness. It is because of who God is and the love He has for us. It is a forgiveness that restores and brings life, purpose, meaning, hope, and grace.

My prayer for you is that you will be able to accept the love and forgiveness of God in all its fullness. Know that it is not and will never be about you; it is about who He is. Rest in the truth, our actions will never be greater than His character. Also, His forgiveness is compelling us to forgive others as well. One day you may find yourself needing to be loving and forgiving to someone else. It will be hard, but He will give you the strength to do the unexpected as well.

God's Love Brings Worship
Matthew 4:8–11

Worship is an essential part of our Christian lives. We worship God in our prayers, in our songs, and in our living. We worship God as a sign of thankfulness and awe of who He is and because of how He loves us. Worship is a response from our hearts and souls and spirits to God's goodness and faithfulness. It is a response to who He is, to His character. He is the only One deserving of our worship.

As human beings, it is a natural need and instinct to worship something—not necessarily God. Many people who do not know the true God worship false gods. Sometimes we may not even realize it, but we might be worshiping our jobs, our families, money, success, or material things. We may not be bowing down to them or singing songs of praise to them, but in our hearts, they hold a place that is meant only for God. Jesus himself was tempted to falsely worship Satan to gain the kingdoms of this world and their splendor. News flash! The world already belonged to Him. Nevertheless, He retorted "Worship the Lord your God, and serve Him only."

Worship is a condition of the heart. And Christ's heart is the model of purity. If we understand the love of God for us, then our hearts will always be filled with worship toward Him. It is like finding out someone did something good for you, something unexpected. Your heart warms and all you can do is thank that person. You acknowledge what they did for you. The same goes for God. He loves us with an undeserving, inexplicable, unchangeable love every day of our lives. It is only natural that our hearts are filled with worship and thankfulness for Him.

Take a moment and think about the love of God in your life. How can you thank Him and worship Him with your life today? Your worship is not only through music but by the way you live your life, the way you treat people, the way you are with your family and friends, the way you talk, the way you act at work or school, the way you drive your car, the way you shop at the supermarket or mall. Think of three practical ways you can worship God with your whole life today.

God's Love Is Our Comfort

Psalm 119:76–77

What would you do if you knew there was an answer for all your problems? Would you take it?

The truth is that the more we know God, the closer we are to Him. We start to realize that in Him, He has all the answers, all the security, and all the comfort we need for every area and every circumstance of our lives. But it sometimes seems too good to be true, right? He asks us to trust without reservation. It's sometimes hard to have faith in a God we cannot see and believe deeply that everything will work out for our good, even when things are not going well in our lives.

God promises us that He will always be with us. He promises us a love that is faithful, steadfast, and irrevocable. No matter what we do, no matter what the chaos of our lives looks like, He loves us with a faithful love. It is a love that is not fickle, because we cannot be comforted by a fickle God. Actually, man is fickle; God is faithful. From the faithfulness of God comes the comfort of God. His promise is that He will always love us and comfort us.

To give comfort is to give strength and hope to someone. And that is what God has promised us. It does not matter what goes on around us—He will always be with us, strengthening and comforting us. In Him, we will always find safety and security. He is our shepherd; He will always protect us and guide us along the right paths. In His comfort, we can find rest and happiness.

God never intended for us to live lonely, sad, or worried lives on our own. He did say that in this life we will encounter trials and tough days, but He also says that He wants to be with us through it all. Loneliness, sadness, and worry are a part of everyone's journey. But use them as a doorway to a deeper walk with Christ. Lay them at His feet. He wants us to know and feel His warm embrace and His comforting love. He sent us a comforter, His Holy Spirit, to guide us and be with us. It is time for us to take advantage of what God offers us and start living our lives to the fullest, knowing that we will always have God on our side.

Lord, may Your faithful love comfort me.

Looking for Comfort
Psalm 119:73–77

What I am about to say may sound strong and negative, but it is a universal, undeniable truth . . . suffering comes with living. Every living thing goes through some sort of suffering in the duration of its life. Animals suffer, plants suffer, humans suffer. It is part of life on this earth. And it is also an undeniable truth that we as human beings look for some sort of comfort to ease that suffering. Everyone is looking for comfort or will look for comfort. There is no way to escape it. No matter what we believe in—and even if we don't believe in anything—we all need comfort. The missionary and the skeptic both seek comfort.

We were made to need comfort. We seek comfort all the time, even when we do not realize it. Sometimes we look for comfort in shallow, quick things. We might go to food for comfort. Some of us go to shopping, technology, TV, movies, pornography, noise, or addictions for some form of comfort. Maybe that quick fix of fake comfort gives us some sort of control over our lives.

But do we value immediate comfort over real comfort? Do we go to the quick things instead of the deep things? Even when we turn to God for comfort, are we looking for something quick, or are we seeking something eternal? C. S. Lewis said that the end goal of Christianity is not personal comfort but a relationship with God. And from that relationship comes the deepest and most real form of comfort we could ever dream of. Seek the relationship first and you will find the comfort.

We have all been hurt. We are all wounded and lonely. We have all felt guilty. We all make mistakes and lack control over so many things in our lives. But we can submit all of that to God, and in return, He promises us His faithful love that comforts us.

We can think of His love as the rope that rock climbers use. It is there whether they need it or not, whether we have a firm grip on life or not. The same thing goes for the love of God in our lives—it does not matter if we succeed or fail, whether we are in joy or in pain, we will always need the security of the comforting love of God. Rest in these truths today.

Where Is Your Delight?
1 Peter 1:6–9

To delight in something is to find great pleasure, happiness, and joy. There are many verses in the Bible that say we find joy when we go through trials and hard times. I often wonder why that is. It sounds somewhat contradictory to find joy while going through a hard time or circumstance. But in the kingdom of God, we are going to find many contradictory things that meet each other on common ground. We have a God who promises us that His eternal love will always give us comfort. He is a God who says if we focus on Him, He will take care of everything for us.

There is a hope that comes with trusting God when we are going through a hard time. It is a hope that comes from knowing the love of God gives us comfort. It is with the result of delighting and rejoicing in God's promises. It may not be easy to find joy or happiness when we are suffering, but we must know that we are never alone in those seasons. The Bible says that we have the Holy Spirit with us as our comforter and that He will be with us forever. It tells us that everything we go through is meant to make us grow as individuals in our faith and help others who will go through the same thing we are going through.

When we delight in something, we want to spend time with it. It may be a TV show, music, the company of friends or family, a good meal, a sports show—whatever it is that brings us joy, we want to spend time doing it. Would you consider taking time daily to enjoy the Word of God and His promises? Think about all the times the comfort of God has given you hope and joy during the hardest moments of your life.

As we learn to delight in the promises of God, as we learn to find joy during trials and hard times, we know we have the promise of His eternal, faithful, comforting love. Remember that God also delights in us with shouts of joy. How wonderful is His love for us!

Submission Brings Comfort

1 Peter 5:10–11

Comfort is not earned; it is received. We can seek it by seeking God, but it is something God gives us in His love, and we receive it. It is a gift and a promise from God to us.

According to Psalm 119:76, we receive the comforting love of God as His servants. To be a servant is to submit to someone else's authority, to accept their authority over us. We submit to the One who created us; we agree that what has afflicted us, He has allowed. We know He is building us up and giving us perseverance through the trials we might go through. We trust that going through these hard times will bring something good into our lives.

As human beings, we are going to find that we have to submit to many things during our lives. We have to submit to laws and regulations, to our parents when we are young, to our teachers when we go to school, to our governing authorities as citizens of the country we live in, and many other things. Do you find yourself more secure when you submit to certain rules and regulations? If your answer is yes, you are right. That is because those were meant to make us feel more secure. They are meant to help us live our lives with a certain order and comfort.

When we submit to the love of God, we will find peace. A great example is the prodigal son. When the son returned and submitted to his father, he rediscovered the love, comfort, forgiveness, hope, and joy that always remained in his home. The father did not leave him standing there alone; he met him. The same happens when we submit ourselves to the love and forgiveness of God. He meets us; He gives us the gift of His love and security.

My prayer today is that we will learn to submit to the will of God and accept that whatever sufferings or trials we may face will bring us closer to His love and comfort. We must understand that submitting to God does not mean we lose our freedom. It means we gain our freedom by living completely surrendered to His love and comfort!

Serving Hands
2 Corinthians 1:3–7

We were made to need comfort, but we were also made to give comfort to others. Second Corinthians 2:4 says, "For I wrote to you with many tears out of an extremely troubled and anguished heart—not to cause you pain, but that you should know the abundant love I have for you." It means our misery becomes our ministry. Our servant hearts become hands that serve others because of the empathy we hold.

God takes our pain and brings healing through knowing Him better. Then we have the empathy to truly care and minister, because we have been there ourselves. God takes our misery and makes it our ministry. No one better to care for a person in grief than someone who has experienced grief and given it to the Lord. No one better at comforting someone going through suffering than the person who went through that same suffering.

During her reign, Queen Victoria heard of a lady who was a common laborer, a peasant, who had lost her baby. Queen Victoria had experienced deep sorrow herself, and she felt moved to express her sympathy. One day she called the bereaved woman to the palace. The lady came and spent time with Queen Victoria. When the lady went back to her house, her neighbors were excited and waiting for her at her door. They asked her what the Queen had to say. And the grieving woman told them that the Queen had said nothing. She simply held her hand, and they wept silently together.

How did the queen know what to do? Because she had been there. She understood. When you know what it is like, you can care at a different level. Let God use your misery to make it your ministry. Let your servant heart become your serving hands.

I pray that today you can receive the comforting love of God in your life in a way so deep that you feel the burning need and desire to share it with others. I pray that you can be a comforter to others through the comfort that God gave you in your pain. I pray that you may be able to understand that every suffering you experienced is not pointless but had a divine purpose to comfort someone else with your empathy and understanding as God loves them . . . through you. Keep your eyes open today for someone in need of comfort.

Supernatural Thirst
John 7:37–39

Creatures are not born with desires unless satisfaction for those desires exists. A baby feels hunger, and there is such a thing as food. A duckling wants to swim, and there is such a thing as water.

King Solomon, who succeeded King David to rule Israel, was famous for his wisdom. Like his father, who wrote many of the psalms, Solomon's writings are also part of the Bible. He wrote Proverbs, Ecclesiastes, and the Song of Solomon.

Solomon was wealthy, educated, accomplished, and able to govern and make alliances. He supervised the construction of magnificent buildings, including his own palace and the temple in Jerusalem. He obtained whatever gave him pleasure. He had 700 wives and 300 concubines. He had everything he desired—power, sex, money, knowledge, accomplishments, popularity, and fame. Yet he felt that pursuing all these things was like chasing the wind. It was meaningless. He was not satisfied. He was still thirsty.

When you have thirsts that are not going to be satisfied through sex, marriage, money, fame, or anything in this world, that is an indication that you've been created for a deeper well. Solomon came to that conclusion and concluded his meditation on the meaning of life by encouraging people to remember their Creator (Eccles. 12:1).

Acknowledge your thirst. Whether you are young, old, or somewhere in between, you've probably felt that thirst that is larger than life, that longing for something or someone you can't name, that desire that shows you still haven't found what you're looking for.

Put aside your need for accomplishment. Put aside your need for ownership, security, and attention. Put it all aside. The world cannot satisfy your thirst. You need Jesus. We all need Him. Hear Him call loudly to invite all who are thirsty to come to Him.

Thirsty for God
Jeremiah 2:11–13

Today is Juneteenth, the day in 1865 celebrating when the final group of enslaved people in Galveston, Texas, heard the news of the Emancipation Proclamation. Freedom had finally come for all. I've been many times to the very spot where the thirst-quenching good news was read by a solider named General Granger. We all thirst for freedom of life and of the soul. We need water, living water.

The human body has three stages of dehydration: mild, moderate, and severe. The first is ordinary thirst. Your mouth is dry, and your brain tells you to drink water. In the second stage, you experience headaches, dizziness, fatigue, confusion, and more. In the third stage, drinking water is no longer enough; medical intervention is necessary.

The story tells of two men who were driving through the desert when their truck broke down. After they drank all the water they had, as the temperature soared, they drank the liquid from the truck's radiator. Tragically, it was lethal.

We can get so thirsty in this world that we will take our legitimate need for God and try to satisfy it in things that are deadly for us. This world is full of broken cisterns where we try to slake our thirst but can't. Malcom Muggeridge, a British author, said this:

> I may, I suppose, regard myself, or pass for being, a relatively successful man. People occasionally stare at me in the streets—that's fame. I can fairly easily earn enough to qualify for admission to the higher slopes of the Inland Revenue—that's success. Furnished with money and a little fame even the elderly, if they care to, may partake of trendy diversions—that's pleasure. It might happen once in a while that something I said or wrote was sufficiently heeded for me to persuade myself that it represented a serious impact on our time—that's fulfilment. Yet I say to you—and I beg you to believe me—multiply these tiny triumphs by a million, add them all together, and they are nothing—less than nothing, a positive impediment—measured against one draught of that living water Christ offers to the spiritually thirsty, irrespective of who or what they are.[29]

Jesus is the living water. He is the only way to satisfy your spiritual thirst. Be reminded on this Juneteenth that He desires to give freedom to our lives and our souls.

Living Water
Revelation 21:6

Jesus invited all who are thirsty to come to Him and drink. Jesus is not like a trickle or a drop of water about to vanish. It is not a gulp or a mouthful; it is much more. Believing in Jesus does not mean you receive temporary reprieve for your thirst. In fact, Jesus said that those who drink of His water never thirst again.

Jesus said He would give people who believe in Him water from the spring of life—that they would experience Him as a spring of water continually bubbling over in their hearts. He also said that whoever believes in Him would have rivers of living water flowing within them.

Springs and rivers are not stagnant. They flow from their headwaters to the sea. They plunge over cliffs, gurgle through the woods, carve channels in the hardest rock, meander over the countryside, rush under bridges, roar as they gain strength and volume, and finally reach the shore. They provide habitats for living creatures and bring sustenance and refreshment to all in their path. Life with Jesus brings abundance and joy.

Do you want that transformation? Drink of Jesus, the living water. Christ is the thirst quencher of the soul. There is nothing and no one else who can satisfy the human soul like He does. Even when we come to the living water of Jesus it doesn't mean we will never struggle with sin or life will be perfect. You will still have to deal with your busy schedule and stress that is waiting around the corner, BUT there is hope.

Jesus is the thirst quencher for the soul. To believe in Christ means to rest your full weight on Him, to have confidence that He is the One who will save you. It means that when it is the long hot days of summer, you still know that the only way to be saved, the only way to walk through the pearly gates, is by believing in Jesus. He is the Shepherd, the teacher, the King of kings, the Lord of lords, and the living water we thirst for.

Jesus Meets Our Needs
Nehemiah 9:19–21

Life is tough. Remember the story of the Israelites? They were enslaved, crying to God for help because of the harshness of their masters. God sent Moses to deliver them from Pharaoh who did not want to let the people go. God sent plague after plague to change Pharaoh's mind. Finally, Pharaoh relented. Then, he changed his mind again and chased the Israelites with his army. The Israelites were trapped between Pharaoh's army and the Red Sea, but God made a way of escape. Moses raised his arms, and the sea parted. The people of God escaped, and their pursuers drowned.

Then Moses led the people through the wilderness. It was a harsh and rocky desert. How did Moses and his people get food and water so they could survive in that difficult environment? God sent the Israelites manna every day. When the people longed for water, God told Moses to speak to a rock, but he struck the rock instead, which angered God. Yet God still gave water for the people to drink.

The rock that Moses struck represents Christ. Struck on the cross, His blood flowed as our spiritual food and drink. At the Passover meal before Jesus' arrest, Jesus held the bread before His disciples and said that it was His body, which would be broken for their sake. He held the cup and said it was His blood, which would be poured out on their behalf. Then He was stricken for our sins. He was beaten on the way to Calvary and nailed to a cross. When He died, He was pierced with a spear, and water and blood flowed from His side. Because of His sacrifice, we can be forgiven of all our sins. Because He rose again, we can have new life. When we believe in Jesus, He sends the Holy Spirit to dwell in our hearts.

Jesus knows what we need. He forgives our sins. He frees us from our fears. He brings life. He brings continual nourishment and refreshment so we can have communion with God through the Holy Spirit. The Spirit reminds us of all Jesus taught and did on the earth. He helps us travel through the wilderness and deserts we face until we reach the Promised Land. Jesus meets all our needs.

If you feel like the Israelites . . . lost in the wilderness or hopeless at the edge of the Red Sea, keep trusting, keep waiting. God will rescue in His timing. I've been there and it's tough but unseen growth is taking place in you. He'll provide and you'll be wowed by His goodness again. Jesus will meet your deepest needs.

An Urgent Invitation
John 7:37–38

It was the last day of the Feast of Tabernacles, and Jesus stood up and loudly declared that anyone who was thirsty could come to Him and drink. He added that whoever believed in Him would have rivers of living water from within. Why did Jesus issue that invitation? Why did He wait until the last day of the week-long feast?

It's important to know what happened before all this. It had been declared that people who believe in Him shall not perish but have everlasting life. He preached. He performed miracles. He extended Himself to those who would refuse Him. In John 5, Jesus experienced conflict. Leaders began to persecute Him because they did not think He should claim to be the Savior. In John 6, despite more miracles, people who supported Him began to leave Him. They found His teaching too hard to accept. Jesus even asked His disciples if they wanted to leave.

John 7 begins with Jesus' brothers. They are going to the feast. They tell Jesus that if He wants to have this public persona as a savior, superhero, and the most popular guy in town, He should attend the feast too. They did not say that because they believed in Jesus; they said it to poke fun. Is it possible to miss Jesus on the way to a religious feast? Apparently so. Kind of like us missing Him on the way to church, while listening to Christian radio. That's exactly what His brothers did. In the midst of all their activity, they missed the Savior.

At the Feast of Tabernacles, the Jews celebrated God's faithfulness to them in the wilderness. The priests who led the celebration would go to the Pool of Siloam each day to draw water. They would walk back with the water and pour it on the altar. On the last day, they would go around the altar seven times.

At the Feast of Tabernacles, on the last day after the priests had poured out the water on the altar, when the greatest number of people had gathered and people were watching even from the rooftops, when He would get in even more trouble with the Jewish leaders . . . do you feel the drama building?

At the pinnacle moment of the feast, Jesus stood and in a loud voice declared that all who were thirsty should come to Him! What's your deepest thirst today? Will you accept His invitation to have your deepest thirst quenched in Him today?

Water Flowing Within
John 7:38–44

We are all looking for something better and something deeper in life; not for short-term satisfaction but for the truths of Scripture to be true. Jesus' invitation is wide open. He says *anyone* who is thirsty. Everyone can come to Him.

Belief in Christ satisfies. Believe that His grace is enough. Believe that He is the One who gives us true security. He is the One we can trust. He is the One who sings the song of victory. He is coming again.

Whoever believes in Jesus, as the Scripture says, will have streams of living water flowing from within. When Jesus promised that, He meant He would send the Holy Spirit to those who believed in Him. This incredible resource of the Spirit within us would happen after Jesus died on the cross, laid in the tomb, rose from the dead, and ascended into heaven. Before then, Jesus had not yet been glorified. But now Jesus has been glorified, and all He promised is available to all who come to Him to satiate their thirst.

When you trust Jesus Christ as your Savior, the Holy Spirit of God dwells in your heart. He lives inside you and empowers you so the living water can flow through you to others.

The Holy Spirit's indwelling results in living water flowing. God's love is poured into our hearts through the Holy Spirit. He is our advocate and teaches us the truth, reminding us of all Jesus said and did. He comforts us when we are sad or worried—when we experience the ups and downs of life. He builds us up. He equips us. He gives us gifts to serve God and serve others. His power flows through our lives. In this world that brings weariness each day, He energizes us. And He helps us bear fruit to please God. Pay attention to what He is prompting you to do this day. Listen to Him so the rivers of life will flow through your life.

Filled to Overflowing
Isaiah 32:1–2

The water Jesus gives is like a spring bubbling up within us for eternal life. It never stops. It does not run dry. Living water flows like rivers within our hearts. It's uncontainable! It spills over in our speech, and it spills over through song. Our hearts are so full that we look for ways to express our gratitude to God. We praise Jesus' name to those around us.

People everywhere are craving. Their parched hearts want living water. And we can share it with them. Through the indwelling of the Holy Spirit, their lives, like ours, are transformed. Where nothing grows and the land is scorched and cracked, God can make green shoots of new life appear. Where there are only weeds and husks and dry stalks, He can make flowers and ferns and forests grow. God transforms barren ground into gardens.

Before God created the first human being, streams watered the ground. When the Lord formed Adam and Eve, He placed them in a garden surrounded by rivers. Many years later, the prophet Isaiah recalled the abundance of this first garden when he talked about the King who will reign in righteousness. That King is Jesus. The book of Isaiah says the righteous King will share His glory. Others will reign with Him. They will be like shelter from the wind, a refuge from the storm, shade in the sun, and streams in the desert. That is an amazing promise! All who Jesus invites to come to Him, no matter how thirsty, humble, powerless, and ordinary they might be, will become with Him—like the thirst quenchers and bringers of blessing.

Thank God for His wonderful plan. Thank Him for His mighty deeds and great promises. He satisfies all who are thirsty. He satisfies all who are hungry. Christ is our spiritual food and spiritual drink. He meets all our needs. Thank God for His unfailing love! Make it your goal today to overflow with thankfulness to God no matter your present circumstance.

Live Boldly but Speak Kindly

Ephesians 4:15–16

Paul tells us to speak the truth in love and the first thing John says in 1 John 2 is "my little children." He is speaking kindly. Then, without being harsh, he boldly declares, "I am writing you these things so that you may not sin" (1 John 2:1). What we learn in these verses is to live boldly but speak kindly. We want to live confidently in our faith, pray for people, share Christ, and take risks in obedience to God. No one has ever lived fully who has lived timidly.

Sometimes, however, we can live so boldly that we forget to speak kindly. Husbands, you need to be men of ambition, going forward in leadership in your families, but don't forget to speak kindly to your wife and children. At the same time, we shouldn't be held hostage by people pleasing. If we do, we won't accomplish much. Being bold will sometimes mean acting in obedience to what we have heard or learned from God regardless of other's opinions.

Have you noticed that we live in a world where we do not speak kindly? Do you ever turn on the TV and everybody is fighting? Many talk shows and news outlets are based on guests verbally attacking each other, then break for a commercial and do it again. It's more entertaining to watch a fight than a conversation.

To speak kindly but live boldly sets a different tone. It does not include being sarcastic, belittling, or humiliating others. It is far from disrespecting authority, tearing down, or putting people down. It has everything to do with speaking the truth in love, building others up, and being the example of what we would ask of anyone else. God has a plan for you, and when you follow His heavenly advice, you are partnering with Him to bring life.

The beauty of Christianity is that you can be an amazingly loving person and live boldly and speak strongly. To be able to put those two things together looks like Jesus.

Good Teaching
1 John 2:1–2

Have you ever wondered why someone is telling you something? Some people just keep talking, and instead of getting to the point . . . they take you for a long ride around every twist and turn. There is never a more comforting thing to hear in those conversations than these words: "I'm telling you this because . . ."

In 1 John 2, John gives us a startling reason for why he is writing. He tells us, "My little children, I am writing you these things . . ." But what are "these things"? They are the truth around the fact that Jesus Christ is the atonement for our sins and that we have to confess our sins to one another and to God. Then he goes on to say, "I am writing you these things so that you may not sin."

That's a big statement since we are going to sin. Unfortunately, we aren't going to wake up tomorrow and never sin again. It is not going to happen.

We can *sin less*, but we will never be *sinless*.

What is John trying to say? Good teaching is intended to keep us from bad living. We need good teaching in our lives. Many of us are taking in whatever the media and the news give us; our minds are being shaped, formed, and molded by the things that are happening in the world.

So where do you get good teaching? It comes from your Bible reading, from mission trips, even from what you listen to, and hopefully, this devotional. At church, we receive godly input from the weekly sermon, at conferences, or presentations. In some churches, adults sign up for Sunday school or Bible classes. There are many options. But you just can't expect to have good living without good teaching. It is not going to work. We need good inflow to have good outflow.

Spend time in God's Word. Take notes. Get something out of the Scriptures. Be encouraged and diligent—you are doing it right now by reading this devotional! Sin destroys direction, kills joy, and shreds relationships. But good teaching gives us direction, fills us with joy, and helps us in our relationships. Walk in God's truth and you'll experience God's power.

Up and in the Right Direction

James 2:14–26

Have you ever wondered when we will stop sinning? We all sin. There is no question about it. But we should stay clear of continual or habitual sin.

We will never get rid of sin in our lives, but we don't want to end up sinning over and over again every day. We may use our condition to be able to relate with others and understand that we all need a Savior, but we must also be able to make some progress and let good teaching result in good living so we can journey on together.

Compare this to your finances. What do you want them to do? You probably want them to go up and to the right. You invest a little bit here, and you want to see some growth or an increased rate of return over time. It's the same thing with your faith. Faith pulls your obedience forward as it increases, and your obedience pulls your faith forward. Faith and obedience both need to grow at the same time.

Some folks say they have a lot of obedience, but they don't have a lot of faith. They are just like the Pharisees in the Bible; they are self-righteous and legalistic. Some other folks have a lot of faith, but they think their faith is personal and don't do much with it. The Bible says that faith without works is dead.

We don't want to be a Pharisee or somebody with dead faith. We want to be people whose faith pulls our obedience forward and whose obedience pulls our faith forward. As I walk with God, every step of obedience is connected by a step of faith. If you don't know if you can obey, just take another step of faith, and your obedience will follow. If you don't know if you can have enough faith, just take a step of obedience, and your faith will follow. They go hand in hand, and they pull one another onward.

Now here's the truth: nobody is perfect. We go up and down every day. Hopefully, we are going more up than down—and in the right direction! Walk today in obedience and faith.

We Have an Advocate
Hebrews 9:15

God our heavenly Father is good beyond our wildest imagination. He has us covered in every aspect of our lives—spiritually, physically, intellectually, emotionally. We can't help but marvel at His love.

Even when we strive to do everything we should, we struggle and will eventually slip and fall. In that moment, it is important to understand that we can bounce back because Jesus has fully paid our debt. Picture a courtroom drama. We are on trial, and God the Son, Jesus Christ, steps forward as our defense attorney. It's true that we are guilty, but He is our righteousness and our payment in the eternal heavenly trial. Jesus is our mediator extraordinaire.

Our assurance is not placed in denomination or church attendance, doing good works, or attempts to be nicer people. No. If we ever sin, we have Jesus to advocate for us. When we struggle with sin, we turn back to Him. That increases our faith, which in turn increases our obedience. And as we obey more, we sin less and keep on walking. That is what it means to walk with God. Remember, we will never be sinless on the earth but we can sin less on the earth. Growth is the cumulative effect of journeying on this path with God every day.

But with Jesus as our defense attorney and mediator, we are safe.

As Christians we are forgiven by God through Jesus Christ who paid for our sins. Trusting is His finished work.

We Will Never Be Alone

1 John 2:1

In the second chapter of 1 John, the apostle John says that in Jesus we have an Advocate. *Paraclete*, the Greek word for advocate, means one who walks alongside of. It conveys the idea that Jesus Christ, through the Holy Spirit, walks alongside of us for the rest of our lives.

Thanks to the permanent company of the Holy Spirit inside us, we know that we always have a friend in Jesus. He bore all our sins and grief. It means that He is right there in the heavenly courtroom saying, "This man, this woman is redeemed because of My blood that was shed for their sin. They are proclaimed innocent in Christ."

Every one of us has felt alone at one time or another. Did you know that 40 percent of adults in America report feeling lonely most of the time? More and more Americans report that they don't have one close confidant or friend. In spite of all the social media and all the connections we now enjoy, people are feeling lonely. Single adults? Lonely. Married people? Lonely. Widows and widowers? Lonely. Old and young? Lonely. You can go to the mall and be surrounded by people, but you still may not have even one friend.

We need someone who cares about us to walk alongside of us. Jesus never leaves us alone. If today you are feeling lonely, without any friends or anyone who cares if you are still breathing, heaven is bringing you a message: Jesus is the One who walks alongside you.

When Abraham Lincoln died, in his pocket he had five things. Among them was a worn-out newspaper clipping about a speech in which someone said, "Abraham Lincoln is one of the greatest men of all time." In the midst of a difficult season, Lincoln must have felt encouraged by knowing somebody was on his team.

As a believer in Jesus Christ, in your heart you carry more than an encouraging quote, you are indwelled by the Holy Spirit. As we walk this journey of life and the seasons of loneliness come, we can know that Jesus is right there with us.

We Have an Accuser
Job 1:8–11

If you've ever watched a good courtroom drama on TV or at the movies, you know that it isn't complete without a prosecutor. In the heavenly courtroom, not only do we have an Advocate in Jesus, but we also have a prosecutor, an adversary, an accuser—Satan. And he is a real spiritual being.

The Bible describes how Satan accused Job, smearing Job's motives for his devotion to God. In the book of Zechariah, the author reveals that Satan stood at the right side of Joshua, the high priest, to accuse him before God. The book of Revelation says that Satan accuses us before God day and night.

It is important to realize that there is an accuser. However, God is greater. When accusations fly at us, God refers the devil to our Advocate, Jesus, who crushed Satan's head at the cross to save us and paid for our redemption with His own blood.

The accuser hates you deeply. He hates your family, your future, and your joy. He will try to keep on lying to you, saying: "You are not a good mom," "You are a sorry dad," "You are single because _____," "If this is marriage, get out," "God is not good; look at all He withholds from you." Or maybe Satan accuses and remind you of your past sins even though they have been forgiven in Christ.

In Revelation 12:11, we read that the saints will overcome Satan by the blood of the Lamb and by the word of their testimony, which elaborates on how they were saved by Jesus. I'm encouraged by the lyrics of a worship song: "Tell the devil no, not today!'" Maybe we could borrow those words as we are walking with God, taking steps of faith and obedience. When the accuser tries to stop us, we can let him know, "Not today. Today, I have an Advocate, I have faith inside my soul. I'm not good at everything. I don't always make great decisions. But Jesus Christ is in my heart, He shed His blood for me, and He has crushed you."

It is time you believe you have a strong Advocate before God. He paid the price for your redemption with His blood. He is your strength, and He lives inside your heart.

Jesus Is Our Pardon
Romans 5:8–11

Jesus can change your life. He loves you. He is the atonement for your sins. He died for you. He wants to change your life and be your atoning sacrifice. He is extremely personal and at the same time, He is global. Jesus not only died for your sins, He died to pay for the sins of the whole world. That does not mean that everyone is saved, but it means that everyone can have the opportunity to trust in Jesus Christ as Savior. We could preach everywhere around the world, but each person must place his or her faith in Christ for salvation. Do you see the difference? It is not that everybody is saved, but now everybody *can* be saved.

Back in 1929, a man robbed a mail carrier. He not only robbed him, but he killed him. The man was sentenced to death, but he received a presidential pardon. But here's the dilemma: the man rejected the pardon. The issue went all the way to the U.S. Supreme Court with this question: If the president of the United States pardons you, can you reject it? The Court responded, "A pardon rejected is no pardon at all. Unless the recipient accepts the pardon, then the pardon cannot be applied."[30]

A pardon has two sides: the giver and the receiver. Jesus Christ has given us a pardon through His death on the cross, through the shedding of His blood. To be saved, we must receive that atonement and say, "Jesus, I trust in You." We are all guilty, but Jesus provides us with innocence through His death on the cross. If we place our trust in Christ as our Savior and the Holy Spirit comes to live in our hearts, we will never be alone. We take a step of faith, and we take a step of obedience. Our lives can become a little topsy-turvy, but in the long run, we grow in this relationship with Jesus. We will never be sinless, but we can strive to sin less as our faith in Jesus Christ pulls us forward in obedience to look more like Him.

Father, I thank You that the accuser is crushed and the Advocate stands for me. I thank You, Lord, that in the midst of many accusations, You fight on my behalf. You fight my battles for me. You have paid the price for me. Thank You!

Secrets to Growing
Hebrews 11:6–10

As people who love Jesus, we want to deepen our relationship with Him, and we want our lives to show it. This is not as difficult as it may seem. Spiritual growth is marked by two interdependent indicators: our faith and our obedience. Our faith pulls our obedience up. And as our obedience grows, our faith grows.

Faith and obedience work interactively to our spiritual benefit. We shouldn't neglect one while championing the other. If you have a whole lot of obedience but not a lot of faith, that is self-righteousness. At the same time, if we claim we have a lot of faith, there should be evidence of it in our lives.

We have some good days and some bad days. No day is perfect, and we don't do everything right. That is why we have Jesus. God is going to stand in for you and for me through Jesus Christ so we can have forgiveness. Grow your faith, and obedience will begin to take care of itself.

Growing in faith and obedience starts by knowing Jesus Christ. Knowing should result in growing. If you say you know Him and don't keep His commandments, you are fooling yourself. Do you think that people should live out their beliefs? Yes, of course. If not, they are inconsistent.

If you say you know Him and then do not follow His commandments, the gap between your words and your actions grows and so does our hypocrisy. When you say something, you should do what you say. When we say we are going to be faithful, we should be faithful. When we say we are going to be there, we should be there. When we say we are going to do something, we should do it. Hebrews 11 is a roster of believers who lived faithfully and obediently. Today, lets follow their example.

Of course, no one does everything perfectly. Even those listed in Hebrews 11 made mistakes, sinned, and some had legendary level checkered pasts. We are all sinners. We all struggle. We will never be perfect until we get to heaven. But as we grow in our relationship with Christ, what we say and what we do should get closer and closer together. Our faith and obedience are interdependent. Take a step of faith and/or obedience today and watch the other grow as well.

Checking Your Heart
Philippians 3:7–11

Knowing God is a key and inviting concept found throughout the Bible. The Creator of the universe wants us to know Him intimately. We should know him as a best friend along with trusting Him as our shepherd.

Often, the word *know* is in the perfect tense, talking about how to have an intimate, growing relationship with Jesus Christ. Our knowledge of Christ places us in His family as well. We are unified with Him and, as a result, a part of His crew, His team, His church, His family! We are called "little children" and "brothers and sisters." Through Jesus, we have become a member of the family of God. And the best way to show that is to live it out.

If we, as members of the family of God, don't keep His commands, we are lying. We are lying to God, which is the dumbest thing we can do because God knows everything. We lie to other people because we are trying to put forth an image that is not us. And we are lying to ourselves.

Self-deception is a big deal. That is where we can get in trouble as believers in Christ. We might think that if our morality is intact, then the authority issues between us and God don't really make a difference. You may be tremendously rebellious in your heart before the Lord and living independent of God, but you are still making it all look right and good. God loves you, He cares for you, and He wants you to come back like the prodigal son.

> *Heavenly Father, I want to be honest with myself. I want to know You deeply enough to hear Your heart. Where am I with You, Lord? What am I saying, and what am I doing? What am I claiming, and how am I acting? Where is my faith, and where is my obedience?*

Jesus Christ Came for Your Heart

1 Samuel 16:7–13

Happy 4th of July! Today, you will see a lot of American Flags. One place our flag is prominently displayed each spring is the Houston Rodeo. As you would expect in Texas, we love the rodeo. Here's how the rodeo begins: a parade of riders carrying flags circle the arena. Everyone dressed in sparkling western wear, the horses are adorned with bejeweled horse tack, looking perfect and the American Flags are held proudly by the riders.

Imagine for just a second that one of those horses at the beginning of the rodeo—the one with the sparkles, the pretty saddle, the mane, and the brushed tail—is a horse from the bareback riding competition. You can't get on it. It looks beautiful, but the heart of the horse is one that will not take authority.

When we lie to ourselves, we become like that horse. We have everything happening on the exterior when people are watching and listening, but our heart is really like a bareback bronco. We don't want anybody to tell us what to do. We sure don't want God to tell us what to do. We don't want to be useful apart from our selfish benefit. We want to do our own thing. That is the difference between a horse that is useful and a bronco that bucks authority. When we don't do what we say or walk according to who we are, we are lying to ourselves, even if we are exteriorly moral.

Rewind in American history to a time when everyone for the most part was considered a Christian. But that really wasn't true, was it? They all just kept it together a little bit better, and maybe they were more apt to go to church. But the issue is not the exterior; the issue is the heart.

The great news is that Jesus Christ came to change your hearts. When your heart changes, it changes who you are. Then you are not lying to God anymore. You are not lying to others anymore. You are not lying to yourself. You are honestly walking with God, and He puts you on a journey of growth so what you say and what you do are consistent. I have been on that journey for more than thirty years. Even though I am still not perfect, I am a lot further along than when I started.

Where are you on that journey of growth with the Lord? Do your words and actions show that you are increasingly useful to the Lord, or is your heart still rebellious? This July 4th seek to be one of the beautiful and useful riders carrying the flag.

Keeping God's Commands

Revelation 22:6–7

Pretend you're guarding a prisoner or keeping a military secret from falling into the wrong hands, as strange as these tasks may seem, God thinks you are the one for the job. In Revelation, we find a blessing for "whoever keeps the words of this prophecy." The Greek word for *keep* means to hold or protect something of importance. It was a word used for guarding a prisoner. How important was that for the guard? Extremely important.

That same word is also in a couple other verses of Scripture you may be familiar with. Peter says in his first letter that we have an inheritance that is imperishable, uncorrupted, and unfading, *kept* in heaven for us. And in 2 Timothy, at the end of his life, Paul said he had *kept* the faith.

When John says, "whoever keeps His word," it means that God's Word is important, real, and true. We keep it as we would guard a prisoner or the most valuable thing we can think of. And when we do that, the love of God is perfected or completed in us. When what we say and what we do connect, an amazing thing happens. We begin to walk with joy in the power of God. We come to realize He is in us, and we are in Him.

When you keep His Word and walk in intimacy with Him, your life will be complete.

Jesus said that if we have His commands and keep them, we love Him, and we will be loved by the Father. Do you see intimacy here? Keeping God's commands will bring intimacy to our relationship with God. And walking in faith and obedience will keep us closer to Him.

Make this your phrase to recite today: "I am going to keep His commands. I'm going to trust Him." In doing so, you will keep His word and live with greater intimacy with Him. There's nothing better!

Being Loved by Heaven

Philippians 1:21–26

The goal of Christianity is not that you just quit cussing, or you are nicer to people on the street, or that you quit doing this or that. Stopping those behaviors is good, but the goal of Christianity is a love relationship with Jesus. You begin to express back to the Creator the love He has for you. When that happens, this beautiful circle starts turning: I am loved by heaven. I love heaven. I am loved by heaven. I love heaven.

Paul said that for him to live is Christ, but to die is gain. With even greater clarity he said, *I am hard pressed on whether I should stay here with you or go to heaven, because it is far better to be in heaven.* We begin to long for a relationship with Jesus. It is not stuff on the earth that drives us anymore. It is hearing this: "Well done, good and faithful servant." Imagine hearing that in heaven!

This is our core motivation: I am loved by God. Because of that love relationship, I am going to keep His commands. They are the best for me, so I am going to walk them out.

Why am I faithful to my wife? I am faithful to my wife because I love her and because I said I would be faithful to her. But the day that I am only faithful to my wife because I said so, not because I love her, is the day that our marriage has intimacy problems. With God, we have a love relationship. We are faithful to God because we love Him. That is the number one thing—not just because He told us to be faithful but because we love Him. Commitment is best rooted in loving desire, not will power.

My love and commitment are connected. That is Christianity. Let's be caught up in a circle of loving heaven and being loved by heaven. Love Jesus, and live it out. And as we live it out, our love for Jesus grows.

July 7

The Joy of Intimacy with God
James 2:14–18

The joy of living out what we believe is growing intimacy with God as He reveals Himself to us. We will only find intimacy through faith and obedience as we grow closer and discover more in Him. Disobedience to God and intimacy with God are incompatible.

When we keep the commandments because of our love for God, we experience His love for us. And He directs us with every single step because we have experienced and seen His faithfulness over time. This makes us better husbands, better wives, better employees, and better employers. Love driven obedience makes us faithful to Him and others.

It is a beautiful display when the church combines "what we say" and "what we do." Words and actions are meant to go together. A group of sayers and doers went to North Carolina on behalf of our church to help with hurricane relief and to clean up houses. Credibility was high because they were from Houston and had personally experienced the devastation of hurricanes.

While picking up supplies in Home Depot, one of the team ministered to a gentleman who didn't know how to "mud-out" his home. After the missionary shared the basics of a mud-out, he shared the gospel right there in the store aisle.

The team also served thousands of meals to people who had lost so much. It is awesome to watch the body of Christ in action. They prayed for people and people prayed for them. They worshiped God by tearing out sheetrock, prayer, and sharing the good news. That is a say-and-do coming together.

They did not go because they had to or because it was mandatory. There was no governmental draft. They went on their own to say, "I want to be there." Even paid their own way. Two in the group owned houses in Houston that had flooded and could tell the people of North Carolina, "I truly know how you feel."

Do you know the joy of bringing words and actions together to love Christ by helping others? Look for an opportunity today and . . . take it.

WWJD

Matthew 10:40–42

Once in a while there comes our way a nagging question: "How do I live out my Christianity?" The answer is as easy as an old cliché. We just ask ourselves, "What would Jesus do?" or "WWJD?" The Bible says that those who claim to follow Christ should walk as Jesus walked. But how did Jesus walk?

Jesus walked slowly, having time for relationships. How many of us bought our house thinking about the people we were going to invite over? But now, we are so busy that we just pull in, close the garage door, and hope no one knocks. We have a mat that says "Welcome," but we don't mean it. The time has come for us to walk slowly and invite people over. Don't you love it when you see somebody whose first priority is relationships?

Jesus walked toward the needy, not away from them, to help them. Let's walk to the least and the lost. Let's be part of their lives. Let's connect with people. Suburban America is not heaven on earth. There are needy people everywhere we go. Let's be friendly, extend a hand, and say, "We are so glad you are here and so glad you are in our lives."

Jesus walked securely in God's love and His plan. If we begin to walk securely in God's plan, there is going to be a depth in our lives that will bring a sense of connection and completeness. This deep growth will hold us true and strong, moving in God's direction.

In the northern oceans, sailors frequently observe icebergs traveling in one direction, even though the wind is blowing strongly in the other direction. How does that happen? Well, we only see the tip of the iceberg. The deep current of the water is stronger than the wind on the surface. Let your depth guide you, not the windy circumstances of the day.

When we follow the commands of God, when our "say" and "do" get closer and closer, when our love and life connect, when our faith and obedience are working in tandem to help us grow, we become people of depth whom the current of God can take against the winds of this world. The Lord and the intimacy of God determine your direction and give you strength to walk as Jesus walked.

Be Wise
Proverbs 31:1–7

Proverbs 31 is a classic chapter for defining a godly woman. But did you know it has a lot to say to men as well? Let's take a look at a few characteristics of a Proverbs 31 man. Ladies, feel free to listen in on some guy talk.

Proverbs 31:1–7 gives us our first warning, which is to be wise. Those seven verses talk a lot about drinking, which I'm sure made some of you nervous, but what the passage is trying to get across is we need to be wise. Speaking to men in particular, we can trip easily over two things: women and wine. All of us have seen men to their detriment fall for these two.

Men have a propensity to fall for women because they are in need of companionship and are stimulated visually. They begin by looking, and then they are tempted and drawn in. It may be through pornography or through a wrong relationship. The same is true with wine. Wine can symbolize escape. We all deal with a lot of pressure and look for an escape. That can be alcohol or drugs.

The temptations to escape are so predictable, so obvious, that God warns men to be on the lookout for women and wine. For men to maintain their purpose of walking with God, they must be aware of those two areas of temptation.

Consider drinking: the more responsibility you have in your life, the less alcohol needs to be part of it. Proverbs is talking about kings here. Nobody wants to see a pilot at the bar before getting on the plane. Nobody wants to hear a surgeon come in and say, "Hey, we are ready for this heart surgery; I usually have a beer or two just to relax." The more responsibility you have, the less you need to be influenced by alcohol. It can cloud our clarity.

Everyone knows somebody whose life has been wrecked by alcohol. In our homes, our kids and grandkids are watching us. We must model a positive way of living life.

Men, be wise about these two obvious temptations. We have seen it with David and Bathsheba, with Solomon and his wives, with our friends. Do not let pleasure destroy purpose in your life. You will find that if you follow the purposes of God, you will discover the delights in your life to be far more in-depth than anything you could have imagined. Be wise. Read and apply Proverbs in your life. Open up the Bible, read a chapter a day, and use it to lead and guard your life.

Speak Up as Protectors

Proverbs 31:8–9

Speak up for those who have no voice, for the justice of all who are dispossessed" (Prov. 31:8). We must all speak up as protectors.

A man with a protective heart does not dishonor women at all; rather, it honors them. God has wired men to be protectors and warriors for good. By the same token, no one is a better protector than mama bear. Ladies, stand up as well to protect and speak for those without a voice.

We need women and men standing up as protectors and providers. The world is a tough place to lack power, age, or experience. Our voices are needed. Guys, it is time for us to be real men. A man nowadays is portrayed in media not as a hero but a bumbling fool. Consequently, we do not have anyone as a model of what it is really like to be a man. Sadly, some men have moved from protectors to predators. Rest assured, God sees and takes note.

Women, we need you to rise and speak up for those who cannot speak for themselves. Ladies of God who say, "No, this is wrong! This is not how we are going to talk in this house. This is not how we are going to act at work. This is not how we're going to live in our society." We do not have to be obnoxious or rude about it, but we do have to step up. We can shine with Jesus and speak the truth in love.

Are we as Christian men and women raising your voice on behalf of people in need? We all need to stand for those without a voice as protectors.

Better than Jewels
Proverbs 31:10–11

W ho can find a wife of noble character? She is far more precious than jewels. The heart of her husband trusts in her, and he will not lack anything good" (Prov. 31:10–11).

Trust is the foundation of any relationship of any value. If you cannot trust someone, you do not have a relationship. How do we have a relationship with God through Jesus Christ? We place our trust in Jesus as Savior. We trust that He died on the cross. We believe that He is the man He said He was, that He is the Messiah. We trust that the Scriptures are true. We trust that He rose from the grave.

The heart of the husband trusts his wife, and she should trust him. Men should honor women. Do you honor women? Do you daily listen to them? Do you daily respect them? Do you receive their wisdom? Do you speak to them in the right tone? Sometimes, we are harsher with the people we love than a stranger on the street.

Ladies, are you of noble character and trustworthy? The beauty of a godly woman is far greater than clothing and makeup can bring. Noble character is from the heart. The inside shining to the outside, a glow unspeakable. Precious jewels of character mark her life. Seek the attention of the Lord and your character will be chiseled in nobility and your life will be trustworthy to those you love.

King Lemuel, mentioned as the author of Proverbs 31, is very interesting. First, he is not mentioned in any of Israel's history, so he is not an Israeli king. Maybe he is a foreign king. Perhaps Lemuel is Solomon's pen name. The name Lemuel means devoted to God. So, the one who is devoted to God is going to be wise, is going to be a protector, and is going to honor women or be a woman of honor.

Be Respectable
Proverbs 31:23

Respect is earned over years and years. It is gathered in drops and lost in buckets.

A woman who has a good man in her home should not disrespect him and cut his legs out from under him over and over again. In doing so, she is creating something she does not want. She may get her way in the moment, but in the end it will weaken her marriage. Men need respect and encouragement. Women need the same and should be shown it.

To become an individual of honor is to be a person who makes wise decisions. To become a person of respect, you need to fly with eagles, not turkeys. You have to be around the right groups of people. Maybe you did not have a good role model in your family. Find somebody in your church, you can look up to, respect, and imitate. Find someone who is respectable—someone you can be like.

In the days when Proverbs was written, all the business took place at the city gates. Men sat like the legislative branch of the United States government. They decided who got in, who did not, and what laws applied. They were the decision-makers. They made the difference. To be a difference-maker, you have to be a decision-maker. You must step forward in difficult time, make wise decisions, and stick with them. Thankfully, in today's world, ladies are difference-makers and decision-makers too. We need both of us.

Respect requires responsibility. We can't avoid it. And respect comes during difficult times, through sleepless nights, from headaches and how you solve problems. You will not get respect because you just want it. Respect comes from how you respond to responsibility at work, at home, at church, and in life. Do you want to gain respect? Make wise decisions.

With the people you love and work with, are you gaining respect or losing it?

Be an Encourager
Proverbs 31:28

How do you speak an encouraging word? How do you give a kind and clear word of encouragement daily to your spouse, your kids, your friends, your employer, your employees, or the person on the street?

Encouragement is best from people who know you the most, and nobody knows you more than your own family. When you give that word of encouragement, it makes a huge, huge difference. Be an encourager. Write notes. Say positive words daily. Shoot someone you love an encouraging text.

There has never been a woman in a marriage counselor's office who said, "I am so sick of this. He tells me I'm beautiful all the time. He tells me he would marry me all over again. He tells me I'm the greatest thing in the world. I'm precious like jewels to him. I want to be out of this." That never happens. What is usually said to the counselor is: "He doesn't say anything. He just sits in that chair watching TV and I don't know how he feels anymore."

Your spouse, your kids, the people around you, they all need to hear a word of encouragement from you. Being a woman is hard; being a man is hard; being a teenager is hard. Positive words are powerful for everyone. There is never a wrong time to encourage. Sincere and specific encouragement can bring healing and courage to those you love.

> Do not withhold good from those to whom it is due, when it is in your power to act. (Prov. 3:27 NIV)

Let's allow our words of encouragement flow freely today!

The Bookends of Proverbs

Proverbs 1:8

They sit on your shelf humbly holding it all together . . . bookends. Without them, books fall into a mess.

There is also a set of bookends in the book of Proverbs—chapter 1 and chapter 31—each framing the fear of the Lord, which is a theme throughout Proverbs. Chapter 1 talks about what the proverbs intend to do in our lives, "The fear of the LORD is the beginning of knowledge; fools despise wisdom and discipline" (Prov. 1:7), while the last chapter says, "A woman who fears the LORD will be praised" (Prov. 31:30). These concepts of the fear of the Lord and wisdom are the bookends of Proverbs.

If there is something we need in this generation, it is the right knowledge along with the wisdom to apply the fear of the Lord to our lives. Remember, knowledge is just information but fearing God is character. In this era of technology, we have tons of information. But only in God can we find the truth. Knowledge without wisdom is just trivial information in our brains. The only way to apply information wisely is through the fear of the Lord in our lives. The reverent fear of God will lead us not only to do the right thing, but with the right heart.

The foundation of life is the fear of the Lord. You can build a skyscraper, but it is not going to stand unless you have a foundation that goes deep. You can have an awesome, beautiful tree, but if you do not have roots that go deep into the ground, it will fall. You must have a foundation. You must have roots—something that goes deep into your life and gives you stability. That something should be the fear of the Lord—a deep abiding respect for who God is and His plan.

We all have bookends of birth and death. But the wise person chooses the bookend of Proverbs—the fear of the Lord—to hold their lives together.

Seeing God with Awe

Deuteronomy 6:1–3

As we define the fear of the Lord, we have to recalibrate our minds. It means to view God with reverence and awe.

Do you see God with reverent awe? Do you realize that God knows every hair on your head and every star in the sky? He knows everything that you and I are going through both wonderful and woeful. He is grander and larger than the mountains and deeper than the sea. Yet He knows every person who has ever lived and every person who will ever live. We can come before this magnificent, vast God. He knows our names, our hurts, and our fears. He deserves our reverent awe.

Where does that reverence of God begin? As humans we usually think everything starts with us, we know better but we feel like we are the center of the universe. The source of aggravation is traffic. Others can wait, I've got something important to do. We all know trials do happen, but when they happen to us, there is a problem with the world. When your worldview begins with yourself, your happiness, and your joy, God becomes an afterthought. Instead of us existing to serve Him, He exists to bless us, and when we can see the blessing clearly . . . uh oh.

Do you think God is there just to bless you and your plans? How can you show the Lord your reverent awe?

When we live in reverent awe, our lives show it. The materials with which we build are ones of godliness. Our deepest hearts exude our works. Our love for Him offers gold, silver, and costly stones, not frivolous wood and hay. From godly awe, we build awesome lives.

God, the Alpha and Omega

Genesis 1:1–5

Would you like a God who does everything but requires nothing? That is what we have created in our society. Consequently, humans are in the middle, in the center, and God is their servant. The whole thing is about us and what God should do for us. That is the world's view, and Christianity has become a psychological self-help movement with Jesus tagged on at the end. That view does not conceive Christianity as the power of God through the Word of God and through the people of God changing lives for Christ. Instead, humans are the center.

What is the right worldview? God, at the center of it all. He is eternal, the Alpha and Omega. We were created, and He is the Creator. See how Genesis begins: "In the beginning God" (Gen. 1:1). It doesn't say "In the beginning humans." God is the central focus.

When you believe there is no Creator, you will end up thinking you are amazing because you are the center of the universe and the greatest thing that has ever happened. Or wonder if you have any purpose at all. The legacy of the luck of evolution dims to the security of being created by a loving God.

But when we realize that God is the best thing that has ever happened, we have reverence and awe for Him. We can say, "Lord, You are incredible. You love us, and You care for us. The foundation of our life is based on You." This is such good news. It is not self-help. It is not will-power. It is not your intellect or strength. It is God's help, God's power, God's strength, God's will, God's desire.

Do you still think you are the center of life? What can you do to make the Lord the center of the universe—the center of your life? That's where true peace and purpose lie, honoring and serving the Creator as part of His creation.

Fearing God Brings Life

Proverbs 10:27–30

Over the next few days, I want to show you four things in the book of Proverbs—in the middle of the bookends of chapter 1 and chapter 31. These four things will give you an understanding of the amazing things that can happen in your life when you have a proper fear of the Lord.

The first is that real life is found only in the fear of the Lord. Proverbs 10:27 states, "The fear of the LORD prolongs life, but the years of the wicked are cut short." It is a fountain of life that will let you live in such a way that you will sleep satisfied. You will be able to lay your head on your pillow knowing you are a person of integrity. God has everything under control, evil cannot touch you.

Joseph Stalin, the dictator of the Soviet Union from 1929 to 1953, lived in such fear of being assassinated that he had eight bedrooms, all with locks. Each night he would switch rooms to stay concealed. On the move to stay a step ahead. Powerful by day but fearful by night. No peace when his head hit the pillow.

Real life, rest, and peace are found in the fear of the Lord. The Lord who grants abundant and peaceful life, something that is not possible when we are the center of our world. Living well happens when God is at the center of your universe.

Today, walk in reverent awe of the One who deserves it and be blessed. I'm cheering for you!

The Source of Confidence

Proverbs 14:26–27

As we discussed yesterday, the first thing the fear of the Lord does is give you real life and peace. The second is genuine confidence in the Lord. Let's dig into that today. Proverbs says that in the fear of the Lord is strong confidence and that God's children have a refuge. It is better to have a little treasure with the fear of the Lord than to have a great treasure that brings you turmoil. In other words, we are better off broke but honoring God than everything at your fingertips but dishonoring Him.

In Christ, we can have confidence that He is higher and greater than any circumstance we face. Someone who fears the Lord says: "I humbly revere You, Lord. I am Yours. I love You. I revere Your judgment; I revere Your great grace, Your great love, Your great kindness, and Your excellent guidance." This mindset is where we will find true, lasting confidence.

Confidence without Christ is veiled arrogance. Why? Because it is a belief based in yourself, your strength and skill. Deep confidence of the soul not just personality is found in the Lord.

As a pastor, I am comfortable speaking in front of people. I'm often asked, "How do you do that? How do you get up in front of all those people each week?" My confidence does not come from my competence. I often pray, "Lord, I do not want my competence in speaking to come from my personality or my confidence from my experience. I trust You alone."

I've preached for more than thirty years, but I do not rest in my experience, and I do not rest in my competence. My confidence is based on believing God has a word for His people.

It's His message. He has a Bible that far outlasts me and outlasts those who will preach and teach it after I am gone. God's Word has lasted throughout all of history and has been taught throughout the entire world. That is where my confidence comes from. If your confidence is in your skill, personality, or experience, at some point that will not be enough.

Is our confidence based on us or the Lord? How can you increase your trust in the Lord today?

Honest and Skillful Living

Proverbs 8:12–14

We have seen that the fear of the Lord brings real life and confidence. Now let me tell you the next attributes the fear of the Lord brings: holiness and humility. Proverbs declares that the fear of the Lord is to hate evil, pride, and arrogance. That's not just disliking them; it's hating them. Whenever God says He hates something, you need to pay attention. He hates what hinders His glory.

Throughout the book of Proverbs, we find the importance of integrity and honesty . . . no unbalanced scales, no stealing, instead, living in a way that glorifies Him. Holiness is a life denouncing evil and humility is a life of honoring Christ. Both are thematic in Proverbs and stem from heartfelt awe of who God is.

The fourth tenet the fear of the Lord brings is skillful living. Solomon wrote, "The fear of the LORD is the beginning of knowledge; fools despise wisdom and discipline" (Prov. 1:7). A fool despises skillful living.

Knowledge is not necessarily wisdom. Many people have a great deal of knowledge. They know a great deal, but are fools. You can be Mr. Smarty Pants all you want, but if you do not have the knowledge of the Lord and the fear of the Lord, you may be a bigger fool than anyone else. The reverent awe of a faithful believer is far more useful and impactful than a wall of framed degrees. Remember, He is God; we are not.

I am in Christ, and Christ is in me. From that place of holiness and humility, I have confidence. I am experiencing real life. Now wisdom provides skill for living that God is guiding. It's His work. Then from that place of trusting in Him, I can step out to make a difference in other people's lives. Remember, you are not the center; God is. And when God is the center of your life, you will make a difference in the hearts of other people.

Are you living honestly and skillfully? With a heart for holiness and humility? If so, then the fear of the Lord is yielding its wonderful fruit in your life.

Three Kinds of Fools
Proverbs 1:5–7

We can embrace the fear of God, or we can be fools. The Bible says that by despising wisdom and discipline, we are fools. There are three Hebrew words in Proverbs that the writer uses for the word *fool*.

The first word means dull and closed-minded, a thickheaded or stubborn person. That word is used forty-nine times in Proverbs. This kind of fool, says things like, "Watch this . . ." Then usually a trip to the ER follows.

The second word for fool refers to someone who lacks spiritual perception. These fools may know everything in the world but not understand how God is at work. They see the tree, they see the fruit, but they are not able to see the root from which they come. They lack spiritual sight.

The third kind of fool is arrogant and flippant, coarse and hardened in his or her ways. That word is used nineteen times in Proverbs. In Proverbs 1:7, that fool—that arrogant and flippant person—despises wisdom. What does *despise* mean? A definition could be "to disdain, hate, and throw off something," saying, "I do not want any of it." When we despise wisdom, we become fools—arrogant, flippant, and hard-hearted. We say, "In Frank Sinatra style, I am going to do it my way." What happens when you do it your way? You get what your way can produce. For some, that might be remarkable, but it is only going to be remarkable for a short time because you are at the center.

When we say, "Lord, I want to do it Your way," true life, true confidence, true humility, true holiness, and skillful living will come to you. That does not mean that your life will be perfect or easy. It means you have connected with heaven, you have jumped into God's river, His stream, Christ's flow. Instead of swimming upstream, let God take you in His power and His strength. Lift up your feet, keep going, and let God do His work.

Let's live faithful not foolish today!

Walk in Wisdom
1 Thessalonians 3:1–5

The last chapter of Proverbs says a woman who fears the Lord will be praised. If we fear the Lord, we are praising Him, and we are cultivating a life of praise. We are also cultivating a life of wisdom.

A skillful life lived in wisdom is our desire. Thankfully, Christ became God-given wisdom for us. His is the treasure trove of all the wisdom and knowledge. Consequently, when we embrace Jesus, we are embracing wisdom to lead us through the thorny paths of life.

In his letter to the Thessalonians, the apostle Paul tells the church that he sent Timothy to encourage them so they would not be shaken by the trials they were bound to face. Paul was afraid the enemy had gotten the best of them, but since their foundation was Christ, he also declared that the enemy had no place there. God knows what you are going through, just as He knew what the Thessalonians would face. God knows what is happening in your life. He knows we need wisdom to walk strongly.

What should we do, then, when trials come? We go to the Lord in prayer to find His wisdom in our difficult times. Everything is resolved in prayer. What will hold your life together is time on your knees before God. In poverty or wealth, sickness or health, you must say, "Jesus, I've got a very short time on this planet, and I want to live skillfully in wisdom. I want to pray so I can live with a reverent awe of You."

Here's the equation: Fear the Lord so you can praise . . . As you praise Him, seeds of wisdom will blossom . . . So you can navigate your trials through prayer.

Step by step we wisely journey.

How Did We Get Here?
Proverbs 5:1–2

It's July, it's hot outside and you may have a tendency to slack on spending time with God. To make sure you continue to "Capture the Moment" in this devotional guide we are going to discuss a subject for the next several days that I bet will get your attention . . . God's plan for sex. Whoa, not your typical daily devotional topic, but God has a lot to say and our culture is really confused. Proverbs 5 offers a lengthy discussion of sexual temptation personified and symbolized in an immoral woman.

First off, when we talk about sex, I want you to know that Jesus Christ can forgive us of any mistakes we have made. If you are struggling with temptation or guilt, I want you to know His grace and love extends to this topic as much as any other. So put your sin and guilt at the cross and walk away.

A good question to ask is: How did we get here? Have you noticed that in the last fifty to sixty years, things have turned upside down? Before the '60s, talking about sex in church would have been a scandal. The right order is marriage, sex, family. Before the '60s we were scared to have sex because you might have to get married or bring shame upon your family. What happened that made a significant change? Birth control.

Birth control accomplished something never before done—it separated sex from pregnancy and marriage. You could have sex, without risk of becoming pregnant. Also our society began to urbanize, instead of growing up in small towns where everybody knew you, people started moving to cities where nobody knew them. Our anonymity was now greater than our accountability.

Then, in the '70s, no-fault divorce. It made marriage a simple contract instead of a covenant. Fatherless homes began to grow at a rapid rate. In the '90s, internet pornography. The web made pornography accessible, affordable, and addictive, which has led to the rise of rape, sex trafficking, sexual abuse, and more.

In 2015, same-sex marriage became legal; marriage was separated from exclusively between a male and a female. We have taken the biology out of it. Now many people wonder is there even such a thing as a male and a female. I could list a thousand other things, but this is basically how we got where we are today.

Prayerfully ponder and seek God for your personal purity today and run from sin.

Run!
Proverbs 5:3–6

In yesterday's devotional, we had a quick review of how we got where we are today in our ideas about sex. Now, think about this. Does God have something to say about it? What is the right thing to do now? What is the truth?

Sex is everywhere. It comes to us a million miles per hour all day long. Advertisers use sex to sell products, even ones that have nothing to do with sex or being sexy! In Proverbs 5, King Solomon said that an immoral woman's lips drip with honey. Though her lips are smoother than oil, they are poison. Her mouth is a double-edged sword. She is headed straight to the grave. She does not even know that her life is crooked and going in the wrong direction.

We must realize that a short-term gain brings long-term pain. Unfortunately, I have been in conversations with folks who have committed adultery. The tears and the sobs are not worth the pleasure that lasted for a brief time. There is not an adulterer I've talked to who would tell you it was worth it; the pain afterward was just too deep.

That sums up Solomon's advice: "So now, sons, listen to me. . . . Keep your way far from her. Don't go near the door of her house" (Prov. 5:7–8). We are called to flee temptation. When you see sexual temptation in the Scriptures, you will always see God's people fleeing from it—taking off, running away, and getting away from it.

Today, do not scroll down to see that picture. Do not click to do a little investigation to see what the story is about. Do not answer the tempting phone call. Do not respond to that text message. We have to flee those temptations.

Married couples, listen, it is better to be thought rude than interested. Our defense begins with not allowing ourselves to be involved in situations that could make us fall. Run to Jesus and don't look back! You will be glad you did.

The Billy Graham Rule

Proverbs 5:7–8

Billy Graham, the famous evangelist, had a rule in order to avoid sexual temptation. It was this: never be in a situation with a woman by yourself.

That does a couple of things. First, it keeps us free of accusations. In today's world your life can be wrecked by just an accusation. Second, it keeps us free from temptation.

I know some of you have to travel for business, and you have to meet with people of the opposite sex. But let me encourage you to do everything you can to not be in a situation where you are alone with another person who is not your spouse. Men, a woman in heels at the office may look better than your wife with a scrunchie in her hair and a kid on each hip. But don't go there. Ladies, the kind words and smile of a man at the office may shine brighter than your hubby at home. But stay clear. The temptation grows as you ponder what-ifs. Run.

If we keep the Billy Graham rule, we will not have a problem because we will have accountability built in. As I said yesterday, it is better to be considered rude than interested.

As we are fleeing sexual temptation, it is also very important to know our weaknesses. We may need to use filters on your computer and your phone. Put your computer in a public place. Parents, keep the electronics out of the kid's bedroom. Also we should have access to every password, every app, everything. Just because our children get a phone does not mean they need an internet browser on it. They can talk and text all day long. Handing our kids that kind of technology is like handing them an encyclopedia with a *Playboy* magazine in the middle and then saying, "Do not read what is in the middle." Remember, you are paying the cell phone, it's actually your phone. So, in a kind caring way, protect your kids.

Do you have a godly strategy with your kids' screens and your screens?

Planning for temptation is one of the best lines of defense. Walk wisely with God today in this dangerous world. Ask, "What would Jesus do and . . . what would Billy Graham do?"

Self-Control Is Your Friend

Proverbs 5:9–18

When we talk about fleeing temptation, the most important and crucial element is the fruit of the Spirit. Galatians 5 describes it as love, joy, peace, patience, kindness, goodness, gentleness, faithfulness, and self-control. How do you battle sexual temptations? Fall in love with Jesus and let self-control, a fruit of the Spirit, flourish in your life. It's not about trying harder; it's about loving deeper. It is important to have great filters and accountability. At the same time, you should not miss the spiritual part of loving God and being satisfied with who Jesus is and what He can do.

Remember, there is a defense and offense regarding God's plan for sex. Why is a good defense so important? Because the price of being careless is higher than your life can afford. It is more than you want to pay. We have to be on the defense because temptation is everywhere. Proverbs is both scary and encouraging, defensive and offensive.

Now, let's talk about the offense. Let's make some baskets and score some points, not just play defense our whole life. How do we move forward in the offense? When Solomon talks about drinking water from our own cistern, from our own well, and that our stream should not flow into the streets, he is talking about the satisfaction of sex we must find only in our marriage. Remember, our greatest defense is our offense. Married folks, you have everything you need in your home with your spouse. There is no need to spill the fountain of your pleasure on the streets or the public squares. You do not have to share it with strangers. Enjoying the love of your spouse is your best counterattack against the enemy.

Do you know that those who are happily married are 61 percent less likely to look at porn? That does not mean you are not going to struggle in your marriage, but it does mean that in a satisfied relationship, there is great protection from the adversary.

Singles, don't worry. God has you in His hand too. He can grant you the self-control to wait. His love is enough.

Are you manifesting the fruit of the Spirit in your life? How is your self-control on a scale of 1 to 10? Are you enjoying the love of your spouse? Are you falling deeper in love with Jesus?

True Pleasure
Proverbs 5:15–16

Regarding sex, most likely whatever you have seen on TV, heard in a song, or seen in a movie has all been wrong. If it had been right, it would not have been done in front of anyone else. That is what is called privacy. Remember, your streams should not overflow in the streets. I want to give you an equation for real pleasure: Privacy + Purity = Pleasure.

Television industry statistics state that since 1998, sex scenes have nearly doubled, and 70 percent of television programming now includes some sexual content. Ninety-two percent of the top ten songs are about sex. If you have heard it, if you have seen it . . . you have seen it wrong. That is not how God wanted it to be. Why? Because true pleasure comes from privacy and purity in marriage. Not that we can't discuss it or learn, but intimacy is not for display.

Today, many believe that pleasure is when you remove privacy and purity and do whatever, whenever you want. Sex is more than physical, and it is more than virtual. It was intended to be spiritual, soulful, and safe.

Parents, we should talk about sex with our children, early and often. Our kids are going to figure out the biology of it, no doubt about that. However, they need to understand the theology and the emotional aspect of sex. The birds and bees also need to include the soul and heart.

It is important to understand men and women have different sexual needs and responses. Women must cross an emotional bridge first, and then they can pass to the physical part. Men usually cross a physical bridge first, and then they are ready to cross to the emotional part. It does not mean that women are not physical and men are not emotional. Their differences are just the way God made men and women and then He put them together to create a balance. Sex is more than physical activity; it is an interaction that is soulful and spiritual with the person you have committed your life to in marriage.

Remember the math today: Privacy + Purity = Pleasure

Safe Sex
Proverbs 5:17

A high school health class will discuss safe sex. But it is more than just prevention from some disease or an unplanned pregnancy. God has something higher, deeper, and better in mind.

A possible journey would be when a guy takes a girl out on a date and treats her well because he considers her valuable to God and her family. As time passes, he takes her on date after date. He can't get her off his mind and she thinks of him constantly as well, until finally he has saved up enough money to buy her a ring. After asking her father for her hand, he gets down on one knee and humbly says, "I am willing to protect you and provide for you. I am willing to give my life for you. Will you marry me?" If she says yes, he puts the ring on her finger! Then they celebrate with both of their families, pick out dishes, and plan the wedding.

Later, they are married before God, their families, and all their friends. Then it can truly be safe sex. Eventually, they may become parents. They will be together through thick and thin, and the expression of their love will be a physical blessing of God. The two will experience great pleasure, intimate privacy, and high purity for decades. Sounds too good to be true. Of course there will be some bumps in the road. But following the Lord is always best.

Let me quickly type the word GRACE! It's possible to honor God, even if you lost your virginity or purity before marriage, were into pornography, or were abused. God can redeem and heal. Your past won't change but your future will!

If you practice safe sex—God's way—you will be in this safe sex zone with your spouse. Embraced and cared for, not taken advantage of.

Sex according to God's plan is truly safe. Safe for the heart. Safe for the soul. Safe for the body. Safe for the emotions. Safe for our self-esteem and self-respect. Safe for joy instead of guilt. It's safe to follow the Lord.

A Loving Deer and a Pleasant Dove

Proverbs 5:18–19

We have talked about enjoying our sexuality in the safety of a marriage based on love—a place where truly safe sex can happen. King Solomon said that our fountain should be blessed and that we should take pleasure in the wife of our youth. Sex is intended to be intimacy without insecurity. That is our best offense.

Proverbs refers to the woman as a loving deer and a pleasant dove. How do you approach a deer? You do not chase a deer yelling, "Hey! Get over here." If you do that, it is going to run! A woman should run too, if someone approaches abruptly. You must approach a deer gently and kindly. Men, women are looking for more romance in their marriage than most husbands are giving them. They are looking for more kindness and gentleness. It is not just a physical thing. It is caring. It is pursuing. Sometimes in our marriages, romance gives way to the mundane.

However, as wives are looking for more romance, most likely husbands are looking for more sexual frequency. When both romance and frequency increase, good things begin to happen in a marriage. You can love one another and care for one another instead of taking advantage of one another. Then you can come together to express your love and find satisfaction.

If you are struggling, ask the Lord for His blessing, praying, "God, we want to walk in our marriage with greater romance, greater frequency. We want to be satisfied in one another." God created sex and He has a plan. If you think that God's plan is wrong and the world's plan is right, look at the results. The world is in chaos and confusion. However, there is forgiveness, faithfulness, and fulfillment in Jesus Christ. God can take your pain and brokenness and restore the years the locusts have eaten.

I am not just calling you to get better filters on your computer. I am inviting you to come to Christ, let the forgiveness of Jesus wash over you, and let Jesus be the strength in your life and your guide in loving your spouse. God has more for all of us if we seek Him.

Let's Build a Firepit
Proverbs 6:27–29

Timothy Ateek at Breakaway Ministries uses this illustration: let's compare sex to a fire that heats and burns. If you go to the internet looking for that fire, you will get an image that you will see, and you will even hear the crackle. But if you tried to get warmth from a screen, that would be crazy, right? The screen is not going to warm you. Pornography is just like that. There is no heat, no intimacy, and no warmth. Visual fire, yes. Warmth, no.

What is God's idea? The Lord wants to put that fire within the right parameters and in the right spot. He takes the firepit of marriage and puts sex there, where it is contained. Then you, as a married person, can say, "I am going to put some logs on the fire" and work on our romance, frequency, and intimacy to make things burn again. Sex is contained in marriage, in the firepit. There is a flame there that we can stoke. We can care for it, and we can help keep this love burning. And knowing the fire is lit and burning, you can walk from this firepit into the world and find strength to face temptation because you are coming from a place of satisfaction. You are full instead of empty when facing temptations.

That does not mean our marriages are perfect. It does mean that we can walk in need but also in fulfillment. Instead of walking in lust, we can walk in a place of love and care. We are in a world that is in chaos, but we have a great defense and a great offense. Let's teach those things to our children and live them out in our own lives.

Are you containing and feeding your fire in the proper place? Don't go to a false fire on a screen. You will never find true warmth. Go to the real deal firepit of God's plan. The proper place of marriage gives security to the soul and intimacy of the heart.

For those of you who are single, don't be discouraged. Trust the Lord that in your stage of life He can still care for your heart.

Ponder how the last several days of discussing God's plan for sex has reframed what the world has hijacked. How has God spoken to you over these days?

The Goal of Parenting
Proverbs 23:15–16

We are shifting gears to a new subject for a few days—parenting. Now don't tune out if you don't have kids. Instead, file this away to use later or share with a friend.

As we look at parenting, the first thing we are going to do is throw off parenting guilt and parenting stress! Instead let's calmly hear what the Lord wants to tell us and how He wants to shape our lives.

Thinking about the influence parents have on their children, I decided to do a little research with my own family. As we sat around the dining room table, I said, "I want you all to tell me something I say you will remember when you leave home."

You can imagine in a pastor's home I have some phrases that we often repeat, like "Be a leader for good, be a leader for God." I also say this: "It is not how you react when you do not get anything but how you react when you do not get everything." Or my classic encouragement, "Your heavenly Father loves you, and so do I."

Comically, the reply was, "Do not use all the hot water." UGH! That's it? I know they will remember the deeper ones as well, but I had to chuckle at their reply. There are so many things we are trying to get across as parents, it can get messy and lost in translation.

Let me ask you a clarifying question: What is our main goal as parents?

King Solomon teaches us that our parenting goal is character, not accomplishment, or in my case, hot water management. It is not about what our kids do; it is about who they are. Our relationship with Christ is the same. It is not about what we do for God; it is about who we are with God and our relationship with Him.

So, we parent for character, not accomplishment. It is not about how many home runs they hit or how many A's they get. It's about godly character. The most important thing is who they are in Christ. Use all the hot water but walk with God!

What are we focused on, character or accomplishment?

Do Not Burn Out Your Kids

Proverbs 10:1

Why is our kids' character the most important goal as parents? Because it will take our kids into marriage and into life better prepared. It will also serve them better than accomplishments. I'm probably going to step on some toes with this one. But trust my heart and be wise enough to ponder your path.

Today, an accomplishment that is battling for character is specialized skills. We want our kid to be the greatest cheerleader, baseball player, football player, soccer player, or band member. There is a coach, trainer, or teacher for everything. Unfortunately, the specialized skills training begins to steal them away from family and church. Life gets so hectic and busy.

Many parents are so busy running their kids to activities that the dinner table is empty and the drive-thru is full. Supper from a sack instead of conversation at a meal. Everyone else is raising our kids instead of us. Remember, the goal is character, not accomplishment.

Time magazine's cover article in September 2017 was this: "Crazy Travel. Crazy Costs. Crazy Stress. How Kid Sports Turned Pro." The article stated that kids' sports are now a $15 billion industry. I have a friend who is a trainer. He trains Major League Baseball players and National Football League athletes. He trains at the highest levels. I asked him his thoughts on kids' sports today. His response was chilling, "For every Tiger Woods, there are a million kids who hate their dad and a half a million kids who hate the sport."

Parents, instead of pushing your kid to be a professional athlete, you may be better off just going with your kid to watch a game, buying a couple hot dogs, and just spending time together. Have fun with your kids' activities and sports. But do not miss church, meals at the table, and conversations. The time you have them in your home is short. Savor every bit of it.

Am I against sports and activities? Absolutely not. I've coached every team my kids have played on. Am I for character building and family time? Absolutely, yes! Be careful, your kids will be gone before you know it. Use the time wisely.

4 Quarters or 100 Pennies

1 Corinthians 15:33–34

There are many traits parents can use to teach their children in order to develop their character. I will list four over the next four days. Truly, these are traits for all of us to practice.

Trait One: Surround yourself with the right people.

Do not underestimate the power of peers, both as adults and kids. Peer pressure is real at fifteen and forty-five. Our God-given desire for community can morph into a dysfunctional need. The result is often running with the wrong crowd. Therefore, we all need to be careful. Parents in particular need to steer our precious kiddos to the right friends. Talking with our kids about the type of friends they should hang out with is crucial.

Of course, we should have friends of all levels of commitment to Christ. But our close friends, our buddies, are best to share the same heart for God. Lots of kids to hang with in the lunchroom but our kids need to choose their Friday night friends carefully, and so do we. Lots more trouble to be had at 11:30 p.m. on Friday night than 11:30 a.m. in the lunchroom. Iron sharpening iron in the best way. Church is a great place to start for your kids finding like-minded friends and fun.

Also, kids with godly friends become tuned in to looking for a godly spouse. That's an entirely different level of importance. Friends are often for a season but a spouse is for a lifetime. Helping our kids realize the importance of the right crew translates into the right companion.

Pray for your kids, pray for a godly wife or husband for them. Set their minds toward what they are looking for in a spouse. It is not about beauty; it is about godliness. Pray not only for your kids but also for their spouse to be, that is somewhere out there.

Teach them the way to choose friends. Put them in the right circle of peers so they will have the right people in their lives. One of my friend's mothers would say "Remember, four quarters is better than 100 pennies when it comes to friends."

Trait one: Surround yourselves with the right people. This is important for all of us and for our kids. How can you put this into action today for you and your family?

Teaching Children Respect
Ephesians 6:1–4

Trait One: Surround yourselves with the right people.
Trait Two: Walk in respect and humility.

Honor your father and your mother" is the fifth commandment, but it is the first commandment that includes a blessing—"so that you may have a long life" (Exod. 20:12). So honoring and respecting Mom and Dad is the key. It is crucial. Disobedience and disrespect receive punishment. While respect and humility receive blessing. Children should respect their parents. They should respect their elders. Also, their teachers, coaches, leaders, police officers . . . can I get an amen? Let me give you a few phrases that will open more doors for our kids (and us as well) than anything else: "Yes, ma'am," "please," and "thank you." If we do not teach proper respect and humility, our children will be ungrateful and greedy. Those qualities don't need to be taught. Like weeds they will just grow.

One thing needed today is teaching our sons to respect women, and it begins with how they treat Mom and Sis. Straight up, "You are not going to talk to your mom like that," "You are not going to treat your sister like that," "You are not going to treat your friend like that," "You are a man of God, who respects and honors women."

Let me give you a thought on humility. We, as parents, need to realize that our kid is not the center of the world. The Duke of Wellington once said this: "The thing that impresses me most about America is the way parents obey their children."[31] Did you catch who is obeying who?

We don't have to do everything for them. It is okay if they get a job and learn to work for the things they want or to make it through college. We should not be running all over to keep them satisfied and then feel parental guilt if we do not give them everything. They should not be the center of our world because they aren't the center of the world. We need to prepare them for reality.

Of course, bless and love them GREATLY, but prepare them for reality by teaching respect and humility.

Celebrating the Highest Things

Proverbs 23:24–25

Trait One: Surround yourselves with the right people.

Trait Two: Walk in respect and humility.

Trait Three: Celebrate the highest things.

King Solomon said the father of a righteous child has great joy, and a man who fathers a wise son rejoices in him. What is the father rejoicing over? His child is walking with God. The highest thing to celebrate as a parent is our kids love for Christ. Better than an award or accomplishment is a love for Jesus in our kids. Parents, we need to cheer for that!

Let your kids know how pleased you are when they love God. They are tuned in to what they sense will please us, and they want to please us. If a girl senses that her mom is proud of her because she is pretty—she gets the right clothes—she is going the beauty route. However, if she realizes that what pleases her mom's heart is that she has a relationship with Christ, then she will focus on that.

Therefore, encourage your children when they are kind. Encourage them when you see godliness coming out in them. Encourage your children to pray and pray with them—not just for them. Discuss God's work at home. When you get to your table, tell them, "You will not believe what God did today," or "Let me tell you about a verse I read today." Make that a point of conversation.

Joshua put it like this: "But as for me and my household, we will serve the LORD" (Josh. 24:15 NIV). Jesus said, "Seek first his kingdom and his righteousness, and all these things will be given to you as well" (Matt. 6:33 NIV).

Your kids could be on lots of teams and in many activities, but when anything starts to mess with your family time, you need to be very careful. I know it is tough but do not sign up for activities that have a Sunday morning attached to it. Model the priority of Christ and His church. If not, your kids get mixed signals of your family's priorities. Clearly, faithfully, joyfully, consistently . . . celebrate the highest things.

Do your kids know that loving the Lord is more important than anything?

Safe Places for Your Kids

Proverbs 23:26

Trait One: Surround yourselves with the right people.
Trait Two: Walk in respect and humility.
Trait Three: Celebrate the highest things.
Trait Four: Handle hearts carefully.

Handling hearts carefully starts when they are little. It starts with reading good bedtime stories. When they get older, it becomes, "Hey! Let's go get a Starbucks together." "Let's get ice cream together." "Let's go on a trip together." Learn to be together and create safe places for them. Handle their hearts carefully. Harsh discipline or a continual lecture doesn't help anything and is actually wounding. Parents, we have to watch our tone and frustration. Yes, there is a need for correction but it best comes through conversation. I've heard it said, "Rules without relationship leads to rebellion."

We must also set a godly example for them. How are we handling the hearts of others? We are not to be travel agent parents who say, "Go live in that land of righteousness, but I will stay right here." We are to be leaders, walking out our righteousness so they can look at us and see what it looks like to be a godly man or a godly woman.

Show your kids how faith and life merge. Is anybody perfect? No. Throw off parenting guilt right now. Throw off parenting pressure and realize that you are not going to be perfect. Nobody is perfect. That gives our kids a reason to need Jesus. Point them to Jesus, and they will see the need to go to Him for an example of perfection. They will see how He carefully handles hearts and in turn they will seek to do the same.

Let your kids catch you praying and reading the Scriptures. Let them see your kindness, your desire to listen, let them see you care. Take a look at your own walk with God. Do you let God "handle hearts" through you in ministering to others?

Handle their hearts carefully, so they will feel safe turning to you and care for others well too.

Crazy Love
2 Corinthians 5:13

True love can make you feel crazy. It can make you do crazy things. Think about the first crush you had on someone. Think about when you first started dating someone. Everything you saw made you think of that person. You were writing poems and drawing hearts on every piece of paper you could find. Did you find yourself acting in ways that were unfamiliar to you? That is what love can do. It can change you; it can make you feel crazy.

That does not mean that the love of God will make you do something illegal or wrong. On the contrary, it makes you act in a good, positive, life-giving way, in a way that for some people might seem crazy. We do things like read a book written thousands of years ago or "talk to the ceiling" when we pray. The love of God causes us to have faith that things will get better even when there seems to be no way out of a bad situation. It means living by faith in God and all His promises. It means believing by faith the blood of Jesus makes us clean as snow and we will have eternal life. It might seem crazy to some, but that is what the crazy, wonderful, and true love of God does in us.

We have received an even more mind-blowing kind of love from God: He sent His only Son to die for us. He is with us every day and indwells us by the Holy Spirit. He made us in His image and has given us all we need as a gift of grace. We find endless demonstrations of the outstanding love of God for us in the Bible. And we are constantly finding evidence of His love for us in our daily lives. Only someone who is head over heels in love would leave ninety-nine sheep alone to go find the one that was lost. That is what God did for us. Jesus is so in love with each one of us that He would do anything to be with us, even die on a cross.

When we know and receive the outrageous love of God in our lives, we start living out that love ourselves. As the love of God infiltrates our lives, our actions at times will not seem logical to others. His love compels us to do things that are no longer about us but about others. And it makes us live a little bit crazy for God and His kingdom.

Compelling Love
2 Corinthians 5:14

The love of God in us is a force that moves us into action. It is not passive, but active. The love of God pushes us out of ourselves. It motivates us to do things—it compels us to powerfully urge someone to follow God's commands, to convince someone Jesus is true, to woo someone to be interested in the love of God.

The love of God compels us to live our lives outside of ourselves. It compels us to live crazy lives for Him, like the apostle Paul did. Once he met God and experienced His love, Paul's whole life changed: from persecutor to preacher. The love of God compelled Paul to live a crazy life—a life that was no longer self-focused but about God's kingdom and God's people. Paul was moved into action.

When someone does something great for us, we feel compelled to be grateful. We do good things out of gratitude for that person and for what they did for us. When Jesus died for us on the cross, it was the greatest act of love anyone could ever do—to lay down their life for someone else. Knowing that He died out of love for us, to save us, should automatically make us live our lives in eternal gratitude. That is the kind of love that compels us. It is the love that compelled Paul to live a crazy life for God.

Paul truly experienced the love of God in His life. Once we experience that same love, it is impossible to keep it to ourselves. The true love of God, experienced, transforms into the love of God, expressed. It is a love that is too wonderful to keep to ourselves. We have such good news to share that we have a burning desire to share it. The love of God is so great, so different than what we are used to in this chaotic world, that we feel compelled to share it with others.

Would you keep quiet if you knew the secret to making the world a better place? Would you keep quiet if you knew a way to make the lives of everyone around you better? Why would you keep quiet when you know the love of God for all humanity?

My prayer for you today is that the love of God compels you into action. My prayer for you is that you can share the great news of God's crazy love with everyone who crosses your path.

Know God
Psalm 46:10

Martin Luther once wrote, "Learn to know Christ and Him crucified. Learn to sing to Him, and say: Lord Jesus, You are my righteousness, I am Your sin. You have taken upon Yourself what is mine and given me what is Yours. You have become what You were not so that I might become what I was not."[32]

The most important thing in Christianity is to know God. We cannot grow in relationship with someone we do not know. We cannot trust deeply in someone we do not know. We cannot find joy in the love of a person we do not know. For us to grow, trust, and find joy in God and His love for us, we must first desire to know Him.

Knowing God can be a feeling and an understanding. We come to know God through His Word, through attending church, and through growing in our relationship with Him. As it is with any human-to-human relationship, so it is with our relationship with God. The more time we spend with Him—praying, praising Him, worshiping Him, reading the Bible—the more we get to know who He is.

The entire purpose of the Bible is to help us know God. The Bible reveals who God is. It reveals His character and His plan for humankind. It is through knowing God that we can receive His love.

Imagine being in a relationship with someone you know nothing about. Could you trust that person or receive that person's love and affection? Consider how you would feel with no clue of where they are from, their name, their likes and dislikes, or what makes them happy or sad. That is not a good way to grow in a relationship. Our relationship with God is the same. An ambiguous force in the heavens is not a joy giver. Thankfully, we have a personal, loving, interested Savior named Jesus!

When we know God, when we seek Him, He reveals Himself and His promises to us. The more we get to know Him, the more we understand Him and discover His perfect love for us and the plans He has for our lives.

Trust in God
Proverbs 3:5–6

To trust someone is to become vulnerable. When we trust someone—a friend, a parent, a sibling, a spouse—we give that person control over a certain area or situation in our lives. When you trust your best friend with a secret, you are giving them control over it. You trust that they will not say anything, but you cannot control them. All you can do is hope that they will not betray that trust. You decide to trust them because you know them deeply enough to trust.

We cannot trust someone we do not know. We cannot trust in something we know nothing about.

The Bible is our source of information about God and His love for us. It is through reading the Bible and having a real relationship with God that we can get to know Him. His love for us compels us to trust Him.

However, there is no way to deeply trust Him without growing in our knowledge of Him. Not just Bible story knowledge but life experience of walking with Him. Through the years I've gotten to know my Lord through the blessing of worship with the right song on my headphones, through times on my knees when life was harder than I ever thought it could be, through times a miracle was so obvious, and through times I wondered if God existed at all.

Faithfulness through the highs and lows are how we get to truly know Him.

What Is Really Important

Psalm 37:4

What is important to us right now might not be important in eternity. In truth, what is important to us today might not even be important to us . . . next month. Sometimes we focus on things that seem like a huge deal at the moment, but later we realize we could have used our time differently and more efficiently if we had shifted our focus to something else. Or if you are like me, we look back wondering why we wasted all that worry on something so small.

When my grandfather was alive, he was devoted to taking care of his front yard. He would spend countless hours every day caring for his plants, the grass, the hedges, and the soil. He worried about the weather and weeds, pine cones and pollen. I loved his passion for his garden. Every visit I would be taken on a tour with every vegetable or change to the yard pointed out. It was a great hobby and kept him busy in retirement.

He and my grandmother are in heaven and the house has been sold (to people that obviously don't enjoy working in the yard). The plants died, the hedges have overgrown and once I saw a car park on the grass. YOW! That definitely would have gotten you written out of the will. But the truth is that what was important to my grandfather is not important to the new owners. That's the way it goes.

But what if we live a life missing what's important to God? That's a complete miss, not just a difference of preference.

Sometimes we get wrapped up in what seems important to us—running errands, cleaning the house, working 24/7, being right all the time—and miss what is really important to God. We miss making a difference in someone else's life. We miss prayer and worship. We miss times in the Word. We miss special moments with family. We miss what really matters.

How can you focus on what's really important today?

Be a Difference-Maker
Matthew 23:11–12

Many of us cope with life instead of being compelled into life. Coping turns us inward, making everything about us and what happens to us. When we are compelled by the love of God, we look outside of ourselves and serve others, making a difference in their lives.

People love difference-makers. When Michael Jordan was playing basketball, he changed the game. He was a difference-maker. Steve Jobs changed cell phones forever; he was a difference-maker. Martin Luther King Jr. was a difference-maker, as he recalibrated thoughts about the value of all people. Mother Teresa was a difference-maker in her love for the poor and in her life of sacrifice.

As believers, we have the love of God, which makes us different from the rest of the world. We have a light shining inside of us that makes us stand apart. We have that compelling love that forces us to be different and make a difference wherever we are. As believers, we are called to be difference-makers.

Jesus was the greatest difference-maker of all time. He taught us that love conquers all and that grace triumphs over judgment and sin. He taught us that the greatest person is the servant, and that the proud will be humbled. He did everything out of love for us. His love is a compelling, everlasting, irrevocable, faithful, and steadfast love.

We find many difference-makers in the Bible. Think of Daniel and his friends in the time of King Nebuchadnezzar. Think of the apostle Paul and everything he did to change the course of history for believers everywhere. Think of Moses, Elijah, Queen Esther, and countless other people in the Bible who made a difference forever.

Let's be difference-makers through our humility and serving others, allowing the compelling love of God to surge through our outreach. May we find ourselves living a life greater than ourselves, serving from a humble heart. May the love of God shine through us like never before! May we live a life of humbly serving others with the same love you received from God.

God Loves Us to Death
Hebrews 2:9

Christ loves us so much that He laid down His life for us. He literally loved us to death! He died so we could have eternal life and live with Him forever in heaven. Think about it: He loves us with a love so deep that He not only gave His life for us, but He wants to spend eternity with us.

Every step Jesus took to the cross on Calvary meant "I love you" to each and every one of us. His love was intentional. It was there since the beginning of time; it was not something that grew with time. His love was always white-hot and meant for us.

Have you ever done something bold for the person you love? Jesus did the boldest thing ever. He changed the course of history for you and for me. He gave up His life for love. He went through a lot of suffering for us. He was beaten, humiliated, denied, and abandoned because He loved us with an irrevocable, steadfast, everlasting, and compelling love.

His love for each of us is personal. He has our names written on the palms of His hands. He does not love us because we are great people or because we do so many great deeds. He loves us because He is love. He loves us because He made us to love Him. His love does not decrease or increase when we do something wrong or when we do something right. It is always there, given to us without reservation and without limits. We will never be able to pay for the love of God; we can never do anything to earn it or deserve it.

He loves us so much that He paid our debt on the cross. And He does not require repayment or charge us interest. All He asks of us in return is to love Him back. And His love is so amazing that even when we choose not to love Him back, He still loves us the same.

My prayer for you today is that you will feel loved by God in a way you have never felt before. May you feel compelled to love others with that same love—a love that does not require anything in return, a love to be enjoyed and given away as a precious gift.

God's Plan vs. Our Plan
Luke 15:11–13

Luke 15 tells the story of 100 sheep and one that gets lost. The Bible goes on to talk about ten coins and one that was lost. A little bit further into the chapter, we read about two sons, and one of them gets lost for a while. This chapter in the Bible shows God getting more personal as He talks about His love for us.

For the next few days, we're going to go deep into the story of the prodigal son. A young man who spends his father's money in a reckless, extravagant way and later makes a repentant return. If we think about the prodigal son, a number of words may come to mind: disrespect, impatience, lust, deception, unfaithfulness, selfishness, carelessness, and recklessness. We see someone whose selfish vision led to a sinking life.

The prodigal son had a thought that most of us have had as well: my plan is better than my father's plan. Sons and daughters may think this about their parents, and all of us can think it about God. My plan is better than my Father's plan.

We may someday face a fork in the road of our lives where we have to decide if God's plan is better than our plan. We can see ourselves standing there at the fork, wondering which way to go. Are we going to follow God's perfect plan for our lives, or are we going to follow our own plan and ask God to just bless it?

C. S. Lewis said, "We are not necessarily doubting that God will do the best for us: we are wondering how painful the best will turn out to be."[33] Maybe the prodigal son's plan was an attempt at more fun or to relax from the chores of home. Or he was looking for someone more jovial than his big brother. Regardless, he hit the road intentionally leaving his dad.

We always know in our hearts that God's plan is better, yet somehow, we do not always want to do things God's way. Sometimes we just want to do what we want to do and hope that God is not paying attention at the time.

Take it to the bank: God always has a better plan for our lives. May we finally come to the realization that His plans are always superior to our plans.

The Grass Is Greener
Luke 15:14–19

The prodigal son chose his own plan instead of choosing his father's plan for his life. His older brother, in contrast, followed his father's plan to work and take care of things at home. Maybe the prodigal son gave in to the oldest temptation in the book . . . the grass was greener somewhere else, outside his father's plan.

We can all look at somebody else's life and think, "I wish I had their car. I wish I had their house. I wish I had their life. I wish I had their job. I wish I had their spouse. I wish I had their gifts. The grass is greener over there." This is such a mistake.

We often think the grass is greener on the other side. Maybe the prodigal son thought, *Look at all this stuff I have with my father, but if I were to go to a distant country* . . . But that distant country is a mirage. It is a mirage of thinking, *If I only had that job. If I only looked like that. If I only had that notoriety, that fame. If I only had that kind of money. If I had all of those things, I would finally be satisfied.* Remember even greener grass still has to be mowed. Our view of a better life isn't always better.

John D. Rockefeller was once asked how much money it takes to make a person happy. He said, "A dollar more."[34] We do not realize that life is life, that things may get hard sometimes, and that truly the grass is not greener in some distant country. We always want more, but often we have more than enough and are not able to see it.

God always gives us what we need. He is always taking good care of us and has the best plans for our lives. He knows what we need and when we need it. He also knows what other people need and when they need it. What others have may be great for them, but it is not what is best for us. The prodigal had plenty and most of all a loving father. Yet his hunger actually ate him.

May we always be grateful for what we have, knowing that whatever we have was given to us by God. He knows what we need before we even realize we need it.

The Journey Back Home

Luke 15:19–24

The prodigal son's journey back home started the moment he left. The day he left home, he started coming back home. He may not have realized it at the time, but the truth is that when he left, he started losing. He started losing his money, all the comfort he had at home, his touch with his family, and most critical he lost sight of what was truly important in life.

When he lost everything he had, he realized he needed to come back home. He did not think he was worthy of his father's love and affection again or worthy of his forgiveness, but he knew he needed to get back home. Back to where it all started. Back to where he felt safe and had everything he needed. Back home where he had taken everything for granted. After venturing into the distant country and spending all his money, he realized that being home was everything he wanted.

Have you ever ventured into the distant country away from God? We all have in one way or another. Some of us may have ventured further and others left but didn't make it too far past the gate. Maybe we turned away from God because we did not get what we wanted. Maybe it was because of a difficult situation in our lives, or maybe because someone we trusted hurt us. Or it was because we just wanted to see what was out there past the fence line. Just a quick "trespass" into sin's field. Not long, just a taste of our plan and not God's plan. Whatever the reason, throughout our lives, we have all wandered away from God, venturing into a distant country, like the prodigal son.

After spending all his money and being left alone, hungry, cold, and tired while feeding pigs, the prodigal son rightly decided it was time to go back home. He had to hit rock bottom to realize that since the moment he left, he was actually on his way back home. Not materially but relationally, it's love we long for not stuff. His heart yearned to go back home where he had everything he wanted and needed. He had to go back to his father's plan for him. And so do we.

God is always pulling us closer to Himself, even when we do not realize it. May we always respond to His pulling and decide to go back home to Him and to His perfect plan for our lives.

The Older Brother
Luke 15:25–32

Perhaps like the older brother, we have never ventured into the distant country. He stayed in the right place but with the wrong heart. An obedient life with a hard heart is a disconnect from the father as well. Not quite as dramatic but a foreign land from the will of God. Maybe we have been following God and doing the right thing for decades because our parents and grandparents did. Maybe we have always gone to church. We have all the right things checked on our lists, but there is a distance in our relationship with God while living under His roof.

Often, our hearts lack tenderness toward God. We follow religious rules, but we do not have a relationship with the Father. We do these things right, but we are not enjoying time with God. We are not praying; we are not fasting; we are not reading the Bible; we are not yearning for a relationship with God. We are good people, but we have a hard heart. And, we wonder why our lives feel so empty.

What we often miss in the story of the prodigal son is that the older brother also took his part of the inheritance. He was just as greedy as the prodigal son. In Jewish culture, whenever you had two sons, two-thirds of the assets went to the older son, and one-third of the assets went to the younger son. The older son got more than what the younger son wasted. However, because of a lack of relationship with his father, the older son seems to harbor bitterness in his heart, despite his outward obedience.

How does that happen? It happens when we begin to lack gratitude. Instead of being grateful for all he had, the older son was bitter because he did not get a fattened calf and a party. Whenever we lack gratitude, we begin to have entitlement. We are not grateful for what we have and feel entitled for what we do not have. We expect things should be done for us and given to us, just like the older brother thought.

The older brother forgot everything his father had was already his. The mirage of greener grass of his brother's welcome home seethed in his hardened heart. Sibling rivalry stole family love. Entitlement stole gratitude. The older brother needs to run to the father too.

Today the Father wants us to run to Him as well. Allow the Holy Spirit to soften our hearts and realize all we have in Christ.

The Love of the Father
Luke 15:20–24

The real change in the life of the prodigal son happened in the arms of his father. The father's embrace broke down every barrier. The father erased every feeling of shame and fear the son had. Everything he planned to say to his father fell apart when he was met with his father's embrace.

Imagine being in those strong field-working father's arms. Imagine feeling guilty, unworthy, dirty, shameful, unforgiven, alone, hungry, cold, and undeserving of love and forgiveness. Imagine having all those feelings yet being met halfway home by a father running to embrace you with such love and grace that all those feelings started to fade and disappear. Imagine an embrace like that. Like a linebacker's hug without the takedown.

The father saw the son coming home and ran toward him, hugged him, and kissed him. He did not let his son finish saying what he had planned. The father's hope was for his son to come back home and feel loved, forgiven, and welcome. It was the same for the older son. When he was angry because the prodigal son was back and they were having a party for him, the father sought out the older son as well, telling him that he loved him. He told him that everything he had was his. He loved both sons well. Just as our Father in heaven moves toward us with love and compassion, this dad did the same.

God's love for us is like that father's love. God loves us no matter what. He never stops loving us. He loves us—every single one of us—with an irrevocable, steadfast, everlasting, and compelling love. He isn't hindered by our past decisions or the things we did or did not do. He wants us to get closer to Him so He can get closer to us.

All the prodigal son needed to do was come back home and all the older brother had to do was walk back in the house. God wants us to do the same—to come back home. He will meet us.

We can rest assured that we have a Father in heaven who loves us unconditionally and will always wait, with open arms, for us to come back home. No matter what we do, He will always love us!

Peter: The Man and the Time

1 Peter 3:13–17

Who was this Peter? A fisherman who left his nets when Jesus called him to be His disciple. Eventually, he became the spokesman for the disciples, which was usually good but occasionally . . . he spoke before he thought.

He denied Jesus three times. This was Peter's worst moment. We know that Peter was not perfect. But the grace moment in that episode was he was restored three times by Jesus. What a lovely God we have! He can take you out of the pit we are in, the hole we have dug, and restore and rescue us.

After the restoration, God had great plans to use him as a tremendous leader. He preached the wallpaper off the walls in the sermon at Pentecost, and thousands came to Christ. God can use our brokenness as a vessel of His power. Really absorb that today. God is far from done with you!

He later wrote the epistle of 1 Peter in approximately AD 63. A letter of encouragement concerning how to make it through difficult times. At least fifteen times in his letter, Peter referred to suffering. He used eight Greek words to do so. He was saying from firsthand experience that there is hope in the pain. God can see you through it and give you a ministry in it.

There is no question that we are going to go through pain. The question is whether we will find hope in Jesus Christ when it happens. Hope in the midst of betrayal, a lawsuit, job loss, cancer, family problems, and anything else, God is there and cares. Peter wrote with experience of pain and suffering because the believers were in a time of physical threat.

It was a dangerous era for Christians. In AD 64, Nero burned Rome so he could rebuild it to his liking. He blamed the fire on the Christians. In AD 67, Roman authorities took Peter and Paul. Many historians believe they were executed that very same day in Rome. Three years later in AD 70, the unimaginable . . . the temple in Jerusalem was destroyed by the Roman army. That was the decade when Peter wrote about the hope we must have in difficult times.

Are you going through difficult times? Have you found hope in Jesus Christ? Trust Him through the trials like Peter did.

Strangers Passing Through
1 Peter 1:1–4

Peter identified himself as an apostle—that means one sent out with a message. His message was one of hope in Jesus Christ, and it was for those who were in Pontus, Galatia, Cappadocia, Asia, and Bithynia. These people were 500 to 800 miles away from Jerusalem. That is a long way from where Christianity started in Israel. No planes or video chat capabilities, just a long, lonely way from home. Christians are always strangers and aliens in this world, but now it was true physically too. And they felt like strangers and aliens, but they knew their citizenship is in heaven not on the earth. As believers in Jesus Christ, our citizenship is in heaven as well.

In this crazy world we live in, there is going to be more craziness. It is far from perfect. There is much sin. That is what happens when people do their own thing. Remember, you are not home yet. You are a stranger, an alien, a temporary resident. You are just passing through. That is why there is awkwardness and longing for more in this life. However, we are called to bring heaven to earth and shine with the gospel of Christ. We find our security in the Lord. Many of us are struggling to try to make the earth a place of comfortable lodging, always just outside of our grasp. But for the heart with a heavenly home, this is a place of pilgrimage.

If you do not know Jesus Christ as your Savior, let me invite you to be a stranger and an alien on the earth, because it is better to be a child of the Father and a citizen of heaven than to be a child of this world and a stranger in heaven.

As a Christian, do not lose sight of who you are; walk with a heart with a heavenly home. Be yourself for God. Many of us are so confused about who we are. We do not know our spiritual gifts and do not honor Jesus as we should. But you will find great freedom in being yourself for God. True, the world is not our home, but Christ is and He placed you here for His purpose.

Here is a powerful declaration: I am seated in heaven, and my identity is found in Jesus Christ. I am going to be a stranger to the temporary things of the earth on this journey. I do not care what anybody else thinks. I am going to honor Him as a stranger and alien in this world because I am just passing through.

The Foreknowledge of God

Psalm 147:5

Where do you look for security in difficult times? In family, government, money? We can find security in the infinite understanding of God, the filling of the Spirit, and the blood of Jesus Christ. Your safety is in the Trinity, not in society.

If you want to find security in society, you will wait a very long time. Society does not have places that are worthy of placing our security. They cannot hold that weight. Your security must be placed in Jesus. What Peter is saying to believers who are 500 miles from their homes, God knows who you are. He has chosen you and knows you from the foundation of the world. It does not matter that you are 500 miles away from home. Our all-knowing God is very aware of where you are, even if you are not in Jerusalem.

God knows everything. You do not have to turn to a horoscope, a talk show, or some political pundit to tell you what the future is. You do not need to have your palm read because His palms have been pierced, and He knows the future. God knows yesterday, today, and tomorrow, and He will never, ever change.

One of the sweetest times as a parent is when your kids think you know everything. A moment will come when they realize that you do not know it all. However, there is never a moment when you will realize that God does not know everything. We can always have childlike faith in the Lord. We can always trust in the fatherhood of God.

We have the identity of a stranger on this earth, but our deeper identity is as a child of the Father. Then we do not have any problem being a stranger in this world. Being a child of God gives us confidence and security. Everyone does not have to like us. We do not have to be invited to every party; we can be a bit odd at times. We can be who we are in Christ. I'm not a stranger to heaven or heavenly things.

God knows everything. Be comforted.

Are you trusting God in every circumstance no matter what? How do you feel understanding that God knows everything about you?

Secure
Ephesians 1:13–14

We have learned that our security is based on the omniscience of God. Paul is saying our security should be placed in the Spirit. When you trust Jesus Christ as your Savior, the Holy Spirit comes and lives inside your heart and changes you. You are different; you are set apart; you are unique.

Singles, you are filled. You are not empty and searching anymore. If you walk into a strange situation, you are secure among the children of the King. Men and women do not walk into a relationship looking for love; they come into a relationship already having found love in Jesus Christ. Women, God has touched you, so no man needs to. He has touched your heart and your soul. Students, when somebody says, "Hey, fill yourself up with these drugs, fill yourself up with this alcohol," you do not have to do it because you are already filled with the Holy Spirit of God. You do not need other stuff. Men, you do not require the approval of others. You are not searching. You are a believer in Jesus Christ and a child of the King.

As a believer, through the Holy Spirit you are set apart, you are complete. You can have joy instead of jealousy. You do not need what the world has because you have what God has given you. Trust Jesus Christ to be your joy so you do not have to look at other stuff with jealous eyes. You are guided in your life instead of guessing. Your circumstances might not all make sense, but you can trust that step by step, God is going to lead you, and you will be a faithful follower.

God welcomes you into His joy. He welcomes you into His guidance. He wants you to find His will. And His will is about who you are more than about what you do. So if you are a child of God who lives filled with the Spirit, you do not have to live empty. It is the Holy Spirit who fills you. You have been set apart for obedience, which is a fruit of the Spirit. The Spirit will help you obey the Word of God; He is your helper. He sanctifies your life in such a way that nobody can touch you.

Are you aware of the presence of the Holy Spirit in your life?

The Blood of Jesus
Hebrews 9:19–22

Our security is in the foreknowledge of God and in the sanctification of the Holy Spirit. And if that is not enough, our security is also in the blood of Jesus Christ. The Trinity gives us security. Scripture tells us that we are sprinkled with the blood of Jesus Christ, and that changes everything. We know it was not just a sprinkling of blood on the cross; it was a dousing. Jesus died, and His blood was poured out.

Moses is pointing us back to the purification rites of the Israelites in the tabernacle and the temple where the priests would sprinkle the blood of lambs and goats to obtain purification for the Jews. Then Jesus stepped forward and became the Lamb of God who was slain, shedding His blood for our sins.

Every one of us is looking for somebody to sacrifice themselves for us. Kids are looking for their parents to sacrifice by attending their events to cheer them on. Girlfriends are looking for a boyfriend who will sacrifice for them. Boyfriends are looking for a girlfriend who will sacrifice for them as well. In our marriages, we are called to sacrifice ourselves for our spouses.

But no one has sacrificed for us like Jesus Christ did. No one but Jesus has poured out His blood; no one else has been falsely accused; no one else has gone to the cross; and no one else has had His palms pierced to give us a future. That is what Jesus did to rescue humanity. He welcomes us and wants us to be rescued by His blood.

To seal our security, we have grace, which multiplies peace in our lives. If you are looking for peace, you first need to discover God's grace. In His grace, you will find the kind of peace that surpasses human understanding. That peace is not going to be simply added to you, but it will be multiplied for you. It will be given abundantly to you in Christ.

I saw these words in a card from a friend: "Life is a test, a trust, and temporary." Your faith will be tested, but you can trust God with your life because you are a stranger and an alien just passing through. Let's be like Peter and say to God, "I want to be Your child."

The Example of Love
Leviticus 19:18

Betcha haven't turned to Leviticus in a while. It's one of the oldest books of the Bible, written thousands of years ago. But it is rich in its roots of something we are very familiar with, "love your neighbor as yourself."

We hear those same words of wisdom from Jesus. It is throughout the Scriptures and finds its beginning in Leviticus 19:18. I bet you even your unchurched neighbor knows about loving your neighbor.

We have heard about loving our brothers and sisters before, about loving those we disagree with and showing them Christ's love, but maybe in our culture, some of us lack practice on really loving each other well. We need to come back for a review. We need to go through the class work one more time and give it a new try.

What makes this age-old commandment new? The love of Christ. More than Levitical instruction, Christ put flesh on it in a perfect way! His mission of love for others is our model.

Jesus Christ is the only person to walk on the earth who is the perfect example of love. To know how to love someone well, we can look at His example. He is not just a prophet, a teacher, or just a nice guy. Jesus is the Son of God who came to the earth to live a sinless life—to show us exactly how to love.

Over the last decades, we have removed Jesus from public conversation and kept Him out of the public square. We have replaced Him with celebrities. We can learn a lot from successful people, from intelligent people in education and the arts. But they are fallen human beings, just like us. They don't provide a good example of what it is like to love someone. Fighting with our neighbor is more in vogue than loving them. The example set in today's world is to spar on social media, go for the jugular in an argument, or let 'em have it. But to love them as ourselves? YOW!

I'm not saying there aren't times to fight, but fight as you would want to be fought with. Kindly and constructively with love. Meaning, don't lose your mind and keep your love.

In all things, love your neighbor as yourself from Old Testament Leviticus to today's life.

Authentic Love
Matthew 5:43–48

Who do you think about when someone says we must love one another? The people around you? Your friends and family? Your Christian brothers and sisters?

As we learned yesterday, when it comes to loving one another well, Jesus is our ultimate example. And what did He do? He taught something like this: "You have heard it is good to love your neighbor, but I tell you to love your enemy, pray for those who persecute you, love those who skip past you when greeting others, and love those who never wave back at you." We are called to love our enemies, those who are aloof and the rude person at the office or school.

The Pharisees, the leaders of the Jewish religion in Jesus' time, were astonished at Jesus. They said, "This guy has dinner with sinners!" Jesus answered that He wasn't sent to the righteous or to the self-righteous, but that He was sent precisely to sinners. We, as well, are called to love sinners.

Peter and Paul in the book of Acts said to not just love the Jewish people. They were going to the Gentiles, the non-Jewish people. We are called to love those who are different from us in ethnicity, religion, and culture. We are called to love those from nations, states, cities, communities, and families who even have historically been our enemies. Even a call for Republicans to love Democrats and vice versa.

Love is not just a flickering feeling. In marriage, it is not so much about feelings or emotions, because those can change gradually or suddenly. Love and marriage are all about choice—our choice to be faithful, stand strong, and build a good relationship together. When we make that choice, then feelings and emotions flow from it. Jesus didn't feel like going to the cross, but He chose to go to the cross. He died on the cross to pay for our sins. The love He demonstrated was deeper than a feeling. And through His death and resurrection, our souls are cleansed. We are called to choose to love.

Are you showing the love of Jesus Christ to the world and to people who are different than you? We get to be part of God's plan—His plan to show His love to the world. We get to be included in that. That's an amazing, incredible impact and . . . difficult way to live!

Time to Throw a Party!
Luke 14:16–24

Today is my birthday and it has me thinking of how to throw a party. Maybe I have a surprise party later today. Probably not, but at least a few cards and texts to say happy birthday.

Our nation, and I bet your city, is tremendously diverse. Different nationalities have their own way of expressing themselves. On a mission trip to the Jackson Heights neighborhood in New York City, our church threw a party for the different nationalities in the area. We partnered with a local church and hosted a banquet for those from India and its surrounding countries.

Food for miles, praise music, and the gospel in their language, a beautiful banquet hall and our team in newly purchased authentic Indian clothes. It was a blast and a blessing! Here are a couple of things we learned about loving our neighbors of different nations.

Do what is important for the culture to reach its people. A morning brunch? A late evening meeting with cake? No food? Lots of food? In our case, food at an evening banquet!

Go where they are, where they live. Jesus came to us. Now it is our turn to go. Many would rather wait for them to come where we are, but the wisest move is to go to their community. Invite everyone. Maybe some would be interested in learning something new, or could use some help. Don't forget homeless people either. As it says in the Scriptures, invite everybody to the banquet; do unto the least what you would do unto the Lord; go and save the lost.

You can't always throw a party so as a family we have gone to restaurants in our home of Houston that are out of our norm. We've been to Afghan, Lebanese, and Nepali restaurants to name a few. It is a ton of fun and great for our kids to go on a mission trip in our city.

Ask questions. Talk about topics you may have in common. Ask how much they know about your culture. Enjoy their company and have a great time. Just love them. Sit and eat. And do you know who will receive the biggest blessing? You!

Outrage and Hate
Proverbs 25:21–22

Proverbs is filled with great reminders of wisdom.
The Lord is telling us to love our brothers and sisters and even our enemies. Love the people around us good or bad. Offer them food and drink to help them. Sometimes this is a challenge in today's "duke it out" media culture.

Have you ever had that feeling? You see someone on TV who says something completely opposite of what you think. And in your heart, you begin to form not disagreement, but feelings of hate. We can disagree all day long, but when hate begins to develop, that is a whole different ballgame.

If we allow hate in our hearts, we can begin to form aggression and darkness toward the people who oppose us. Our hearts begin to become angry, and we don't do what Jesus told us to do. He said to walk in the light in a way that we can really shine with Jesus. He wants us to show the love of God.

The Greek word for *hate* means to spit at one's heart in disgust. In our society, the media would like to keep us in a place of outrage, tension, and hate. When we keep stoking the fires in our hearts, someone just has to disagree with us on any issue, and the fire of anger comes out of us to char them. But what Jesus is saying is that He wants us to love them. We can still adamantly disagree but still love in Christ.

If you love people, does that mean you never disagree? No. Of course, you disagree. Does that mean you never fight for what is right? No, we fight for what is right, but we fight right. Do you see the difference? We fight right, as we fight for what is right.

As believers in Christ, we can love people we vehemently disagree with and show them the love of God. To do that, we have to be able to say, "Lord, I want to love people with Your love despite completely disagreeing with them. Jesus, You have to do it through me. I want to walk with You, and I want You to live life through me." Don't let your love grow cold. Warm it up with prayer and kindness toward someone you disagree with.

Making a Way for Love

Colossians 3:8–13

An article in the October 4, 2018, edition of *Outreach* magazine quoted Ed Stetzer as saying, "A lot of people have lost their lives to outrage and are losing their ability to relate to other people. People are being discipled by their cable news stations. They are being shaped by their social media feeds, producing more and more waves of division."[35]

Are we being dragged by those waves? Where do we stand on love? If you are married, where is your marriage right now? Are you getting pulled into tension and outrage with your spouse? Your family? Your brothers and sisters? Your church family? Your friends?

We can allow the love of God to do something in our lives so we are able to love well. We need to love our spouses, our families, our fellow believers, our friends, and even those who are outside our normal, little circles in which we live.

What can we do in a practical way? The first thing we can do is get rid of the gnawing in our hearts and then receive healing. In the Lord's Prayer, we ask God to forgive our trespasses as we forgive those who trespass against us. That means we must forgive those who have wronged us. Forgiveness is our best bet to keep our love flowing strongly. Our obedience will restore our own well-being and our ability to love. Once healed, we can move on and love freely again. That way, we let God do His work in our lives, and we can walk in the light and share God's love.

When God's people consistently walk in the light, sharing His love, others will experience the love we show. That will shape our minds to know that our love is real. Little love gestures can go a long way into other people's hearts. Give them a Bible or bless them by letting them use our parking space or sharing the gospel with them. That will have a cumulative effect that sometimes will lead the person to give their life to Jesus. It doesn't matter how different they may seem from us or our background and life experiences.

To walk in the light in a great way is only possible through Jesus Christ!

Love Can Change Everything for Good

John 8:12

What happens to us when we begin to walk in darkness and live with a heart of hate? We don't like anybody but us. Darkness and hate begin to inhibit our relationship with God and our relationship with other people. Darkness brings blindness; we lose clarity of direction and start stumbling like when we stub our toe while wandering through the house in the darkness.

Whenever you sense a disagreement is turning into a feeling of hate, whether it is toward someone on TV or someone around you, get back into the light. If we walk in the light and in love in an active relationship with Jesus Christ, we begin to see the path clearly. Then we trust God to fight for us, and we allow Him to do His work in our lives.

When the world is trying to keep us in hate, Christians look different because, through the cross of Jesus, we want to remain in the love of God. Love is defined in Paul's first letter to the Corinthians chapter 13. Love was shown by God sending His only Son to give us everlasting life. Love is produced by the Spirit who lives inside of each believer.

When we are friends with nonbelievers, even if they stand on the other side of things, we will have many opportunities to shine the love of Jesus on them. Maybe we can even get to pray with them, letting them experience God personally. Loving nonbelievers doesn't mean we have to negate our faith or compromise and believe some universalistic idea. Jesus will work in their lives in an amazing way. Let's go with the love of Christ and the light of Christ and not let hate form in our hearts.

Is there hate in your heart toward someone or something? Are you staging fights in your mind, exchanging verbal barbs with someone? I must admit I've had some good fantasy fights in my head—no matter the subject, I get the final victorious word. But once I'm back in reality, all I've done is fueled my anger. How do we break loose to walk in the light? Christianity 101: tell God you are sorry and you need His strength.

Living Right

Acts 17:16–17

The book of Acts was written by a doctor named Luke in about AD 63. It is a continuation of the book of Luke. In the first twelve chapters, the main human character is the apostle Peter; in chapters 13 through 28, it is the apostle Paul.

In chapters 1 through 7, the story moves like an earthquake from the epicenter, Jerusalem. Then it moves to Judea and Samaria for chapters 8 through 11. Finally, it goes to the ends of the earth for chapters 12 through 28. Like an earthquake, it moves out geographically. This progression is also seen with people groups. First, the gospel goes out to the Jews; then to the Samaritans, who are half Jew and half Gentile; and then further to the Gentiles. It is said that we should study the book of Acts at least once every five years.

In this devotional, I want you to see that it is possible to live right in a culture gone wrong. We do not have to live away from the culture; we must live godly right where God has placed us.

Definitely, the world in the time of Acts was very different from the world today. In the book of Acts, the divide between the culture and God's people was even worse. Paul shows us what we are supposed to do in that situation. When he saw all the idols people had, he knew it was not honoring the one true God because idolatry is sin, and there is no good for anyone when you disobey God. Sin is very expensive—you have to pay a great price for it. We live in an era when the world celebrates sin and intimidates righteousness. Sin is always loud and repetitive, but it is without reason and without foundation.

God has given us His Word that speaks about the redemption He has provided for us. The Word shapes our worldview. We should not be intimidated by the world but be able to move further in the ways of the Lord.

What is your worldview? Is it that we have a small God and a big world? Or do you believe that we have a big God and that this is His world? The way you see this, your worldview, will make a significant difference in the way you behave in this crazy society we are living in.

We Have a Big God
Acts 17:5–6

If you believe that we have a small God and a big world, you will hide out or give in. If you hide out, you will be afraid of everything and remain only within the walls of your house or your church. If you give in, you will end up doing the same things the world does. You will agree with sinful behaviors or just fade away into the busyness of life. Neither hiding out nor giving in is the right thing that works long-term for us or future generations.

If your worldview is that we have a big God and this world belongs to Him, you will walk in faith and hope. God knows what is happening to everyone everywhere. He is big enough for the whole world. He is the Creator of the universe. That is the size of the God we have.

Can anything of this world intimidate God? No. He is not dead. And this world, even though it seems to be lost, is still His world. You can walk in faith, in hope, and in strength. Paul stood in the middle of all the idols of Athens and felt troubled, and that made him speak boldly about Jesus to the people there. Earlier in Acts 17:6, Jason and the believers are persecuted for . . . wait for it . . . an incredible description of impact . . . they were persecuted for "turning the world upside down" with the gospel!

J. B. Phillips, a famous British Bible scholar and translator, said this about the church in the book of Acts:

> This surely is the Church as it was meant to be. It is vigorous and flexible. . . . These men did not make "acts of faith," they believed; they did not "say their prayers," they really prayed. They did not hold conferences on psychosomatic medicine, they simply healed the sick. But if they were uncomplicated and naive by modern standards, we have ruefully to admit that they were open on the Godward side in a way that is almost unknown today . . . these men have turned the world upside down.[36]

But perhaps because of their very simplicity, perhaps because of their readiness simply to believe, to obey, to give, to suffer, and, if necessary, to die, the Spirit of God found that He could do His work in them and through them.

A. W. Tozer, a noted American pastor and author, wrote, "The man who comes to a right belief about God is relieved of ten thousand temporal problems."[37]

Nothing Intimidates God

Acts 4:16–22

How do you see yourself? What is your internal and external view of yourself? Are you more than a physical being? In the world, people think that everything is just carnal. They encourage you to get whatever you want materially. The whole goal of their lives is to stimulate their nerve endings. If it feels good, do whatever you want.

But we are more than mere physical beings; we have a soul. That is why we are sad when pets die and grieve far more deeply when our spouse dies. There is something in us that is different than what we look like, something that is deeper. It is the soul, the fingerprint of God. How does evolution evolve a soul? How does evolution give a personality? We have a personality because we have a personal God.

Is life just about us? Can we do whatever we want, or are we called to live dependently on the God who created us? We should live depending on God, a resource that is higher than our very small resources in the world. That is our God, who is bigger than the world—a world that belongs to Him because He created it.

The culture in the time of the book of Acts was even worse than today's culture regarding the worldviews people had. There was violence; Stephen and James were killed. There were efforts to silence the disciples; the Jews did not want the disciples to speak in the name of Jesus. They were jailed; three times they were put in prison. But there were also angelic prison breaks. God broke the chains and set them free. You may feel like you are jailed, but God can break your chains, and bring you freedom in Jesus Christ.

Humanity's sin nature pushes against God. People push away the One who loves them the most. People call evil good and good evil; they have darkness for light and light for darkness; bitter for sweet and sweet for bitter.

But the world cannot intimidate God. When people fight against the Holy Spirit, they will always lose. God always wins. They may seem like they win short-term, but their end is either salvation or destruction. Let's surrender to His mighty power and love. Let's hide in Him as a loving and never-intimidated Father.

Amazing Things Still Happen
Acts 3:1–8

Even though the culture in the time of the book of Acts was against God, Jesus still did amazing things through the disciples. Jesus throughout the Gospels healed the sick. Through Peter in the book of Acts, He healed the lame man who was at the gate of the temple. Jesus miraculously healed the heart of a persecutor of the church called Saul of Tarsus on the road to Damascus.

Jesus is the good news. There is hope for you no matter how bad the world is treating you.

Jesus unified communities. There was great joy in Samaria when the crowds heard Philip and saw the signs he performed in the name of Jesus. Jesus unified families. All of Cornelius's family received the Holy Spirit and were baptized when Peter was brought to speak about Jesus.

Jesus saved sinners. He came to the earth to die on a cross to save us. Thousands were saved by Jesus due to the preaching of the disciples.

The world will never stop the work of God. He is still in control and is doing amazing things. Nobody can intimidate God! Hear that with your heart not just your ears. Nobody, no bully, no authority, no loud mouth . . . nobody intimidates God.

If you are like me, perhaps you like to see the seen. I know that God works in the unseen, but I want to see His work in the seen. I want to see people coming to Jesus; I want to see the healing when people pray for it. It is hard to see what God is doing, but I have to trust that He is working. You have to believe that He is working in your heart. He is working on your children. He is working on your spouse, even if you cannot see any change. He is unintimidated and unstoppable in his movement.

If you turn to the culture today, you will think God does not even exist—that He is cowering in the corner. But He is still working. He will not be intimidated!

Impactful Acts

Acts 4:23–31

It is important to trust in God's work even when we do not see what He is doing. How can we see Him moving? Consider the ingredients of impactful Acts.

When the disciples were asked by the Sanhedrin to stop speaking in the name of Jesus, they did not pray for revenge against their enemies. They prayed for three things.

First, they prayed for bold love. The disciples loved each other so much that they said something like this: "If I have something you need, it is yours." Today, the world should know we are Christians by our love. We must love people who believe in Jesus and those who do not. We must love the person we agree with and also the person who disagrees with us about everything. That is the difference in Christianity.

Second, the disciples prayed for bravery in their clarity. They were clear in their work. They were clear about what they needed to pray for. They were clear on their message. They had just one message, and it was Jesus. There was no confusion about that. They persevered and pushed back against the culture. We have to push back against our culture as they did—not in anger but in love.

There are going to be jokes at your office that you must not laugh at. There are going to be things that everybody is going to do, but you are not going to do them. Many times, you will have to go against the current. If people can be bold about their sins, which wreck their lives, why can't we be bold about Jesus, who saves our lives?

And third, the disciples prayed to be true in their devotion. They were not playing a Christian game. They were living for Jesus. Do you just repeat the same things over and over when you pray? Pray with your heart, not your lips. Have you ever fasted? Have you ever turned off the TV to spend time in the Word? Have you ever made a sacrifice to be with Jesus? I'm sure you have, and God will use it. Be genuine in your devotion.

If you pray for these three things—love, bravery, and devotion—you will see life from another perspective. You will know that God is at work, and nothing can intimidate Him. You will see that it is possible to live right in a culture gone wrong.

Difficult Passages
2 Timothy 2:14–15

Some teachings are addressed to the heart and touch your emotions. Others are addressed to the feet and encourage you to take some action. And still others are addressed to the head and make you think and affirm your beliefs. Today, I will appeal to your head because I will discuss how to think through a passage from Scripture that may be difficult to understand. There are many portions of the Word of God that are hard to comprehend, and if you have not faced any of them, perhaps you are not reading your Bible enough.

Let me give you five instructions on how we should approach a difficult passage.

1. *Is the passage intended to be descriptive or prescriptive?* For example, we know that Moses went to a burning bush, but that does not mean that every time God speaks, we must see a burning bush. This account is descriptive of the journey of Moses, but not prescriptive for the people of God.

2. *Is this an unusual incident or a biblical theme?* For instance, another example from Moses, he led the people out of Egypt through the parting of the Red Sea to freedom. Yes, freedom is a biblical theme, but how he did it is not necessarily how it is going to be done today.

3. *What is the context in the biblical book or in the Bible as a whole?* For example, the book of Jeremiah is different from the book of Ephesians. We need to look at them differently. But there is also context; we must pay attention to how a Scripture fits with the whole Bible. Does it appear in different parts of the Bible, or is it occasional?

4. *Dig deeper.* Look at the grammar and sentence structure. You might need to look at the original languages. Some verses are very clear, but others need more attention. Do not stay at a superficial level.

5. *Use clear texts to understand confusing texts.* Mark Twain reportedly said: "It ain't those parts of the Bible that I can't understand that bother me, it is the parts that I do understand."[38] Many things are very clear in Scripture, and we can use those clear things to then study the unclear things. Let's not be detoured by difficult passages; let's dig deeper and find God faithful.

The Pleasure of a Change of Seasons
Daniel 2:20–21

Why is it that we enjoy and look forward to the change of seasons in the weather but dread it in our lives? Living in Texas we usually have basically two seasons, summer and winter. Fall and spring are just the weekend when the front comes in to usher us to the other end of the spectrum. Right now, in September, we are waiting for that cold front!

The city becomes alive with the new briskness, everyone is talking about it. "Feels great outside, doesn't it?" The sweaters are beginning to move from the top shelf in the closet to the drawer in the dresser. A new season is on the horizon and the Christmas carols are just a couple of months away. The change of seasons brings freshness and anticipation when it is in regard to the weather but fear and "Oh no" when it is in regard to our life.

We are looking for some sort of cruise-control, to find a speed and highway we are fond of, and tap the button to maintain. Fortunately, life is a bit more exciting, frustrating, and scary at times. God brings different seasons to the soul just as He does to the trees. Walking in faith is a walk that acknowledges each season is from Him and one in which He can be found.

Only enjoying the spring's freshness and avoiding winter's chill is not a walk of faith. It is a statement of lack of trust. It incorrectly says, "The Lord only giveth and never taketh." Some of the greatest gifts come in the coldest times. Walking through the seasons with God, confirms His authority to brown and blossom the leaves without our approval. I have found a beautiful completeness to this Weatherman, what He browns, He will one day blossom.

> "Every branch that is fruitful, I prune so that it may become even MORE fruitful." (John 15:2, my paraphrase)

The changing of seasons without apology brings a different wardrobe and a new feel. Be excited about the armor He has dressed you in and anticipate the quest He has before you. We all want a "beach bum" Christian experience, an umbrella in the sand as the waves roll in. But that isn't reality. Seasons, jobs, emotions, homes, and a lot more changes. Walk the road, summer or winter, walk the road, browned or blossomed, walk the road, without cruise-control, walk the road. Anticipate change in your life, welcome it, and savor its new taste, trusting that this brisk change will bring a new freshness in His time. Be encouraged by Daniel 2:21: "He changes the times and seasons."

Ice to H2O
Matthew 28:7–29

I suppose in an unconscious attempt to get in touch with my sensitive side, I read a poem by Elizabeth Doten entitled "In a Hundred Years." The premise was the ground will again be level in a hundred years. The rich and poor today will both be gone in a hundred years, the swords of the brave will be rust in a hundred years and on it went. In this beautiful and insightful poem one line in particular, pierced deeply:

"Are the trophies they've reared and the glories they've won
Only castles of frost-work confronting the sun?"

I almost could not finish the poem, "Castles of frost-work (that's ice for the poetically challenged) confronting the sun." What a spot-on picture of our earthly successes! Castles—intricate, painstaking castles—hand-carved, glistening in the sun, but melting away drip by drip.

As I read that line, my heart sank with the thought of the castle villages I've built in the kingdom of Gregg. "Oh Lord, I'm sorry for the times I have yearned for the attention and stolen the praise. No doubt my castles have moved and melted quickly from December to August. I was also reminded with how quickly life passes.

But with every true repentant whisper, God reveals how to trade the counterfeit of sin for the real McCoy. The melting of my castles highlights the importance of building His kingdom, not mine. The best way to do that is through discipleship! We are all melting away and it's true, in a hundred years the sun will be victorious. BUT! Passing on our faith is like dipping the pitcher in the vat of water that remains and refreezing it again in someone else's life. Who are we pouring into? Discipleship is an intentional effort to pass truth to the next generation. To "keep frozen" the Living Water of truth for the sunrise of the next generation! The tragedy is not in melting castles but evaporated water. Pass your faith on.

Catchin' Fish and Leavin' Nets
Luke 5:1–11

The story of fishermen turned followers is familiar. These guys stood tired from a long day's work and Jesus was asking them to do it all over again. He wanted to put the boats out in the water and go farther out. Imagine leaving the office at 8 p.m. after a solid twelve hours of work and there stands Jesus saying, "Let's go back to the desk for another couple hours." "You can't be serious." "Yes, back in and even further out."

Once again God was right, and man was wrong. The deep water brought a huge catch. A net-breaking, boat-sinking catch, send-for-help catch. On their own, they caught nothing. Under Jesus' leadership, more than ever imagined. It was as if your W-2 climbed so high you paid twenty friends' house notes for the month.

Then in verses 10 and 11 the entire story spins around. If the episode ends in verse 9, we say "Oh yeah, if I try nothing, but let God lead then the big deal will go through." Not so fast . . . The blessing was definitely there, but then the ol' switcharoo. Jesus moves us from earthly to eternal in our perspective. "From now on you will be fishers of men." The goal of their occupation and life switched in an instant from feeding the stomach to feeding the soul. God wants our eyes on the catch that matters, the souls of men. Each day we are making choices of what we are fishing for. When we pull up the anchor, head out in the water of school or work, what are we hoping to catch? Are we fishing for people's approval, our comfort, more money, or the lost?

He has placed us in a *specific* boat, sailing *strategic* waters, for *significant* fishing! Verse 11 shows how this type of fishing changes the saltiest of fishermen, "So they pulled their boats up on shore, left everything and followed Him." At the pinnacle of their career they left it all to follow their All in All. Jesus was so incredible they left at the top of their game. The greatest catch was nothing compared to following Him. Holding out for God's best instead of the world's "good enough" is worth the wait. Loving and following Jesus no matter the weight of the nets is normative Christianity. Nets, even full nets on the best day dim in comparison to following Jesus as fishers of men. "Lord, take us to deep waters for significant fishing, no matter the cost!"

Ponder these questions:

- What am I fishing for most days?
- Why are the souls of men the most rewarding catch?
- What is an example of a net He is calling me to drop to follow Him?

A Super Man
Philippians 4:13

You know the plot by now. An evil foe wreaks havoc on the world. His powers are too great for any mere human to defeat. The planet needs a savior—somebody who can stand up to evil and win.

But where will they find such a person? Perhaps a strong military leader or a government official can do the job. Whoever it is, he must have plenty of resources, big muscles, a cape, and some impressive gadgets.

Actually, no. Our unassuming Savior comes from a small town and a humble profession. He is not well-known for most of His life and has no military experience, political clout, or money. Some consider him a lunatic or a myth. Many fail to see the need for Him in the first place, and few realize that His Father sent Him to the earth for the purpose of saving them. They are content with the way of the world just as it is, thank you very much.

Who is this super man? Jesus Christ, of course. This small-town carpenter went toe-to-toe with Satan—the greatest enemy the world has ever known—and won. Jesus defeated death itself—once and for all.

Unlike Superman, Jesus makes His supernatural strength available to anybody who wants it. Once you have it, you can do anything through Christ (Phil. 4:13). You won't walk on water or feed thousands with one picnic basket (John 6), but you will be able to take on life's challenges with strength unlike anything else the world has to offer.

This offer comes with a price, of course. Anything worth having always does. Simply put, Jesus wants your life. Your desires and ambitions, careers and relationships—all of it. In exchange, you will receive His strength and eternal life, as well.

What's the first step? Admit that you have sinned and ask God to forgive you (He will). Second, believe that Jesus died on the cross and rose again (He did). Third, confess that Jesus is the Lord of your life (He wants to be). Fourth, live in His super power!

"Look! Up in the sky! It's a lunatic! It's a myth! No, it's Jesus Christ—the real Super Man!"

Physical and Spiritual
Matthew 9:35

Jesus went out to towns and villages to do two things. First, He preached and taught. He prioritized spiritual needs. Second, He healed people of their sicknesses and diseases. He met their physical needs. What Jesus did is what difference-makers must do: minister to both physical and spiritual needs.

The Bible also teaches this in James. It warns us not to say, "God bless you!" to a hungry man and then not give him some food. If you say, "God is with you" and talk about the Lord but do not give that hungry man the food he needs, he is not going to listen to you.

Meeting physical needs allows us to meet spiritual needs. They go hand in hand. Do not pray before the meal and then tip only 6 percent. Be a person who blesses others. The more you meet others' physical needs—the more you care—the more you can make a difference in people's lives.

One day, when my daughter was little, she came up to me at home. I guess we had the air conditioning on too low because she said, "Daddy, I'm freezing. Can I snuggle with you?" For dads, that is a dream moment. Yes, my prayers had been answered, right there, for my daughter to ask to snuggle with me.

We started snuggling. I had my arm around her. I was rubbing her arm a bit, trying to warm her up. She said, "Oh, Daddy, it feels so good. I'm getting warmer!" Then she said, "You are a difference-maker!" I said, "You've been listening in church! All right! Way to go, girl!" What happened in that little microcosm, that little scene, is that her physical needs were being met as I snuggled with her. Warming her arms helped warm her heart to the words of God I had spoken.

When we minister to and care for people when they have physical needs, at that moment their ears begin to perk up. It is then that a Christian is reaching out with the kind of love that Jesus showed. It is then that people will ask, "Tell me more about this Jesus." Jesus makes a difference in us so we can make a difference in someone else.

Jesus, open my eyes to the needs of those around me and help me make a difference in Your name.

Help for Heaven
Matthew 9:35

You become a Christian through faith in Jesus Christ. You make an exchange of His life for your sinful life. You put your faith in His death and resurrection. You ask Him to be your Savior. And then, once you are a Christian, you live as one. You walk out your actions. Our identity precedes our actions. We have a phrase we use around our church: "As we go." It means that what we do flows out of who we are.

What actions should flow from our identity? As Christians, we help people go to heaven. Difference-makers meet both physical and spiritual needs. Our ministry is not limited to helping people with their physical needs. Our goal is not to make the earth a better place to go to hell from.

It is not enough to just help people. Even if everybody was well fed and had access to clean water or all the clothes they need, having one's physical needs met does not change one's soul. If it were true then suburban America is heaven on earth. We have more than we need. Just look at our closets. But we know there are divorces, addictions, pornography, and sin in nice neighborhoods too. The world is a bizarre place, quickly becoming crazier and more chaotic. It is not sustainable. Something has to be different.

As Christians, we help people. Yes, of course! But that is not all we do. We do not just engage in social activity; we engage in soulful activity. The world says life does not matter. It says a human being is just a freak of nature and that we are no better than a dead dog when we die. But Christians know each person has a soul. You were knitted together in your mother's womb. Each and every life matters to God.

We help people, and by meeting their physical needs and declaring truth to them, we help them go to heaven. As we go, we become like Jesus.

God, fill me with Your love so I might not just help, but help people go to heaven.

September 9

Weary and Worn-Out
Matthew 9:36

Jesus felt compassion for the crowds because they were weary and worn-out, harassed and helpless. If we are going to be difference-makers, we must ask this: Do we have compassion for the crowds?

I confess that sometimes, when I see the news, I don't have compassion. I think, *This is chaos. This is crazy. I am aggravated with you people. Why can't you get a clue?* At other times, I get ticked off. I hope it is a righteous anger. But the Lord wants us to have compassion.

Of course, no one should break the law. I am not saying that in the least or trying to be soft on crime. But people do make crazy decisions because they are hurting, wounded, or confused. They have had all sorts of problems in their lives. We must recognize this and have compassion even as we stand for truth.

Sin makes people worn out and weary. There is a truth to that. Sometimes, people who sin think it is the sin that is making them cool. But in just a few decades, their bodies are wrecked. Sin literally wears us out. It creates a weariness. It can even lead to medical problems.

The Bible teaches that sin brings death. I met with an adulterer, a man who had cheated on his wife. He said, "It is exhausting." He said it was a relief to be found out because the sin of his double life was exhausting. Sin is exhausting, but following God is exhilarating.

We all sin, but there is forgiveness in Jesus Christ. Many Christians have made decisions that they are not proud of in a lot of different areas, but Jesus has the power to forgive sins. He has compassion for us. There is hope in Jesus Christ. He makes a difference in us so we can make a difference in His name.

Jesus, please give me a heart like Yours, full of compassion.

Jesus, Our Leader

Galatians 6:7

Moved with compassion for the crowds, Jesus said they were weary and worn out; they were sheep without a shepherd. People without a leader do not know their purpose. They do not know where they are going or what they are doing.

If you do not have direction, you will wander into fields where you should not go. That is why we ask in the Lord's Prayer for Him to forgive us our trespasses as we forgive those who trespass against us. We have walked into the wrong field. We have begun to feast on what was not ours to feast on. We have trespassed across a boundary line.

Jesus said the crowds were sheep without a shepherd. He stepped forward as the Messiah to say He was their leader. He was not chosen by the Sadducees or the Pharisees but by God the Father.

God sets up the government, the church, and the home. He sets up authorities and establishes laws. We must respect the leaders with authority in our society. We must honor them, stand behind them, and pray for them. When there is an election coming up, whether it is to elect the mayor or the president, we must decide what kind of people we want to elect. Will it be a leader with some good ideas or a leader who is also following Jesus?

God is the supreme leader, but we have removed God as leader. We are in chaos because we do not know who to follow. God will not be mocked; we will reap what we sow. Leaderless equals purposeless which becomes chaos and confusion. We have racial issues, moral issues, security issues, and all sorts of things. But when we fall in love with Jesus, we realize the color of our skin does not matter. It can be black, brown, white, or even blue or purple! It does not matter; what matters is the soul and what God is doing to change it. God does not look at the exterior; He looks at the heart. If we want to relieve racial tension, let's keep our eyes on Jesus.

Leaderless equals purposeless. Difference-makers have a leader. They have a purpose. To be a difference-maker, make sure you are following Jesus.

God, help me to follow You.

"Kind of" People
Matthew 9:37–38

Jesus said that the harvest is abundant, but the workers are few. The problem is not with the harvest. Many people realize they have a need of the soul. The problem, according to Jesus, is that there are few workers. He says to pray that God would send out workers into His harvest.

Jesus tells us to pray for difference-makers. They are people who say yes to God. They are the ones who stand up and pray, "I want You to call on me, Lord. I want to be the one who makes a difference in my city, my nation, my world. I want to be a person that says yes to God."

There are not enough yes people. There are not enough people who are stepping forward to say, "Yes, I'm in. I want God to do something in me and through me."

Many Christians are not yes people when it comes to the things of God; we are "kind of" people. We are kind of committed to the Lord. When asked to give, we answer, "You know, I've given in other ways." When asked to go, we say, "I'm for missions, but I'm not going to go on a trip. I like my pillow. I like my blanket." If asked, "Are you going to share your faith?" we answer, "It is just so hard; at work we cannot really do that; no." If asked, "Are you going to teach your kids about God?" we say, "Well, I do not want to force anything on them. I just want them to choose for themselves one day."

As *kind of* people, we are kind of in it, kind of out of it. We are a little bit scared and a little less faithful until finally we become hiding people. Hiding from God, responsibility, and ultimately joy.

But to follow Jesus, we must see the crowds with compassion, not hate. We must recognize that they are weary and worn out. They have no shepherd. And we, who have a Shepherd, must pray.

> *Lord, I want to be a yes person to You. I want to follow You. And as I follow You, Lord, You will bring people in my path who I can minister to and care for. I want to share Your greatness with them. I trust that You will have a harvest, Lord, as You work through me.*

Pray for Others
Ephesians 6:18

How do you become a "yes to God" person? You pray for others. Praying for others increases the yes in our hearts. Interestingly, in this Scripture, Jesus does not say, "Okay, let's all step out, let's go for it." He doesn't command, like a military leader, "Everybody, charge!" What Jesus says, instead, is something like this: "I do not want you to reach out before you have looked up. I do not want you to go out before you have gone up. I want you to pray. I want you to pray that God will send workers out in the field." Jesus is not asking you and me to pray for ourselves; He is asking us to pray for somebody else.

Pretend you are in business and that you pray, not for yourself, but for other men and women in business this week, that they would make a difference through their work. You pray, "Lord, I want to pray for all the business people. I want to pray, God, that they will make a difference, that they will realize it is not just about making money, it is about You placing them in a position of influence. I pray that business people will take the opportunity to share Jesus Christ when it is appropriate and bless their associates. I pray for the business community in this city to be difference-makers for good and for God."

When you start praying that way, as a person in business, guess what happens? You ask, "How can I pray for everyone else to do this if I am not doing it?"

If you are a teacher, pray for teachers. If you are a principal, pray for principals. If you are an administrator, pray for administrators. As a pastor, I should pray for pastors. As you begin to pray, you will want to be part of it because your heart is moved. Pray for missions, and you will end up going. Pray for America, and you will vote. Pray for your family, and you will grow in love. Pray for your church, and you will begin inviting people there. Pray for the harvest, and you will begin to share.

Do you see what God does? When you begin to pray for yes people, you can become a yes person. You can be a difference-maker.

Lord, stoke my heart through prayer.

Be a Yes Person
Psalm 32:8–11

Are you a "Yes to God" person, a "maybe" or "kind of" person? A while back, I went to the funeral of a deputy who was shot in Houston. He was an officer of one race who was killed by a man of another. I sat in the service with other pastors from our community. We sat as a pastoral block, representing all different races, to say we love Jesus. We did not care who was black, white, brown, green, purple—it did not matter. We sat together in unity, as pastors all created in the image of God, committed to the gospel.

It was a powerful funeral. The crowd was mostly made up of uniformed police officers, guys and gals with guns, sitting at the funeral of a comrade.

The preacher said something like this: "If you are going to stand against evil and to protect the community, then stand right where you are so we can pray for you." Those men and women stood up right away. There was no hesitation. They could not get up out of their seats fast enough. And those of us who were not police officers, who are not in the line of fire, were inspired. We had goose bumps on our arms. It was powerful. I thought, *This is what yes people look like.*

Jesus calls us in the same way that preacher called those officers at the funeral. He calls us to make a difference. He calls us to meet others' physical and spiritual needs. Does He call us to be obnoxious? No. Does He call us to be winsome? Yes. Does He call us to be harsh? No. Does He call us to be compassionate? Yes.

As Christians, we help people, and we help them go to heaven. We walk as difference-makers in a world that is in great need.

Jesus, help me be a difference-maker in Your name.

Live Heart-Healthy
Isaiah 1:1–4

My daughter gave me a milk chocolate peanut butter cup. She said, "Daddy, it is *healthy*!" The wrapper had the word *organic* on it, so it must be good, right? Organic makes everything okay: the sugar, the fat, and more.

We love buzzwords. If something is organic, hybrid, biodegradable, or gluten-free, that makes it okay. One of the big phrases on all sorts of foods right now is *heart-healthy*. God also wants us to be heart-healthy. He wants us to have hearts that are spiritually healthy. Physical health is important, too, but if you live organic and gluten-free and all those cool words but don't have God, you're missing something crucial.

To look at what God says about being heart-healthy, we are going to look at Isaiah for a few days, the 23rd book of the Old Testament. Isaiah is amazing in that it mimics the whole Bible; it is like a Bible within the Bible. There are sixty-six books in the Bible, and Isaiah has sixty-six chapters. The Old Testament has thirty-nine books, and there are thirty-nine chapters in the first section of Isaiah. The New Testament has twenty-seven books, and there are twenty-seven chapters in the second section of Isaiah. They even focus on the same themes: God's righteousness, justice, and holiness in the Old Testament and the first part of Isaiah; God's glory, compassion, and grace in the New Testament and the second part of Isaiah. The name *Isaiah* means the Lord saves, and that is also the message of the Bible.

The book was written between 740 BC and 700 BC. Isaiah 1:1 tells us that the prophet saw this vision during the reigns of Uzziah, Jotham, Ahaz, and Hezekiah. His ministry spanned forty years throughout the rule of four kings.

In Isaiah, the word *holy* comes up thirty-three times. Isaiah emphasizes that God is holy, and that because He is holy, God is serious about love and sin. The more you get into God's love, the less desirable sin is going to be. And the more you get into sin, the less desirable God's love is going to be. To stand up as difference-makers, we need to be heart-healthy.

Lord, heal our hearts so we can put away sin, love You, and be holy.

Cold Hearts
Isaiah 1:1–4

What does a loving parent do? Does he or she say, "Hey, kids, go and play on the freeway. It is not a problem. Do whatever you want— whatever you think is right." Now, that is crazy. That's not love. Or does that parent say, "Stay away from the street. Look both ways. Cross at the crosswalk. Make sure the light is red and the sign says it is okay to walk."

God is our Father. He is serious about the dangers of sin and loving enough to warn us. Isaiah 1:2 says that God raised up children who rebelled against Him. God did everything for them. He raised them, provided for them, and blessed them. And yet, they turned their backs on Him. They refused His goodness and said they wanted to do their own thing. They preferred sin. We have done the same thing. Sin hinders love.

When we sin, our hearts grow cold. Can you feel that in you? I feel that in me. A cold heart is not heart-healthy.

All of us are overwhelmed with bad news. We get bad news from the internet, the TV, and the radio. We hear about bombs going off, people getting shot, and others being killed. I do not even want my kids to watch the news. Bad news is everywhere, anytime, all the time. Our hearts grow cold because we cannot handle all the negative news. It is just all too much emotionally.

So instead of praying about the tragedies and being broken for the sin and pain we see, we watch news almost like it's entertainment. We want to see what happens in the scandal. We want to follow the bombing and see what takes place next. The news becomes an entertainment drama instead of breaking our hearts. Our hearts grow cold, in part because we are overwhelmed.

It has been said that if you live in a graveyard too long, you will stop crying when someone dies. Am I saying we should cry over every news report? No. We do not have the emotional capacity to do that. But am I saying that we should not have cold hearts to people hurting? Yes, I am. We should care when people suffer. We should care about the tragedies going on in our world. And we should care about the sin that brings them about.

Lord, make us sensitive to the dangers of sin.

Serve Orphans and Widows

Psalm 82:3–5

Loving the orphan and the widow is not an option for the Christian. There are things that are kind of optional. You may be good at hospitality; well, I am not. Maybe teaching is your thing while it might be a struggle for others. God has given everyone different gifts. But all throughout the Scriptures, we find God commanding us to care for the widow and the orphan. At different times, the prisoner and the stranger are "included" as well. The point is, God cares about people who are defenseless. He wants us to defend them.

I am not saying that widows or widowers are not strong people. Because they have faced hardship, they may be stronger than any of us. I am saying that God has called us to work on behalf of the orphan and the widow. They need us, as the body of Christ, to be their defenders.

God gets really specific. He commands the people of Israel, and us, to care for the orphan and the widow. God has blessed our church for 175 years, partly due to our emphasis on supporting widows and orphans. We help widows. Every one of our deacons has a widow assigned to him that he connects with, cares about, and makes sure is doing well. We also have a ministry to widows to help them with whatever is needed. Regularly, we organize a day for the men in our church to serve others. Our men come together, dressed in work clothes, and show up at widows' houses with power tools. They paint, they fix, they do what is needed. Our budget includes giving to our denomination's retirement program, which helps widows.

We help orphans. We have been part of funding more than 200 adoptions! We help orphanages and orphan ministries. We have a full-time staff member at our church who is in charge of adoptions, orphan care, and foster care.

Part of living heart-healthy is being a person who is not selfish, but selfless. Living heart-healthy means not focusing on ourselves, being defensive, or protecting our turf and our stuff. It means stepping forward to defend somebody else. Be on the lookout today for someone you can bless.

Lord, I want to make a difference. Help me stop doing evil, start doing good, and help widows and orphans.

Hearts That Hide
Isaiah 1:16–20

Sin makes your heart cold. Then, it makes your heart hard. A third thing that sin does is cause us to hide. Instead of embracing God and others, we hide.

Sin isolates you. With some sins, it is far easier to sin in solitude than it is to sin in a group. Sin moves you into the dark. It is much easier to sin at midnight than it is to sin at noon. We think, well, now that it is dark, maybe we can enter in, and nobody will know. It gives us a hard heart. It gives us a cold soul. We hide instead of embracing God and embracing others.

When you are alone, the enemy comes and takes out your knees. When you are in a place of darkness, he comes and takes out your life. God, in contrast, wants to bring you to the light and to the community of the people of God.

Isaiah tells a vision about the people of Judah and Jerusalem. They were sinning against the Lord, and they knew it. So, what did they do? They began with their own works. They tried to get rid of their guilt and trouble by making sacrifices to the Lord. But Isaiah 1:11 shows us what the Lord thought about their efforts. They were useless. They were detestable.

The people of Israel said something like this: "Let's just go to church more. We have a heart problem, so let's just try to do some spiritual things." All of us have lived that facade before. We have pretended with actions when we know our hearts are cold and hard.

But God says something like this: "No, no, no, no, no. I am not asking for your exterior. I am asking for your interior. I want to make a difference in who you are, because who you are will affect what you do." God wants to warm and soften our beating hearts. He wants to bring us to the light and to the community of the people of God. And then He wants to fill us with life and love so love can become the basis for our actions.

Lord, do not let me hide. Make my heart-healthy.

Stop Doing Evil
James 4:7–10

No one has done you more harm than . . . you. Blaming someone else is often the cool thing today—it has been for a long time. The practice goes right back to Genesis. "Well, who gave you the apple?" "My wife did." "Who gave *you* the apple?" "The snake did." "Who made the apple tree?" "God did." "The fault is not mine. Somehow, the fruit got eaten."

Do you know what the number-one killer is in the United States? Every year, 610,000 people die of heart disease. One out of every four deaths are due to heart disease. It is the leading cause of death for both men and women. We are dying physically because of bad heart health, but we are also dying spiritually because of bad heart health. And most of the time that's because of bad decisions on our part. Thankfully, God has the solution. He has told people since the beginning to stop doing what is evil and start doing what is good.

Stop doing evil. If it is not glorifying God, if it is not giving you passion for Him, if you wouldn't do it in front of your mamma or your daddy, if you wouldn't want all of us to know, then stop. Quit looking at that, doing that, going there, acting like that, thinking that. Just quit it. Just stop. That is how you begin to live heart-healthy. Stop doing evil. John Owen, a theologian, said it like this: "Be killing sin or it will be killing you."[39] This is possible because of the power of Christ. His power in you can give you the strength to stop the evil and start the righteousness. More than will power it has to be God's power.

Jesus Christ died on the cross to pay for our sins. Trust Him, and His blood will make you pure in God's sight. Christianity is an exchange. You take your ugly heart and exchange it for the righteousness of Christ. Have you made a trade with Jesus? Have you been born again? Are you living with a new heart?

Sin brings death, and love brings life. If we are going to be heart-healthy spiritually, if we are going to be difference-makers, we must repent of sin and stop doing evil. Then can we walk with God more closely and joyfully.

Lord, I am sorry for my sin. Help me get my heart right.

Start Doing Good
1 Peter 4:7–11

No one has done you more harm in your life than you. No one has done you or me more harm than what we have done to ourselves. Our own decision-making is often contrary to God's plan. Romans 6:23 says that the result of sin is death. We aren't accountable for people's sins against us, we are accountable for the sin we've chosen.

But at the same time, no one has done you more good than God. He has given you and me a bounty of love, a feast of righteousness, and all kinds of blessings. He provides our every need—not every want, but every need. God has given us everything, just as He gave it to the people of Israel and Judah. And yet they and we have turned our backs on Him. Our nation has received blessing upon blessing. Just look at the hand of God on our history! Yet we continue to sin. God's first command through Isaiah is to stop sinning. Stop doing evil.

God's next command is to start doing good. God is very clear about this. Isaiah 1:17 not only tells us to do what is good, but to learn it, to seek justice, to fight against oppression, and to defend and help those who need it.

You see, it is not enough to just say, "Stop doing evil." That's like telling a hungry man to quit eating. If you do not eat, you starve. The thing is, you do not need to starve.

Sin hinders love, and love hinders sin. God does not just say, "Don't sin." He offers an alternative. He does not just issue a negative command; He wants positive action. He wants that cold, hard heart to change. He wants our hearts soft and warm and to beat with purpose.

Lord, I want to invest my energy in doing good and not evil. I want to make a difference.

Hard Hearts and Harsh Words

Proverbs 21:23

My son was headed to church camp, excited about a week of worship and service at the beach! As his small group of seven to ten teenage boys assembled, he said, "Rule #1, don't get me in trouble." Great advice for those boys and even better advice according to Proverbs 21:23 for our words. "Okay mouth, Rule #1: don't get me in trouble." It is so easy to break that rule though!

The book of James 3:2 hits it squarely too: "If anyone does not stumble in word, he is a perfect man" (author paraphrase). Well, I've lost that one from the start. But, the effort is worth it because words matter . . . really matter. They matter in our friendships, vocations, parenting, and marriage.

See harsh words stem from hard hearts. One degree at a time, like a slow cold front blowing in our hearts chill and harden. No one plans on or wants a hard heart, it's a slow fade unnoticed until it sneaks out of mouths.

We diagnose the hardness when our tone changes. Tone is a big deal in friendship and marriage. "Close the door" and "CLOSE THE DOOR!" are way different. Tone is cutting; a subtle jab; a passive swipe. We can become a real expert at it. Married folks, have you ever allowed the tone and the words to lure you in and a few minutes later you are not really sure what you are fighting about? Our hard hearts became sharp tones and Rule #1 is broken and we're in trouble.

Here is what we need to learn: just because we think it, does not mean we should say it. I'm not encouraging a lack of transparency but an abundance of wisdom. Before you let loose, examine your heart for hardness, consider your tone, decide if it is even worth bringing up. When we are young, we think it is best to just say it, no matter how much we hurt our friend, coworker, or spouse. That, however, is not always the best thing. We need a filter of wisdom and self-control.

After more than twenty years of marriage, I have learned that everything I think does not need to be said; neither does everything Kelly thinks. A friend of mine says, "Always tell the truth but don't always be telling it." Our hearts need to be laid before the Lord. We need to pray,

Lord, keep my heart soft. Grant me the strength to not wound with my words. May they be a tool of encouragement, not a weapon against those I love.

But God
Ephesians 4:21–24

A deep desire in our hearts will always be met in something God has provided. That is because God put a thumbprint on every human life; we have been created for God and by God. We will never be satisfied with anything less. Therefore, our deepest desires are not desires for sin. They are desires for the things of God.

We are born in sin, but when we accept Jesus into our lives, when we embrace the new life He brings within us, we begin living new lives as new creations in Christ. We stop walking like sinful creatures and accept new life, new hearts, and new minds from God.

When we start walking with God, we are changed. We can all live lives of sin and far away from God, but God shows up and changes everything. "But God" is such a powerful phrase. It is what changes all things in our lives. When God shows up, He makes a difference. He comes and makes us new so we can start walking in a new way.

I was anxious, "but God" gave me peace.

I was lonely, "but God" was with me.

I was confused, "but God" directed my path.

I was in need, "but God" provided for me.

We can live our lives minding our own business, worrying about everything, living dark and meaningless lives, but God shows up and makes everything different. He turns our lives upside down and gives us purpose, a new life, a new way of walking, and a new way of seeing life.

God shows up and nothing stays the same. He changes our old self into a new one, our old ways of walking into new ways. He leads us into a new life. That is the truth that is Jesus. That is the truth of the cross. Christ died for our sins, for our old nature, and resurrected us into new people, transforming us into new men and women through His sacrifice.

When that "but God" moment comes, nothing can stay the same. It changes the course of our lives forever. As we begin to live new lives as new men and women, God transforms our way of thinking. We begin to see things differently, we begin to speak differently, and we treat people differently because we start seeing things the way God sees them.

I pray that while reading this devotional, your "but God" moment will come and change your life forever!

Understand the Old Self and the New Self

Ezekiel 11:19–20

We need to understand what the Bible calls the old man and the new man. All of us are born in sin; all of us are born with our own desires. The old man, or old self, means walking in *my* strength, on *my* path, for *my* glory. There is no room left for anyone else but me. The new man, or new self, is completely different. Living life as a new person means walking in God's strength, on His path, for His glory. It is living our lives for God, completely surrendered to Him. It is leaving sin behind and following in Jesus' footsteps.

There is an old self, the natural man of Adam, and a new self, the spirit man of Christ. The difference between the two is faith in the cross and the resurrection of Jesus Christ. It is not just going to church or doing what is right. It is not getting shined up. It is understanding that once we were lost, and now we are found. Once we were blind, and now we see. Once we were in the dark, on the broad road of destruction, and now we are on the narrow road of life. Once we were without God, and now we are indwelled by the Holy Spirit through Jesus Christ. Do you see that?

We might believe that it is enough to just stop cursing in order to live life as new men and women in Christ. Yet we can have the purest language and not know God. There is a difference between the old self and the new self. We are not just the same person with a different coat and a new pair of boots. We are no longer who we were. We talk differently, we walk differently, we treat people differently. We understand the sacrifice on the cross and start living our lives with a different mindset. We walk as Jesus walked as we allow Him to live through us.

It is when we really know God and understand the sacrifice of Jesus on the cross that we start living new lives. It is through faith and through having a real, honest relationship with God that we begin to walk in a new way, leaving our old way of life behind.

Understanding the difference between the old self and the new self will help us grow as believers in Christ and in our relationships with God.

Live today thankful for new life in Christ and walking in your new identity in Christ!

Grow Up
Romans 6:5–11

There comes a time in our lives when we need to put aside the old self, the old way of thinking, our sinful nature, and grow up spiritually into new men and women we already are in Christ. We need to realize that we are not who we used to be. There comes a time when we need to leave the old self behind and know that, as we abide in Christ, we need to start releasing what is within us.

What is our old way of thinking and sinful nature? According to the apostle Paul in Ephesians, it is pointless thinking, darkened understanding, exclusion from the life of God, ignorance, hardened hearts, and callousness when we lose the capacity to feel shame. It is being impure, and greedy—with a constant desire to want more and more of the things that do not come from God. It means having an appetite for sin.

Sin is an appetite, and the more we eat from it, the more we are going to want it. That is why it is so important for us to leave our sinful nature behind.

Whenever we begin to have the sinful appetites of our old self, we need to remind ourselves that is not what we really want and not who we really are. We do not want sin if we are believers in Christ; and even if we do not believe in Christ, we do not want a life of sin, either. Even the most sinful person is looking for God.

Can you imagine the owner of a business saying that he wants his employees to be ignorant, impure, greedy, hard-hearted, and always thinking about pointless things? Even if he is not a Christian, he will want his employees to be like the new man or woman in Christ, not like the old one.

Thankfully this passage in Romans 6 says we have been set free from the power of sin. We can live joyously for God. I pray we can put aside our old sinful nature and grow up spiritually. Embrace our new life in Christ, leaving sin behind and following in His steps.

Renew Your Mind
Romans 12:1–2

The Bible tells us that we need to renew our minds. Have you ever wondered why that is? It is because what we think is what we become. In the Old Testament, it says, "For as he thinks in his heart, so is he" (Prov. 23:7 NKJV). What we think about is what we are going to yearn for and what we will become. René Descartes famously wrote, "*Cogito, ergo sum,*" or "I think, therefore I am."[40]

What we think about is also what we worry about; what we worry about is what we are afraid of, and that will become our idol. What do you think about? Do you think like a Christian (taking every thought captive to obey Christ), or do you think as the world thinks and just add a Christian tagline or motto to your thoughts?

When we renew our minds, we start to think in a Christian way. This changes the way we do things. It changes the way we parent, how we treat our spouse, how we talk and act in our workplace, and how we live our lives. It is not enough to just keep thinking the same way we used to think before, adding a few touch-ups and shining it all up. That will not make a difference. We need to renew our minds entirely.

It is so important for us to understand that the way we think affects our lives. It is the difference between living a life of worry and anxiety and living a life of freedom and peace. I want to encourage you to read the Scriptures and fill your mind with the Word of God. Worship and listen to preaching. Fill your mind with the things of God, so it will be renewed in a godly way, and then you will respond to things in a godly manner.

I realize this is easier said than done. But it has to be a fight we continually wage. So much is coming at us each day, so much to worry about. This is all the more reason to renew our minds. To seek an obtainable peace in Christ. He loves you and is in control. Let your mind rest and renew in Him.

Put On the New Self
Galatians 2:20

As a dad of a daughter, my appreciation for shopping has grown. More than new clothes, it is time with her and the fun of seeing the smile a new outfit can bring. A change in our look or style can be exciting but it will fade. The exterior never completes us. Styles and taste change but the needs of the heart remain.

God has made us new in our soul, not just improved in our style. A lot of things can give us a new style, but only Christianity can give us a new person. Put on the new self, and God will do something amazing. Release what God has put in your life through the Holy Spirit. When you put on the new self, you allow God to work through you.

When we put on the new self, we are being transformed into the likeness of God, who created us perfect in His image. But we chose our own path for our own will and glory. We walked along that path for a long time, and then we came to the cross. Hopefully, we accepted Jesus Christ as our Savior and put our faith in His death and resurrection. Now we have a new self. God wants to take us back to when we were pure, when He first created us. He wants to wash us clean. He wants to dwell in us. He wants to walk with us as He did in the garden with Adam and Eve before they sinned.

The new self is God doing something on the inside and our salvation coming out for all to see. God puts a desire for Himself in our hearts and minds when we begin walking as new men and women in Him. The Bible says, "Take delight in the LORD, and he will give you your heart's desires" (Ps. 37:4). As we put on the new self, God gives us new desires and renews our minds. He gives us a new appetite for the things of God.

I pray today you walk in a new way, as the new person God intended you to be. May you embrace salvation through the sacrifice of Jesus on the cross and start living and thinking in a completely new, godly way.

A new self, not just a new style.

Fully Known
Psalm 139:1

Psalm 139 is a very poetic and famous psalm. David declares in this psalm that God is everything. He is all-powerful and everywhere for every time and every moment. We are to lay our lives before Him.

God is also all-knowing and all-interested. You might say, "Yeah, I know God's all-knowing. Of course. He's God!" But do you know that God is not only all-knowing but also all-interested? He not only loves you, He likes you. He not only cares for you, He wants to be part of what is going on in your life.

This is so important for us because every human desires to be known and to have friendships. All of us, introverts and extroverts, long for different levels of friendship, but everybody wants a friend, wants to be known, and wants to be cared for.

One of my best friends since sixth grade and I have this phrase that we use together: "Fully known; fully loved." That is the way we describe each other. I know everything about him. He knows everything about me. I fully love him, and he fully loves me. It is the same with the Lord, just at a deeper level. He fully knows everything about you, and He fully loves you with everything He is.

We crave to be known. It may be through selfies on social media. We may be looking for fame through acknowledgments of our accolades, our accomplishments, or our trophies. Everybody wants to be known, and God says, "I know you, and I like you."

It does not matter how many followers you have on social media; it matters who you have as your leader. If you have Christ as your leader, knowing Him will give you more satisfaction than a million followers will ever give you.

God wants you to know that you are fully known and fully loved by Him.

Walking in the Light
Galatians 2:11–14

One of the worst feelings a human can experience is feeling ignored. I listened to a podcast from a retired CEO of Ritz-Carlton, and he made this statement: "We train our people so when they're walking down the hall, if they get within six or seven feet of a customer, they are supposed to say, 'Good morning, Sir. Good morning, Ma'am.'"[41]

The employees are trained to look at customers in the eye and acknowledge them in the hall. They understand the psyche of men and women because they understand that the worst feeling is to be ignored. Have you ever been ignored? Sure you have!

Have you been to a party and it seems like everybody else knows each other? Have you walked up to somebody that turns the other way? All of us have been in a spot where we felt like we were blending into the wallpaper instead of being part of what was going on.

God is saying to you, "You'll never be ignored by Me, because My eyes are on you, and I know right where you are."

God's knowledge of us is intimate. His intimacy does two things; it invites us and repels us. It invites us when we understand how God knows us, and we respond by saying, "Yes. I want to be known by my Creator and God. I need a place to pour out my deepest thoughts, a place for forgiveness of my hidden sins. I need a place to connect." I am invited to understand that He searches me and knows me. He knows when I leave, what I say, and what I do.

But if God knows everything, then it also repels me because it is a little scary to think, *If He knows everything, I don't know how close I want to get; He may start changing things. I want Him to know which things are changeable and which are not.*

Everything is on the table before God. He can see anything. Even the things that I think are in the dark, God can take those and change them. His love invites me to trust Him.

Far from ignored by heaven, our loving God knows all and still cares deeply. Let Him have His healing way, experience His deep love in every area of your life.

What about the Pain?
Psalm 139:7–12

God's intimate knowledge of us invites us, but it also challenges us—it moves us back. If God knows everything, then I am safe and satisfied. But if God knows everything, how do I reconcile the pain and the tragedy in my life? What do I do with that? Will I lean further in, or will the pain and tragedy push me further out?

In John 11, Lazarus dies. The Bible says two days passed before Jesus went to Lazarus, whom He loved. He waited two days. Why did He delay? He delayed so He could show the glory of God in an even greater way. Mary and Martha—and you and I—do not like God's delays.

I do not like the moments when I feel like I must say, "God, You should be doing something to help me." I am not sure how to adapt that into His sovereignty. There is part of the sovereignty of God that repels me when I say, "Why does this happen?" And then there is the part of God's sovereignty that motivates me to say, "God, You know that it's happening, and I've got no other place to flee."

We are going to see that same tension with David in the next devotional. David is thinking about fleeing. You might not have seen this before in the Scriptures, although you might have considered fleeing.

David's thinking might have been something like this: "I don't know if I want to stay here. What would happen if I fled? Well, if I go to the sky, He's there. If I go to the bottom of the ocean, He's there. Wherever I go, He's there!"

This knowledge is going to comfort us eventually. God is always present and always powerful. It does not matter where you are, where you're going, or where you've been. God is always present and always powerful. David ponders fleeing, but he realizes that it is impossible. God is omnipresent—everywhere. He is omnipotent—all-powerful. David says, "I can't go anywhere. God is already there."

So wherever you are hurting, quiet your heart and find Him there. He is God. His name will be glorified in your situation.

Lord, even in the midst of my pain, walk me through it. Amen.

God's Handiwork

Psalm 139:13–18

God is everywhere, and He is the Creator of all we see. The heavens declare His glory. The skies declare the skill of His hands. David said, "You knit me together in my mother's womb. I praise you because I am fearfully and wonderfully made" (Ps. 139:13–14 NIV).

Psalm 139 can answer so many questions that we have in our culture right now. People have removed the Creator from society and have lifted up creation. Many are looking for the fruit of the Spirit without the Spirit. People want to have love and to be kind, patient, gentle, and faithful, but they do not want to receive the fruit of the Spirit from the Spirit. If we remove the Creator, we cannot just tell everybody to be nice to each other.

Climate change will not be the motivation for one person to love another. Saving the seals is not going to get the job done to bring true harmony and fellowship. Real love happens when we realize there is a Creator who has put His fingerprint on our lives. He is saying: "I am the Creator, and I want you to learn to love Me first. Then you can learn to value and love others."

We all have value because we have been knit together by the same loving Father in heaven. Our skin color does not make any difference; I can love you, and you can love me because the same God who loves us has knit us together.

When we love God as He loves us, we are able to step forward and love across racial lines. He can make things brand-new. God brings a loving perspective for all of us. We are created in His image. Children of one Father!

It is not willpower. It is the power of His love in me saying, "I want to follow through on the fingerprint of God."

Precious Value
Psalm 139:13–16

Psalm 139:15 answers this question: When does life begin?

Life begins when it is knit together in a mother's womb—in that place—as sperm and egg come together. God knits us together as male or female. God's knitting is so intricate that Sir Isaac Newton said, "In the absence of any other proof, the thumb alone would convince me of God's existence."[42]

God said He has put a fingerprint in you and on you. That is why humans are valued. What brings value to anything? An exterior statement brings value to something. Gold is worthless unless everybody wants it. Land is worthless unless somebody is going to build a shop or a house on it.

God has put His fingerprint on us and says that we are created in His image. That is why you can drive past roadkill, but you would never drive past a dead person. It is different. All creatures are not the same. God's image is on you and me.

This knitting that comes together in a mother's womb reveals our great value. God can do great things in us. He can move through us and move our minds and our hearts so we can love people whom we didn't love before.

God can do more than we can think of or even imagine. We can walk in the paths that He has prepared for us to live out His plan. God is at work; it happens through the knitting. You have been intricately created by God, and that gives your life a precious value.

We also have His most valuable gift of love, which comes through Jesus Christ and what He has done for us. When we understand how valuable we are to Him, His thoughts will be our greatest treasure and will enable us to walk in His ways.

God, You knit me together so wonderfully! Move my heart and my mind to follow through on the continuation of Your plan and Your will for my life. I am ready to follow Your fingerprint. Amen.

Valued
Psalm 139:16–18

In Roman culture in the first century, baby girls were often unwanted. The parents would take the baby to the outskirts of the city and leave her there. The precious little girl's cries could be heard from the city, and two groups would run out to get the baby. Whoever won the race got the child. One group consisted of brothel owners; the second were believers in Jesus Christ. Early Christians would run, rescue, and care for that child.

If you look at the end of slavery, you find the church there. Look at the history of the Civil Rights movement in our country, and you will find the church. When you see people with the cross in their heart, you will see people who sacrificially care for their brothers and sisters. This care comes from their understanding of the Scripture that says we have been knit together by God, and we are therefore valuable.

Where does value come for humans? What makes us different from a cat or a dog? It is the fingerprint of God. Not only does He love you, He likes you. He created you and has a plan for you. His thoughts about you are as numerous as the grains of the sand of the sea. Nobody else thinks of you that much!

I really like the reminder of the phrase, "You wouldn't worry what people thought of you if you knew how seldom they did." It is true! But God is telling us the opposite: "As the sand of the sea, so are my thoughts toward you. That's how much I love you. In the midst of the pain, My thoughts are toward you. In the midst of joy, My thoughts are still toward you. I have thoughts toward you because I have woven you together. You have eternal value as My creation." This realization of personal value charges the understanding that others are valuable too. Therefore, Christians ran to the babies, and abolitionists ended slavery. The value of all people is precious to God and the church.

Everything in us is crying out, "I want to be known . . . please notice something special about me!" Where does that come from? It comes from a Father, God, who knit you together, who is still thinking about you this very moment. He is so in love with you.

God knows who you are; He sees how special and valuable you are. He has a plan for your life, and He is at work. Trust Him.

The Examined Life
Psalm 139:19–24

David begins the last part of Psalm 139 by separating himself from enemies of God. He says something like this: "God, I despise your enemies. I'm not like them; I'm completely on Your side."

Then, in verse 23, David tells the Lord to search him and know him. Let's compare verse 1 with verse 23. Verse 1 says, "LORD, you have searched me and known me." That is a fact, just the way it is. Verse 23 is an invitation that stems from humility: I want You to "search me, God, and know my heart."

It is exactly what happens in our lives. We begin to understand that God is everywhere, all-knowing, all-interested, ever-present, and that we are precious in His sight, created by Him in His image. When we understand there is something different about us that is not in a cow, a monkey, or a dog, then we understand the intrinsic value God places on us. When all of this knowledge begins to sink in, we begin to respond to the Lord with requests and respect.

Here is our request: "Lord, search me and know me. Test my heart. See if there's any anxious way in me, and lead me in the path of everlasting life. I want You to speak to my heart, God. What's in there? I can't even rightly judge myself, Lord. Where am I off? Where are my lusts becoming something I'm trying to justify? What are my prejudices, Lord? What still needs to be crucified in me? I'm requesting that You would do that, Lord."

Here is our respect: "God, because You are a loving Father who thinks about me more than I can fathom, speak to my heart and reveal Yourself to me. I respect Your leadership in my life. I'm going to follow You even when it's not convenient or I don't necessarily like it."

It is called living the examined life. He knows everything about me, and He does not want my heart to get away with sin. He is interested in me pursuing the dreams He has for me as I trust that He is God. I know He can fill my heart with praise and joy and my mouth with laughter as I give Him everything that is in my heart.

Let Him search you today. Then respond with requests and respect.

October 3

Real Life
John 15:1

My first missionary journey that opened my eyes to the nations was a trip to east Asia. We talked to people who were in English classes and answered questions about America. I wrote on the board that I was from Texas. The students with a smile started calling out words like *cows*, *horses*, and *cowboy hats*! They asked me if I had horses, and I explained that most people don't own horses in Texas. I added that I was a graduate of Texas A&M University and that our mascot was an Aggie. They did not grasp that at all, so I explained that it had to do with agriculture and farmland. They huddled together, and after much effort on their part, they translated the word *aggie* to . . . *peasant*! Later I found out this was a word for the lowest rung of their society who works in the field. Not real flattering but we just went with it.

I use this illustration because I want you to see how sometimes we take God as the gardener of our hearts and souls and move Him down to the lowest rung. He only gets to garden where we give Him permission. We are above Him, and we want Him to tend to what we want. We never actually say this, but we live like this: His gardening happens only when He has been given approval by "the big boss"—us.

Whenever God gardens or clips branches in ways we don't agree with, we get offended and say, "God, I want the blessing that this person has" or "I don't want the trial that I have; I don't like it." "Lord, here is the fruit that I want You to plant. I want You to water it on Monday, Wednesday, and Friday, but I want You to leave it alone on Tuesday and Thursday." We make God into a peasant—one who follows our orders—instead of us following His orders.

In John 14, Jesus gets us ready to trust the Gardener by talking to us about the Holy Spirit. Jesus tells us that the Holy Spirit is our Counselor, our *Paraclete*—one who walks alongside. He is part of the Trinity. With the Counselor's help, we are able to say, "Lord, You prune, clip, and plant as You want." In doing this, we will find real life. Then John 15, Jesus writes His role on the classroom chalkboard . . . a good and wise gardener. As you walk through the day, let Him do His work.

Our Union with Jesus
Revelation 22:13

The Lord is able to weave things together in a profound way. As the Alpha and Omega, He can see it all . . . even the middle. I feel like I'm in the middle a lot, already started but not quite finished. Thankfully, I can trust Him with it all.

Here's a few connectors the Lord has given to teach us He is trustworthy in the middle.

The books of the Bible connect with each other to prove God's points. What is the first thing God created? Light! Then, in the first chapter of John's Gospel, John the Baptist tells us the first *I am* statement about Jesus when he says that Jesus is the true Light. Genesis and John just connected to prove God's point.

Then in John 6, Jesus says, "I am the bread of life" (v. 35). What did the Israelites eat when they were in the wilderness journeying through the desert? Manna—bread from heaven. Jesus says He is the true bread, and when we eat of Him we will never go hungry again.

Jesus makes another declaration in chapter 15. He says, "I am the vine" (John 15:5). This is the seventh and *last* "I am" statement from the book of John.

When we come to the table for the Lord's Supper, we have bread and wine—the fruit of the vine. From the first to the last statement, we declare who Jesus Christ is—He is God, not a peasant. Jesus is the first and the last, the Alpha and Omega.

When Jesus tells His disciples He is the vine, He is saying, in essence, "I am a huge connection point to you." In the book of Isaiah, we learn that Israel is supposed to be the true vine that blossoms with His fruit. Israel's disobedience prevented this and Jesus took the place of Israel, to be the perfect vine. Israel's and our redemption come from Jesus. His obedience bears the fruit of righteousness. Salvation comes through Him.

When we declare in our culture that Jesus is the true vine, it means He is the only way to heaven. He is not *a* vine, He is *the* Vine. He and the Father are one.

God has woven the Scriptures together in an incredible way! He is in control of the beginning, the end, and even the middle.

Peasant or God?
John 15:7–8

Is God the gardener who can tend to your soul, or is He one that needs your approval? Is God the one you hire to be your yardman, or is He the one you give your field to own it? These are vastly different roles. If you hire Jesus to be your yardman and do some things for you, through His grace He will show you a few things. However, when you give Jesus your land, you might say, "Lord, I don't like tomatoes, so please don't plant tomatoes." And when He plants tomatoes, you realize, "I love tomatoes!" When He says, "I want to make this a pecan orchard," you say, "I'm not really into pecans, but I am going to trust Him." In doing this, we say, "Lord, You are the true Vine! I trust Your wisdom and will."

The greatest blessings in my life were those things I was afraid to give up. I was so afraid as a teenager to give my life to Jesus because I did not want to lose my friendships. Now, I have so many friends that I cannot remember everybody's name.

God had to peel my hands off my dream to be a businessman, which is a great calling. But God said, "No, vocational ministry is what you are going to do." What a blessing it has been! Now I can say, "Lord, my life is Your field. You are not my worker; You are not my yardman; You are not a peasant. You are my Lord. I am Your child; I am Your servant; I am Your son."

This is easy to say on Sunday at church but not so easy on Monday morning when the Gardener cuts off the branches that bear no fruit and prunes the branches that do bear fruit. The Gardener does this with two kinds of storms in our lives: correcting storms and perfecting storms.

Correcting storms take the vineyard vines out of the ground and train them to run along the trellis so they can get the right amount of sun. The perfecting storm is for the vines that are bearing fruit, but the Gardener wants to produce more fruit in them.

Ask yourself today: *Which type of storm am I in need of? Am I off course and need a course correction? Or am I walking with Jesus and the perfecting storm is chiseling my character to look more like Christ?* Neither are fun, but the Gardner can use them to tend our lives and hearts.

Fruit Bearer
John 15:1–2

If you are not bearing fruit, you are in the muck of life. The Gardener wants to come and lift you up and put you on the trellis where you can grow. You will never be satisfied in your life until you are on the trellis and out of the mud. A believer in Christ, indwelt by the Holy Spirit, is not meant for the mire or the muck of the ground. We are meant to bear fruit. Whenever we see our lives dragging in the dirt, we need to realize that is not what we were meant for. God wants to lift us up. If we think He is a peasant and we are the boss, we will never let Him do it. If we allow Him to lift us up, He will then place us high up where He can show us off for His glory. As He places you there, He will say, "This is what I meant for you, My child."

Jesus is the true vine, and the Father is the Gardener. The Gardener takes those who do not bear fruit and lifts them up out of the muck. He knows that grapes do not grow well on the ground. Pumpkins and squash might, but grapes don't. Believers don't. Would you allow Him to lift you up and place you on the trellis of growth? That is where you will get the sunshine you need.

Both types of believers—those who bear fruit and those who do not bear fruit—will have an aha moment when they say, "Why am I doing this? This might work right now, but it won't work in the long run!" At that moment, wake up and let the Gardener lift you up.

Believers who are bearing fruit are in need of perfecting storms. They are on the right path, and on that journey, they are being perfected, made better and stronger. They are given the opportunity to grow and exercise faith. When the Gardener prunes, we say, "Lord, don't prune away the leaves. Take the thorns instead." We get nervous about pruning because we love today's leaves more than tomorrow's fruit. But we walk by faith not by sight.

How is He shaping you? How is God showing you that He is the master gardener? Seek to love tomorrow's fruit more than today's leaves; you will begin to be perfected in Christ.

Blossom with Jesus
John 15:3–5

When we surrender to the Gardener, God might not start picking at the leaves; He might start picking at the petals. When He does that, don't get upset. Sometimes, God prunes the whole thing. And in those moments, you say, "Lord, why?! Do You even love me?" There have been times in ministry that I have felt like I was holding only stalks and stems after pruning. I had to go back and remember that He prunes because He loves. And every branch that is fruitful He prunes so we can become *more fruitful*. He is not pruning because He is upset with us. He is perfecting us. He has a trade coming for you. Your stem is about to become a bouquet that is a pruned heart that begins to blossom with Jesus. When you blossom with Him, God is able to do His work in ways that you never expected.

The Gardener is doing His work. He is not our servant, we are His. Do you see Him as a servant to your happiness? Or do you see Him as the Gardener of your soul?

Pray this: "God, my heart is Your field, and I give You everything I have." I lay it down before You so You can do your work in me. If that is true for you, it will hurt when today's leaves are gone, but you will love tomorrow's fruit more. Choose the fruit.

Are you bearing fruit? If you are not, would you allow the Gardener to lift you up and put you back on the trellis? If you are bearing fruit, would you stand firm in the pruning? Allow God to prune your heart and your life. It is painful but purposeful. Which group are you in? Correcting storms or perfecting storms? Either one has the same Gardener. Allow Him to do His work in your life.

> *Jesus, I give You great thanks. God, make my heart into a garden. Tend my soul. Speak to me, Lord. May my faith grow even though it hurts. Do things in me, Lord, that I do not want You to do in my flesh but that I trust You to do in my spirit. In Jesus' name, amen.*

We Are Washed Clean
Colossians 3:1–4

We are called to set our minds in the heavens. Focusing high not low. Just like roses are not made to be in the mud, a vine is not supposed to be in the muck. Grapes are not meant to grow on the ground as pumpkins do; they are made to be lifted up on a trellis. Christians are not made to live low either, because Jesus lives inside of them through the Holy Spirit. Their lives are meant to be lifted up from sin.

We have times for pruning. The Gardener takes things away so we can be more fruitful. We must learn to love tomorrow's fruit more than today's leaves. He prunes us so we can be on display for His glory.

In John 15, Jesus gives us a vineyard illustration with vines growing, and He presents us with the choice of abiding or not abiding in Him. If we do abide in Him, our lives will bear fruit; if we don't, our lives won't accomplish anything eternal.

Jesus begins by saying that we are already clean by the word He has spoken to us. We are forgiven in Jesus Christ. Our identity in Jesus is key to understanding the part about abiding in Him. If we just jump to abiding without realizing we are clean, we are going to work to try to earn our salvation and His blessing.

Many people think incorrectly about what it is to become a Christian. They think that a relationship with Jesus is on an installment plan. Just do a little good along the way and receive a little forgiveness along the way. But the gospel is far better than that. When we pray the prayer of forgiveness and ask Jesus into our hearts, trusting Him as Savior, at that moment we are washed clean—completely forgiven! As Colossians 3:3 says, "For you have died and your life is hidden with Christ in God."

When we receive forgiveness, it is not like: "Now that I have a little bit more forgiveness, I am cleaner." This thinking is incorrect. Cleanliness does not come in installments. Forgiveness and cleanliness are a one-time deal. When we receive Jesus Christ as our Savior, we are made clean—righteous. We trade our life for Jesus' life. Our sins are given to Him, and His righteousness comes to us. We are not earning cleanliness by abiding in Him. We are responding to who we are, and that changes what we do. We are clean in Christ; therefore, we abide in Him.

Clean Feet
John 13:6–10

If you are a believer in Jesus, you are not a sinner who does saintly things every once in a while. You are born again. You have been made new. Jesus Christ, through the Holy Spirit, lives inside of you. You are clean. You are a saint who at times sins, and when that happens, Jesus gives you a way out—confession leads to being completely clean.

As believers in Jesus Christ, our greatest desire is not to sin. If you are in Christ, you have been born again, and what you really want is righteousness. I want to do things that honor God. I want to know God better. That's why you are daily reading the devotional; you desire to grow in Christ. Be encouraged. That understanding is different from "I know I shouldn't do bad things, but I really want to." Where is your want? Understand that you have been made clean.

God is a holy God. He has never thought about doing anything wrong. He is completely pure. He made us in His image. We were made without sin, but we chose the wrong path; we lied, and we sinned. Now we have a holy God and sinful people. What did God do? He sent His Son Jesus Christ to die on the cross for our sins so everyone could be made clean in Him. It is not in us but in a relationship with Him that we are clean. That is how we begin our journey—this Christian walk of abiding. We do not have to earn our salvation; we do not have to get clean on our own. He has given us cleanliness in Jesus.

That is what it means to be a Christian—forgiveness of sin and Jesus living in our hearts. All we have to do is respond and say, "Lord, I know I have done things wrong. I want You to come into my heart and make me clean." When that happens, change happens in your life. Picture a bride dressed in her clean, beautiful, white gown or a military sailor dressed in the cleanliness of dress whites. In Jesus, we are dressed in white, and we are clean. We are made clean in Him. We are not trying to earn a new nature; we already have one. From that knowledge and understanding, we then step into abiding, connecting to the Source.

Lord, thank You. In You, I have been made clean. Now I can rest in Your love.

Good Soil
John 15:4–5

A story has been told about a school that had a fire. When the alarm went off, the kids thought it was a fire drill, so they were excited to miss class for a while. As they got out of their classrooms, they realized that smoke was coming through the hallways. They went out into the parking lot, and the teachers began to count noses. The principal then realized that some of the kids did not make it out. They tragically did not survive the fire.

The principal and teachers vowed to rebuild the school and set up a state-of-the-art sprinkler to keep this from happening again. As time went by, a janitor was walking around the newly remodeled school doing some inspections. He realized that even though they had the best sprinkler system money could buy, someone had failed to connect it to the water source. They had everything in place but had no connection to the water!

I give you that illustration as we talk about abiding because you also can have everything in place but not be connected to the source—Jesus Christ—and nothing is going to work. Life is never going to satisfy you because sin can never satisfy. No accomplishment can satisfy.

Jesus extends this invitation to us: "Abide in Me, and I in you" (John 15:4 NKJV). To abide is to experience a restful residence and a desperate dependence. We rest in the Lord. We trust in God that He is the vine and we are the branches. We are just a conduit, a pipeline for His glory and for what He wants to do. It is not our choices that matter; it is His choices. We yield as the vine takes His glory to the fruit. We are just the branch that it comes through. We are desperately dependent upon Him and restfully resident in Him. He has made us clean.

We are not encouraged to bear fruit but to abide. If we abide in Christ, desperately dependent on Him, restfully residing in Him, then the fruit will take care of itself. If we focus on bearing fruit, we will not abide in Christ. We may die trying to bear fruit, and we won't get to know Jesus any better in the process. It is in abiding that we find out who we are in Him.

Today think of Jesus as the water source and your life as the sprinkler system. How can you allow Him to flow through you in a greater way?

Abiding vs. Achieving
John 15:5–7

L et me take the bull's-eye of abiding and put a ring around it to illus-trate the concept. The first ring is the difference between abiding and achieving. We are called to abide, not to achieve. When we abide, we trust God and allow Him to do His work through us.

We live in a culture that is very achievement driven. We drop our kids into the "achievatron" because we never want to see any potential left on the table. Many of us are addicted to our cell phone screens, checking our email in the midst of conversations with people we love. Our actions say something like this: "Let me NOT spend time with my loved ones in order to get with someone I barely know and see what they need." Do you see the fallacy? Do you perceive the addiction? Don't seek achievement; seek abiding.

The addiction trickles down, and we put it on our kids. We put headphones on a pregnant woman's belly, trying to teach the baby an appreciation of music. As soon as a baby can eat Cheerios, we count them in Spanish because we want the baby to learn a foreign language. By the time the baby is six, he or she gets a tutor; by eight, he or she has specialized in a sport and has a former pro athlete as a trainer. These are not bad things in themselves. But often, we focus on achievements and accomplishments instead of training children in character. We are trying to "achieve" great kids.

The goal is not to achieve but to abide. As I abide in Christ, my godli-ness will make me a better father. Then, I will be able to achieve greater things with my kids. If I abide, I walk with Christ and honor God. I live restfully resident in Him, desperately dependent upon Him. That makes me a better husband, employer, or whatever it is that I do. I have been made clean. I am attached to the Vine, and He is just coming through me to bear the fruit.

C. S. Lewis said, "Put first things first and we get second things thrown in: put second things first and we lose *both* first and second things."[43]

Remember the ring around the bull's-eye of abiding? The first ring is this: Are you just trying to achieve? Or are you aiming for the bull's-eye of abiding in Christ?

My Identity in Christ
1 Peter 2:9–10

There is a difference between our roles and our identities. Your identity is a son or daughter of God as a believer in Christ. Then you have your roles: a spouse, a father, a mother, a grandparent, an employer, or an employee. If your whole identity is wrapped around your vocation, then when you retire, you will not know what to do with yourself because your role has become your identity.

Everyone calls me Pastor Gregg, and I love it! But there will be a day when I will not be a pastor. My identity is that I am a child of God through my faith in Christ; my role is that I am the pastor of a church. Do you see the difference? If I get to where I think my identity is being the pastor of the church, I am going to miss my true identity in Christ. My identity in Jesus keeps the role of the pastor in the right place.

Our identity as a child of God makes us a different kind of person as we walk in our roles. We mix up our role and our identity because we seek to achieve rather than to abide. We lift up our role because we don't understand our identity. Then, when our vocation comes to an end or someone else comes along and takes the baton in our vocation, we are left without a sense of identity.

In an interview with *Vanity Fair*, Madonna said, "My drive in life is from this horrible fear of being mediocre. And that is always pushing me, pushing me. Because even though I have become somebody, I still have to prove that I am somebody. My struggle has never ended and it probably never will."[44]

When we do not understand our identity, we will not understand our role. As children of God, Jesus calls us to abide in Him, and then we will bear fruit.

Aim for the bull's-eye of your identity in Christ, then you will achieve His plans and fulfill the roles He has given you.

Restful Residence
Isaiah 30:15–18

You have a big meeting Tuesday, so you stay up late preparing your presentation, making everything happen. Knowing that if you don't get the deal, you are not going to get paid, the stress grows. The weight of the world is on your shoulders; it feels like it is all up to you.

Or you can say, "Lord, I give You this meeting. I want to trust in You with my preparation because this is a big deal for our company. I give it to You, Lord. I want to begin my day by spending time in Your Word. I want to see and understand my identity in You is safe. I am clean and forgiven, and nothing can ever be taken away from me. Even if I lose this deal, I am dependent on You. You are my Provider, I rest in You, Lord. I give You this meeting; please let me do my best and trust You whatever the result."

Tuesday at the meeting: Allow God to speak through you and use your preparation. After the meeting, you can say, "Lord, I trust in You as my provider. I am not looking for a prince to provide because I have a King! It's all in Your hands. I just want to live for Your glory."

The difference in the two scenarios is resting in the Lord. An intentional focus or trusting in His plan and His power through us changes everything. Sure, stress will still come; adrenaline is useful at times. It is good to have the thrill of a challenge but the trusting of the result. Let's give it our all but depend on the fact that God is in control.

Let's take resting in the Lord's work from another angle . . . parenting. A mom wakes up in the morning, and the whole day is about getting the children's shoes on and making sure they get to their activities on time—frazzled, hurried, stressed, with a thousand things to do. Or the day can have the same ingredients but each one is seen as a blessing instead of a task. Let it take ten more minutes yet be enjoyable. Nurture instead of chase the kids. So as parents, we are able to set a tone of peace and trust.

No doubt, this is easier said than done. I'm often guilty of running instead of resting. But I'm trying. Join me in swimming upstream, seeking to rest in Him.

Costly Stones
1 Corinthians 3:11–15

Understand that you are clean, that you belong to God, and that you are NOT the Vine. You don't have to be worried about the fruit; you are the branch. The fruit will take care of itself. If you abide in Christ, fruit will come. If you understand your identity, you will walk further in your roles. If you focus on seeking achievement in your roles, you won't stand on a firm foundation. You will never be the parent or the husband or the wife you desire to be.

The choice is ours: trust in Christ or walk in our own strength. If we do not trust in Him, we are like a state-of-the-art sprinkler system, disconnected from the water source. *Nothing* of eternal value will be achieved in your life. You may rule the world, but when you die, it will be over. You will not have an eternal legacy.

Today's verses remind us fire will test each person's work. On Judgment Day, we will stand before the throne, and all we accomplished will be tested. If we did not abide in Christ, like a puff of air it will all be gone! If I'm not abiding in Jesus, I am not passing down eternal things. I may accomplish great things on the earth but not eternal things.

True achievement comes from true abiding. Abide in order to achieve. Rest in your identity in order to fulfill your roles. Then we can accomplish great things for the kingdom of God. Our kids will be blessed by eternal things, not just temporary things. The eternal fruit will come through abiding; it will change how we influence the people around us. Then we will stand on Judgment Day and say, "Lord, here are my gold, silver, and costly stones of accomplishment through abiding."

Unintended Consequences

Isaiah 50:7

The budget does not allow for new furniture, so you decide to rear-range your living room to meet the need you have for change. You push the sofa, causing the end table to move and the lamp to fall off and shatter. You think, *Wait a minute. All I did was push the sofa. How did the lamp smash on the ground?* You keep moving things and decide to move the dining room table. When you do, it moves the bed in the bedroom, and it goes cockeyed. You begin to look more closely at things and realize that in between each piece of furniture is a rope. When you pull the rope, it pulls on something else. Everything is interconnected, and you learn a new concept: *unintended consequence.*

You didn't mean to push the sofa and break the lamp—that was an unintended consequence. You didn't mean to move the bed when you moved the dining room table. It was an unintended consequence. That term might come in handy when it happens at your next family gathering. Everyone in your family is going to bring some food. You've never liked broccoli, so you're bound to walk up and say, "I don't really like broccoli." You're then going to hear Aunt Thelma say, "Well, I don't really like you" (she made the broccoli). You didn't know that when you pushed the broccoli away, there was a rope connected to your aunt's heart. It was an unintended consequence.

There is an unintended consequence when we do not set our focus on Jesus Christ. As Isaiah puts it, "set my face like flint" (Isa. 50:7), mean-ing determined. Jesus tells us that if we do not focus on Him, we will accomplish *nothing*. Do you intend to accomplish nothing for your family, coworkers, or friends? No! We intend to accomplish great things.

To truly raise your kids in the way of the Lord, you have to focus on the Lord. Mom and Dad are great parents when they're focused. When we don't focus on the Lord, we end up with unintended consequences.

Are we going to be people who live by unintended or intended conse-quences? It is our choice of focus on Jesus or not.

Christ!

Colossians 1:15–20

Jesus gives us a positive intended consequence of being restfully resident, desperately dependent on Him: *prayers become intimate and are answered.* Here is part of a 1,500-year-old prayer called St. Patrick's Breastplate:

> Christ with me,
> Christ before me,
> Christ behind me, Christ in me,
> Christ beneath me,
> Christ above me,
> Christ on my right,
> Christ on my left,
> Christ when I lie down,
> Christ when I sit down,
> Christ when I arise,
> Christ in the heart of every man who thinks of me,
> Christ in the mouth of everyone who speaks of me,
> Christ in every eye that sees me,
> Christ in every ear that hears me.[45]

Does that sound like a focused prayer? When we say, "Lord, I want to trust in You," He refines our prayer life. It's no longer about our comfort but about His kingdom. There is something higher than our comfort. Our discomfort is God's advantage. The more uncomfortable I am, the more I need God—the more I must trust in Him—the more I turn to Him.

A second refinement of our prayer life is that it begins to move from being about needs to being about our relationship with God. When we go out to eat, I like to tell our waiter, "We're about to pray for our food. Is there anything that we can pray for you about?" Waiters at times say, "I'm good; I don't need any prayer." That is how many Christians think about their prayer lives—"All is well. I don't need God . . . until I need Him."

God wants to move us from need-centered to relationship-centered prayer, to where we ask for what He wants. Try it now as you finish reading.

To Glorify God
Colossians 4:2–6

Saturday evenings I look over my sermon. I lie down on the floor in my home office with my Bible, computer, and notes. Sometimes, I have worship music on. I look over my sermon outline, and I pray. I have done that for about thirty years now, ever since college. I was reminded of my unspoken hope thirty years ago: "Dear Lord, I'm going to speak to a bunch of people tomorrow. Don't let me look bad. In Jesus' name, amen."

That used to be my goal and sometimes, to be honest, I still think that. But the usual Saturday night prayer is: "Lord, thank You that I get to speak to people; let me know more about You. Let me understand more about You. Let me walk in You. Let me abide in You. I am so thankful that I've been able to sit down here with a notepad, Bible, and an outline, and I've found You faithful every time. I know You. You're Jesus. You're the Savior. You're faithful. You've gifted me to be used for Your glory. I just want to rest in You." Those types of relationship prayers are different from "God, do something that keeps me from being uncomfortable."

Christ wants to refine our prayer life so it is based on a relationship with God. Our prayers become intimate, and the answers flow as we understand that it is all about Him. It's not about getting God on our program. That is not the point of prayer. It is about us getting on God's program. That's the point of prayer!

The deeper we walk with the Lord, the deeper our prayer life and vice versa. Today, spend a little more time in prayer than you usually do. Talk to Jesus about your gratitude to be in relationship with Him. As you do, consciously go deeper.

Agreeing with God
Matthew 7:15–20

Glorifying God is a vast concept. What does it mean? There are many definitions, but let me share this one with you: We glorify God when we stand in agreement with God. We say, "What Your Word says, Lord, I believe. I'm going to live my life like that." That brings Him glory. "Everything God says about Himself, I believe." That glorifies God.

I stand in agreement with God. And when I glorify God, He teaches me His disciplines—He makes me a disciple. Discipleship is a continuous process of agreeing more and more with God. You might go to a Bible study, and you might learn to agree to a greater extent with God. You hear a message, and you agree with God. Glorifying God then results in bearing fruit.

In college, I took a class in botany, the study of plants. I'm a very talented botanist, I want you to know that I can identify an orange tree spectacularly . . . if there are oranges hanging from the branches. I can look at an apple tree from thirty yards away, and if there are apples hanging from the branches I can say with confidence, "That's an apple tree!" I'm sure my botany professor would be proud! Truly, I'm not even sure tree identification counts as botany, but you get the point.

We are great at identifying the tree correctly if we see the fruit connected to it. Dear Christian, you will be identified as a disciple of Jesus if you bear much fruit. People should be able to look at a believer in Christ and see the fruits of the Spirit: love, joy, peace, patience, kindness, goodness, gentleness, faithfulness, and self-control.

People should look at you and say, "Look, it's a Christian." But what is really confusing is when somebody says, "I'm a Christian" and there is no evidence—no fruit. They hear "Christian," but there is no fruit to show for it.

Jesus says that you will bear much fruit, and people will know that you are His disciple. You don't have to announce you are a Christian. You can show it with the fruit of Christ's life in you. People can identify His disciples from thirty yards away and say, "I see great peace in him; I believe he is a Christian." "I see great joy in her; I believe she is a Christian." That brings God glory.

The Father's Love
Romans 8:29

Jesus wants us to experience the Father's love and joy.

Walking with God brings deep understanding of the Father's love for you. Jesus wants us to know this so our joy may be complete. He is so good to us! Faith achieves love and joy. We understand and experience the love of the Father and the love that Jesus gives us when we persevere.

God wants to bring joy, *deep joy*, into your life. That is the intended consequence of walking by faith. If our earthly parents know how to give good gifts, how much more does our heavenly Father know how to give us good things. On the road with God we get to know Him in prayer and glorify Him in our lives. It's abiding deeply to achieve greatly. Then we become His disciples and experience His love and His joy so we can respond something like this:

> Christ be with me,
> At the dinner table,
> At the ballfield,
> At school,
> At the office,
> In my marriage,
> In my singlehood,
> In my friendships,
> In my church.

The joy of a life lived for Jesus! Will we live intentionally or unintentionally?

> *Dear God, I want to know You better by living restfully, trusting fully, and bringing You glory. I trust You to make a disciple of me as I abide in Your Son. In His name, amen.*

Greatest Sacrifice

James 2:23

Faith is to be restfully resident and desperately dependent upon Jesus. He is the Vine, and we are the branches. If we just rest in Christ and allow Him to flow, we will have great fruit coming through our lives. The call is not to bear fruit; the call is to rely. In doing that, we will achieve greatly. I am not talking about worldly success but about bearing eternal, lasting fruit.

It is amazing to think He calls us friend. We have to rely on Him, trust in Him, and rest in our identity in Christ—not in the roles of husband, wife, or student. We must rest in the identity we have through a relationship with Jesus Christ, whom we received when we trusted Him for salvation. As we abide in Christ, the fruit will come in our lives. It is a natural outflow.

Jesus wants us to love each other as He has loved us, with sacrificial love. Great love shows itself in great sacrifice. While we were still sinners, Jesus died and paid for our sins. He sacrificed Himself for us so we could each be called a friend of God. Because of the great sacrifice Jesus made for us, what we do in response isn't really a sacrifice. When we forego things and give them away for Christ's sake, we receive so much back from the Lord.

Jesus lets us know that we have friendship with God through the sacrifice He made on our behalf. Our friendship with God is shown through our friendship with others in making sacrifices for them. Sacrifice and love go hand in hand. If you are not sacrificial in your actions, in your way of thinking, in the things that you do, then you really don't have love.

Deep love is shown best in deep sacrifice. Those we love the most, we sacrifice for the most. Parents with children know this because there are days when the whole day is spent doing kid stuff. There is also great sacrifice in marriage. We sacrifice for one another, saying, "I choose to put your interest before my interest."

Jesus, "who for the joy that was set before Him endured the cross" (Heb. 12:2 NKJV), put our interest first—the greatest love, the greatest sacrifice.

Sacrificial Love
John 15:9–13

There were a few fourteen-year-old girls hanging out on boogie boards on a lake in Florida. All of a sudden, an alligator bit the arm of one of the girls and dragged her underneath the water. She began to pry herself loose from the alligator with her other arm. She popped out of the water and saw that every one of her friends had left in panic—except one, her best friend Amanda, who pulled her to shore as the gator followed them. If Amanda had not chosen to stay, the alligator would have killed her friend.

In the Greek language, there are three primary words for *love*:

eros—romantic love

phileo—friendship, brotherly love

agape—God's love

John 15 uses the word *agape* for deep feeling, but love at its core is a decision. Does it mean there is no emotion? Absolutely not. The emotions of love are throughout. However, we need to understand that God's love is a decision. He decided to stay when the alligator of sin tried to pull us under.

Jesus Christ says, "Greater love has no one than this: to lay down one's life for one's friends" (John 15:13 NIV).

The greatest possible love is Jesus Christ on the cross. In John 15, the resurrection is coming in a few days. Jesus is saying something like this: "I'm going to the cross, and you need to know that I love you greatly. Remember that as I give my life for you." If Jesus had not died, we would never have been able to be in a relationship with the Father. Today is particularly special to me. October 21, 1986, I trusted Christ as my Savior. So today is my spiritual birthday! What a blessing to experience Jesus' love and sacrifice.

Jesus sacrificed for us, and as friends we sacrifice for other friends. I want to be the kind of friend Amanda was when the alligator bit. Sacrificial love might look different for you and me today. Maybe we have to decide to reach out to a neighbor. Maybe we choose to stay in our marriage or workplace even though it is difficult to do so. Regardless of the action, let the heart be love.

A Friend of God
Exodus 33:7–11

Jesus Christ can meet our innermost need—love. As believers, we decide to keep our lives pure for Him. Leaving sinful things behind is not a sacrifice, though it may feel like it. But we lay them down because we want to know the greatest love there is. Jesus Christ laid down His life for me. When we realize the love of God, renouncing things is really not a sacrifice.

Jesus, the Son of God, calls us friends. That is amazing! Why? There are only two people in the entire Old Testament whom God called friends: Abraham and Moses. Jesus gives a blanket statement to us all, through Jesus Christ, each one of us, every one of us, can become a friend of God.

Moses spoke to the Lord as a friend. It's incredible that we get to do the same thing. Prayer is a friendly conversation with the greatest friend ever. A tent of meeting is available 24/7 to every believer. Through the cross we have moved from enemy to friend.

Moses and Abraham walked in relationship with God. Others just went to the synagogue and kept the Law the best they knew how. They did not have a friendship with God. Jesus said He was going to lay down His life for you and call you His friend. The reason He can call us *friend* is because He made it possible for the Holy Spirit to dwell in our hearts through salvation.

In Him, we have the power to walk in love and leave behind our sinful nature and all the things that came along with it. They have no place in our lives anymore. We get to walk in friendship with God.

God's friends: Abraham, Moses, and _____ (insert your name here).

God Calls Me Friend
John 15:14–16

Let's lock this down another notch. God calls you and me friend. This happens when you realize that you don't have a relationship with God through Christ, so you ask Jesus to forgive your sins and wash you clean. The Holy Spirit, who is part of the Trinity, comes and lives in your heart. Then you get to be called a friend of God.

Often we are more comfortable with the concept of being servants of Christ than friends of Christ. Please receive this: God not only loves you, He likes you. He is and wants to be your friend.

There is no better friend than Jesus Christ. He is the best friend you could ever have. You discover it the most when you lack friends the most. Student, will you stay at home on a Friday night when everybody else is doing something that will not honor God? Will you choose to stay home and say, "Jesus, You're better." If you do that, you'll find in Him a friend. How do I know? Because I did it many times in high school and college. If you choose Jesus to be your friend, He will be the best friend you could ever have. And I think seeing your faithfulness He just might provide amazing friends that ARE doing the right thing. You'll have a lot more fun, I promise. So good to know we are not just His servants; we are also His friends. Friends are fully known and fully loved. He knows you fully and loves you fully.

Jesus doesn't owe us anything. He chose us and wants us to be His friends. I experience His great love—*agape* love—because I am His friend. Now, the greatest thing I can do is serve Him. Friendship does not do away with service; it empowers it. A friendship with God allows me to serve in a way that I can truly abide. I am not serving to earn His love or please Him to gain some kind of benefit. Jesus and I are already friends, so I am completely secure in my relationship with Him, and now I serve from it. That is security in Jesus.

I want to sacrifice in my friendships on earth so I can show God's love in the way I serve them. God is not asking what you can do for Him, because that will simply accomplish nothing. God wants you to see what He can accomplish *through* you, by the power of the Holy Spirit who inhabits you, because His friends accomplish lasting fruit.

Discover God to Know His Will

John 15:15

Jesus says, "I do not call you servants anymore. . . . I have called you friends" (John 15:15). I know I'm saved because I've trusted Jesus; I'm not earning my salvation—now I'm a friend. If I am a friend, I will know my Master's business, and He will tell me everything I need to know. "I have made known to you everything I have heard from my Father" (John 15:15).

Why do we so often pray, "Lord, what is Your will? Is it a right turn or a left turn? Is it speak or remain silent? Is it do this or do that? This car or that job?" If we are supposed to know the Father's business, why are we so confused about so many things? We have incorrectly defined the Father's business as what we do, instead of who we are.

Primary question: Who are we? We are children of God. What are we supposed to do? Trust in Jesus. This is the business of God. We often want the specifics of the doing, not the generals of abiding. We want the specifics of the mission so we can execute it on behalf of God instead of the general aspects of the task being God's. Choose general trusting over specific doing. Walking by faith not sight. The goal is not answers from God, but a relationship with God. And as you discover God, you will discover His will. Find the God of God's will, and you will find the will of God.

If you know the Father's business of resting in Him, then you will know who you are—His friend! If you are a friend, you will know what to do and how to serve. If you are only about what to do, you may begin to think, *God, you owe me something. You have to tell me something, God, because I am still a private and don't have a relationship with my leader, so I just want orders.* Jesus then says, "I did not die on the cross to make you a private; I died on the cross to make you My pal, and I've called you friend. When you get to know Me, you will know who you are in Me, and then . . . you will know what to do."

Fruit That Lasts
John 15:5

You and I, standing in friendship with Jesus, will bear fruit for our families, our lives, in everything we do. From the strength of our relationship with Jesus, we are able to walk in our lives—in marriage, in singlehood, at school, in our neighborhoods, in service.

When we speak of our friendship with the Son of God because of His grace—knowing we sinned but His death paid for our sin—we are making a huge statement about Christ. Being about the Master's business is being about faith in Jesus Christ. We are friends with God, so we live out this relationship serving Him with all we are and have.

In Christ, we are saints. Now saints still sin, but we are not defined by that. We did not choose the Teacher; the Master chose us, and He asked us to journey with Him for eternity. If you walk in this friendship with Jesus, you will have fruit that will last. Abiding will turn into fruit. Walking in friendship with Jesus will yield fruit that lasts. Love and friendship leave a lasting legacy.

Jesus Christ is the best friend you and I will ever have because He laid down His life for us. He did that so the Holy Spirit could live in our hearts and He could call us friends. By being His friends, we get to know Him and love Him. As we love Him, we serve Him. We abide deeply so we can achieve greatly. Don't get these two mixed up. He is not asking what you can do for Him, but what He can do through you. Then you can rest and watch Him do His work.

Then guess what happens . . . You are the friend that stays true when hard times come. You are the friend who stays when your friend or coworker is in need. You're the one who shines with Jesus. Your life will have a lasting legacy.

You can be a friend of God, which impacts your friendship with others.

There Is More
Ephesians 1:7–10

Since you're reading this devotional, you want to grow spiritually. Something inside is telling you, "There is more."

We all need to grow spiritually. Our walk with God is not linked to our natural, physical age. Becoming older doesn't mean we are more spiritually mature. Some teenagers are more spiritually mature than their parents or other adults.

As we grow older, shouldn't we be growing more spiritually mature at the same time? Shouldn't we be different than when we first started, more mature after walking with the Lord for years? John is going to show us, through the symbolic representations of a child, a young man, and a father, the different stages of spiritual maturity.

Imagine a graph where the vertical values represent obedience, and the horizontal values represent faith. Hopefully, our faith is pushing our obedience up. We are not perfect, but we are moving up and to the right.

Our relationship with God starts with forgiveness through Jesus Christ. To obtain forgiveness, we first need humility. We must admit that we've sinned. Why wouldn't we admit that we have sinned? Basically because of pride, which is contrary to child-like faith.

We must realize that we have not done everything perfectly or lived a holy life—we have sinned. Then we humbly come to the Father, the One we have displeased, and ask for forgiveness through Jesus Christ on account of His name. It's not on account of our works or by going to church or by trying to be nicer people.

We admit we will never be able to do more good than bad. Therefore, heaven is based not on our works, but on Jesus' death on the cross and His grace. It is not in ourselves; it is through Jesus Christ. Our relationship with God is formed through forgiveness. We now have a relationship with the Father, as little children growing in faith.

With this in mind, Ephesians 1 blows us away—riches of grace, heavenly blessing, redemption, forgiveness, purpose, and MORE! Ponder the "more" of God today and let your heart be overwhelmed.

A Tremendous Battle
Romans 8:15–17

What is the best thing about being a little child? The only thing you need to know is that you are part of a family. You don't have to do anything but feel safe in your home. Unfortunately, not every person felt the love of a family. Maybe you have some wounds in this area. That's what makes my next sentence so important. A relationship with God the Father through the Son of God, Jesus Christ, makes you part of a heavenly home, God's family.

We have seen that when a heart is fatherless, problems multiply. When we trust in the forgiveness of Jesus Christ, the Father comes to our hearts, which changes everything. We as little children can each crawl up in the lap of God and say, "Yes. He's my Father."

But it might be a very big temptation to stop there. Many people got saved years ago but haven't grown spiritually since then. God does not want us to stay in this childhood stage. He wants us to grow and move toward being men and women of God.

Life is a tremendous battle against pride, sin, our own base desires, the devil, and the world. Sins like pornography and anger do not have to be part of our lives forever. But we will not gain the victory through our willpower. We are to fight for right. Spiritual men and women have conquered the evil one. We can be victorious through Jesus Christ. The devil bruised Jesus' heel, but Jesus crushed Satan's head.

The battle requires us to stand our ground in God's love. The devil and the world use the media to rile us up and make us fall in the way of outrage and hate. Instead of disagreeing in love with others, they want us to hate the very people Jesus sent us to love. We must stand and say, "No. We are going to fight for what is right, but we are going to fight right—in love without hate."

What gives us the ability to do this? John says, "I have written to you, young men, because . . . you have conquered the evil one" (1 John 2:14). How? Through the cross of Jesus Christ, we are able to move into the love of God. Battling sin is difficult. But here is the great news: You can actually conquer it through Christ. You don't have to live in that place. You may never be sinless, but you can sin less. You can win, because you are safe and secure in the victorious family of God.

One Conquering Weapon
Hebrews 4:12

After being born again into the Father's family through Jesus Christ, we can grow into men and women of God. As such, the Lord wants us to know that we are in a battle. Therefore, He gave us a special message. He said that we are victorious. He has revealed to us that our victory tool is the Word of God, and in it we see the future—that God has something bigger for us.

We go through the battle because we know that all things work for the good of those who love Christ. No one can snatch us from His hands. In difficult times, He can take us through the Red Sea like Moses.

Maybe you've heard these sayings: "Seven days without God's Word makes one weak" or "You'll either find a worn-out Bible or you'll find a worn-out life." Some of us are still spiritual children who think we don't have time to read the Bible. Make time. That is the most important thing you could possibly do. Maybe you don't read the Word because you don't understand it. No one understands everything. It is a difficult book. But we can go to the Father and pray, "God, I need Your help. Let me understand your Word. Let it wash over me." Then, go to the New Testament and start reading. That is all you have to do to begin.

God's Word brings the victory. The Word of God is the weapon over sin. Victory comes by reading it, studying it, obeying it, living it, resting in it, remaining in it, abiding in it.

All of us could do better with our Bible reading. Be encouraged that you are reading this devotional right now. Way to go! Keep it up! Put the Word in your mind and in your heart, and let God do something in you. That is how you move from a little child to a man or woman of God.

Heaven is counting on men and women of all ages to rely on God's Word in the battles and to stay true spiritually. We are not talking about age progression; we are talking about spiritual maturity. Believers, we have conquered the evil one through Jesus!

The Inner Change Challenge
1 Kings 19:1–8

Today begin planning a time you can take the Inner Change Challenge. We are all so busy and we need to experience the spiritual discipline of having a time of solitude with God. If you want to join this challenge, plan to be still before the Lord for an extended time at some over the next two weeks. Hopefully, it will become a consistent part of your life.

Set aside some time to get alone with a journal, a Bible, your headphones, and some music that can lead you to process with the Lord. Take out your calendar and plan when you are going to spend this good time with God. Take some time for the spiritual discipline of solitude. In 1 Kings 19, we see an encouraging account of the refreshment in a difficult time Elijah experienced.

Inspired by Elijah, every month for years now I've set aside the better part of one day to be with the Lord. I call it "Time with the Father." I like to say on that day I "work on the ministry not in the ministry." Instead of daily to-do's, I focus on the big picture including my heart. I'm asking what's the longer look at life and how am I "really" doing.

During this time, set aside your social media, your texting, and your email. Better yet, just turn off your notifications. You can be sure it will all be there when you come back! Emails seems to be eternally with us, ugh.

Be still before God, and let an inner change happen in your heart. We are acquainted with the verse that says, "Be still, and know that I am God" (Ps. 46:10 NIV). But do we know what the rest of the verse says? "Be still, and know that I am God; I will be exalted among the nations."

Stillness results in impact. Take the Inner Change Challenge and be still for a time. Get away with God, spend some time letting the things in your heart settle, and you will come back as a better dad, a better mom, and a better employee or employer with a new vision or new thought, or whatever you need.

If you just stay on the hamster wheel, nothing will change. To fight the battle, spend time alone with God to get into His Word. Experience inner change and refreshment.

Spiritual Parents
2 Timothy 2:1–2

We are a long way from Mother's or Father's Day, but we can still celebrate spiritual mothers and fathers. They are believers who have made their relationship with God their main focus—their joy comes from pouring into others. That kind of spiritual maturity is not reached with age. They can be older people who may have just started their walk with God or young folks who have already made their relationship with the Father their priority, either way they want to raise up disciples.

Another way we can spot spiritual fathers or mothers is that they no longer put themselves into the spotlight. Their main passion is to minister, teach, or care for somebody else.

Just as it is natural for parents to place their attention on their children's well-being and development, spiritual fathers and mothers try to make sure the next generation of believers can grow up in a loving environment until they are ready to minister to others and do something for God in a greater way.

We become models of humbleness and kindness, able to teach and patiently endure evil, and truly listen. We give those who want to love Jesus the training and opportunities to continue with the work of God in their own particular style.

God the Father, is always reminding us how much He loves us. He tells us things like this: "I love you. I got you. I am journeying this path with you. Trust in My forgiveness. Oh, I know it is a battle, but I have conquered the enemy. You just stay here. Stay close. We are going to be victorious. You will never be sinless, but you will sin less. I will begin to use you and your story to minister to others."

So how do we put this spiritual parenting into practice today? We simply minister to others for their benefit, not yours. Be an encouragement to someone's spiritual growth.

October 31

Don't Love the World
Matthew 6:19–21

Are you familiar with this scene? Suddenly, you enter a huge department store. Your claim is that "I am not really into things." That's good church talk, but after a few moments in the store, your real cravings begin to show. Straightaway, you see that _____ you've always wanted.

Matthew warns us of moths and rust while marketers remind us of what all the neighbors have. We can get mixed up when we say that we are going after God but then get pulled in by materialism and pride. We all need food to eat, a place to live, clothes to dress according to the local weather, and some means of transportation and communication. Taking care of our material needs in the right way is hard because we are all surrounded by many things to spend our money on. They can grab our hearts and lead us down a path of loving the world more than God.

I remember when I was a teenager and went to the dealership to get my first brand-new car. I couldn't believe it was finally happening, a brand-new car! Few things are more exciting than a new car. That 1989 Mustang (unfortunately with a 4-cylinder engine) was as good as it could get in my eyes, I was the king of the world, until I drove out of the parking lot of the dealership. All of a sudden, a Corvette went by. One look at it, and my Mustang just didn't feel quite as good.

But isn't that life? You get something and think it is great until you see a better one . . . a better house, a better whatever. Comparison typically brings disappointment. I could have compared my new car to the junky ones on the road, but somehow it was the Vette that caught my eye. We are all tempted to compare up. And sometimes we begin to chase those things instead of the Lord. John says really clear: "Do not love the world" (1 John 2:15).

What is at stake is lost gratitude and intimacy with God. Love God more than what moths and rust can eat. Be pleased with the things you have, enjoy new purchases, but love Him more.

Love God More
Matthew 7:3–5

While living in this world, we will need food, shelter, clothing, education, and a means of communication and transportation. Sure, it is great to have nice things, but we don't want that to steal our hearts. When we are caught up in things, our whole life switches into upkeep mode; we can forget about doing what God wants. We know what we would have to do if we were going to keep this place and this lifestyle. So we have to be careful that the Lord comes first and that we love Him with all our heart. As I grow older I feel the pull to "manage my lifestyle" in tension with full surrender to God.

Some of us have become expert identifiers. We know which people have spent too much and gone too far. Then, we try to say what we would have done instead. "If I had that much money, I would drive _____, I would live _____, I would eat _____, I would wear _____." Do you know what the Bible says about that? Remove the plank from your own eye before you remove the speck from somebody else's eye.

We know the "why" behind all the things we have and how we have arranged our lives. We can explain why we purchased these things and why we think our heart was right when we did so. But in other people's lives, we do not understand the "why." We only see the "what." So, we become judgmental. It is a slippery slope. When we do that, we are unknowingly trying to deflect attention from our own hearts. That should be a warning sign to us. Whenever we catch ourselves acting as expert identifiers, we should realize that an inner inspection is due.

James tells us that whoever wants to be the world's friend becomes God's enemy. Our goal is to love God more than the world. God can bless you. God can give you nice stuff. You can have a nice house and a nice car. You can have nice clothes. But don't let those things ever capture your heart and get in the way of following God's will.

As we are going, moving, and shaking, we start doing better. Sometimes we get paid more, have more disposable income, and can buy nicer things. All of that is awesome, but don't let it capture your heart. Don't be a friend of the world or try to remove the speck in someone else's eye before the plank in your own.

The Lust of the Flesh
1 John 2:16

When talking about the battle against materialism and pride, John shows us three areas where we need to keep our hearts in check: the desires of the flesh, the lust of the eyes, and the pride in possessions. The Bible doesn't state that certain things, experiences, or honors come from the world and not from the Father. Instead, it says that it is in our attitude toward these things, not the things themselves, that we have to be on guard for.

We can see how all three of these pitfalls came into play in one verse of Scripture—Genesis 3:6. That verse tells us about the first sin. Here is what it says:

Then the woman saw that the tree was good for food . . .

What is that? Lust of the flesh.

. . . and delightful to look at . . .

Lust of the eyes.

. . . and that it was desirable for obtaining wisdom.

The boastful pride of life.

In the first sin, we see all three of the dangers that John addresses in 1 John 2. The first one is the lust of the flesh, which is where our old nature and our new nature are at war. The Bible says that Jesus Christ died on a cross so you could receive Him as Savior and place your faith in Him alone. When you do that, you receive a new nature in Jesus Christ. That means you have an old nature before you trusted Christ as Savior that desires the sinful, but you also have a new nature through the Holy Spirit that desires the godly.

No matter what you already have, your old nature will always be craving something more. But your new nature can be satisfied in your relationship with Jesus Christ. He gives you living water so you will never thirst again. He gives you the bread of life so you will never hunger again.

The reason we don't practice sin—not that we will ever be perfect—is because we have been given a new nature that desires other things. We have been given a new nature in Jesus Christ that desires the things of God.

The Lust of the Eyes
2 Peter 1:4

The same thing can be godly or sinful depending on your viewpoint. Sleep is a great gift of God, but laziness will wreck your life. Sex is a gift from God in the intimacy of marriage to bring a husband and wife together and express their love for one another, but pornography is destructive. God blesses us with opportunities, experiences, relationships, and even material things. But just devouring stuff and needing bigger and better every moment is a problem that takes us far from Him.

The lust of the eyes is a big deal. The Bible tells us that one fateful day when King David should have been off at war, he saw Bathsheba bathing on the rooftop. God's will for David's life was to be at the battlefront with his army. He didn't go. He was in the wrong place at the wrong time. What happened then? He committed adultery and then murder. What we see affects what we do. What goes into our eyes is crucial for what comes out of our lives. What are we taking in?

Jesus said that our eyes are the lamps of our body. If our eyes are good, our whole body will be full of light. But if our eyes are bad, our whole body will be full of darkness. What we put before our eyes is crucial. It affects us.

In the taking of Jericho, Achan took some of the spoils that he shouldn't have taken. When he explained what happened, he saw these nice things. When he saw, he wanted them, and then desire turned into action.

Men and women, sometimes we are going to have to close our eyes during the commercials, even if it's during a baseball game.

What we put into our minds and our eyes affects what we do. It affects us. Looking at the wrong things will be detrimental. What goes in can affect the way we think. We are very visual. Look out for the lust of the eyes, because it affects what we do. When we desire to follow God, our desires are different. The Spirit motivates us to seek after God. Look to Him, gaze upon Christ, and the true desires of your heart will surface.

The Pride of Life
Esther 4:13–14

Middle-aged men and women are advised to take regular stress tests to make sure their hearts are functioning well. If we put electrodes on our spiritual chests to measure the health of our hearts as we run the race of life, when would they beep? They may beep the loudest when we are boasting in the pride of life.

The boastful pride of life is basically a desire to impress. How many of us would do what we do if nobody was there to see it? Would you iron your shirt or get dressed up if you lived on a desert island? Probably not. We do a lot of this for everybody else.

We know what we have and what we do. But sometimes, we love to sneak certain things into our conversations to bolster our insecurities. That's a sign that we are gauging our worth by comparing ourselves to others, that we are seeking to please others instead of God.

We should lift up our eyes and see the value that God has given us, for we are fearfully and wonderfully made. God has positioned us where we are and has given us abilities and gifts. Be true to yourself and be the best you can be for Jesus. Live in the new nature and clothe yourself in Christ. Let your eyes be set on the things above, not on the things of this world. If we let God do great things through us, it will make a huge difference.

God will put you in the place He wants you to be. Esther ended up in the palace, but she had a purpose there. Did God put you in a palace? Good, but don't get so used to palace-life that you will never live anywhere else. And if you are not in the palace, don't get bitter thinking that everyone in the palace must be a bad person. You don't know what God is doing in their lives, how they got there, or why. We need to love Jesus enough so we can be anywhere and glorify God. When we restrict ourselves to what is familiar and comfortable, that ends up being a problem. That will negate missional living in our lives.

At the same time, if we can be in a place that we are not used to, either up or down in society, and shine for Jesus, then we are able to glorify God anywhere we go.

Live for What Lasts
James 1:9–10

The Bible says that a rich man just fades away in his pursuits. Instead of longing to be like the rich, we should want to rise up and live for the things that last. It doesn't matter if we are in the palace, in poverty, or somewhere in between; the Christian life is a call to eternal impact, not just personal pleasure. Our legacy is defined by what we can give back. The number-one thing for us has nothing to do with this earth. The number-one thing for us has everything to do with heaven and Jesus Christ. That is where we can find our security, our faith, and our hope.

Have you ever seen a junkyard? At one point, every one of those cars was brand-new. Should you have a car? Of course, but you can't live for that. It will be smashed one day. Do you know that twenty years from now we are going to laugh at ourselves for what we are wearing now? Styles change, live for the things that last.

God is calling us to have an interchange in our hearts of darkness for light and of lies for truth. Where are you? Take a step and let God work in your life; begin to live out God's will for your life. It is better to be in the heart of God's will than in the heart of the world's will. Go about the things of God and live for the things that last. Then, no matter how hard it gets, you will run and not grow weary, you will walk and not faint, you will fly with wings of eagles, and you will live in God's will.

We are surrounded by material pleasures at our fingertips and filling our eyesight. It can be on your doorstep by just clicking a button. New and better houses go up every day. But, may we long for a city whose architect and builder is God.

Father, may our hearts beat for You so that when You bless us, we share the blessing and give You the glory. May we be givers and live for the things that last. May we be humble and not prideful. Every one of us is rich compared to the rest of the world, even when we don't feel like it. Let us long for more of You.

The Heart, Not the Address

Acts 2:1–13

In Luke 24, Jesus was sending His disciples to the nations. But I want you to understand where the disciples' power came from. When we get to know God's heart and His love for the nations, and when we begin to understand that our identity is in Him, we begin to grow a heart for impact. Our hearts want to spread the love of God. Incredibly, we are not alone, God gives us His Holy Spirit to help us complete this mission. The Holy Spirit is where the power comes from.

I encourage you to read Acts 2 to understand Pentecost. God did not want us to do this life with our own power. His desire was that we live through His power. Through His Spirit, we are transformed and begin to love like He does. When the Spirit of God lives in a believer, he or she automatically becomes a missionary. Can I give you a synonym for the word *missionary*? It's *Christian*. If you're a Christian, you are a missionary. Being a missionary does not mean you have to live on the other side of the world. Every believer is a missionary regardless of where they live. A life on mission is about your heart, not your address.

Whether you are a student or an adult, you have a weekly routine. Does living a daily routine outside of a "foreign mission field" mean you can't make an impact?

If a life on mission is about a foreign address, then our lives are not living out God's plan. If it is only about going to your nice office to make money to keep your lifestyle going, then it's less than He desires. But a life on mission is about the heart, not a location. Whether you are a doctor, a teacher, a retail salesperson, or a waiter, consider your workplace your ministry. I could say the same thing about me. There are a lot of foreign cities where I could be a pastor, but God uses me to make a difference where He has placed me.

Listen to the Spirit and where He is guiding you to complete the mission Christ created you for. You may be called to go to a different country, or you may be called to reach people in your workplace. Through the Holy Spirit, you have the power to make a difference right where God has put you. That is your mission field.

Living in the Last Hour
Matthew 24:42–44

Matthew reveals in chapter 24 of his Gospel that we are living in the last hour. According to the Bible, the end times run from the resurrection of Jesus Christ to His return. We don't know when Jesus is coming back, but we can see that we are closer today than ever before.

Jesus said there are six signs that the end is getting near: false messiahs, wars, natural disasters, persecution, turning away, and good news about the gospel. False teaching looks like something good, but when we get one degree off course, we end up miles off down the road.

There has been an increase in wars from 1870 to date. And there are more earthquakes, hurricanes, and tornadoes since 1950. Today, it is more dangerous than ever to be a Christian. In countries that used to be open, people lose their jobs just for being Christian. Open Doors USA reported that we are at the worst levels of persecution in modern times. Persecution is now hitting nearly every continent in the world.[46]

In 2016, the Center for Studies on New Religions determined that in 2015, 90,000 Christians were killed worldwide for their beliefs. Nearly a third were killed at the hands of Islamic extremists. The study also found that as many as 600 million Christians were prevented from practicing their faith in 2016.[47]

Americans with no religious affiliation grew from 8 percent in 1990 to 20 percent in 2012. A large percentage of the increase is among young people. Currently, 35 percent of millennials do not identify with any religion. That is twice the number of the previous generation who didn't identify with any religion. And back even another generation, there were only 11 percent who did not identify with any religion.[48] We need to reach millennials for Christ.

On the other hand, the number of unreached or unengaged people groups went down from 3,800 in 2011 to 700 in 2015. It is the fastest drop in the history of Christianity. Even though this is awesome, it also confirms that the end is getting closer and closer. The more we know about Christ returning and what is taking place, the more our Christian character must grow.

Who Is the Antichrist?
Ephesians 6:12

What is the Bible talking about when it mentions the word *antichrist*? There are three things the Bible talks about when referring to the word *antichrist*. One of them is the Antichrist, who in the book of Revelation is called the beast.

The second meaning of antichrist is a spirit that is against Jesus Christ. Do you sense a spirit "against Christ" in today's world? Believers are getting fired for their faith. In some places, believers can't mention Jesus' name or talk about God or the Bible. Prayer, Bibles, Christian artwork, monuments, engravings, names, and more are being removed or substituted. Biblical and moral stances are being repealed or revoked by legal means.

When good is opposed, we may often wonder why someone would be opposed to it. The Bible says that we are not wrestling against people but against various ranks of evil spirits. Satan, the prince of darkness, the prince of the air, is active in this world. There is a spirit "against," of opposition, that has been pushing back the things of the gospel, the things of the kingdom, and the things of Christ. A. W. Tozer said, "Satan hates your God. He hates Jesus Christ. He hates your faith. You should be aware of the devil's evil intentions."[49]

The third kind of antichrist mentioned in the Bible is the false teachers of the day. In New Testament times, they were called Gnostics. Some embody the spirit of antichrist and begin to teach false things. False teachers often look like angels of light. False teachings are everywhere, masquerading as good imitations of the truth.

We as believers in Christ strive to be sweet, nice, peaceful, agreeable people. The downside to this is that we can be very naïve about discerning lies from truth. The purpose of false teaching is to take people away from God. In any teaching you hear, make sure it is talking about Jesus, confirming the deity of Christ, and the truth of God's Word.

Be on the lookout today for the lies and plans of darkness and pray for God's power to prevail.

The Qualities of the Antichrist

Daniel 9:27

The book of Revelation says that the Antichrist will be symbolically represented as a beast from the sea (Rev. 13:1–10). The Bible also says no one knows the day that Jesus will return (Matt. 24:36). Satan always has someone ready to be the Antichrist.

In the early church, the Caesars of Rome would rise up and declare themselves gods to be worshiped, trying to take the place of God. So early Christians thought one of them would surely be the Antichrist. In more modern times, people thought Napoleon could be the Antichrist since he was taking over Europe. People also thought Hitler could be the Antichrist since he went against the Jews and tried to take over Europe. Hitler was definitely a good candidate.

People through the ages have made the strangest estimates using the number of the beast mentioned by John (Rev. 13:18). They claim to know who the Antichrist is by a creative use of numbers. Believe it or not, somebody figured out it was JFK by adding the letters of his name after giving the letters of the alphabet certain values. Some people in the 1980s thought Ronald Wilson Reagan was the Antichrist because his first, middle, and last names had six letters, not to mention that he was shot and didn't die. According to these methods, the Antichrist could almost be anyone. I took Revelation in seminary and our professor worked a math problem on the chalkboard, which was odd because there's not much math in seminary. Well, the equation worked out to my professor's name totaling 666. I don't think I was taught Revelation by the Antichrist! Then again wouldn't that be interesting to hear the Antichrist's take on end times.

Nevertheless, there are four qualities of the Antichrist: 1) He will be eloquent and winsome. 2) He will be a complete deceiver, ruthless to the core. People will need and admire him. 3) As a leader, he will masterfully bring peace to the earth and establish a treaty with Israel but afterward he will break the treaty. 4) He will set himself up in the new temple that will be built in Jerusalem and will command people to worship him. In the book of Daniel, it is called the abomination of desolation. All of this will happen during a seven-year period of time called the tribulation.

Don't fear; instead remember, Satan and God are not equal. Christ will be victorious over the Antichrist and all evil! We can trust in Him today and for the days to come.

False Teachers

1 John 2:19

Our times are filled with false teachers and false teachings. All of those who know Jesus as Savior must know the truth in order to avoid being deceived.

John says that some will leave the faith. That means that some are in the church but not in Christ. If you are in the church but you don't know if you are in Christ, this devotional doesn't end with you trying to figure out who the Antichrist is or what will happen in the not-so-distant future. It doesn't matter what denomination you belong to, how many days or years you have been in the church, or if you are a deacon or a staff member—you need to be in Christ.

Just being in the church will not make a difference for your eternity. On the other hand, being in Christ will change your life and bring the Holy Spirit to dwell inside of you. This is important because at the rapture, Jesus will take His people to heaven. The reason the tribulation starts at this point is because the Holy Spirit will be taken out of the world along with the people of God He indwells. The man of lawlessness will run rampant, because there won't be anything left to hold him back anymore.

Yes, there will be an Antichrist, but there is a Christ who can save and rescue you to be forever with God. Do not miss a relationship with Jesus. He was nailed to a cross and died for you. He received the wages for your sins to wash you clean so you can not only be in the church but in Him. Pray this from your soul, from your heart, and with your voice:

> *Father, I thank You that You are here. You are great and mighty. I no longer want just to be in church. I want to come to You in Christ. I know that I have sinned and chosen wrong. Jesus, You are the Savior. It is not through my efforts. You lived perfectly and never did wrong. I place my faith in You. Your death on the cross was for me. Wash me clean. Forgive me of my sins. Be my Savior. Thank You for saving me. Thank You that the Holy Spirit now lives inside of me. Thank You that You've got me.*

A Rich Life
John 15:18–21

A rich, real life—from the soul out—is found by abiding in Jesus Christ. Abiding is being desperately dependent and restfully resident in Him. It is not up to our efforts or willpower. The Christian life is resting in God, dependent on Him. We aren't called to bear the fruit, just to rest in the Vine. He is the Vine, we are the branches. The fruit will take care of itself. We abide deeply to achieve greatly and eternally. If we do not abide in Him, we will accomplish nothing.

God has moved us from being only servants to enjoying friendship with Him. We are friends of God. We may know the Father's business—abiding. If we abide, seeking first His kingdom and righteousness, then all the things we need will be added unto us.

Throughout this devotional, we have talked about the encouraging, wonderful news of abiding in Christ. Now, let's consider the downside of abiding. Jesus lays out struggles for us because struggles strengthen. God's strength will come through us if we can rest in Him.

In discussing the relationship of the believer with the world, John 15 uses the word *hate* seven times in ten verses to talk about the emphasis of persecution. If you really walk with Jesus Christ, there are tremendous upsides, but there is also a downside when persecution comes.

Jesus is light that expels darkness. He reveals our sin. Jesus says that if the world hates you, keep in mind it hated Him first. In Greek, the verb tense for the word *hate* means "to continue on hating you," or "has hated you and still hates you." Jesus then adds, "A servant is not greater than his master" (John 15:20).

Light expels the darkness. When those who are in darkness are around a true believer in Jesus Christ, both the message and messenger can receive push back. But others will respond willingly by trusting Jesus! That makes it all worth it.

The Struggle Is Real
John 17:14–18

A vine has to struggle to get the best fruit.

Jesus is the Vine, we are the branches. Just as the Vine has to struggle, we are going to struggle in order to render the best fruit.

Vineyards are found in places where there is great heat in the day and great coolness at night. In America, most of the wine comes from the West Coast. The weather is hot during the day, and in the evenings, it cools down. That is how the grapes rest, and that is how they struggle. If it is hot all the time or cool all the time, the fruit will ripen or die too quickly. A vine has to struggle to get the best fruit.

Jesus is saying here that He is going to struggle. He is going to be beaten, whipped, falsely accused, and nailed to the cross. And then He adds that we shouldn't think we are going to be any greater or any different. We are going to go through persecution. He calls us a servant here because friendship and servanthood go hand in hand. The greater the friendship I have with Christ, the more I want to serve Him.

We have to abide to please God rather than people. All of us have varying desires to please other people. This may be a key part of our struggle. Most of us can identify the person we most want to please. But if we are going to really walk with Christ, we need to let go of the need to please others. If you belong to the group that wants to please the world, the world will love you as its own. But Jesus says, "Because you are not of the world, but I have chosen you out of it, the world hates you" (John 15:19).

The world likes shelves to place people in categories. It likes to label a person, classify a person, and put a person in a pigeonhole. Anyone who does not conform to the pattern will certainly meet trouble. When you and I declare, "No, we won't conform. We're going to follow Jesus, abide in Christ, and make decisions differently," we are surely going to be met with trouble.

Abide in Christ to please God, not people. Struggle when needed in order to produce the greater fruit.

Spirit Living
John 15:20–21

Everyone loves the fruit of the Spirit. It doesn't matter who you are. Who doesn't want it? If you were to say to any married couple, "Do you want love, joy, peace, patience, kindness, goodness, faithfulness, gentleness, and self-control?" the couple would say, "Yes, we do!" (Gal. 5:22).

What if we said to employers, "What kind of employee do you want?" They would no doubt say, "Boy, I'd like to have someone who's patient and kind with clients. Someone who's faithful to show up at work. I'd like someone who's self-controlled and disciplined and makes sure they're on task." Everybody loves the fruit of the Spirit, but they do not always love the route to gain the fruit of the Spirit. That is the difference.

The route is connecting, yielding, and surrendering to the Vine—obedience to Christ. Those outside the desire to please God do not say no to the attributes of the Spirit but to Jesus Christ and surrendering to Him. The fruit of the Spirit comes through abiding—abiding is surrendering.

Do not take difficult people personally; expect it. This is normative Christianity. The servant is not greater than the master. It comes with the territory. If you are the president of a bank, you must expect complaints. It doesn't have anything to do with you. If you work in retail during Christmas, standing behind the cash register with customers who are upset, remember that they're not upset with you as a person. They're upset with whoever is behind the cash register at that moment. My role is a pastor. And I must remember that whoever the pastor is will receive a compliment, an encouragement, and yes, a not-so-encouraging criticism. It's the position, not the person, that brings persecution.

When we realize that our position is in Jesus Christ and that Christ is our identity, we cannot take things personally. We must respond with the fruit of the Spirit. Abiding in Christ and shining with Christ in a difficult interaction is the key.

Let me remind you that Jesus Christ was crucified. Many people did not like Him. We love Him in the church. The world does not. When we look like Jesus, we are going to be met with some opposition. Expect it! Do not be surprised by it.

Entrust Your Heart in the Struggle

Acts 5:41

We must acknowledge that our culture has turned toward disrespecting God. You will realize the world has changed in the past years with news such as this:

- A Wisconsin federal judge made a decision to declare the National Day of Prayer unconstitutional.
- The New York City Department of Education banned the display of the Nativity during Christmas, but the judge found that the display of a Jewish menorah and an Islamic star and crescent were okay to display during Hanukkah or Ramadan since those symbols were considered secular.

That is disrespectful to God, not just to human beings. We may want to cry that we are victims, but we have the victory in Jesus Christ! We are not victims of any government or any individual. We are reigning on high with the King of kings and the Lord of lords.

As we know, Jesus Christ ultimately went to the cross. When He did, the world cried, "Victory! We crucified Him!" But on day three, the stone was rolled away, and Jesus Christ came out victorious! And 2,000 years later, the church is still here abiding in Christ.

It's a challenging world that stands against the ways of God. It's a struggle . . . Great believers struggle. Great parents struggle because they don't just let whatever happens, happen. Thankfully, great fruit comes from great struggle. Jesus endured a great struggle on the cross, but He had great fruit through the victory of the resurrection.

So when we go through difficult times, if anyone mocks you, your cry should be "I consider it an honor to be named with Jesus." God says throughout His Word that we are blessed if we are insulted because of His name. Peter, when speaking about Jesus' suffering, tells us that "when he was insulted, he did not insult in return . . . but entrusted himself to the one who judges justly" (1 Pet. 2:23).

When you struggle, don't be alarmed, discouraged, or dismayed. Entrust your heart to Jesus Christ and say something like this:

Lord, I have victory and strength in You. You're the Vine. I'm just the branch. I trust You, God. I'm struggling right now. Would You help me?

Vines vs. Grass
Luke 6:27–28

A vine has to struggle to get the best fruit. Vines grow differently than grass. Grass is put on the topsoil and only grows down a few inches to receive its nutrients. In contrast, vines are often grown in rocky areas on mountains and hills. Vines are forced to go 2 to 4 feet underneath the topsoil to get the deeper nutrients and bear sweeter fruit.

Are you a Christian who is growing like grass or one who is growing like a vine? Topsoil, skipping like a rock through life or digging deep through the rock to discover the unseen blessings? Great fruit comes from great struggle. If you are struggling, hang in there.

In 2011, New York's Court of Appeals banned churches from using public schools for worship services. The U.S. Supreme Court refused to hear the appeal filed by the church. The schools were empty on Sunday mornings, but the city still banned the use of schools by "paying good money" churches. It looks to me like the government needs as much money as it can get. From a spiritual side, it was also a bad decision because the churches were a blessing in the neighborhoods in which they were planted. They were abiding in Christ, producing the fruit of the Spirit where they worked.

Struggle strengthens. Christians entrusted that court ruling to the Lord, prayed, and filed an appeal, although it was not heard. They believed that God would do greater things through the churches than could ever be imagined. Did they think they were going to shut down the church by a court ruling? No, Jesus said, "I will build my church, and the gates of Hades will not overpower it" (Matt. 16:18). Struggle strengthens the faith and the believer. It sends them out stronger. Christians pray, walk, and trust more. They dig deeper!

The churches that were evicted grew stronger because of this trial. In the end, the services they provided while they abided in Christ were exactly the fruit of the Spirit the city of New York needed. Thankfully, a new court ruling allowed New York City churches to again meet in public schools for worship services!

Walk with God in love, joy, peace, patience, kindness, goodness, faithfulness, gentleness, and self-control, and God will take care of you. Embrace the struggle for righteousness. When faced with a struggle, remember . . . be a vine, not grass. Great fruit comes from great struggle.

Abundant Life

Hebrews 10:32–39

I love this quote by Scottish philosopher Thomas Carlyle: "No pressure, no diamonds."[50] In the Christian walk, there is going to be pressure. Jesus said, "They will treat you this way because of my name" (John 15:21 NIV). So, abide to endure.

In 2005, Chinese officials from the Public Security Bureau invaded a church Sunday school room. They found thirty kids meeting inside and led them into their vans. As the children got into the vans, they began singing to the Lord. Upon arrival at the police station, the officers took the children into an interrogation room, and the children continued to sing. The Chinese officers said they would be released if they would write "I do not believe in Jesus" 100 times. But instead, the children wrote, "I believe in Jesus today. I will believe in Jesus tomorrow. I will believe in Jesus forever."[51]

When parents came to pick them up, they were told to renounce Christ to be able to take their children home. Some of them did, but one woman, a widow, refused to deny Jesus. The officers reminded her that they would not release her twin sons unless she denied Jesus. She said, "You will just have to keep them, because without Jesus, there would be no way for me to take care of them."[52] The irritated officers told her to take her sons and go home.

How do we sail boldly into the wind to make a difference in the world we live in? We hide in His name. We abide to endure and to become genuine disciples of Jesus Christ. Then we will become fearless leaders in politics and the arts, in New York City, in Washington, DC, in the oil industry, and in medicine. We will be leaders who are genuine followers and will stand strong. If Christian leaders trim their sails, what will happen in our world? If the fruits of the Spirit are our calling card and we are politicians, CEOs, moms, and dads who are not afraid to sail into the wind and sing in the midst of persecution, then the world will know Christ.

Do not feel sorry for Jesus. He intentionally went to the cross. When they mocked Him as a king, He knew He was the King. The world lifts up pride and mocks prayer; it mocks truth and embraces lies; it mocks life and loves death. Look at the things we do as a culture. Choose the abundant life that Jesus came to give us and don't shrink back.

His Heartbeat

Colossians 3:3

We all know that a bag of potato chips is one-third full and two-thirds air. Sometimes that is our faith. We can be even worse—one-fourth full and three-fourths air—when any kind of struggle comes along. We get mad at God and say, "How could You do this?!" Remember, all of Jesus' friends were poor and died for their faith. It has been said, "If this is how You treat Your friends, no wonder You have so few of them!"

As we conclude our look at abiding in Christ, I give you one more powerful illustration: Gordon and Norma Yeager were in a bad car accident. When the ambulance took them to the hospital, they were put in the same room. They were hooked to machines, side by side. As they held hands, Gordon passed away. Norma was still holding her husband's hand when the family saw Gordon's EKG monitor—and there was still a heartbeat. The children wondered why a heartbeat was still registering on the graph when their father wasn't breathing. A nurse told them that his wife's heartbeat was coming through his body.

Abiding is holding the hand of the Savior, so the pulse of God comes through our lives for the world to see. It is not our job to keep our spiritual hearts beating. We just hold the hand of Jesus, and the heartbeat of God comes through. When that pulse comes during persecution, we show that He is worthy of it. When the pulse comes through in blessing, we thank Him.

You suffer in your marriage, and you stay married—you are committed to your spouse. You suffer in parenting, and you stay a good parent—you are committed to praying for your kids. You think you will not be able to go any longer, but you say, "Lord, I'm just going to keep holding your hand," and the heartbeat of God comes through. There is no greater joy than real life found in Him.

Suffering is the downside of abiding. But it is nothing when compared to the upside. You are not a victim; you are victorious in your life in Christ. Hold the hand of the Father, and you will be an abiding, full-potato-chip-bag kind of Christian.

Thank You, Father, for the real life that is found in abiding in Jesus. Amen.

God of History
Ephesians 3:14-21

Be amazed by the Lord today.

With that in mind, I want to draw your attention to the time line of history. The year of King Uzziah's death and the year of the founding of Rome was 739 BC. The Old Testament tells how Israel went into a decline. It declined so much that in New Testament times, the Israelites—the Pharisees, Sadducees, and everyone else—did not recognize the Messiah—Jesus—when He arrived. But Rome was strong, their power began right here in Isaiah in 739 BC, "the year King Uzziah died."

The book of Isaiah chronicles the decline of Israel due to their disobedience. As Israel declined, you have the rise of Rome, which God knew 739 years in advance that Jesus Christ would show up on the earth. The Jews won't recognize Him, and the Romans will be powerful enough to crucify Him. But the Romans will also have built roads throughout all the ancient world so the gospel of Jesus Christ would be able to go forward to the ends of the earth.

I want you to see history. Around 2000 BC, we have Abraham, Isaac, and Jacob. In about 1000 BC, David and Solomon rule—the high point of the nation Israel. Then Solomon disobeys the Lord, and after his death, the Israelites end up with a divided kingdom: Israel in the north and Judah in the south.

As Rome was starting in 739 BC, Israel was declining. That is where we are at this moment, when Isaiah sees a vision. God shows up in the darkest of times, doesn't He? God loves bad odds. And Isaiah is amazed by God. What God will do in the next centuries is amazing. What He wants to do in you and in me is absolutely amazing as well. He may be starting something that won't blossom in your life until way later. Be faithful today, trusting in fruit tomorrow.

Ask yourself: Am I amazed by God? Am I overwhelmed or underwhelmed by the gospel? Do I receive God's blessings in expectation or in gratitude?

It's mind-blowing amazing to see and ponder how God worked in history. He is complex and strategic in every way. God connects dots and builds time lines with heavenly craftsman precision. Seeing His hand in history strengthens my belief in His hand in my life.

Amazed by God
Isaiah 57:15–16

Isaiah is called to be a difference-maker. He sees a vision and says, "I saw the Lord" (Isa. 6:1). He sees Him high and lifted up . . . filling the temple in heaven . . . with seraphim calling Him holy, holy, holy. Holiness is a huge thing and God is a huge God. He can't be contained, not even in the ark of the covenant. They traveled through the wilderness with the ark. They could put it—and God—in a tent. Yet, Isaiah says that God is so big that the train of His robe fills the heavenly temple. God defies our expectations.

In his book *Miracles*, British author C. S. Lewis put it like this:

> It is always shocking to meet life where we thought we were alone. "Look out!" we cry, "it's alive." And therefore this is the very point at which so many draw back—I would have done so myself if I could—and proceed no further with Christianity. An "impersonal God"—well and good. A subjective God of beauty, truth and goodness, inside our own heads—better still. A formless life-force surging through us, a vast power which we can tap—best of all. But God Himself, alive, pulling at the other end of the cord, perhaps approaching at an infinite speed, the hunter, king, husband—that is quite another matter. There comes a moment when the children who have been playing at burglars hush suddenly: was that a real footstep in the hall? There comes a moment when people who have been dabbling in religion ("Man's search for God"!) suddenly draw back. Supposing we really found Him? We never meant it to come to that! Worse still, supposing He had found us?[53]

God is real. He is seated upon a throne, the train of His robe filling the temple in heaven, smoke all around Him, angelic beings flying around. God is holy, and Isaiah sees Him. We all have this little box that we place God in. What happens when we see God for who He is, not who we want Him to be?

Be amazed by the Lord. Seeing God changed Isaiah's life. His mission became telling people about the greatness of God. He saw God anew, and the way he saw Him anew changed everything else he saw.

Are we amazed by God, or have we put Him in a box? Do I see God as He really is?

Holy, Holy, Holy
1 Samuel 2:1–2

How do we become a person who makes a difference in your community? We become a difference-maker by being amazed by the Lord, like Isaiah was. He saw the Lord, and his response was, "Woe is me!" (Isa. 6:5).

It is not measured between people. God is the standard. Spirituality is how people measure up compared to God, not each other. God is holy, holy, holy. And when we realize His holiness, we say "Woe is me!"

God is different than we are. He is so holy, holy, holy that seraphim cover their eyes in humility. They cannot even look at Him. This is the only place the word *seraphim* is mentioned in Scripture. It means "burning ones." The seraphim, in response to the purity and holiness of God, cover their eyes. They cover their feet out of respect. They fly around God, chanting one to another, "Holy, holy, holy" (Isa. 6:3).

I just did a word search in my Bible program. I typed in the word *holy* to see every Scripture that has this word in it. I received fifteen pages in 12-point font. The printout does not even show the whole verse; it just shows every phrase that has the word *holy* in it. When I saw this, I was blown away. God is not just nice or good. He is holy. The Scriptures do not describe Him as only love or only grace. But from His holiness comes His grace, His love, and His justice.

The seraphim cover their faces, not daring to look at God. Meanwhile, we think that all we have to be is nicer than somebody else and God will be pleased with us. But a holy God requires holiness, and that is only found through Jesus Christ. When you think about these Scriptures—holy, holy, holy—it changes everything, doesn't it? God is holy. He is righteous. He is set apart.

Do I measure my spirituality by comparing myself to others or to God? Do I know what it means to be holy?

Power to Shake Foundations

Psalm 95:1–7

Can you imagine being amazed with God, seeing Him as holy for the first time? Maybe it's similar to seeing color for the first time. I watched a video online of a colorblind father putting on special glasses that allowed him to see color for the first time ever. His entire perception of the world changed. He choked up with tears (and I did too) when he looked his child in the eyes for the first time. Never seen before was the beautiful blue of his precious son's eyes. He sat speechless.

A new vision creates a new perspective of life. And here's what results: it creates praise. The result is praise! We are wowed by our new reality, just as we should be with our ancient yet present God.

Praise has the power to shake the foundations. We see it in verse 4 of Isaiah 6. It says the foundations of the doorway shook at the sound of the seraphim's voices, at their praise, and the heavenly temple filled with smoke. What an amazing thought! Praise has the power to shake foundations. Psalm 95 shouts with worship as well.

When we see God holy and lifted up, when we see Him for who He is, we begin to praise. We begin to say, "Lord, I am amazed at what You have done. You are so mighty. You are the God of history. You have a plan. You have all of this in your hand."

We want to say, with Isaiah, "God, You are high and lifted up. You are holy, holy, holy. You have everything in Your hands. You are preparing the earth for the coming Messiah. Lord, we just want to give You praise. We want to give You praise because we are amazed by You."

Like someone seeing color for the first time, let's see God afresh. Let's praise Him for His goodness!

Not, Not, Not
Isaiah 6:5–7

There's a big difference between God and humanity. Isaiah understood this. He saw God and exclaimed, "Woe is me!" (Isa. 6:5).

In our society, do we understand the difference between God and human beings? Or have we thought that we are God? We begin to play God, don't we? We think we have no boundaries, that we can do anything and go anywhere.

We are not God. We have our little categories that make us think we are better or different than others. *I am smarter. I have been to more places. I have more stuff. I have more money or less money. I have more education or less education.* All of these little things separate us, but what happens when you die? As you stand before the holy God, you have none of these aspects that separate you from other people and realize God doesn't grade on a curve. That is a scary place when you have built your whole life on what separates you from other people and what makes you special. But suddenly you are naked—not physically, but spiritually. It is you and God. You are completely alone, and at that moment, you need Jesus.

It is Jesus who steps in front of you and the Holy One. In His holiness, God sees that you are clothed in Christ. And now you realize the difference between God and humanity. You say, like Isaiah, "Woe is me. . . . I am a man of unclean lips and live among a people of unclean lips" (Isa. 6:5).

Notice the order. Isaiah first realizes his personal uncleanliness, then he realizes the corporate or societal uncleanliness. Incorrectly, we have reversed it. We say, "Look at our society, how bad everyone is!" But we ought to be saying, "Look at my own heart, how bad it is!" There may be lust out there, but there is lust in my thoughts too. There may be greed out there, but there is greed in me. When I first see that, I can then say, "Lord, have mercy upon our people, because we, as humans, are streaked and stained with sin." God is holy, holy, holy. I am not, not, not. And I need forgiveness—forgiveness in Jesus Christ.

Am I relying on what makes me different from others? Am I blaming others to take attention away from my own sins? Am I hoping God grades on a curve or am I relying on Christ's righteousness to make be holy through His forgiveness?

The Power of Pride

2 Chronicles 26:16–21

In 2 Chronicles 26, we learn about the fall of King Uzziah, who died in 739 BC, the year Isaiah had his vision. Years before Isaiah's vision, in 791 or 792 BC, Uzziah became king at just age sixteen. I've been around a lot of teens but I have never seen a sixteen-year-old ready to be king! Plus, Uzziah reigned for fifty-two years. When he sought the Lord, God gave him success.

In 2 Chronicles 26, we see that King Uzziah has numerous warriors, towers, and more. He had catapults and weapons built to shoot arrows from the towers and corners of Jerusalem. His fame spread, and God marvelously helped him. Unfortunately, it was about to change.

When King Uzziah became strong, he started saying, "Awesome is me. I've got armies, I've got gardens, I've got all sorts of stuff, and I'm famous. I am the man!" After fifty-two years on the throne, his pride was taking over. We need to be so careful as our experience grows to never give pride a foothold.

God loves the humble. God loves the weak. Uzziah was no longer either. He became strong because of the blessing of God. He grew arrogant, and it led to his own destruction. Uzziah strutted into the temple to offer incense to the Lord. But the kings did not offer up incense; that was the priestly role. But King Uzziah strolled right into the temple and began offering incense to the Lord. Leprosy broke out on his forehead. His pride was his downfall and he had to give up his throne to his son and live separated in a different place until he died.

Let us be warned that even after fifty-two years, the devil can take us down. We may start thinking we're something, but we'll be nothing by the end of the week. I'm not saying God's going to strike us with leprosy. What I am saying is that we should be humble and grateful to God Almighty.

To grow in Christ, choose humility in the midst of success. We do not walk into the temple and act like God really got something when He got us. No, we got something when we got Him. Be humble before God in your success. Stay in the lane of humility not pride.

Ask yourself: *Am I grateful, or am I full of pride, like Uzziah; or am I humble, like Isaiah?*

A Vast Difference
Isaiah 66:1–2

Numerous times I've led the Houston Texans chapel service. I am always excited but also humbled. Let me tell you how keenly aware I am of the differences between me and the NFL players on the team. There is no thought in my mind that we are the same. When they sit down, they are almost taller than I am standing up. The average weight of a lineman is 310 pounds; my weight is about as much as the leg of one of these Goliaths.

We are different. Vastly, vastly different. Professional athlete and a preacher! Let me tell you, those are just differences between people. But when you look at the differences between God and people, it's even greater.

I don't want to stand before a holy God to try to justify myself. I need Jesus to be my clothing so when God sees me, He sees His Son. God is holy; I am not. I can't be saved through good works. I can only be saved by receiving the grace of Jesus Christ, praying, *Lord, I need You and I trust You. You and I are different. I need Christ—the Son of Man and the Son of God—to be in my heart, to be the difference-maker.*

Be amazed and humbled by the Lord. Praise God that we can have a relationship with Him and that He has a plan. See God for who He is and yourself for who you are. God and man are vastly different, He is completely other. But God lovingly sent His Son to bridge the gap between us. Thank You, Lord!

A Graceful Touch
Isaiah 6:1–3

Isaiah had a vision of the Lord surrounded by seraphim in 739 BC. This is the only mention of seraphim in the Bible. Each seraph had six wings: two wings covered their faces to show humility; two wings covered their feet in reverence; and they used two wings to fly. One seraph called out to another, "Holy, holy, holy." The holiness of God amazed Isaiah.

Today live as one astonished by the Lord. Realize the difference between God and human beings, between NFL players and pastors as we mentioned yesterday. Isaiah recognized that he was a man of unclean lips, living among people of unclean lips. You and I—we are not God. God has plans; we have problems.

Notice that Isaiah specifically said, "I am a man of unclean lips" (Isa. 6:5). Where Isaiah acknowledged his sin, God forgave. It is difficult to do two very important things. First, acknowledge we have sinned. Second, to receive forgiveness by grace. Our tendency is to slightly justify our sin and try to make it right on our own. But He's not intimidated by our sin. He makes us clean by His loving grace. Just receive it.

Isaiah in religious effort didn't climb up to the altar to try to pull out the burning coal with his hands to become holy. In grace, the seraph brought the coal to Isaiah and touched his lips with it. Matthew 12:34 says "for the mouth speaks from the overflow of the heart." God wants to work deeply in Isaiah before He works clearly through him. As believers we have received a graceful touch.

Do I see the holiness of God and the contrast of my sin? Am I willing to confess my sin to receive God's graceful touch?

Purifying Fire
Exodus 19:16–18

In Isaiah, we have the lips of the prophet Isaiah being touched by flaming coals from the altar. In Acts, we have the touch of the tongues of fire on the apostles to enable them to preach the gospel of Jesus Christ. On Mount Sinai in Exodus "the LORD descended on it in fire" (19:18 NIV). There's a connection. Fire is throughout the Scriptures typically representing purity. Think about some point when you've had a splinter. Someone lit a flame and put a needle in the flame to purify the needle. Fire brings purity.

Many years ago, before we had kids, my wife and I spent a summer in East Asia. We stayed on a college campus and ministered to the people there. It was a great, amazing, mind-blowing time in our lives. We became really comfortable there. We'd jump in a cab and head downtown even without a translator. That's a big step for two Texans. We could not speak the language, but we had a little book and could point to words we knew.

Our hosts told us, "Here's how you know where to eat: always eat where you can see fire. If you can see the flames and the food coming out of the fire, no problem. If you cannot see fire, don't eat it." Why? Because the fire is cooking and purifying the food, and then you can digest it and not get sick. We want to dine on the things of God, because His is a fire of purity.

The fiery coals touched Isaiah's lips, and in Acts tongues of fire rested on the people on the Day of Pentecost as the pure gospel was proclaimed to the impure world. God's purifying touch has to be on all we do.

The throne of God has an altar with flaming coals. Because God is holy, holy, holy. You could also say He is pure, pure, pure. God's primary attribute is holiness. It is not love, and it is not grace. God is holy, and from His holiness come His love and grace. That is why you have a Holy Bible with a Holy Spirit with a holy God who sent a holy Savior, to make us holy . . . even the angels cry out, "Holy, holy, holy."

Do I see God's holiness and purity? Am I willing to submit to God so He can burn away the impurities in my life?

A Willing Heart
Jonah 2:7–3:3

Something we all want is to have a willing heart and a willing life. We see it in the prophet Isaiah's response to God. Can you see Isaiah raising his hand? He is forthright as he declared, "Here am I. Send me" (Isa. 6:8). I want to be used by You, God. Believers do not hide from God's will; they say, "I want to do Your will, Lord. Here I am! Send me." Be like Isaiah instead of Jonah. Isaiah was a quick yes. Jonah had to go through the digestive system of a whale to get with the program.

A single mom and a ten-year-old girl came to our church. The fifth-grade little girl wanted to start a Bible study at her school. Her mother checked with the school and the assistant principal said, "Yes, have a Bible study here. We'll even give you a room to meet in." Her mom encouraged her to invite her friends in faith and just see what God would do. They went together to "See You at the Pole" where people gather around the school's flagpole to pray at the beginning of the school year. Six people assembled around the flagpole, and this girl said, "I want to start a Bible study at our school. Would any of y'all like to come?"

She's making a difference. "Here I am! Send me!" No one told her, "But you're only ten." God can use kids. Her mother did not say, "You're too little. Wait until later." The administrator did not discourage her either. Instead, he said, "Let's do this. I've been put here for a purpose." And so this whole thing came together, fifth graders gathering for Bible study at a public school because of three people who said, "send me." The assistant principal, the mom, and the girl. Way to go, team!

Whether you are a parent, single adult, student, a teacher, or an administrator, you have a huge opportunity to make a difference wherever you are. Whatever your age, even in the formative years of life, you can make a difference. Pray for the people you see as you walk down the hall. Be humble and be helpful. Be with people; love them and care for them; invite them to church. Sit and eat with people who are alone, and God will use you in great ways. The fields are ripe for the harvest, and you just need to say, "Here I am, Lord. Send me." A willing heart is the first step.

Today ask: "What are You calling me to do, God? Am I making excuses not to do it instead of simply obeying You and stepping out in faith? Lord, my heart is willing today and my answer is yes!"

November 28

Send Me
Colossians 3:14–17

At our church, we have a ministry called "Men Serve." It's typically a Saturday morning when men serve the widows of our church. Guys bring their sons, for a wonderful, multi-generational endeavor. We gather power tools and energy drinks and head to multiple widows' houses to paint, pressure wash, do yard work, and make minor repairs.

One of our single men was getting married. He decided that for his bachelor party, he and his groomsmen would participate in Men Serve and bless a widow. Absolutely amazing! Not too many single guys want to do manual labor to serve a widow for their bachelor party. The widow found out about it and gave him a button that said, "Best groom." She baked a little cake and offered apple cider to the groom and his groomsmen. A little wedding celebration before they made repairs and then prayed together.

I didn't do anything like that on my wedding weekend. It never even occurred to me, but what a difference can be made when we step up and say, "Here I am. Send me (and my groomsmen too!)."

All of us realize the brokenness of our world, but many of us say, "Oh yeah, send them. Somebody should go on a mission trip. Somebody should share their faith," we say. "You should do that. No, it can't be me. I've got all these other obligations. Somebody should volunteer to serve the widows at the church. But if you knew my schedule, it just wouldn't work out." But at some point, "Here I am, send *them*" needs to become "Here I am, send me."

Will you answer the spiritual needs of this world with the right response? Christian men and women are to express a willing heart and a willing life. They live intentionally, listening to the Holy Spirit and humbly proclaiming and demonstrating the gospel in word and deed.

Am I saying, "Send them," or will I say, with Isaiah, "Here I am, Lord, send me"? How can God use you today to impact another?

Wherever God Leads

Proverbs 16:1–9

I mentioned a few days ago speaking at an NFL chapel. Such fun. I had another special experience speaking at the Bowl game chapel service at my alma mater, Texas A&M. Since it was for the Texas Bowl, the service was at a downtown Houston hotel.

Football chapels always make me nervous. What do I have in common with these world class athletes? I played one year in middle school on the B team and here I am before a college bowl game! But I trust the Lord has led me to the opportunity.

Before the chapel service, I was praying, "Lord, help me connect." Driving to the downtown hotel, I was sitting at the light when a Houston metro bus went by. The origination stops and the destination stops are written on the side of the bus. This one said, "Downtown and West Oaks Mall." West Oaks Mall was where our family went growing up. Most of my high school clothes and shoes were purchased at that mall.

I felt the Lord speak to my heart: "I have taken you from when you were as a kid at West Oaks Mall to downtown to speak at a NCAA Bowl game day chapel. There is a bus of grace. If you say, 'Here I am, send me,' and get on and let Me drive, I will take you places you never imagined."

I was so encouraged that the Lord had my life in His hand. He was taking me to the place He wanted me to be. Today, let's express a willing heart and a willing life. Get on the bus and let God take you wherever He wants to take you. Say to Him, "Here I am, send me. I want to go where You want me to go."

Am I listening intently to the Lord? Can I hear His voice in the midst of the noise? Can I get on the bus of His grace and calling and let Him drive?

Lord, Where Are You?
Isaiah 40:21–25

For the next several days, we will camp in an important chapter of Scripture, Isaiah 40. Isaiah 40 helps us in the present and looks into the future. It is a prophetic statement that the Lord gave to Israel and Judah through Isaiah. The Lord is like a quarterback throwing a long pass, and the people of God—the receiver—run underneath it and catch it. The Lord warns His people that they will go through a time of exile. In the first thirty-nine chapters, the Israelites have been hearing about judgment and the coming exile. Even after the exile, many years later, they wondered, "God, have You left us? God, are You still here with us?"

Have you ever gone through anything so bad that you wondered where God was? Do you ever look around and see other people happy with life while you are walking through grief? Have you asked, "Lord, where are You?" Does it seem like everyone's business is awesome, and yours is in the tank? "Lord, where are You?" That is where Israel and Judah was. Through Isaiah, the Lord was throwing a pass to them so each one of them would know, "Okay, You are with me." The Lord wanted them to know this: "I am there with you. Even if you do not notice, even if it does not seem like it, I am with you."

When we take our eyes off of God, we tend to see our circumstances negatively, and our problems magnified. No doubt problems are real and they need to be solved.

In times of trouble, some think Satan and God are equals. Almost like, Satan is the bad part, and God is the good part. But Satan is not a rival to God. He is a created being; God is the Creator of the universe. Satan may have bruised Jesus' heel, but Jesus crushed his head. God and Satan are not equal. God is unrivaled, there is no one like Him. He is above our problems and He is higher and bigger than our circumstances or our problems, and He knows the future.

Let's trust God is with us and has our future in His hands. Keep running the receiver's route because the pass is on its way!

Grasshoppers
Isaiah 40:21–22

Isaiah 40:22 says that "God is enthroned above the circle of the earth"—meaning the horizon. In 700 BC, getting past the horizon was unheard of. They did not have supersonic planes or global imaging satellites. When Isaiah says God is enthroned past the horizon, encircling the earth, and the people of the earth are like grasshoppers, that's a big statement for his day. We have all been on a plane and looked down and said, "Look at the little cars down there! Look at the little people! They look like ants!" To God, we look like grasshoppers.

But do we respond as grasshoppers? By saying, "God, You are unrivaled." The question is not whether God is rivaled in the cosmos. The question is whether God is rivaled in our heart. Are you and God in rivalry? Are you and God in a win-lose contest? Are you going to push your will instead of His will? We have a God that sits encircled above the earth, and we are like grasshoppers before Him. He is greater, He is more, He is encircled above.

Imagine what we look like bringing our little grasshopper rivalries with one another before Him. Imagine what we look like strutting around saying, "I'm a little bit taller grasshopper" or "You are an ordinary grasshopper, but I am a famous grasshopper. I am a powerful grasshopper. Look how high I can jump." We are still all grasshoppers!

Isaiah says, "Do you not know? Have you not heard? . . . God is enthroned above the circle of the earth" (Isa. 40:21–22). The Lord is great. He is amazing. He is the One who is higher than all our problems. God is unrivaled. God is huge. He has no equal. He is holy. Do you not know, have you not heard, have you not seen? He is enthroned above. People are like grasshoppers before Him. He is vast, but thankfully He is also interested in us. The God of the universe is interested in us grasshoppers—in little ol' me and in little ol' you.

Do I see the greatness of my own grasshopper self, or do I see the greatness of God? The bigger my view of God's power, the smaller my view of my problems.

Lord over Leaders
Isaiah 40:23–24

Isaiah 40:23 says that God reduces princes to nothing and makes judges useless. God is greater than the leaders of the earth. Is God a Republican or a Democrat? Neither. He is the captain of the Lord's army. He is the Creator. He is above the leaders of the earth, yet He wants to use leaders for His glory and society's good.

Before he became a famous Christian author, Chuck Colson was part of President Richard Nixon's administration. Obviously, that did not go too well, and Colson was sent to prison. He came to Christ there and later had a prison ministry. He was an amazing man of God. He once told the story of being in Rome, looking at the ruins of the Roman Senate. He thought back to the Roosevelt Room, which was right across the hall from the Oval Office, where staff members would sit around a huge mahogany table. Henry Kissinger would sit there with senior aides at 8:00 a.m. each day and say, "Gentlemen, we are going to make decisions today that will affect the course of human history." So as Chuck Colson looked at the Senate ruins in Rome, his mind went back to that mahogany table. He asked himself, *Where will that table be 2,000 years from now compared to the rock of Jesus 2,000 years from now?* Political decisions impact history, but not like Jesus impacted eternity.

Leaders are like grasshoppers, and that table will be sawdust one day. Jesus is the King of kings. God is above even the greatest leaders. Yet if we read further in the New Testament and in the book of Proverbs, we see the importance of having leaders who lead in the right direction and the problems that arise when they go in the wrong direction.

Of course, when we have elections, we should pray, and we should vote. We want to put good men and women in charge, people who will lead our city, our state, and our country in a direction that honors the teachings of Scripture. Isaiah 26:1–4 says that when we have leaders who trust in the Lord, our city, our state, and our nation will be strong and at peace. It is biblical to pray for our leaders. Yet the Lord God is the eternal Rock. He is the leader we ultimately follow.

Do we put our trust in fleeting things like human leaders? Or are we investing in a kingdom that will last?

A Sign of God
Isaiah 40:26

A Russian cosmonaut was shot out into space. From his capsule, he made this comment: "I see no sign of God." Think about that. He is out in space, seeing the stars, and looking back at this blue marble where there is just enough oxygen, just enough carbon dioxide, and just enough gravity to not just have life but to have human life that can reason, think, love, care and make a difference. But he blurts out, "I don't see God." Why? Because we see what we want to see, don't we? That is what it really comes down to, isn't it? Out in space, you can see God clearly by looking at the cosmos. But this man said, "I see no sign of God."

Looking at Isaiah 40:26, God says He created all the stars and called them by name. Not a single one is missing. Who can compare to God? Who could possibly be His equal?

Think of a time you were in the countryside when you saw the stars. No light pollution, clear skies, and wow! A sky full of stars. By current estimates, there are 100 billion galaxies. Just in the Milky Way galaxy, there are at least 250 billion stars. Look up galaxies on YouTube to see the grandness and the greatness of God. Look up the Sombrero galaxy or the Pinwheel galaxy. They're gorgeous. There are billions of stars, and God says He calls each one of them by name. Because of His great power and strength, not one of them is missing. The heavens declare His glory. That's the God who also knows your name.

Now, smarter people than me have determined how many stars there are in the universe. The number is 10 to the 23rd power. That is 1 with 23 zeros behind it. Try to write that down, it's a huge number.

How can a cosmonaut sail through space and say, "I see no sign of God"? The sheer number of stars and their beauty testify to His existence and grandeur. Sometimes we only see what we really want to see. But God is all around us. He knows every star and calls them all forth.

Tonight, even if you live in the city, step outside, look up, and say, "Wow"!

A Star Lit for Me
Genesis 15:5–6

Rich Mullins was one of my favorite Christian singers growing up. He had a song called "Sometimes by Step." The chorus says, "Step by step You'll lead me, and I will follow You all of my days."[54]

The song also includes this phrase, based on Genesis 15:5: "Sometimes I think of Abraham, how one star he saw had been lit for me." I heard that, and I realized that one of the stars Abraham saw in the night sky represented me; I am a spiritual descendant of Abraham. Not that I am Jewish, but that through Jesus Christ I have been grafted into Abraham's family. Abraham and I believe in the same God and in Christ we are brothers. It's pretty amazing to think about.

I was speaking at a student camp over a weekend and thought of that song lyric one night. If one star was lit for me, I thought I should pick one out. I looked up and chose a star. It was going to be my star. Every time I saw it, I said, "That's my star, Lord. You know where I am, and You know who I am." And I would think about God's greatness and power.

Another time, looking at the sky, I thought, *I want to get married.* I picked out another star that was right next to my star to be my wife's star. I didn't know who she was or where she was at that time. I didn't even know her name. But I prayed, "Lord, bring her to me at the right time. Protect her, keep her, let her grow in You." Now I have the best wife on the earth. Kelly is a blessing upon blessing. One night we were looking at the stars. I told her the story of when I picked out a star for myself, and she thought that was cool. Then I said, "I also picked out that one for you. There are our stars, together, right there." She gasped and hugged my neck.

There we were, looking at the stars, snuggled together on that starry night. We picked out stars for our kids next to ours. Now each of my two kids have a star. Our family is together on the earth and in the heavens. We told them, "God loves you. He knows you by name. We want you to know that you can look up wherever you are on the earth and know that you are loved and part of a family on the earth and in the heavens."

Tonight, go outside and pick out a star that has been lit for you and ones you love!

Vast and Precise
Job 39:1–4

Think how big the sun is. You can take 109 Earths and line them up across the sun.[55] Yet our sun is just a medium-sized star in one of 100 billion galaxies.

God is so vast that He knows every star by name. He knows all that has happened and will happen. God is so precise that He knows the number of hairs on your head and every word on your tongue before you say it. He is so grand that He could do anything in your life, but He is so strategic that He will only do what is in accordance to His plans for you.

A key to spiritual growth is appreciating God's transcendence, or vastness, and His intimacy and precision.

Incorrectly defining His grandeur, we say, "Transcendence. Oh, God is so big. He is so distant. *God, You handle heaven, and I will handle the office.* He is so transcendent that He is up there—somewhere."

Or we might focus on intimacy so much that we imagine God is deeply involved in our problems. He gets stressed out when we cannot find a parking spot at the mall. He is so into us and all our problems that all we do is pray about them and never think about others. We so personalize our Savior that we can no longer transfer our Savior.

Spiritual growth happens when you exclaim, "God, You are amazing. You are so vast, and I am a grasshopper. You are God Almighty, transcendent, resplendent." Spiritual growth also happens when you say, "You care about my innermost needs. I want to share with You things I have never told anyone else. I want You to work deep within me to redeem my past and transform my misery into my ministry." That tension is where spiritual growth happens.

Do you see that the vast, transcendent God of the universe cares intimately and precisely about little ol' you?

Look Up
Jeremiah 32:17–19

When I was in college, I worked at a summer camp in the tall piney woods of east Texas. A beautiful place on the lake surrounded by trees reaching for the sky. The counselors would park their cars in the staff lot hidden in the woods distant from the cabins. On the infrequent but coveted off-nights, my counselor friends and I would drive into the nearby small town for a hamburger. The night would end with riding my mountain bike from the staff parking lot back to my cabin.

In those woods at night, it is darker than dark. The route from the lot to the cabin was just a long road lined with high pine trees and no streetlights; you could only see about fifteen feet. As I rode my bike through the darkness, trying to get back to the cabin, since I could not really see where I was going, I just looked up. By looking at the trail of stars in the heavens, I could see the tree line. With my head cocked back, I rode my bike looking up at the brilliant twinkling stars in the sky leading me home. Gorgeous and symbolic.

This is a great picture of how we are to live life—looking up. One person put it like this: "Look at others, and you'll be distressed; look at yourself, and you'll be depressed; look up, and you'll be blessed." How do you find security in life? You do it by looking up, not around. You find security not in comparison or in what's going on but by looking up, seeing the stars, and remembering who made them and knows them by name.

Look up, today! God is vast and yet He loves you and me. The God of the universe and little ol' me, in Jesus Christ, come together in relationship. That is grace! The bigger you see God, the more you will appreciate grace. The more you appreciate grace, the more your heart will live a life for this grand God. He calls the stars, and He calls you.

Are you looking up at the Lord or out at the darkness? Is your security in the God of grace? If you are not sure where you are in the dark . . . look up and discover the trail of stars leading you home.

Walk on Water
Matthew 14:22–33

Your goal as a believer is to follow Jesus' path. It is hypocrisy when Christ is on one path and Christians are on another. Paul said, "Follow my example, as I follow the example of Christ" (1 Cor. 11:1 NIV). You are called to lead. Whether you are leading in your home, at work, in your city, or elsewhere, your leadership will be based on your followship. He is using you and working in your heart, and it is through Him that you will lead and serve others well.

In Matthew 14, you'll find a story about Jesus and His disciples. He had just finished feeding a crowd of 5,000 people when He led His disciples to sail. Instead of joining them, He chose to pray on the mountainside. The disciples fear grew as they encountered a storm. When Jesus saw their struggle, He walked across the water and went to them. He immediately said, "Have courage! It is I. Don't be afraid" (Matt. 14:27).

The disciples were startled. They believed Jesus was a ghost. "'Lord, if it's you,' Peter answered him, 'command me to come to you on the water'" (v. 28). I love Peter because he was the one who would jump out there. He wanted to go with Jesus. Jesus told him to come, and as Peter climbed out of the boat, he began to walk on the water toward Jesus. The Scripture says that when Peter saw the strength of the winds, he became afraid, began to sink, and cried out to Jesus, "Lord, save me!" (v. 30). Immediately, Jesus reached out His hand, caught him, and said, "You of little faith, why did you doubt?" (v. 31).

Jesus immediately reached out for Peter, and He will do the same for you, even if you doubt. Jesus is your Savior. Meaning He delights in saving us for eternity, of course, but even compassionately grabbing our hand in trials, stress, grief, cancer, discouragement, depression . . . He loves to save. He forgave our sins and loves us more than we could ever know. Let's walk in grace today because of His love for us. Give Him your hand, as He reaches out to you.

Don't focus on the wind and waves, keep walking through the storm with your eyes on Christ. His eyes are on you.

Get out of the Boat
Deuteronomy 31:6

Just as Peter is called to courage in the New Testament account in Matthew 14:22–33, Joshua is called to courage in the Old Testament to step into leadership after Moses. God calls him to step out of the boat. As a follower of Christ, have the courage to get out of the boat.

What does the boat symbolize? It symbolizes the comfort zone we all have. Think about Peter. He was a fisherman. Do you think a fisherman is more comfortable in or out of the boat? If you're a good fisherman, your comfort zone is in the boat. That's how you catch the most fish. I know there's wade fishing and other types of fishing, but in the kind of fishing that Peter did, you sail out onto the water with nets to get a big haul of fish. And the most comfortable choice is to stay on the boat.

The disciples' comfort zone was staying in the boat. Yet Peter climbed out, believing Jesus would help him. What is your comfort zone? Leaving it behind does not always mean you must leave your job and move to Timbuktu as a missionary. Sometimes, leaving your comfort zone looks like leaving guilt. We get so comfortable with guilt that we don't want to walk in forgiveness. We get so comfortable with unforgiveness that we don't want to walk in forgiveness. We get so comfortable with sin that we don't know what it would be like to pursue holiness. We hesitate to trust God with our money. What would it be like to become a generous person, tell someone about the gospel, or spend daily time with the Lord?

Whatever your comfort zone, Jesus is calling you! Get out of the boat, go for it, and walk in courage. You were made to step out in faith and walk on water. You were made to follow Jesus in a miraculous way. You were made to courageously follow Jesus in such a way that His glory and power are evident to all. When you just sit back in the boat, you miss out on shining with Christ.

In the Old Testament, these words were said to Joshua as he took over Moses' position: "Be strong and courageous" (Deut. 31:6). Pray this passage over your life today. Get out of the boat. Get out of your comfort zone. Get uncomfortable. You are strong and courageous in Jesus!

Stay Focused
Matthew 14:28–29

Peter also taught us this: Stay focused on God's kingdom and place everything else in God's hands. What happened when Peter stepped out of the boat? He began to walk on the water toward Jesus, but when he saw the strength of the wind, he became afraid, began to sink, and cried out, "Lord, save me!" (Matt. 14:30).

What are you focusing on? Is your focus on Jesus? On the kingdom of God?

Like Peter, we can lose our focus and begin to sink in our relationship with Christ. At first, Peter focused on Jesus. That is all he needed to do. "Seek first the kingdom of God and his righteousness, and all these things will be provided for you" (Matt. 6:33). We place Jesus first by seeking Him.

When Hurricane Harvey hit Houston, we had more than twenty staff members and 700 church members with flooded homes. One night, the Spirit led me to reposition every ministry of our church for disaster relief. We needed laser focus to make it through this. We no longer had a music or student ministry, we had musicians and students focused on helping people who had lost their homes. Every ministry was charged with disaster relief. We put our focus on the urgent need in our city. Such an impact was made, we received praise from our Mayor, Senator, and Lieutenant Governor, thanking us for our work as a church. It was an awesome testimony of what we can do when we solely focus on Jesus.

In the book *Tozer for the Christian Leader*, there's a paragraph about focusing:

> The important thing about a man is not where he goes when he is compelled to go, but where he goes when he is free to go where he will. A man is absent from church Sunday morning. Where is he? If he is in a hospital having his appendix removed his absence tells us nothing about him except that he is ill; but if he is out on the golf course, that tells us a lot. To go to the hospital is compulsory; to go to the golf course, voluntary. The man is free to choose and he chooses to play instead of to pray. His choice reveals what kind of man he is. Choices always do.[56]

I am not picking on golfers. We all make choices, and they reveal our focus. Choose to focus on Jesus and walk on water with your eyes on Him.

Grow in Grace
Matthew 14:28–31

W hen Peter stepped out of the boat, he got his focus off of Jesus and didn't realize who had the real strength. The Creator of the wind is much stronger than the wind, but Peter focused on the wind and began to sink. Did Jesus get mad at Peter? No, but He did ask, "Why did you doubt?" (Matt. 14:31). But actually, that's a statement of compassion. As Peter sank, Jesus immediately grabbed him and lifted him out of the water.

Here's a key point we can learn from this passage: grow in grace. We are so hard on ourselves. Often harder than God is on us. Yes, step out of the boat, yes, stay focused and yes, you will sink at times so . . . grow in grace.

God is a gracious God. Do you find that you are harder on yourself than God is on you? We often live with guilt, but God forgives in a moment. He already forgave you on the cross of Jesus Christ when He said it is finished. Forgiveness has already been offered; we just have to take hold of it.

The grace of God is so real. Think of grace as an acronym that stands for this: God's Riches at Christ's Expense. It's the fact that you don't deserve it, you didn't earn it, but you asked for it, and God gave it. If you feel like you have been sinking, let Jesus pull you out. It's a finished work on the cross and readily available to us.

Receive God's grace. No one gets it right all the time. Later in the Gospels, we see that Peter denied Christ, but we see in the book of Acts that he also became the leader of the early church. Leaders who stand with great strength sometimes sink, but Jesus lifts them up. I've preached a lot of imperfect sermons, but do you know what? I'm glad about that. That gives room for God to move. This devotional guide is far from perfect and there are plenty of better writers, but I'm out of the boat trusting the grace of God. If I get it all right, then where's the need for Jesus? When I'm weak He is strong.

You're not going to do it all right. You're not going to say the right words to your spouse every time. You're not going to think the right thoughts every time. You and I will see the wind and . . . sink. But He is there to lift us. But you can rely on His grace, knowing that there is for-giveness. Often, we have too high of a standard for ourselves and too low of a threshold for the grace of God. It's okay to do well, but God's grace is there for you on days you don't do so great.

Jesus, Your Savior
Titus 2:11–14

Do you know the gospel, the good news, is all throughout Scripture? We could go to countless passages concerning God's grace. Thankfully it is spoken of everywhere. We see it in the garden of Eden as God covers their nakedness, and grace is the final word of Revelation. Then in the middle of the New Testament, Titus tells us that God's grace extends to us all. Grace is what makes a truly Merry Christmas.

As we inch closer to Christmas each day, it is REALLY good news that God sent Jesus to planet Earth, to the manger, born of a virgin. Then thirty-three years later, on a hill called Calvary, Jesus Christ died on a cross. Even on the cross, He lifts a prayer for us and those who were crucifying Him. "Father, forgive them, because they know not what they are doing" (Luke 23:34). He prayed for the soldiers who were killing Him. He came, if you will, off the cross and to the resurrection to come to you and to me as we're journeying in this thing called life.

Do you know Jesus as Lord and Savior? What this means is that you declare, "Jesus, I know I have sinned. I trust that You died on the cross. You rose from the grave, and Your hand is extended to me from heaven. Forgive my sin, I want to grab Your hand, and I want You to be my Savior."

Salvation takes two things: believing and receiving.

Believing Jesus is God's Son who has come to save, and receiving by faith His gracious forgiveness. If you trust Him, my friend, you will find grace like never before. The best Christmas gift ever. You can pray right where you are, and His hand will reach out and grab you in that moment.

If you are already a believer, ponder His grace and share the good news of Christmas. Someone you will encounter today will be sinking, maybe so slowly they don't even realize it. Kindly share the good news of Christmas and the cross, that there is a Savior extending a nail-pierced hand to save.

When You're Wet
Matthew 14:32–33

It took courage for Peter to step out of the boat, but he became misfocused and sank. He taught us a valuable lesson . . . worship when we are wet. What does this mean? It means to worship God even when we have failed. I have found sweet moments with the Lord when I have been worried and anxious and chose to put on some worship music. The peace that comes over me in that moment is incredible. My focus shifts from the problems on this earth to the person of heaven.

I'll never be a good singer, but I can be a great worshiper. Listen to music that praises His name and sing to the Lord. There are moments when tears stream down my face because I know I have sunk, and God has rescued me. I sit and worship Him for saving me. I worship Him because He is worthy. He also grabbed your hand and saved you when you were sinking.

Often, we think that worship is what we do on Sundays. We get shined up, put on our best duds, comb our hair, and brush our teeth to go to worship at church. It's not necessarily a bad thing. But know even in the boat after you've sunk in the waves, you can worship when you're wet. You can worship in the midst of failure. You can worship at 2:00 a.m. crying out, "Dear God, help me." The Christmas music that surrounds us during this month is a great tool for worship. Let the songs be more than nostalgia but true lyrics bringing true worship.

The passage says, "Then those in the boat worshiped him and said, 'Truly you are the Son of God'" (Matt. 14:33). Keep focused and growing even in the hard times. And do you know what I like about this? Whose worship do you think was the deepest? I'm going to just take a guess that it was Peter's because he was the one who had stepped out of the boat.

Peter stepped back in the boat, rescued by the Lord, and worshiped. And truly they realized Jesus was the Son of God.

Worship God through your failures. Worship God after sinking. Worship God when you are wet.

This, Too, Shall Pass
Matthew 14:32

The passage in Matthew where Jesus walked on water concludes like this: "When they got into the boat, the wind ceased" (v. 32). And here is the last step we can apply from this story: this, too, shall pass.

Whatever you're going through, it, too, shall pass. Feelings pass. Trials pass. Storms pass. Things come and go. The sun sets. Remember what you were worried about last year on this date? No, you probably don't, not unless it was something truly life changing.

Life can be compared to moving clouds. Some clouds come through, and they are dark; others are wonderful, big, puffy clouds. But clouds are always moving. The winds continue to blow and the earth continues to spin and clouds continue to move. I know there are days that feel as if the dark clouds will never move, but let me encourage you. This, too, shall pass. As we see in this Scripture passage, the storm came to an end.

Hang on and remind yourself often of this story. You will step out of the boat, remain focused on Jesus through the storm, allow yourself to grow in grace, worship your Savior who will never forsake you, and be encouraged with the understanding that it, too, shall pass. Your storm will end. If not on the earth, then in heaven.

At Cambridge University, a lecturer named Mark Ashton Smith was kayaking off the coast of England. The kayak capsized. He clung to his boat and reached for his cell phone that he had in a Ziploc bag. He was going to call his dad. But he's off the coast of England, and his dad is training British troops in Dubai, 3,500 miles away. Why would he call his dad who is so far away? Because his dad had military connections to relay his son's Mayday to the Coast Guard in England. In twelve minutes, a helicopter hovered over the kayak. Let me tell you something: call your Dad in the storm. Call your Father in heaven. It may feel like He's 3,500 miles away, but call Him, He will rescue you. No matter how far you feel from God, He is right there. Call out to Him and let Him do a work in your life.

We are called to be followers of Christ. Did Jesus have blue skies every day? No, but He remained faithful to God the Father through it all, and He changed the world. You will encounter storms in life and they will pass. Remain faithful to Christ and take the necessary steps to strengthen your courage in the storm.

French Fries and a Blessing

Proverbs 19:17

What does it mean to follow in Jesus' footsteps and live a life like He lived? One thing for sure is it means to love the poor.

How do we respond to those who cannot be a financial blessing to us, those who do not have the resources to help us out? We know that having more money in our wallets does not give us any more dignity before God. And it does not give us any less standing before God if we do not have a lot of money. We have all been made in God's image. That is what gives us value.

Something that was a real blessing to me was the time some women in our church befriended a woman who was homeless. The women in the church began to minister and care for her. And the homeless woman became part of the church and sat with the women. When I drove underneath the bridge, I would roll down my window and call out to her, "How are you doing?"

She would yell back, "Pastor! How are you?" And all the homeless people would say, "He's your pastor? What church do you go to?"

We became friends. It was a wonderful thing. I pulled up one day by the bridge, and she had a gentleman with her. I told them I had a little time on my hands and asked if I could take both of them to lunch. They loved the idea, jumped in my car, and I drove to McDonald's. Now, I am not saying you should allow any stranger or homeless person in your car—stay wise and safe—but we had built a relationship for some time. Quite frankly, it was a lunch different from the usual ones I have. I sat across from this couple in my starch shirt from the office and they in tattered clothes smelling of car exhaust and we talked. We talked about life, Christ, and the French fries. What a blessing to my life probably more than theirs. Two people who could not buy me anything, blessed my life.

This Christmas season, see the poor and help them. I'm sure your church has a route to do so. Let's be a blessing and we will find we are the ones who will be blessed.

Take the Bad Seat
Luke 14:7–13

Jesus told a parable to teach us humility. He noticed how the Pharisees chose the best places for themselves. Let me paraphrase what He told them: "When you are invited to a feast, don't sit in the best place. Someone more important may have been invited. Then the one who invited you will come and say, 'Give your place to this other guest!' You will be embarrassed and will have to sit in the worst place."

Jesus knew that everyone was looking for the most important seat. In that specific culture, the most important seat was the center seat on the couch. In our culture, the most important seat is at the recliner with the remote control, right? Regardless, we are usually polite enough to let the seat go, but our hearts can still struggle with an unspoken "me first" attitude.

Jesus desires humility. He told the people to take the worst seat, not the best. He continued by saying something like this: "When you give a dinner, don't invite your friends and family and relatives. If you do, they will invite you in return, and you will be paid back. When you give a feast, invite the poor, the paralyzed, the lame, and the blind."

Does this mean you can't have a Christmas dinner anymore with your loved ones or coffee with a friend? Absolutely not. That is not what Jesus is saying. He is telling us to not be part of something only to try to get something back.

Christmas time provides a great opportunity to break the "What's in it for me?" mindset. All of us except Jesus have that mentality at times. If I scratch your back, you will scratch mine. If I do this, you will do that. We unknowingly seek reciprocal relationships, and Jesus wants to break that mindset. President John F. Kennedy said it differently, "Ask not what your country can do for you. Ask what you can do for your country."[57]

Jesus wants us to give and bless others without expecting anything in return. I'll give you an action point . . . buy a Christmas present for someone who most likely isn't going to or can't buy one for you.

December 16

When We Love with No Return
Philippians 2:3–5

A few examples to start us off. Marriage is not about what our spouse can do for us but about what we can do for our spouse. Church should be a blessing, but we are there to serve others. At work, walk the extra mile without expecting anything in return.

Selfishness is: "Give so I can get." It can also lead to manipulation in our relationships. Subtle strings begin to attach, especially in those close everyday relationships. The math adds up so quick when we are together often. We have to be careful not to keep score of our good deeds versus the one we love's deeds toward us.

No closer of a relationship or better for score keeping than marriage. Therefore, we need the reminder, marriage isn't a 50/50 deal. That's a shaky marriage from the start. A marriage is best built on each spouse giving 100 percent. And 110 percent is even better. In any relationship, there will be moments you don't feel the love coming back to you. It's true in marriage, friendship, and raising kids.

Parenting is a blessing, but it is also a one-sided love at times. I can assure you the gifts on Christmas morning will be 10 to 1 in favor of the kids. We are all fine with that but in other ways, it is hard to be the one who keeps giving. Your children will never give you as much as you give them as far as what you can buy. That is just how parenting works, yet it is still a blessing in so many other ways.

Jesus wants to break this mindset of one-sided love and break the selfishness of believing that giving has to be reciprocated. Our church like many others, hosts a Christmas Store for those in need. As the gifts are given, no one from our church is wondering *Where's mine?* The blessing is in the joy of giving without receiving. Let's take that missional attitude into our day today. Consider others more important than yourself.

Jesus wants us to love without expecting anything in return. He wants us storing up eternal treasures in heaven not on the earth. Can we begin to practice giving of ourselves without expecting anything back? This Christmas allow Jesus to break selfish expectations. Let Him transform your mind and your heart to bless someone else at home, church, and work.

The Poor
Leviticus 23:22

Jesus said, "When you host a banquet, invite those who are poor, maimed, lame, or blind" (Luke 14:13). What did He mean by that? People with disabilities can actually do great things because they're amazing people. Our church has an incredible special needs ministry. I'm blown away by their abilities and love. But in that agrarian society, if you were blind or if you could not walk well, you were not able to work in the fields. The disabled were often relegated to begging.

Jesus was asking His listeners to go and invite the people who could not reciprocate. True love is an exercise in humility.

We want to minister to the poor as well, those who are in need financially. There are three groupings of impoverished:

1. *Those in generational poverty.* That's defined as poverty over two generations. They are people who, in their poverty, aren't sure how to live any other way.

2. *Those in situational poverty.* That's when something happens that causes a person to be poor. It may be an illness, the loss of a job, or a divorce. Sometimes it is bad choices such as alcohol or drug abuse. No question about it, you can end up in poverty by making really bad choices. But some people are in situational poverty that was not due to their bad choices; something detrimental or devastating occurred to knock them off their feet. A catastrophic event happened that they could not escape. They were living on the edge of poverty, and the event sent them over the edge. We should not come along and tell them, "Well, you need to get back on your feet." Instead, we should say, "How can I help?"

3. *The working poor.* There are people who are employed and still struggling. They are working two to three jobs. For example, at a restaurant, you might hear the waitress say, "You know, I have kids at home, and this is my second job." *Ding! Ding! Ding!* Whenever you hear of people going through those sorts of struggles, they are probably the working poor.

Throughout the Old and New Testaments, you will find God commanding us to reach out to the poor, no matter the groups. Let your heart lead you. As you bless others, you will also be blessed.

Honor God

Proverbs 14:31

The one who oppresses the poor person insults his Maker, but one who is kind to the needy honors him" (Prov. 14:31). Proverbs is a great book about monetary issues and the poor in particular. When we help the poor, we are actually honoring God. We insult God when we look down on someone who cannot give us anything back. Yet we honor God by honoring those in need.

A few things to consider as we reach out:

1. Be wise and safe. Use wisdom and discernment when helping others.

2. Acknowledge that as much as you can give to a person in need, there are some people who will not want to change. They will not want to change their situation and may even reject the gospel when you share it with them. But that's God's concern not ours. We just need to stay faithful and let Him handle their hearts.

3. There are some people who may take advantage of you. That is why it is so important to ask the Spirit for wisdom. Loving the poor does not require you to walk around handing out money. Boundaries are necessary and an appropriate thing in ministry. Christian enablers are not helpful long-term.

4. Understand that some may want the help but will take a very long time to make changes. That may be due to addictions or habits. They may need to enter some sort of rehab or vocational training to really get back on their feet. Giving them a bottle of water or a meal will help in the moment but won't be enough long-term. They will need strategic guidance to truly get out of their situation.

Father God, I want to honor You, especially as Christmas approaches. I want to be Your hands and feet here on the earth and I want to love people. I want to honor those in need. Guide me with Your Spirit so I know where to begin. I want to see people with Your eyes, Lord, so I can help them. Fill me with wisdom and compassion. In Your name I pray, amen.

Spiritually Poor
Matthew 5:3

You may have a desire to love the poor, but you may not know where to begin.

Volunteering is a great way to help. Volunteer some of your time to serving the community. There are many organizations that reach out to those in need and could use your help. For example, a woman in our church knits little booties by the dozen. She donates them to a pregnancy center, and pregnant women can take them for free when they get a sonogram. A touch of knitted love in a challenging time.

Others in our church work diligently in our Faith Centers giving food and clothes away. Some tutor, teach, coach, counsel, and pray for the under-resourced. We aren't just helping with temporary physical needs but the needs of the soul, sharing Christ at every turn. Volunteering is about using your giftedness and expertise to help others. It is about sharing your resources and knowledge with those who need it. Sometimes it is simply about sharing your time to bless somebody. We are all busy, but we can make time to go feed the hungry, love orphans, tutor children who cannot afford tutors, or hang out with students who are in need of a friend. There is so much you can do for your community. Make volunteering a New Year's resolution.

I encourage you to connect with an organization through your church that ministers and is faith-based. They not only provide food for the hungry and clothes and shelter for the homeless, but they also share Jesus Christ with them. People who go there will have the opportunity to know Jesus as their Savior. They will have the opportunity to listen to the good news and choose to trust in Christ.

The goal of the Bible is for people to trust Jesus Christ as their Savior for all eternity. Ministering to the poor is an on-ramp to sharing the gospel because every human being is spiritually poor. Until we trust Jesus Christ as our Savior, we are spiritually poor. The apostle Paul wrote that Jesus became poor on our behalf. He who was rich became poor so that we who are poor spiritually can become rich spiritually. When you trust Jesus as your Savior, when you receive Christ, you have a relationship with God, and that gives you spiritual wealth. It might not change your wallet, but it changes your eternity.

Eternally Rich

Acts 20:32–36

Christmas touches our hearts to help others in need materially and spiritually. We share Jesus because there is not only economic poverty but also spiritual poverty. We give a cup of cold water in Jesus' name. Sure, we want to help people materially, but that is just an on-ramp to helping them eternally. We want the Lord to come into their life as they place their faith in Jesus. It's a powerful and eternally life-changing moment.

If you are spiritually poor, I want you to know that Jesus Christ loves you, and you can place your faith in Christ alone. He can save your life and your heart. You can trust Jesus. If you have come to Christ and are experiencing His wealth in your heart, continue to use your giftedness, share your resources, give of your time, and bless others with the good news. Think about how God can use you to help others.

Some people won't have the means to pay you back. But God will bless you. In a world that's always thinking of the best investments and how to make more money, Jesus is saying to give to those who cannot give you anything in return. Your repayment will come with eternal rewards. Isn't that great? There is no need to brag. God is delighted in how you love others in secret.

We know it is better to give than it is to receive. We stop looking for the payback and care for those in need. Breaking the mindset of "What's in it for me?" is a key to joy. Serve and love the elderly, the poor, the hungry. Being God's hands and feet here on the earth, results in eternal benefits. The book of Proverbs says that being kind to the poor is a loan to the Lord. You are giving to the Lord. Here is a truth about being a Christian: Our rewards are greater and longer than anything the world can give. It's not just for today; it's for all of eternity.

Pray this prayer as you begin to live a life loving the poor:

> *Father, I thank You that You came to me in my spiritually tattered rags. I pray that I never become too good to love others or busy to see them. You wrapped us in forgiveness, love, and grace, and Father, in that same way, may I have compassion for others. Lord, let me be in tune with how I can bless them. I trust You. Use me. Do Your work in and through me. In Your name, amen.*

A Little Blue at Christmas Time

Ecclesiastes 4:9–10

We can get a little lonely around Christmas. So much that there are songs like "I'll Be Home for Christmas" and "I'll Have a Blue Christmas without You." Thankfully Jesus cares deeply about relationships. He is a great friend when we long for companionship.

Loneliness, in part, is because we have a God-given need for friends. We are wired for friendship, to be connected to one another. That is why throughout Scripture, Jesus talks about friendships, shows His love for the disciples, and His love for the crowds.

The sad truth is that humanity and society are struggling with loneliness more than ever. Great Britain just appointed a Minister of Loneliness to address the concern. An article called "Why Millennials Are So Lonely" stated that 30 percent of millennials (ages 23–38) always or often feel lonely. About one in five people in this age range say they have no friends, while 27 percent say they have no close friends, and 30 percent say they have no "best friend." These numbers are considerably higher than the other generations surveyed.[58] It appears the decline is most prevalent among millennials. Loneliness is a huge problem.

It's a challenge to live in the modern world, our devices that supposedly keep us so connected often disconnect us. Virtual connection can't replace true connection. The funny thing is that when we feel isolated, what do we do? We go right back to our devices that in part brought the divide. It is a vicious cycle that goes around and around.

Billy Graham, the famous evangelist, once said, "Loneliness is no respecter of persons. It invades the palace as well as the hut. . . . The kind of society we live in can contribute to loneliness. Mobility and constant change tend to make some individuals feel rootless and disconnected."[59] Mother Teresa said, "The most terrible poverty is loneliness and the feeling of being unloved."

If you are a little lonely this Christmas, reach out to a friend and your truest Friend. His heart is for you. Also reach out to others and minister to them. Christmas can be a lonely time. Trust Jesus to meet you where you are with a heart of friendship.

Some Are a Challenge
Matthew 11:19

Three days from Christmas we need to be reminded not everyone is easy to be around, even family. Jesus was a friend of sinners *and* saints. Sometimes, as believers, we think that we are only supposed to befriend the saints, right? We form our little cliques and believe we should not hang out with any of those people we view as *sinners*. Let's face it; some people are more enjoyable than others—usually because we share things in common. This makes it fun to be with them but hard to reach out to others. Jesus, of course, is the greatest example of reaching across the aisle to others. He was a friend of sinners.

In the Gospels, including the book of Matthew, we read that Jesus was a friend of tax collectors, sinners, drunkards, and gluttons—so much so that people told Him, "You must be just like them."

You see, Jesus Christ did not hang out with sinners to justify and participate in sin. He stepped into their lives to make a difference. He wanted to shine in such a way that they would be able to see something better, something greater. He wanted to show them that there was more than the lifestyle they were living.

In Proverbs it says, "Don't make friends with an angry person . . . or you will learn his ways and entangle yourself in a snare" (Prov. 22:24–25). We have to show care, but we also have to be careful. Do you ever get around somebody and start complaining like they complain? You get mad like they get mad? You begin to gossip like they gossip? They just pull that out of you. We can get pulled down. If I were to stand on a chair, it would be easier for you to pull me down than for me to lift you up. We have to be aware of our tendencies and temptations.

We can get influenced and all of a sudden become materialistic, angry, or gossipy. Then the sea has come into the boat. Bad company corrupts good morals. George Washington said, "Associate yourself with men of quality if you esteem your own reputation, for 'tis better to be alone than in bad company."[60]

This Christmas, Uncle So-and-So will still be a challenge. Get prayed up and reach out.

Friends of Saints

1 Samuel 18:1–4

As Christmas approaches, let's continue to look at the way Jesus connected with people to get us ready for that family meal. Jesus was a friend of sinners, but He was also a friend of saints. In the book of John, He called His disciples His friends. In Revelation, He is knocking on the door, wanting to dine with the church of Ephesus. Bottom line, He wants to be with us.

Obedience brings greater friendship with God. If you obey Jesus, you are going to walk with Him in greater intimacy and friendship. I have been walking with the Lord over thirty-five years now. Jesus is my best friend. I have grown in that friendship and relationship with Him in good times, bad times, up times, and down times. His friendship means more to me than any other friendship on the earth. But the intimacy of my friendship with Him grows when I am obedient and listening to what He says.

Your proximity with God, never changes. The Holy Spirit lives in your heart. God is not way over there and you way over here. Nevertheless, the intimacy in your relationship with God can change. That intimacy is based on being a listener and follower of Christ. Stable proximity inspires and promotes deeper intimacy.

Jesus was a friend of saints; Jesus was a friend of sinners. You probably have a little of both coming over for Christmas. Hang in there; for both we sacrifice, share, befriend, connect, and love. How's the balance? Are you surrounded by friends who do not walk with God and are struggling to stay afloat? Or do you have so many friends from church there's no one to reach?

I came to Christ when I was sixteen years old. I didn't know many people who went to church. Everybody I knew was partying. I had my fill of sinners, among which I was the chief. Then I started to discover some saints. In college, I had the perfect balance. However, when I went to seminary, I went way over in the saint category. Since I am a pastor I have a bunch of saint friends, and I love them all, but I have to work on having friends outside the church because my vocation has sheltered me.

Striking the balance at Christmas and beyond creates a balance of ministry and encouragement.

The Close and the Crowds

Matthew 9:35–36

Christmas Eve is a time to gather with close circles. Our schedule is family around the dinner table and church for a candlelight service. Close friends and family at the table and a crowd at the church is a good recipe on Christmas Eve. Jesus was a friend of both the close and the crowds. The close were those who were around Him a lot, but He also made friends with the crowds. Through the Scriptures, we see Jesus taking an even smaller group from the twelve disciples on a mountainside or deeper into the garden.

You and I need close friends. A Russian proverb says, "An old friend is better than two new ones."[61] It does not matter how many Facebook friends you have. Not all of them are real friends; many are acquaintances. Keep a few friends close, just like Jesus did. Invest this Christmas Eve in those close friendships and family—there is lots of growth in these special moments.

In Matthew, we also read that Jesus felt compassion for the crowds. Crowds of friends are a blessing too. The crowd could be acquaintances at the office, friends on the football team, or friends at church for the candlelight service. We need big friendship groups too—a Christmas party!

What Jesus models is really the balance between being an introvert and being an extrovert. Extroverts tend to like crowds, and introverts tend to like just a few close friends. It's the picture of my marriage. I'm an extrovert and love to be with lots of people. My wife likes it a little bit smaller. When we go to a party or outing, she will ask, "How do you walk around and talk to everybody at the party?" This is what I tell her: "I'm shallow, you're deep. That's how." Ha! While that's not completely true, she does prefer a deep conversation with a handful, and I like a crowd.

Jesus was the perfect blend of extrovert and introvert—close and crowds. We see Him go away in solitude on the mountain. We see Him teach a small group of disciples. But we see Him on the hillside having compassion for the masses. Jesus was that perfect connection, and that's what the church has to be. Christians should connect with the close and the crowds. We want to reach the world, but at the same time, we want to have small groups, Bible studies, and cups of coffee where we connect with one another on a personal basis. It's the crowd and the close that add to the joy of Christmas.

Merry Christmas!
Matthew 1:22–23

Merry Christmas! A day to celebrate His birth with family and friends. Here's the good news of the best present ever. We can be friends of God through Christ. We think it's cool to be friends with somebody that's rich or famous. Even better, we get to be a friend of God. We think it's cool to be friends with somebody who's popular. We get to be a friend of God. We think it's cool to be a friend of some athlete. So what? We get to be a friend of God through Christ. That's amazing. That's what Christmas is about.

Job said when he was in the prime of his life, the all-powerful God was his closest friend. The Scriptures also say that Moses spoke to the Lord just as someone speaks with a friend. In James, it says how Abraham became God's friend. Simply embrace the thought that you get to be God's friend. How does this happen? It's through Jesus, His Son, who came to the earth. And if you will place your faith in His death to be the payment for your sins and receive Him in your heart as your Savior, you will be connected to the Father. His friendship brings the merriest Christmas.

You place your faith and trust in Jesus and allow the Holy Spirit to live inside of you. And now you have a Friend who is closer than a brother because He is in your heart. Here's what is amazing about that. He is all you need. You can live without envy because you do not need what others have. You don't have to worry about being rich enough or pretty enough or this or that enough. You can stand in confidence knowing that Jesus is your place of security.

You can step out with the saints, the crowds, the close ones, the introverts, and the extroverts and know that your heart and foundation are still in the Savior. God is the Friend who speaks to you in the silence. He speaks to your soul. Jesus loves you. He's the greatest Christmas present! Immanuel, God with us!

Billy Graham said this: "There are thousands of lonely people in the city and in the country, who carry heavy and difficult burdens of grief, anxiety, pain, and disappointment; but the loneliest soul of all is the man whose life is steeped in sin."[62] Sin will put you in solitude. Jesus came as a baby, lived as a man, and died as payment to forgive our sins so we don't have to be lonely. Jesus wants to be your closest Friend Christmas morning and beyond. From that closeness, you can then take a step out in any direction because you have firm security on the Rock of Ages, Jesus Christ. Merry Christmas, as you spend time with your eternal friend, Jesus.

December 26

Thank God for Friends
Proverbs 27:17

The day after Christmas can be a letdown. We can feel sad and a bit lonely. If you're struggling to connect with friends, let me encourage you to pray to Jesus and ask God to give you one more Christmas present: good friends. We all need a few good friends in our lives.

Remember, Jesus, who is your silver dollar friend meeting all your needs, provides friendly quarters. He will provide pennies, too. But let the silver dollar of Jesus be your number-one friend. He changes everything and provides what we need. There's a wonderful old hymn that goes like this:

> What a Friend we have in Jesus,
> All our sins and griefs to bear
> What a privilege to carry
> Everything to God in prayer!
>
> O what a peace we often forfeit,
> O what needless pain we bear,
> All because we do not carry
> Everything to God in prayer![63]

Oh, what a friend we have in Jesus. He can provide the friends you need. It changes everything to trust in God. He begins to change you, and you become a friend to others.

Someone once wrote this: "I went out to find a friend. I could find no one there. I went out to be a friend, and friends were everywhere." When we strive to be a friend, that's how we attract friends. We are not meant to do life alone on the earth. God wants us to have friendships. I encourage you on this day after Christmas to push through the "letdown" with this prayer:

> *Father God, thank You for being my friend. You know the blessing a friendship is to others, so I ask that You provide that one friend in my life. I put my trust and faith in You that You will provide the right friendships in my life. Give me the wisdom to also be a good friend to someone. In Your name I pray, amen.*

You Are a Friend

Proverbs 17:17

As this year comes to a close, I want to encourage you with four things Christ showed us about friendships. They're a good example of what our friendships should be like:

1. *Compassion*. Jesus looked out on the crowds with compassion. The more you know and reflect Jesus Christ, the more compassion you will have for others. Whether you befriend saints or sinners, you will be able to come around them with compassion, not judgment.

2. *Conversation*. Jesus had deep and meaningful conversations with others. As we grow in our relationship with Christ and have Christian friends and friends who do not know Christ, we should be able to ask others how they are doing. It is okay to interact with each other on a surface level, but we should be able to have real conversations, ones that touch the soul. We should build one another up.

3. *Be loyal*. If we walk with Jesus as our friend, we're going to be loyal friends. When you text someone who is going through a hard time, tell them you are praying for them. Or get a cup of coffee with a friend and be a loyal friend in good and hard moments. We have all gone through difficult times. Will you "run in" when it feels like everybody else is "running out"? That makes a huge difference.

4. *Growth*. If you are walking with Jesus as your number-one friend, there will be growth in your life in being a friend. The people you interact with in your friendships should also be motivating you to grow. You should have friends in your life who challenge you to simply be better. My wife and I are around incredible older couples in our church, and we say, "Let's be like them."

Jesus loves the saints, the sinners, the crowds, and the closed-off. He wants to be your friend. When I came to know Christ as my Savior at sixteen years old, I was so worried that the Lord would take my friends away. More than thirty-five years later, I want you to know that I did lose some friends. You are not going to walk with God and not lose some people along the way. But the Lord will see you through.

Trust Jesus, He is your friend. He will give you the strength and ability to be a friend to others. Allow God to do His work. People need friends. You need friends. We can work these things out as followers of Jesus Christ. Head into the new year as a compassionate, conversational, loyal, and growing friend.

Our World or the World

Revelation 7:9

L et's end the year with a focus on others. It's so easy to live in "our world" and forget about "the world." There are errands to run, Christmas presents to return, and New Year's Eve plans to make. All good but not a big enough perspective. God is not only interested in "our world" but "the world." He is a global God with a global heart and at work worldwide every moment.

For example, did you know God has been at work in South Korea? The gospel first reached the Korean people through foreign missionaries in 1885. God has been on the move—the number of believers in South Korea is amazing. Forty years after Korea sent out its first missionaries, 27,436 Korean missionaries from various denominations served in 170 countries.[64] Isn't that amazing?

How did God call so many missionaries out of Korea? Well, they had a church tradition of deep prayer. At 5:00 a.m., before heading to work, believers would show up to pray. They would ask the Lord to do what He wanted to do with their day. God ripened their hearts to send them to the nations, and now the Lord is using them all over the world.

There is a Japanese proverb that says, "A tiger dies and leaves his skin; a man dies and leaves his name."[65] Korean Christians live knowing that their name is "believer in Christ." That is their identity, so they choose to leave a legacy of sharing the gospel.

Three things we should embrace about living life on mission:

1. Jesus has a heart for the nations.

2. If you are going to be a follower of Christ, you will also have a heart for the nations.

3. The Word of God says that every nation, tribe, and language will stand before the Lamb and praise His name.

We are called on a mission to spread the good news.

Embrace a Life on Mission

Luke 24:46–49

In the book of Luke, Jesus says that the Messiah will die and rise again, and after that, the forgiveness of sins will be preached everywhere. You, a follower of Christ and a child of God, are called to preach His name. Not necessarily like your pastor but in accordance with your giftedness. What a joy to have an eternal purpose on the earth.

Life on mission is to be embraced, not feared. Do not be afraid that God is going to send you somewhere you do not want to go. Surrendering to God is the blessing of all blessings of your life. God will do amazing things in your life if you simply trust and surrender to Him. You will find His joy and purpose as He sends you across the street or across the ocean.

We like to keep God at arm's length, not just because of foreign missions but because we are a bit nervous of what God will do with our lives. Let's lay down the anxiety and anticipate the plans of our heavenly Father who loves us more than we love ourselves. Embrace living on mission. End the fear. When God calls you, you will have more joy in your life than your plan. God will do His work through you, and it will bless your life. God will use you in a great way.

Here is what happens in our life: there's a tug. It's like a tug-of-war between faith and fear. Do you feel that in your life? I feel it with the little flag in the center of the tug-of-war rope. It goes over to the fear side, and we say, "Oh no, oh no!" And then it comes back over to the faith side, and we say, "Oh yeah, God can do it. God will do it!" We want faith to win over fear.

A follower of Christ is growing toward a deeper life of faith. Life comes with challenges. But you can trust God. He's got you.

I feared surrendering my vocation to God for a while. "Anything, Lord, except ministry or being a pastor." Now I can't imagine my life any other way. It's one of my greatest joys to serve Him. No need to fear the plan of a loving heavenly Father. As the year closes, look back on His faithfulness to you. It will help encourage you to keep walking by faith.

Fellowship
2 Corinthians 13:14

Fellowship comes from a Greek word that means "to have in common." Have you noticed that many churches throughout the nation have a room called the fellowship hall? When the church meets in the fellowship hall, what does that usually mean? Most of the time it means eating together, but it also means relating and connecting with one another. Fellowship in the church is interacting with your brothers and sisters in Christ. As fun and enjoyable as that can be, we also need to fellowship within our communities.

Many of us are getting ready for parties to welcome the new year and celebrate the one that has just passed. Many of us have witnessed moments of hatred and division, but we should focus on what we have in common. We can share values, appreciation, and love for one another. Fellowship with action is showing we care for each other. Examples are to give, encourage, and pray for others. That is fellowship with action. Celebration comes naturally when Christ is the foundation of our gatherings.

That is the foundation the apostle John was laying when he said, "What we have seen and heard we also declare to you, so that you may also have fellowship with us; and indeed our fellowship is with the Father and with his Son, Jesus Christ" (1 John 1:3).

Fellowship means "to have in common," but before Christ, we truly had nothing in common with God. God is eternal. We have a birth date and a death date. God is all-knowing. We use and need the internet every day. God never tires or sleeps. We need sleep, and then we need coffee! You get the point. We had nothing in common with God until Jesus came to the earth. He is Holy; we are sinful.

Jesus was a man and lived the life that you and I could not live. We needed Jesus to be human and die the death He died, shed the blood He bled, and rise from the grave so we can accept Him in our hearts as our Savior and rise from death to eternal life in heaven. We not only have eternal life now through Jesus Christ, but we can have fellowship with God.

Jesus is the bridge that connects us from this earth to heaven. But it's deeper than that. Now we can connect and celebrate with others from the heart because of the commonality we have with God. They will know us as believers through the love we spread. We will connect from the heart with others because of the fellowship we have with God. Having fellowship with God allows us to share the heart of what He is doing in us. Fellowship with God means having a heart in common with Him. There is no room for hate or bigotry. God's heart lives through us, which allows us to love others well.

You Are Called to Adventure

Luke 24:49–53

The last day of the year and the last words in the Gospel of Luke. Let's end with a heart set on adventure. In 1910, Andrew Murray, a Scottish missionary to South Africa, said at the World Missionary Conference, "We shall need three times more men, four times more money, and seven times more prayer."[66] There is definitely still a great need throughout the world. Theodore Williams, founder of the Indian Evangelical Mission, said in 1965, "We face a humanity that is too precious to neglect. We know a remedy for the ills of the world too wonderful to withhold. We have a Christ too glorious to hide."[67]

We have an adventure that's too thrilling to miss. God wants your life, your job, and your mission to be an adventure. If God has called you to move, that's awesome. If He has called you to be in vocational ministry, say yes. If He has called you to go on a mission trip for one week, go! Wherever He is calling you, wherever He has placed you, do the best job you can to minister and share His great love.

Never forget about this world. There are so many people who need to hear and know the love of God. They need the good news. We can get so concerned about our own children that we forget there are orphaned children throughout the world. God has given us the obligation and responsibility to make a difference in our homes and in the world. We have our chance.

When God changes your perspective, He changes your priorities. When your priorities change, your actions change. When you place your trust and faith in Christ, the Holy Spirit comes into your heart and dwells inside of you. That changes you. Your priorities are no longer about making sure you get what you need in life. You begin to love nations as the Lord does. When there is an opportunity to give to world missions, your heart will desire to give. When you hear about a mission trip to serve orphans, your heart will want to go. We have four choices with missions: giving, going, praying, or disobeying.

The Bible teaches that if we fall in love with Jesus, we will make the nations a priority. We will make missions a priority. We will make church a priority. A life on mission is about having the right perspective of the world. It is about having the right priorities. It is about letting our priorities change what we do. Let's end this year ready to go in the new year on mission with God in the office and in the home, across the street and across the ocean!

Notes

1. Franklin Graham, *Through My Father's Eyes* (Nashville: W Publishing Group, 2018), 90.

2. Thierry Steimer, "The Biology of Fear- and Anxiety-Related Behaviors," *Dialogues in Clinical Neuroscience 4*, 3 (September 2002), 231–49, https://www.ncbi.nlm.nih.gov/pmc/articles/PMC3181681/.

3. "Corrie ten Boom Quotes," *BrainyQuotes*, https://www.brainyquote.com/quotes/corrie_ten_boom_381185.

4. "History of the Reformation," *History World*, http://www.historyworld.net/wrldhis/PlainTextHistories.asp?ParagraphID=hnl.

5. St. Augustine of Hippo, "Article #15," *Confessions*, in "Our Hearts Are Restless, until They Can Find Rest in You," *Christian History Institute*, https://christianhistoryinstitute.org/incontext/article/augustine.

6. "John Calvin," *Goodreads*, https://www.goodreads.com/quotes/80297-man-s-nature-so-to-speak-is-a-perpetual-factory-of.

7. "Reach Your City," *Impact Your City*, https://www.bible.com/reading-plans/14207-impact-your-city/day/6.

8. All quotes in this study from the Declaration of Independence are taken from "Declaration of Independence," *USHistory.org*, http://www.ushistory.org/declaration/document/.

9. "David Livingstone," *Goodreads*, https://www.goodreads.com/quotes/64830-i-will-go-anywhere-provided-it-be-forward.

10. John C. Maxwell, *Thinking for a Change: 11 Ways Highly Successful People Approach Life and Work* (New York: Hatchette Book Group, 2003), 230.

11. https://lifewayresearch.com/2019/07/02/few-protestant-churchgoers-read-the-bible-daily/

12. *Nelson Glueck, Apologetics 315*, https://apologetics315.com/2009/07/sunday-quote-nelson-glueck-on-archaeology/.

13. Mark Twain, *Goodreads*, https://www.goodreads.com/quotes/85747-it-ain-t-the-parts-of-the-bible-that-i-can-t.

14. Mandisa, "Unfinished," from *Out of the Dark* (2017), *MusixMatch*, https://www.musixmatch.com/lyrics/Mandisa/Unfinished.

15. Warren W. Wiersbe, *The Wiersbe Bible Study Series: 2 Peter, 2&3 John, Jude: Be Aware of the Religious Imposters* (Colorado Springs, CO: David C. Cook, 2013), 18.

16. https://www.today.com/parents/youth-sports-referees-across-us-are-quitting-because-abusive-parents-t126087

17. https://www.businessinsider.com/this-is-the-potential-of-solar-power-2015-9

18. Robert J. Morgan, *Red Sea Rules* (Nashville: Thomas Nelson, 2001), 7.

19. Morgan, *Red Sea Rules*, 96.

20. C. S. Lewis, *The Problem of Pain* (New York: Harper One, 1996), 91.

21. "Corrie ten Boom," *Goodreads*, https://www.goodreads.com /quotes/70125-never-be-afraid-to-trust-an-unknown-future-to-a.

22. C. S. Lewis, *The Complete C. S. Lewis Signature Classics* (New York: HarperOne, 2002), 54.

23. Andy Stanley, *Enemies of the Heart* (Colorado Springs, CO: Multnomah Books, 2011), 113.

24. Erwin W. Lutzer, *When a Nation Forgets God: 7 Lessons We Must Learn from Nazi Germany* (Chicago: Moody Publishers, 2010), 124.

25. G. K. Chesterton, *Orthodoxy* (Norwood, MA: Plimpton Press, 1908), 186.

26. Elesha Coffman, "What Luther Said," *Christianity Today*, July 8, 2019, https://www.christianitytoday.com/history/2008/august/what -luther-said.html.

27. Eric Metaxas, *Martin Luther: The Man Who Rediscovered God and Changed the World* (New York: Viking, 2007), 375.

28. "Johann Sebastian Bach Quotes," *Gokodreads*, https://www .goodreads.com/quotes/search?utf8=%E2%9C%93&q=Where+this+is+not +remembered%2C+there%E2%80%99s+no+real+music+but+only+devilish +hubbub&commit=Search.

29. Malcolm Muggeridge, *Seeing through the Eye: Malcolm Muggeridge on Faith* (San Francisco: Ignatius Press, 2005), 97.

30. Justice Thurgood Marshall, in Tony Evans, *Tony Evans' Book of Illustrations* (Chicago: Moody Publishers, 2009), 111.

31. "Edward VIII Quotes," *BrainyQuote*, https://www.brainyquote .com/quotes/edward_viii_106978.

32. https://gracequotes.org/quote/learn-to-know-christ-and-him -crucified-learn-to-sing-to-him-and-say-lord-jesus-you-are-my-righteousn ess-i-am-your-sin-you-have-taken-upon-yourself-what-is-mine-and-given -me-what-is-your/

33. https://www.bible.com/en-GB/reading-plans/2047-when-god -doesnt-make-sense/day/3

34. https://www.azquotes.com/quote/919457

35. Rob Wilkins, "Ed Stetzer: Good News in This Age of Rage," *Outreach*, October 4, 2018, https://outreachmagazine.com/features /evangelism/34490-good-news-in-this-age-of-rage.html.

36. J. B. Phillips, "Preface," *J. B. Phillips New Testament, in Larry Tomczak, Reckless Abandon* (Lake Mary, FL: Charisma House, 2002), 61–62.

37. A. W. Tozer, *The Knowledge of the Holy* (New York: HarperCollins Publishers, 1961), 2.

38. "Mark Twain Quotes," *BrainyQuote*, https://www.brainyquote.com/quotes/mark_twain_153875.

39. John Owen, Mortification of Sin in Believers, in John Piper, "How to Kill Sin," *Desiring God*, https://www.desiringgod.org/messages/how-to-kill-sin-part-1.

40. René Descartes, *Principles of Philosophy*, 1644, in *"Cogito, Ergo Sum,"* *Wikipedia*, https://en.wikipedia.org/wiki/Cogito,_ergo_sum.

41. "Building Vision with Horst Schulze, Part 1," *Andy Stanley Leadership Podcast*, https://omny.fm/shows/andy-stanley-leadership-podcast/building-leaders-with-horst-schulze-part-1.

42. "Isaac Newton Quotes," *Isaac Newton.org*, http://www.isaacnewton.org/quotes.jsp.

43. C. S. Lewis, "First and Second Things," June 27, 2017, *C. S. Lewis Institute*, http://www.cslewisinstitute.org/First_and_Second_Things.

44. Lynn Hirschberg, "The Misfit," *Vanity Fair*, April 1991, 198.

45. "St. Patrick's Breastplate," *Our Catholic Prayers*, https://www.ourcatholicprayers.com/st-patricks-breastplate.html.

46. https://www.opendoorsusa.org/christian-persecution/world-watch-list/

47. https://us11.campaign-archive.com/?u=060e80f6eebfc8804f8049bad&id=c0d75f13c6&e=88b938d3be

48. https://www.pewresearch.org/fact-tank/2015/05/12/millennials-increasingly-are-driving-growth-of-nones/

49. A. W. Tozer, *Tozer for the Christian Leader: A 365-Day Devotional* (Chicago: Moody Bible Institute of Chicago, 2001), 4.

50. "Thomas Carlyle," *Goodreads*, https://www.goodreads.com/quotes/409109-no-pressure-no-diamonds.

51. "Kids of Courage," *The Voice of the Martyrs*, https://www.kidsofcourage.com/?p=5845.

52. "Kids of Courage."

53. C. S. Lewis, "What If God Is Alive, Not the Impersonal Life-Force of *Star Wars*?" July 2012, *C. S. Lewis Institute*, http://www.cslewisinstitute.org/What_if_God_is_Alive_Reflections.

54. "Sometimes by Step" by Rich Mullins on the album, *The World as Best as I Can Remember*, 1992, Edward Grant, Inc., 1991, Kid Brothers of St. Frank Publishing.

55. Tim Sharp, "How Big Is the Sun? | Size of the Sun," Space.com, October 31, 2017, https://www.space.com/17001-how-big-is-the-sun-size-of-the-sun.html.

56. A. W. Tozer, *Tozer for the Christian Leader: A 365-Day Devotional* (Chicago: Moody Bible Institute of Chicago, 2001), 28.

57. John F. Kennedy, "Ask Not What Your Country Can Do for You," *John F. Kennedy Presidential Library and Museum*, https://www.jfklibrary.org /learn/education/teachers/curricular-resources/elementary-school-curricular -resources/ask-not-what-your-country-can-do-for-you?gclid=EAIaIQobCh MIuNvBmfqA5AIVwf_jBx3ACA5REAAYASAAEgIK6fD_BwE.

58. https://www.psychologytoday.com/us/blog/compassion-matters/201909/why-millennials-are-so-lonely

59. Franklin Graham, *Billy Graham in Quotes* (Nashville: Thomas Nelson, 2011), 224.

60. George Washington, "The Rules of Civility," *George Washington's Mount Vernon*, https://www.mountvernon.org/george-washington/rules -of-civility/article/associate-yourself-with-men-of-good-quality-if-you -esteem-your-own-reputation-for-tis-better-to-be-alone-than-in-bad -company/.

61. "Russian Proverbs (About Friendship)," *Inspirational Proverbs, Quotes, Sayings*, https://www.inspirationalstories.com/proverbs/russian-an -old-friend-is-better-than-two-new/.

62. Billy Graham, *Peace with God: The Secret of Happiness* (Nashville: Thomas Nelson, 2017), 82.

63. "What a Friend We Have in Jesus," *Hymnal.net*, 789, public domain.

64. https://www.imb.org/2018/02/09/south-korea-mission-movement/

65. "Japanese Proverbs," *Inspirational Proverbs, Quotes, Sayings*, https://www.inspirationalstories.com/proverbs/japanese-a-tiger-dies-and -leaves-his-skin-a/.

66. "What They Said about World Evangelism," *Bible.org*, https:// bible.org/illustration/what-they-said-about-world-evangelism.

67. Theodore Williams, in Gregg Matte, *Unstoppable Gospel: Living Out the World–Changing Vision of Jesus' First Followers* (Grand Rapids, MI: Baker Books, 2015), 28.

Also available
from Gregg Matte

Difference Makers

**Difference Makers
6-Session Bible Study**

What is our purpose in this life? Can we really make a difference? Pastor and author Gregg Matte believes we can.

You were made for more than watching. You have a history-changing, difference-making, life-giving, Spirit-empowered legacy to leave. As Jesus works deeply in you and clearly through you, you will be a difference maker.

AVAILABLE WHERE BOOKS ARE SOLD

Meeting needs, changing lives

|>> SEND Relief

Every purchase of *Capture the Moment* is providing **three meals for people in need** through Send Relief.

Connecting people in need with people who care, Send Relief is the Southern Baptist compassion ministry that meets physical and spiritual needs around the world.

Learn more at **SendRelief.org**